To the E~~nds of the Earth~~

Ranulph Fiennes was born in 1944 and educated at Eton. He was commissioned into the Royal Scots Greys in 1963 and completed attachments with 22 SAS Regiment in 1966 and the Sultan of Oman's forces in 1968 and 1970. He has led many major expeditions. *The Guinness Book of Records* described him in 1984 as 'the world's greatest living explorer'. In 1982 he became, with Charles Burton, the first man to reach both North and South Poles overland. He led the first circumpolar navigation of earth in 1979/82. In 1990 he achieved, with Dr Stroud, the world record for unsupported northerly travel and in 1993 the first unsupported crossing of the Antarctic continent, which was also the longest unsupported polar journey in history. He has received an Honorary Doctorate of Science, the Founder's Medal of the Royal Geographical Society, the Polar Medal with bar from the Queen, and the Sultan of Oman's Bravery Medal. He is the author of ten books including the No. 1 UK bestsellers, *The Feather Men* and *Mind Over Matter*. He lives with his wife on their farm in Somerset.

Other Books by Ranulph Fiennes

A Talent For Trouble
Ice Fall in Norway*
The Headless Valley
Where Soldiers Fear to Tread*
Hell on Ice
Bothie, the Polar Dog (with Virginia Fiennes)
Living Dangerously (autobiography)
The Feather Men (No. 1 UK bestseller)
Atlantis of the Sands
Mind Over Matter*

available from Mandarin

The author would like to express his sincere thanks to all of those involved in the Transglobe Expedition and who are not fully acknowledged in this edition.

The expedition is also indebted to a large number of companies and individuals without whose support or advice it would not have taken place.

To *the Ends of the Earth*

TRANSGLOBAL EXPEDITION
1979–82

RANULPH FIENNES

Mandarin

For Poul Andersson whom we will not forget

A Mandarin Paperback
TO THE ENDS OF THE EARTH

First published in Great Britain 1983
by Hodder & Stoughton Ltd
This edition published 1995
by Mandarin Paperbacks
an imprint of Reed Consumer Books Ltd
Michelin House, 81 Fulham Road, London SW3 6RB
and Auckland, Melbourne, Singapore and Toronto

Reprinted 1995

Copyright © 1983 by Sir Ranulph Fiennes
The author has asserted his moral rights

A CIP catalogue record for this title
is available from the British Library
ISBN 0 7493 1911 9

Printed and bound by Firmin-Didot (France),
Group Herissey. No d'impression : 31568.

Foreword

by His Royal Highness the Prince of Wales

I was lucky enough not only to be present at the start and at the finish of the Transglobe Expedition in London but also to be able to meet Ran Fiennes and his team when the Benjamin Bowring was moored in Sydney Harbour. For someone who participated in what I suspect were the only comfortable parts of the entire voyage to write a foreword may seem presumptuous. I am however delighted to be able to record my admiration for the extraordinary ingenuity, courage, imagination and sheer hard work of the entire expedition. I know that Ran himself would acknowledge that the party would never have left London, let alone returned there, without the work and support of the Committee at home and the incredibly generous help and sponsorship of so many different individuals and companies. This is of course true, but it is also true that notwithstanding the immensely important contributions made by everyone else, the ultimate success of Transglobe was due to the efforts of those who carried out this unprecedented adventure. How they endured the hardships that confronted them or survived the astonishing risks they took is beyond my comprehension. Their exploits have added another stirring chapter to the long history of polar explorers, whose heroic example has contributed greatly to man's knowledge as well as stimulating the imagination of countless people all over the world.

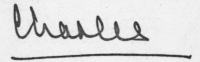

Contents

Maps

The Transglobe Expedition, 1979–82

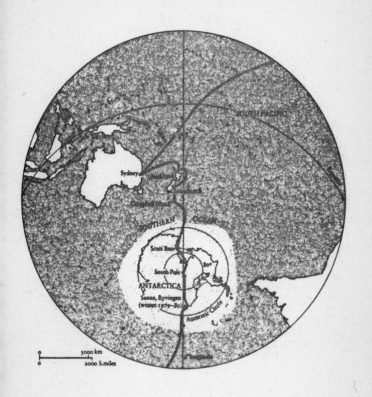

SOUTH PACIFIC

Sydney

Southern Ocean

SOUTHERN OCEAN

Scott Base

South Pole

80°

ANTARCTICA

Sanae, Ryvingen
(winter 1979–80)

Antarctic Circle

0° longitude

3000 km
2000 S.miles

1

Ginnie's Idea

1972–6

Great floods have flown from simple sources.

WILLIAM SHAKESPEARE

In February 1972 my wife suggested we travel around the world.

I looked up from the boots I was polishing with a mixture of spit and black Kiwi in readiness for a weekend with my Territorial SAS regiment.

"Ginnie, we can't pay the mortgage. How the hell can we go round the world?"

"Get a contract from a newspaper, a book publisher and a TV company." She was peering into the simmering Irish stew. I knew it was Irish stew because that was, with very few exceptions, the only dish she had produced since our marriage eighteen months earlier.

"They won't be interested," I replied. "Everybody goes round the world."

"They all do it horizontally."

I glanced at her, not understanding. She continued to poke at the stewpot without elaborating. "Of course they do. There is no other way." I tried to keep the sarcasm out of my voice. Our life together was at the time a series of minor volcanic eruptions touched off by the tiniest sparks. "You can't get over the top because of the Arctic Ocean and the Antarctic icecap happens to cover the bottom."

She stopped prodding our supper and looked up. "So?" Her glacier blue eyes were on me, unblinking.

"So no sane person even tries to do it. If it were possible it would have been done. All oceans have been crossed west to east, north to south, solo, on rafts, backwards and sideways. All major mountains have been climbed and all rivers travelled up to their source and back down again. People have gone round the world by horse, bicycle and probably by broomstick. They have parachuted from over 30,000 feet and gone paddling to the deepest spots in the deepest seas. Quite apart from strolling around on the moon."

I spat for emphasis at one toecap but it went inside the boot.

She was unimpressed. "You are saying it can't be done because it hasn't been done. Is that it? That's pathetic."

"It may be pathetic but it's practical. Even to look into the possibilities would take months. We know nothing about polar travel. Nothing. How do we pay the gas bill if I spend months in libraries and polar institutes doing the necessary research? Answer me that."

The matter continued to be thrashed out over the Irish stew and by bedtime had become a tender topic.

It might seem odd in the twentieth century to plan and carry out expeditions as a means of making a living, yet I'd been doing just that for the last two years. I hadn't consciously chosen such a life; it had just worked out that way.

In 1943, four months before I was born, my father died of wounds received not far north of Monte Cassino whilst commanding a tank regiment, the Royal Scots Greys. When I was sixteen, I decided to make the army my career too. I'd inherited my father's title but not his brains, so the Royal Military Academy at Sandhurst was out. However I managed to scrape through Mons Officer Cadet School and into the Greys on a three-year short service commission which I spent ploughing about Germany in tanks, canoeing along European rivers with brawny Jocks and langlauf skiing in Bavaria. All this gave me a taste for travel.

Then in 1965 I saw an SAS recruitment notice. The Special Air Service did not normally accept short service commissioned officers with but two years' experience. Still, there was no harm in trying. Their selection course in North Wales was an interesting experience. At first there were fourteen officer applicants and 130 other ranks.

After a week there were six officers and forty-two other ranks. Most of the survivors were hardened soldiers from the Parachute Regiment, the Royal Marines and the toughest infantry regiments. Tank people like me were the scum of the earth, but I was still around one month later when we were down to three officers and twelve men. Finally I passed into the SAS and began a special training in demolition.

I collected over the weeks a certain amount of plastic explosive, detonators and other such bric-à-brac. A civilian friend in the wine business was at the time incensed by the outcry in England's prettiest village, Castle Combe in Wiltshire. The village was, he said, being ruined by concrete and sandbags because 20th Century Fox was turning it into a film set for *Doctor Dolittle* with Rex Harrison and Samantha Eggar. Since the villagers' protests were going unheard, my friend devised a plan to destroy the mock lake the Fox people had built and thereby publicise the whole outrage. My part would be to provide the explosive side of the affair. No one would be hurt but the point would be made.

As it was, the police were tipped off in advance and pounced. I evaded capture but my car did not. Needing to report at camp the very next morning for a jungle training course in Borneo, I approached the police. Far from releasing my car they put me up for the night in Chippenham jail. At the subsequent local Assizes I was heavily fined and Colonel Wingate Gray sacked me from the SAS.

After a year back in tanks I volunteered for a two-year posting to the Sultan of Oman's Forces. With thirty Muslim soldiers, some phosphorous grenades and ten light machine guns, I learnt what real soldiering was about: not at all the romantic existence to which I had looked forward so much. I found that to kill a man face to face, even though to delay by a second would mean one's own death, was a foul experience. I saw too what man could do to man in the name of ideology: what befell those Muslims, young and old alike, who failed to switch their allegiance and join the Marxists. I saw backs that had been burnt with hot charcoal, eye sockets from which the eyes had been gouged with sticks.

Nonetheless I think I would have stayed in the army had it been possible, but I had already stretched my original three-year short service commission to eight and that was as far as it would go.

What to do in civvie street – that sand sea beyond the secure khaki oasis which had been my home and the confines of my thinking since schooldays? With no business connections, no qualifications and no unearned income, I could not linger. My only skills lay outside the city. I had enjoyed the planning and the organising of adventure training. But, in the army, taxpayers had provided the funds, the transport and the paid participants.

Starting small with a journey to a Norwegian glacier, a hovercraft trip up the Nile and the transnavigation of British Columbia by river, I made contacts with some fifty companies willing to help, either through altruism or in return for publicity. In 1970 I married Ginnie. We worked well together but craved a bigger challenge than the rivers and mountains of the early expeditions.

In the summer of 1972, after three months' study in geographical libraries, we took Ginnie's circumpolar idea to my literary agent, George Greenfield. George acted for John le Carré, David Niven and many other notable writers but his particular interest was, and is, the field of exploration. Through his ability to interest publishers and newspaper editors in the rights of proposed expeditions, he has helped to make financially feasible such journeys as Vivian Fuchs' crossing of Antarctica, Wally Herbert's crossing of the Arctic Ocean and Francis Chichester's solo circumnavigation.

George explained to us that we faced three main problems: time, money and the need for government approval. The *only* journey ever made across Antarctica had taken four years of full-time planning, two years of travelling and had cost a million pounds. The leader, Sir Vivian Fuchs, was a man of great polar experience. The only bases in Antarctica were government-run scientific outposts. None looked kindly on helping unauthorised visitors. Nor were commercial sponsors interested in such a remote and frozen area. The only crossing ever made of the Arctic had been accomplished by Wally Herbert in 1968 with three companions and forty huskies, after four years of planning and a sixteen-month slog. Ignoring any problems we might have crossing the Sahara or with other parts of our route, it would seem that the polar zones alone might take us twelve years to cope with.

We left George's office and sat in silence with two cups of coffee at the nearest sandwich bar.

"Well?" said Ginnie.

"Yes." I agreed.

We were looking for a challenge and no one, but no one had ever reached both Poles, let alone traversed both polar regions.

W. H. Smith used to produce six-inch tin globes. We bought one and pencilled out various possible routes. It did not seem worth the risk of mounting the whole scheme in the knowledge that, at any minute, political permission might be withdrawn, so we rubbed off all the pencilled routes passing through the USSR. Only one line remained — just off the Greenwich meridian.

On the principle that the shortest route is a straight line between two points, we decided to plan a journey which adhered to the Greenwich meridian unless a good reason cropped up to add mileage with detours.

The Arctic Ocean, though less remote than Antarctica, appeared to provide more difficult travel conditions. Better to leave it till last. Our route from Greenwich then would go south through Europe across the Sahara to West Africa, by sea to Cape Town, then on to Antarctica.

By chance, close to where the meridian touches Antarctica's coastline, there is a South African scientific base called Sanae (standing for South African National Antarctic Expedition). From the region of Sanae our pencil line skimmed over some 1,400 miles of white nothingness to the South Pole and, on the other side of the world, jinked north to a New Zealand coastal base named after Captain Scott, thence up the Pacific along the International Date Line all the way to the Bering Strait between Russia and Alaska.

At this point we made a critical route-planning decision. Wally Herbert's Arctic Ocean crossing was made from Point Barrow in Alaska up to the North Pole then down to Spitsbergen. I had no wish to emulate his route. There was one other possible start point on the North American coastline: Ellesmere Island in the Canadian archipelago. To reach it from the Bering Strait I traced a line up the Yukon River to Dawson City, then north to the Mackenzie River and down to its mouth at Tuktoyaktuk. From there to Ellesmere Island my pencil ran east then north along the coast between various islands for two or three thousand miles. This was the largely icebound corridor known as the North West Passage, made notorious in the nineteenth century by the deaths of over 200 explorers and pioneers along its barren shores. From Ellesmere Island the route ran on to the

North Pole where it rejoined the Greenwich meridian for the last stretch back to England.

Man had reached the moon, yet none had travelled to both Poles in one expedition, let alone trod the course of the earth's polar axis. We would try to correct this omission.

A friend in Los Angeles told us of four Americans who had travelled to the North Pole in 1968 on snowmobiles. One of them, Walt Pedersen, now intended to reach the South Pole overland and become the first man to reach both ends of the earth. He had a few years' start on us, planning-wise, but perhaps we could still beat him to it. The Norwegians had by four short weeks beaten the British to the South Pole in 1911. The Americans had beaten several British essays to the top of the world when Peary claimed 90° north in 1910. Some say neither Peary nor his rival American claimant, Cook, reached the Pole. Nonetheless, if they didn't, Plaisted – Walt Pedersen's leader – certainly clinched American priority in 1968.

The longest single stage of our planned route, some 1,000 miles to the South Pole, along the zero meridian, was one of the last remaining truly unexplored regions on earth, so what we were considering probably amounted to the last major polar challenge: the joining up of the feats of the Antarctic, Arctic and North West Passage pioneers into a logical conclusion with the Sahara, Atlantic and Pacific thrown in for extra measure.

Patriotism in the mid 1970s was no longer openly considered a worthwhile motive. To admit to it was to invite denigration and scorn. Perhaps I was born too late in the scheme of things because to me a man's country can be worth living for, dying for and 'doing' for. Later on more tangible benefits to be gained as a result of our venture, mainly through scientific research work in the polar regions, became apparent, but initially our sole reasoning was the acceptance of challenge for its own sake.

George Greenfield had made it clear that without the blessing of the British government we could not hope to receive help from any base in Antarctica. Without such help the journey would stand little chance. So my next visit was to the Foreign Office. The so-called Polar Desk, a sub-office of the Latin Americas Department, was housed near Waterloo Bridge. I wore my grey pin-striped suit and got an old regimental tie out of mothballs. The gentleman I was to meet looked after Great Britain's reponsibilities north of the Arctic Circle and south of the Antarctic Circle virtually by himself. He was an ex-biologist and, quite apart from his diplomatic position, was a leading figure in Antarctic circles owing to his past activities with the Falkland Islands Dependencies Survey (now called the British Antarctic Survey). He made it plain that I would get to Antarctica, much less cross it, over his dead body.

That meeting, I think in retrospect, finally removed my last doubts as to the desirability of pursuing the whole endeavour. This pillar of the establishment had flung down the gauntlet. As far as he and, I later discovered, a number of other Antarctic pundits in the country likewise were concerned, I was to be blocked at every turn. He knew where I would have to go, whom I must approach and lost no time in putting the word about in those quarters.

For the next four years we were to batter our heads against an unyielding wall of officialdom. But, practice making perfect, we got quite good at it. The eminent Foreign Office gentleman died some five years later.

It is best, when chatting people up, to have a firm date to aim for. Then sponsors are less inclined to think you are building castles in the air. Obviously, we could not get going in a year. But two might be possible. So, early in 1973, we drew up plans to depart in September 1975. The Royal Greenwich Observatory celebrated their Tercentenary in 1975; thinking of a neat tie-up we visited the Observatory. Owing to pollution Greenwich skies are no longer good for observing stars, so the Observatory has moved, lock, stock and Isaac Newton's telescope, down to the clear skies of Sussex and the spacious grounds of Herstmonceux Castle.

Normally, I find my full family name, Twisleton-Wykeham-Fiennes, a bit of a burden, but as far as our standing with the Observatory's Director was concerned, it could do no harm, for he was keen on local history. Back in 1066 my ancestor, Count Eustache de Boulogne, had been appointed number two to William the Conqueror before the attack. King Harold, defending Hastings, was inhibited by a Norman arrow in his eye. Cousin Eustache grabbed his chance and, according to the Bayeux Tapestry, removed the royal head with a clean sweep of his axe. William was grateful and the Fynnes or Fiennes clan flourished. Later Fiennes folk, five centuries back, had built Herstmonceux. So the castle's present inmate agreed to a tie-up between his Observatory and our voyage.

How long would the 37,000-mile round trip take? Well, it is only possible to cross the poles during *their* summer and it would only be possible to take a boat through the North West Passage when the sea-ice had begun to break up in mid-July: so these three absolutes controlled our timing.

If we started going south in September, we might reach the Antarctic in January in time to set up a base camp for the winter (end of year one) and so be ready to start to cross in November, the very moment the days got warm enough. With luck we'd be across to the Pacific and up to the Yukon by mid-July in time to spend our second winter in Canada (end of year two). We would then start to cross the Arctic as soon as it became warm enough to travel in March. With continued luck we would be back in England by September. End of year three.

With luck, with luck. But from the start we must plan against *bad* luck and allow an extra year down in Antarctica for another winter, another attempt, just in case. Take an umbrella with you and it won't rain. Plan for the worst and we might do it all in three years.

By the time the enormity of our self-imposed undertaking had fully sunk in, with the slow unearthing of more information, we had spent a year doing nothing else. We were like rolling stones. Having gone a little way down a hill, the realisation that the hill was more like a mountain with no yet visible bottom was not going to stop us.

For the first year we lived in a basement flat in Earls Court just behind the underground station, a grotty, noisy spot.

"We need an office," Ginnie said. "With a free telephone. There's no way we can set up everything here. The cost of phone calls and postage alone will be crippling."

"I'll ask the Colonel," I said. "There must be spare space in the barracks."

The 21st SAS Territorial Regiment is based in the Duke of York's Barracks in Sloane Square. Mistakenly, the IRA believed that regular Special Air Service men used the place and had recently bombed it twice, both times damaging the Victorian brickwork but not much else.

The Colonel was sympathetic: he liked the idea. As a territorial or weekend soldier, I was a regular attender in charge of a troop. My earlier explosive sins with the regular SAS had been forgotten – or so I thought. But 21 SAS and its Scottish territorial counterpart, 23 SAS, are administered by a Brigadier who also commands the regular regiment. When my Colonel asked permission for the SAS to sponsor the expedition in general and to provide barracks space for our office, memories were revived. Was it the same Fiennes who caused trouble six years previously? It was. How do we know he's changed his ways? We don't, but his scheme sounds worthwhile. We'll back it officially *only* if a responsible SAS man oversees Fiennes. They obviously had a wry sense of humour because the man they chose was Brigadier Mike Wingate Gray, now retired; the man who had slung me out of the SAS. Surprisingly, he agreed to become nominal boss of the venture to keep me in the paths of righteousness.

They gave us an office, an attic room in a disused indoor rifle range. There was no window and no light bulb but, on the plus side, it was so quiet you could hear the mice pass wind and – there was a telephone. Ten days, two light bulbs and some purloined furniture later, the Quartermaster visited us without an appointment and found Ginnie using the telephone (to a potential stationery sponsor).

He looked at me.

"That is a telephone."

"Yes," I agreed. "Would you like some tea? We've installed a kettle."

"That telephone is not on our establishment; it was removed last year."

My blood ran cold. The telephone must be guarded at all costs. I decided not to annoy him.

"That's correct. It was removed. Do you take milk? Sugar?"

The Quartermaster drank his tea but next morning our phone was gone. The advantage of a territorial unit is the number of civilian professions represented. One of my men had a friend who knew a Post Office technician. Late one night, after minimal fiddling with the wiring, a new phone was installed and kept in a desk drawer when not in use. We were back in business. By the end of 1973 a mountain of equipment from some two hundred sponsor companies was stored around the barracks in half empty garages and armouries.

When dispirited by a bad morning of sponsors saying 'No' we could always listen to the Irish Rifles recruits downstairs learning to play the bagpipes or watch the cast of *Upstairs Downstairs* rehearsing in the old gymnasium next door.

When our finances grew serious one of us would disappear for a while to recoup. I spent three weeks doing an 'expedition' in the London sewers in the company of a well-built blonde actress as part of the BBC *World About Us* series. Ginnie went to Oman for a month to live as a nominal third wife of a local sheikh in order to write a feature for *Woman's Own*. For two months I went to Brunei with a detachment of the regular SAS on a jungle tracking course – the same course I had missed by a day seven years before, owing to the *Doctor Dolittle* débâcle. In the evenings and at weekends I lectured to schools, universities, ladies' luncheon clubs and borstals about previous expeditions.

During the day we gathered equipment for the polar crossing and wondered how we were going to obtain a Hercules C130 transport plane with skis. Let alone a ship. Robin Knox-Johnston, single-handed yachtsman of common sense and experience, said the cheapest ship, second hand, that he advised for a voyage such as we envisaged would cost £350,000. We would also need fuel: thousands of gallons of it.

I visited Sir David Barron, top executive of Shell, in their sky-scraper beside the Thames. He was friendly and tried hard to press my case with the rest of his Board – to no avail. BP were also negative, so I approached the only other British-owned gasoline company – ICI Petrochemicals. After a year of correspondence they agreed to help.

The Army Mountain and Arctic Warfare Committee saw an opportunity, at no cost, of prolonged cold-weather tests for recently developed clothing and rations. Through them we obtained Arctic food, excellent polar clothing and 300 equipment parachutes.

To travel over the ice we must have dogs or machines to pull our sledges. Wally Herbert, Britain's most experienced polar traveller, wrote: "The partnership of man and dogs is the safest form of surface travel in the Arctic Ocean when beyond the range of light aircraft . . . If a dog dies, he and his food supply are eaten by his team mates and the team carries on."

Dr Geoffrey Hattersley-Smith, one of the few men to have worked with machines and dogs along the edge of the Arctic Ocean, stressed that his dog team could move a great deal faster over patches of rough ice than any type of snow machine. The superiority of dogs over machines for day to day travel in areas of broken polar ice was never in doubt, whoever we asked. Dogs do not refuse to start in low temperatures, nor do they break down and waste weeks, not just days, of good travel weather as a result. But when I wrote to Wally Herbert in 1974 for his advice, his answer had been adamant. We should *not* use dogs unless we were prepared to spend a year or two learning how to handle them.

Further prolonged delay whilst we learned to master the difficult art of dog driving and dog care was not easy to accept. Moreover, our expedition would, of necessity, be under some public scrutiny and the media can be quick to spotlight any real or imagined cruelty to animals. Although our intentions might be humane, the results could misfire. A Japanese polar expedition flew 180 huskies from Thule to Alert in specially built cages but the dogs panicked in the air and 105 died. Wally Herbert bought forty dogs in Qânâq but on the way back to his base a quarter either died or chewed through their traces and deserted. So, having weighed the pros and cons, we decided to use snow machines. Even if they made travel more difficult over the Arctic Ocean, they were financially and administratively within our scope. Dogs were not.

When a man who has never sailed, but wants to, goes to a boat show he is confronted by a thousand different shapes, sizes and types. Bewildering, especially if he's uncertain of the conditions in the seas he will eventually visit. I too was bewildered when I discovered the plethora of snow machines on the market. To help myself I categorised all of them into two groups: snowcats, bigger machines with closed driving cabins; and snowmobiles, little ones with no protection from the elements. Previous homework indicated our sledge loads would be around 1,000 pounds so the machines selected must be able to pull that weight in soft powder snow or on ice and have protection to save us from exposure. Yet they should be light enough for two or three people to manhandle.

I opted for an Austrian snowcat big enough for two passengers in a little raised cabin. Since this looked like a groundhog on the Sugar Puffs cereal packet that's what we called it.

I knew even less about the pros and cons of sledges, except that if they broke up everything would come to an abrupt halt and wood repairs in low temperatures can take up a lot of precious time.

Wally advised me: "I personally would *never* take a metal sledge. A sledge must be flexible and easy to repair as well as strong." The Antarctic travellers I spoke to said the same thing. Nonetheless, keen to take advantage of anything the twentieth century might offer, I approached the British Steel Corporation. They were interested.

How would Austenitic 316 special steel stand up to extreme temperatures? Using thin tubes welded by hand to the design of Professor Noel Dilley, four 8′ 6″ sledges for the Arctic and four 12′ 9″ sledges for the Antarctic were fashioned by young BSC apprentices as part of their training, under the watchful eye of expert steel welder, Percy Wood, recently retired. "We'll show these wood merchants a thing or two," Percy muttered as the sledges were handed over. Later the sledges were coated at great heat and Tufnol runners affixed by Plastic Coatings with Araldite epoxy and self-locking GKN bolts.

Meanwhile, my attempts to get approval for the Antarctic plans were going nowhere fast. The crossing plan depended on Hercules transport aircraft dropping parachutes with fuel and food. Only the RAF could provide this aid but they would not do so without the Royal Geographical Society's approval of the plans. The RGS Committee would not even convene unless the Foreign Office gave them the green light. They would not. Impasse.

After two years of turned-down proposals, my military patrons, the SAS, were becoming impatient. When any aspect of my plan was criticised, I altered it and re-applied. But the Foreign Office simply found new criticisms.

I was learning. Learning how not to approach the Foreign Office; how not to contact individual British polar experts. While I honed my technique, I concentrated on finding people for our team. We could forget aircraft crewmen since, if the RAF did help, their Hercules would be fully manned. The ship's crew would have to wait for the moment. My first target was the land team, those who would travel across the Poles and all the jungles, deserts, swamps and rivers in between.

Previous journeys had made me a firm believer that the fewer people involved the better, since human beings seem to be badly designed for getting on with each other. Shove them together in a confined space and the sparks will usually fly: witness the one-in-three divorce rate. Three or four seemed as small an ice-travel team as we could get away with.

Colonel Andrew Croft, well-known in polar circles, was in the early days almost the only member of those circles prepared to be seen to help and advise us. On the ideal number for a travel group, he said: "With three men, two can gang up against the leader. My experience suggests that you as leader should only decide whether to have two or three companions *after* you have seen your potential colleagues in action during Arctic training." This seemed sound advice. However no one would let me go to the Arctic for the moment, so Snowdonia would have to do for selection and training.

Between 1972 and 1978 120 volunteers tried their luck. Some lasted no longer than the interview stage. I had a stock approach which I called the 'black talk'.

"If you want to join, you must apply to the Territorial SAS Regiment in the corridor just below this attic. They have a weekend selection course in Wales."

"What, just the weekend?"

"No, twelve weekends and a final two-week test in the hills. You will need to get rid of your beard and some of that hair, of course."

If this last point did not get rid of them at once the black talk continued. "If the SAS accept you as a trooper, come back again and we'll have another talk. If you are still keen, you must leave your job and help us here full-time to get the expedition going."

"What's the pay?"

"Pay! We don't have pay. This is an expedition. There is no pay."

"But you say the journey may last three years. How do I live?"

"The expedition will last at least three years. But it could be that we aren't ready to leave as planned in 1975. If so, we just keep working till we are ready. We only work in the day times normally, so you can get a job in the evenings and at weekends to keep alive."

"What if you can't get the support? You've no ship, no aircraft, they say."

"We *will* get going one day."

"Yeah, but if I'm going to give up my job, I won't get it back again. I've got to be sure there's at least going to be an expedition."

"You can be."

"You're a captain and a Sir. You don't need to work."

This one made me swallow. "I may have a title but I don't have any income except what I earn. I lecture at £65 a time plus travel. Evenings and weekends. Ginnie and I don't entertain, we don't drink. We don't have a home life. *This* is our life. You either commit yourself or you don't."

The bulk of them we never saw again. But some made it into the

Territorial SAS and worked on and off to help us, although few made the final decision to fling in their jobs altogether.

Whoever made the grade I took on weekends in Snowdonia each winter and spring from 1973 until 1976 to train for the annual army race, the Welsh 3000. Usually there was freezing rain, thick mist and strong winds, sometimes snow and ice. Starting on the summit of Snowdon, the whole team practised covering twenty-five miles to the top of thirteen Welsh peaks over 3,000 feet within twenty-four hours, carrying twenty-five pounds of safety gear on their backs. In 1974 we won in the record time of seven and a half hours and brought the Territorial cup back to the Duke of York's Barracks in triumph. It wasn't a perfect method of selecting people for polar travel but the best I could manage at no expense.

I wasn't after physical prowess but reaction to stress and strain. I looked for good nature and patience. Ginnie and I might not have either but there wasn't much we could do about that: at least we could ensure that the rest of the team were suitable. Once I'd found my paragons, I hoped that the army would train them as astro-navigators, mechanics, radio operators and medics at no extra cost.

George Greenfield now suggested a cautious approach to Sir Vivian Fuchs to obtain his personal support. His advice was that no one would take us seriously until we had gained polar experience. Tentatively I approached the Foreign Office, suggesting that I'd like to do three months' icecap travel in Greenland, followed by five months' Arctic training further north. This was turned down. I simplified my request and asked only for three months in Greenland. At long last I received approval in principle. Perhaps they would let us go further north after we'd shown ourselves to be responsible in Greenland.

The RAF, I discovered, operated three polar navigation flights to Thule in Greenland each summer and they now agreed to take our cargo but not us, although we were Territorials. Much more helpful was Colonel Paul Clark, Air Attaché at the US Embassy in London, who nodded sympathetically at my tale of official delays and agreed to get us to Greenland in a USAF plane for $2,000. Paul Clark was later to give up a promising career to join us as an unpaid deck-hand.

The long weary years in the attic were nearing an end. They were an investment we had made of our own free will. We had learned patience and in the process had grown much closer together.

I blame no one for the stonewalling. The army did what they could to help but they, like us, were hidebound by the Foreign Office. And the Foreign Office had long since learned that to keep private individuals out of Antarctica, which was their unwritten duty, they had only to rebuff all approaches until the applicant gave up.

2

Polar Apprenticeship

1976–7

Failure has no friends.

JOHN F. KENNEDY

One day a well-dressed man with an air of mild debauchery stalked into our office. Oliver Shepard was tall, dark, in his mid-twenties and keen to join us.

Mentally I denounced him as unsuitable on sight. For a start I remembered him from Eton days as a pompous-sounding character with pompous-sounding friends. We had joined 21 SAS at the same time but seldom met. For three years I had seen nothing of him but heard on the grapevine that he had expensive tastes, was intermittently separated from his wife and lived a life as far removed from expeditions as chalk from cheese.

A quick interrogation revealed that he was working for a wine and beer distributor, managing their Chelsea pubs and enjoying a good salary complete with Volvo estate car and healthy expense account which was reflected in his paunch. Altogether not a propitious background for our purposes, but there was no harm in letting him try his luck. So he rejoined the Territorials and began to suffer weekends in Snowdonia.

Mary Gibbs came to us through friends of friends. She was dark and pretty and Ginnie got on well with her. Not able to join the SAS, she signed up with a Territorial hospital unit based in the barracks. Ginnie was likewise attached to a signals regiment.

Geoff Newman, tall and fair and powerfully built, gave up a printing job to join us, and, in October that year, Oliver took me to a local drinks party to meet one Charlie Burton who had just left a job in South Africa. The next morning Charlie turned up at the barracks in an old tweed overcoat, smoking an evil-smelling briar. He and Geoff had finished their SAS selection courses early in 1976. In March the six of us went training in the Cairngorms. I ran through the basics of cross-country skiing for the umpteenth time, how to erect a polar tent and how to cook dehydrated rations. Again, I wondered how long *this* group would last.

I need not have worried. All seemed ideal; indeed, they improved with time. Geoff and Mary became quietly attached. Oliver and Charlie, both extroverts and accomplished beer-drinkers, developed a close and lasting friendship. They took my initial black talk in their stride. I therefore decided to take them all to Greenland: the men would trek, Mary and Ginnie would act as radio base camp. Oliver now took up residence within the barracks, sleeping on our office floor and eating expedition dehydrated rations. His paunch disappeared.

Andrew Croft asked me to supper one night. The key Foreign Office man was also there, not our initial bête noire, but a younger, friendlier man who had taken over the Polar Desk. He was prepared to help not hinder, but warned us it would be a long uphill struggle and the main expedition's chances would depend on our success or otherwise in Greenland.

Spring fled by and the team trained hard. Charlie and Geoff were accepted into the SAS as troopers. Ollie and I were captains. Ginnie and Mary in their separate outfits were privates.

Ollie took numerous courses. On 25th April his diary recorded: "I am now a doctor." On 18th May: "Now I am a dentist." This after a one-day course with the Royal Army Dental Corps.

"What's the secret of good dentistry?" I asked him.

"You've got to be cruel to be kind," he said.

I made a mental note to keep my teeth well away from him. Two weeks after his general hospital attendance Ollie was itching to get at our appendixes, but two years later, out on the ice, it was all he could do to remember which side they were on.

In the past expeditions for me had been hermetically sealed units.

You left England, carried out your set task and returned; *all* the team went too; none stayed behind as UK representatives. But things were different now. Work towards the main circumpolar venture must continue whilst we were away training in Greenland, so Mike Wingate Gray and Andrew Croft, together with Peter Booth, a friend from previous travels, agreed to carry on in London.

Ginnie, our communications planner, would be unable to telephone them from polar bases, so she visited the Cove Radio and Navigation Department of the Royal Aircraft Establishment at Farnborough. The three officers there, with the permission of their departmental boss, agreed to act as Ginnie's UK radio base. They would then phone Andrew Croft or the others in London. This way we could have speedy communications, even from the Poles, whenever ionospheric conditions were favourable.

We arrived in Greenland in late July 1976 but the RAF didn't arrive with our sledges and two groundhogs until August, so I proposed to squeeze two experimental journeys into what remained of the short summer season. First, an eighty-mile loop journey passing through two known crevasse zones, and secondly a 150-mile trek into the interior of the icecap along fissured slopes parallel to the coast.

If all went well with our untested machines, steel sledges and inexperienced participants – and if the weather held – I hoped to complete both journeys in time to face the Royal Geographical Society's Expeditions Committee on 1st November, well primed with details of the experience we'd gained in order to press for permission to go further north for more Arctic training.

I decided to take Oliver and Geoff on the first loop journey and Oliver and Charlie on the second, as our tent was designed for three. I suspected that three would prove ideal for the Arctic and also thought it best to leave one male with our otherwise all-woman radio base. Oliver, who had been with me longest, was a good radio operator, a sound medic and a solid, if somewhat snappy, person and I now wished to groom him as our future groundhog mechanic. During the course of the two journeys I would probably decide between Geoff and Charlie.

For over a month Oliver, Geoff and I slogged our way over crevasses and fissures in freezing temperatures. I skied ahead with one eye never far from my compass, prodding hard at the snow with my ski stick to test the surface, whilst Oliver and Geoff followed behind in their groundhogs. We learned to make camp in a blizzard, to replace broken sprocket wheels in below-zero temperatures, to navigate in a whiteout, to remain amicably jammed together in a tiny tent in a snowstorm for days on end. By the end we felt confident that we could travel far and fast in groundhogs over inhospitable terrain. Geoffrey turned out to be quite the opposite in temperament to Oliver but both seemed tough and resilient and both remained cool under pressure.

Ginnie met us at the edge of the ice sheet on our return and gave a depressing account of Charlie's behaviour. He'd been morose and idle in camp, spending long hours on his mattress in the hut reading cowboy books. She then departed taking Geoff with her and I gazed at Charlie with a somewhat jaundiced eye. We hoped to spend six years of enforced togetherness in tough circumstances, if all our plans materialised, so could not afford to carry any laggards. Hostilities must not be allowed to thrive either.

Oliver and I began the second inland journey with critical glances at Charlie but he showed no signs of evil humour. Instead he seemed happy to be away from Thule; he pulled his weight at whatever we did and was unusually quick at copying our actions for, with our earlier journey behind us, we thought we were experts. This might have annoyed Charlie but he never showed it. When disaster threatened he turned up trumps.

We'd been travelling for several days when we hit a field of crevasses. The first I knew about it was when one of my ski sticks' broke straight through the surface snow and disappeared. My arm followed up to the shoulder. With slow movements, carefully keeping my body weight over both skis, I moved away from the small black hole in the snow, the only indication of hidden danger. I cursed myself for a fool. The trouble was we had been taking too long over this second journey and were trying to push on too fast. It was a misty day and getting dark now but this was no place for travelling in poor visibility. I was descending a steep slope without any idea of what lay below. The angle was too great for a groundhog to get back up, if need be, and too steep to pitch our tent.

I waited for the groundhogs to catch up and explained our predicament. Both drivers gave the thumbs up and travelled on in first gear, using the steering brakes as sparingly as possible and I skied carefully on in front. The farther we descended, the darker it became. It seemed an age before the slope levelled out and only then, when I was well and truly committed to the valley, did it reveal its unpleasant nature.

I kick-turned my light Norwegian skis and langlaufed back up my trail. Suddenly a groundhog appeared with Charlie half out of its cab. Oliver, he said, had gone down a crevasse.

At first I could see nothing. Charlie pointed to a vague line of darker gloom. I skied towards it. Oliver's groundhog had a flag on its cabin roof and it was this that Charlie had seen. The rest of the vehicle had disappeared from view. Then cresting the rise, I saw the trapped groundhog and, catching my breath, came to an abrupt halt. My ski tips hung over a narrow canyon in the snow which led zig-zag fashion to the hole that engulfed the machine.

Gingerly I inspected the fissure and could see no bottom to it. Oliver had been driving almost parallel to its course when his groundhog's right-hand track had punctured the rotten bridge concealing its presence.

The vehicle must have lurched sideways and downwards. Fortunately, for the moment at least, the left-hand track had caught upon the lip of the crevasse and balanced there. But the least movement could dislodge the machine and send it plunging downwards.

As I watched, Oliver began to wriggle out of his tiny cabin door, his parka catching on the controls as he did so. The groundhog rocked to and fro; snow fell away from the bank which held it and Oliver, realising his danger, redoubled his efforts. Soon he was on the catwalk beside the cab and, keeping his weight central, edged towards the safer side, away from the void. Each time the machine lurched and slipped a bit, he froze. When it quieted he moved eel-like nearer terra firma. He did well, escaping without disturbing the machine. Now we had only to pull it out, an event we had long prepared for. Oliver, without the safety of skis, stayed where he was. I moved over to Charlie and beckoned him forward.

On paper we had agreed on the best method of recovery: a straightforward pull by the still mobile groundhog using Kevla, a tow-rope endowed with a great deal of elastic strength. Once enough elasticity was induced by the towing machine, the other should by rights pop out of its predicament like a cork from a champagne bottle.

Charlie reversed, then slowly nosed through the mist into the best approach angle. He was perhaps eighty yards from Oliver and well away from the crevasse when it happened.

The only noise was a sharp thud as Charlie's head hit the windscreen. I watched fascinated as the snow unzipped in front of me, revealing a long black cavern.

The groundhog was moving slowly at the time and Charlie was quick. He slammed on both steering brakes as he felt himself fall, coming to an abrupt halt as his vehicle jammed its upper catwalks between the lips of the new crevasse. Then, unseen, the moon edged behind the southern hills and the darkness was complete. By torchlight and wary as long-tailed cats in a room full of rocking chairs, we tested the snow yard by yard until we came to Charlie. He was out before we reached him and unlashing his tent from his leading sledge.

We made camp between the two crevasses, hoping that the spot we chose was solid. We were tired, many miles from anywhere, and caught between an escarpment we could not climb and a deeply crevassed valley through which we must travel to escape.

For two days we shovelled, dug, chipped and cursed. At first the task had seemed beyond us. To extricate the groundhogs from their dizzy perches meant moving them backwards or forwards. Yet the slightest movement in either direction would only serve to widen the gap in the delicate snow bridges and send the machines plunging downwards.

Oliver's diary records: "We spent the day roped together as crevasses are all around us. One, close to the tent, is about five feet wide and has infinite depth."

After many hours, we completed tunnels for our aluminium crevasse ladders well below the sunken groundhogs. The recovery operation was dicey but it worked.

Our timetable was now well into the red. Winter and darkness was upon us. The journey back to Thule was splattered with crevasse alarms, boggings, and many breakdowns. But Oliver always coped. With spindrift settling down his neck and some of his fingers split from the nails back to the first knuckle, he continued patiently and thoroughly, 'botching up' where he had no spare part to do the job. As he worked Charlie watched, helping where he could. Oliver was often short and sharp with him but he ignored this. He decided it was just 'Ol's way' when embroiled with details and lived with it. Theirs was a close and easy friendship. Luckily, however, the two did not form an alliance against me. In the back-of-beyond where there are no links with normal life, friendship is important. Two things I believe saved us from the 'triangle' situation.

Both men were strong individualists and at all times stuck rigidly to their independent theories on how things should best be done. They did not experience the temptation of forming a united front for the sake of it or the better to disrupt my own way of doing things. When each disagreed with my theories he did so separately and openly, avoiding the behind-the-back consultations which are the most poisonous ingredient even a short expedition can suffer.

Secondly, I had been through life without feeling the need for close friends: probably due to a youth spent amusing myself as my three elder sisters had different tastes. Most days I could speak to Ginnie on the radio or at least listen to her morse signals, so there was never a feeling of personal isolation. I had been lucky enough to be able to select with care individuals without malice. Such people are surprisingly rare. With Charlie, the 'malice content' was minimal: with Oliver, non-existent.

We returned to Thule not a day too soon. The weather clamped down on the icecap and stayed there, a grim, grey blanket hiding the whole feature from the camp. But the wind spilled down the valley, battering at the man-made installations and tearing through Thule to lash the icebergs and the black islands beyond.

Once again six in number, we stored all the kit, cleaned and greased for the winter, and told the authorities, Danish and American, that we hoped to be back in about three months' time to transport all of it by plane to Alert.

I returned from Greenland fit and weighing 185 pounds. Over the next three months in London, the most harassing I can remember, I lost fourteen pounds without exercise or a diet. My first grey hairs also sprouted during this period.

Back in the office the detailed costs of the circumpolar expedition were mounting. I realised that no one would give millions of pounds of equipment to a group of nobodies who'd merely messed around on the fringe of some icecap. The only way we might ever obtain the tremendous sponsorship our ultimate journey required would be by conducting a more impressive feat in worse conditions. A journey to the North Pole was the obvious choice.

I went before the Royal Geographical Society's Expeditions Committee who questioned me closely on many technical details of our time in Greenland and posed a wide variety of questions from astro-navigation to personality differences. Then I asked permission to try for the North Pole itself, leaving England within three months.

Whilst I waited for their answer I set about rethinking our means of ice travel. The groundhogs had superior pulling power to most snow vehicles but on bare sea-ice they were impossible to control: the metal tracks, unable to dig in, had slithered about sideways or even backwards. The Arctic is not a solid continental mass like the Antarctic, it consists of a delicate skin of ice covering a deep ocean; bare ice would frequently occur so it would be essential to have a vehicle which could grapple competently with a slippery surface.

There are more individuals in Britain who have climbed Mount Everest than have travelled even briefly on Arctic sea-ice. I contacted one of the few who have, Geoffrey Hattersley-Smith, and he recommended me to try a Canadian Bombardier snowmobile called a skidoo which had a 640 cc air-cooled Rotax engine made in Austria. I telexed the Bombardier company near Montreal who would not sponsor us but were happy to sell us four machines with £500 of back-up spares and despatch them immediately to Resolute, 600 miles south of Alert.

Oliver travelled to Austria where the engines and gearboxes were manufactured for a quick training course. This took place in German, a language of which Oliver had little knowledge, but he was ever an optimist.

The RAF would not fly our gear from Thule to Alert so I must find money to charter a Twin Otter ski-plane to do so and for resupply drops on our journey to the North Pole.

An old friend of mine was an ex-soldier who lived and worked in Arabia. At the time he was visiting London and he offered to introduce me to his friend Dr Omar Zawawi, an Omani who had built up a business in Zanzibar and subsequently in Europe. Dr Omar, a charming man with a wealth of good humour and razor-sharp perception, interviewed me at his Knightsbridge house. Nothing escaped his dark brown eyes. For two hours I described our aims and our problems.

He approved of free enterprise. He had read and enjoyed a book I had written about Oman. Most of all he was grateful to the individual Britons who had risked their lives for the freedom of his country. The upshot of the meeting was a dinner at which he introduced Ginnie and me to a Yorkshireman, Jack Codd, the Managing Director of Tarmac International. A month later we received £58,000 from Dr Omar and Jack Codd, as well as promises of support for the main circumpolar journey.

Scandinavian Airline Systems now said that they would take us and our baggage from England to Thule and back again. As a rule they sponsored only Björn Borg, the local tennis hero, but two coincidences attracted them to us. Their trade name was 'SAS' and the start date of our polar training journey coincided with their celebrations to mark the twentieth anniversary of their first trans-polar flight.

At long last the Royal Geographical Society's approval came. Now all we needed was Canadian army permission for us to use some old shacks of theirs at Alert for our base camp and permission from the US to land at Thule to collect the gear we'd left there.

Speed was essential. We had to reach Alert by January in order to move in the necessary 31,000 pounds of fuel, food and equipment and set up a self-contained base in permanent darkness and sub-zero temperatures. We must set out for the North Pole before 15th March to have any hope of success. Most North Pole attempts end in dismal failure because they mistime their journey – the last effort had only got three miles from its starting point.

As we dashed hither and thither fixing up equipment, greasing, painting and packaging, weighing and listing tons of sponsors' stores, we were constantly interrupted by our need to earn money in order to eat and our need to fulfil our Territorial Army duties. On three evenings a week I lectured; every Tuesday evening found all six of us in khaki in various London drill halls; Oliver, Charlie and Geoff had to spend two precious weeks in Bavaria on an SAS course whilst I had to parachute into Denmark by night to make a mock attack on NATO installations. Our polar experience was not widened by these activities but we earned our use of the office space at the Duke of York's headquarters.

Five short weeks before we must leave England, I flew to Canada to ask for their permission to use their Alert shacks. This they gave most willingly, only requesting that we be totally self-contained and self-reliant, that we produce proof of insurance cover up to £100,000 for search and rescue costs, and that we keep clear of security areas at all times.

Three weeks to go and still no permission to land at Thule from the Americans. Then a telegram came from the US authorities in Thule to the US Air Attaché in London stating that "the request to visit Thule" had been granted. Later we were to discover that this had been intended for some anthropologists, not for us, but not knowing this at the time, we felt the elation of a break-through. We could now try for the North Pole. The circumnavigation of the world looked a distinct possibility. Much had hinged on that one muddled telegram . . .

Two weeks to go and I decided to ask HRH Prince Charles if he would agree to be Patron of the Transglobe expedition. No harm in asking. So I wrote a letter requesting this honour and took it by hand to Buckingham Palace. It was raining gently and few tourists were about. I asked one of the sentries at the gate where I should go regarding the matter of Royal Patronage. The soldier was unable to speak, so I moved round to the left flank where there appeared to be a tradesmen's entrance. My identity card saw me past two policemen but a security officer stopped me well before I made it to the main palace. He relieved me of the letter. "Don't worry, sir. I'll make good and sure this reaches His Royal Highness. A fine day to you, sir." I had been politely seen off.

On 26th February Oliver, Geoff, Charlie and I set out for the North Pole. Three days later we were stuck after only six miles. The new Bombardier skidoos refused to start, no matter what we did to them with blow-torches, heaters and even hot tea. When we moved our clothes cracked. Soon Ginnie informed us on the radio that Alert had just recorded its lowest ever temperature and that the United States were experiencing the coldest winter ever known. It was 1977. No normal year.

When the temperature reached −51°C, I sensed impending failure, for we had got to average ten miles a day every day to reach the North Pole before ice break-up, but the vehicles kept refusing to start under such abnormal conditions. Then Geoff became unusually quiet and his feet soon lost all feeling. Whilst I skied back to Alert for help, the others tried to massage some life back into his yellow-white toes. When I returned with the base commander, a mechanic and an aircraft heater to 'dry out' the skidoos, we decided to return to Alert to manufacture built-in heater systems for each skidoo before going any further.

On the journey back to base, Geoffrey was wearing woollen gloves, heavy quilt gauntlets and thick leather outer mitts but instead of stopping every so often to swing his arms, he kept going for fear that the engine of his skidoo might stall. Six of his fingers became completely numb with frostbite. When we left Alert again on 10th March, it was without Geoff.

We could get the skidoos going in the mornings now, but there was much time to be made up so we travelled hard, sometimes ten or eleven-hours a day without a break in exceptionally low temperatures, made worse by a wind chill factor which on occasion reached —105°. To right tipped-up sledges, to re-lash equipment and tinker with faulty engines in this degree of cold was unpleasant.

Nights were bitter with frozen sleeping bags to thaw out in a perishingly cold tent. I couldn't sleep, dreading the moment when at intervals throughout the night, it was necessary to turn over and the layer of frost particles from my breath dropped off the bag lining and slid down my neck.

As we left the coast and struggled inland over the broken ice rubble of the semi-frozen sea, the wind chill factor increased, an icy blast whipping at us, freezing the liquid on our eyeballs.

We had been warned that we would come across high pressure ridges of ice at a rate of some seventy a mile, stretching for at least thirty miles: these we would have to hack through with ice axes. But the unprecedented ferocity of the winter of 1977 meant that it was very much worse than our wildest imaginings, with the pressure ridges far more frequent, seemingly unending and the areas in between chock-a-block with chaotic debris. We had to hack a path through every inch of this, wide and smooth enough to take the skidoos. At low temperatures the human body, making no allowances for the encumbrance of bulky clothing and footwear, works at four-fifths of its normal efficiency; with Geoff gone and Oliver constantly attending to the skidoos, it meant that all the chopping had to be done by Charlie and me: just two pairs of hands, two axes, bashing at the ice for mile upon mile.

Each time the axe struck, bits of ice flew about. But so little ice for so much activity. Feather-soft snow lay over cracks in between ice blocks and we kept falling into these. Charlie disappeared up to his shoulders on one occasion. On another, one of my boots became stuck in a cranny. We laughed weakly at each other's predicaments. To strike a stance from which gainfully to use the axe it was often necessary to dig out a flat platform first. Otherwise the act of swinging the axe had us sliding all over the place. The exertion meant taking deep breaths of freezing air and this gave a burning sensation in the chest.

The reflected glare made me want to wear my tinted glasses but they either misted up or my nose was exposed to the wind, depending on whether my facemask was up or down. Since my nose was already raw I gave up the glasses and never wore them again until, weeks later, the temperatures warmed up to the −20s.

After seven hours and two hundred yards of axe work we trudged and slid back to the tent. Oliver was sitting on a skidoo cleaning a sparking plug. He did not appear to notice our return though we approached from the direction he was facing.

"How's it going, Ol?" Charlie offered.

Oliver looked up sharply and I noticed the whites of his eyes were completely bloodshot.

"I don't seem able to see much," he said, "and it's not just my squint."

"Could be a touch of sun blindness," I suggested.

He shook his head. "There's no real pain, just a general blur." Oliver did not blame the glare. He thought it more likely that cooker fumes were the cause.

Our tents each had a ventilation hole at the peak but these became quickly clogged with ice, despite daily attention and, because of the extreme temperatures, the fumes seemed loath to rise. As all the carburettors were cleaned with petrol in the other tent, the fumes were worse there. The other two's eye problems doubtless started first because of this.

I remember one night particularly clearly because a number of little things went wrong. It was no exceptional experience and the others certainly suffered the same sort of troubles.

After a supper of dehydrated chicken chunks and carrot flakes, I chewed at my daily Mars bar. A sizeable piece of filling came out of one tooth and I swallowed it. The cavity left a rough edge which a raw piece on my tongue kept touching.

As was our custom, I used a polythene bag after supper to avoid going outside. I propped this up, after securing the neck with a double hitch, at the end of my sleeping bag. Normally by morning the bag would be frozen solid and easy to bury. But that night the bag leaked over the end of my sleeping bag.

Soon after I had placed my metal one-pint mug, full of ice slush, on the cooker, my eyes began to sting. This grew quickly intolerable, as though a spike was being screwed in behind the upper lid of each eye.

I lay on my back to see if that lessened the pain. In doing so, my feet kicked the cooker and the mug fell over on to my only two dried items – a khaki facemask and my blue Damart mitts – which I only wore at night.

Not seeing much, for my eyes were watering, I grabbed the hot base of the metal mug. For long minutes in the dark I thought of nothing but my eyes. I squirmed about, pressed my eyeballs with my mitts, knelt and looked downwards, even scraped frost off the tent liner and held it against each eye in turn. But the feeling of grit lumps moving about under the lids persisted: even intensified. And the tent grew quickly colder.

I lit the candle which came with the day's rations and propped it on the cooker board, the only flat space in the tent. Not thinking, I picked up my spoon from the end of the bed and received another cold burn through a hole in the mitt.

One eye got better for a while and I determined to drink hot cocoa before trying to sleep. I kept the half-gallon petrol can well away from the inner tent lining which, by nature of its breathability, is made from a material that is also highly inflammable. As I filled the cooker tank, a second unseen spurt escaped to the groundsheet and flowed away in several directions. This had happened several times before, but I had always noticed it in time to mop up the spillage before lighting up.

Perhaps because of my eye problems that night I lit the cooker without noticing the rivulets of petrol.

There was a sudden *woomf* as the fumes and the liquid ignited. None of the flames was as yet touching the inflammable liner, so I tried to smother them with the bag. Each time I moved the bag to a new area, the place I'd just snuffed out caught fire again. I grabbed for the Chubb fire blanket always carried in our camp boxes. The fire was soon out but my second mug of cocoa water had tipped over and acrid black smoke curled about the tent.

The lace which tied the inner sleeve of the tent in place had frozen solid. Eventually I cut it open to let the fumes out. The rest of the night was a succession of long minutes to be lived through.

That was the first of many nights that my eyes kept me awake. I can remember no dentist, limb breakage, nothing in my life, which caused such a memorable sensation as the 'eye thing' during our first month on the Arctic Ocean.

Part of my trouble was obviously the absence of my tent partner, Geoff, and his body warmth. Soon I moved in to share with Oliver and Charlie, which made rather a squash as we were all over six foot. Any bit of snow left on your clothes after brushing down in the entrance area was likely to fall on someone else's gear and cause a good deal of unspoken indignation.

Since I was next to Oliver I found myself silently cursing him on many occasions for the most paltry 'offences'. By nature impatient and selfish, I must have been an exceptionally objectionable tent companion. Fortunately for our continued survival as a workable team, the others possessed more easy-going natures.

For many days our average progress was half a mile to the north and, to achieve even that, many miles of through-way to the west, east and south had to be axed. Any attempt at cutting a route due north, whatever the obstacles, had soon proved unrealistic.

Long journeys on foot in all directions always preceded the making of our 'Burma Highway', since there was little point in hacking our way through solid ice when a perfectly good passageway just *might* run along a few yards away to either side. Indeed, the feeling that, if we hauled our way over just one more wall, we might be rewarded by some treasure such as an open paddock, prolonged many a useless recce journey, slithering, sliding, plunging into sharp-edged crevices hidden by drifts and always wary of the creeping attack of frost on cheeks and nose.

The twin aches of hunger and thirst travelled with us. The hunger was each day with coffee for breakfast and nothing but deep-frozen Mars bars or a packet of pellet-like Rolos and eight sweets aptly called Fox's Glacier Mints. The Mars bars were heavenly once you managed to gnaw off a piece small enough to close your mouth over and suck. But they were also tooth killers. By the end of the following June, when we returned to London, we had between us lost a total of nineteen fillings.

Oliver had been trained to take out teeth and fill up holes, but despite the professional-looking set of dental instruments which he would show Charlie and me with loving pride from time to time and despite the unpleasantness of our gaping holes, neither of us ever approached him to undertake molar repairs of any sort.

During the day we thirsted for fourteen hours in the arid atmosphere of a polar desert with nothing to drink but little balls of snow. Little lollipops of ice looked nicer but I avoided them after once cutting a thin sliver off a big block. I put it in my mouth. There was a fizzling noise and stinging sensation. I felt around with my mitt and removed the ice. I tasted blood. For days afterwards my tongue remained raw where the ice had burnt it.

Travelling up front and needing to look constantly at the horizon for the line of apparent least resistance, I wore no goggles. My eyes were shielded from the lethal glare by the ice beads which formed on my eyelashes. I learnt never to rub these off until either eye could see nothing at all and then only to remove enough to unstick the lashes.

As the weeks went by, we were increasingly made aware that we were travelling over water. As the temperature rose, the composition of the ice-pack weakened. Then, when the wind blew, the ocean beneath us moved with the currents and with the natural swell of all seas in response to the moon's pull. At night only a groundsheet and a thin Karrimat separated the ear from the ice and we could hear each vibration, crack or thud: it was unsettling.

On 4th April, Oliver's skidoo broke down. This was nothing new as we were averaging nine or ten breakdowns daily. Charlie stayed to help and, leaving my sledge with them, I carried on with skidoo and axe to work on whatever obstacles lay ahead. I noticed the sky was darker than usual. The lane I followed ran north east, narrowed into a bottleneck alley and then to a wide paddock.

As though a vice had squeezed the whole paddock inwards, the floes which formed its floor had broken and tipped at various angles. Sea water had flowed into the low parts and, in the middle of the paddock, several of the floes had floated apart. Here the water seemed to be freshly frozen over. It looked passable.

I left the skidoo ticking over and walked forward to check.

The ice felt spongy at first, then more like rubber. Without warning it began to move. A few feet ahead black water gushed up and spread rapidly over a wide area. I stopped at once but the water rushed past me, covering my boots and, perhaps because of its weight or my involuntary movements, the whole mass of new ice began to rise and fall as though a motor boat had passed by. The undulating movement of a swell approached in slow motion and as it passed under me the ice rind broke up beneath my boots and I began to sink. Fearing to disturb the ice further, I remained rigid like a mesmerised rabbit.

As the water closed over my knees the remaining layer of crust broke, and I sank quietly and completely. My head could not have been submerged more than a second for the air trapped under my wolfskin acted as a lifejacket. At first I had no thoughts but to get out at once. But the nearest solid floe was thirty yards away.

I shouted instinctively for the others, then remembered they were a good half-mile away on the other side of many slabs and ridges. I leant both arms on the new ice that hung suspended under two or three inches of water. Then kicked with my boots to lever my chest up on to this fragile skin. I succeeded and felt a rush of hope. But the thin skin broke beneath me and I sank again.

I tried several times. Each time I clawed and crawled until half out and each time I sank I was weaker. My mind began to work overtime but not constructively. Perhaps a passer-by might see me and throw a rope. The realisation hit then like a bombshell. There would be no passer-by.

Was it deep? A vivid picture of the Arctic Ocean's floor mapped in the *National Geographic Magazine* flashed to mind and gave me a sort of watery vertigo. Yes, it was deep. Directly under my threshing feet was a cold drop to the canyons off the Lomonosov Ridge between 14–17,000 feet below.

I vaguely remembered that sailors on the Murmansk convoys reckoned on survival in the waters of the North Sea for about one minute before the cold got them.

This thought brought back the words of an SAS lecturer on survival: "Never struggle. Don't even try to swim. Just float and keep as still as you can. Give the water trapped in your clothes a chance to warm up a bit, then keep it there."

So I tried doing nothing except paddle my arms to keep afloat. But, at a great distance it seemed, I sensed a numbness in my toes. My inner boots filled up, my trousers were sodden. Only in the wolfskin could I 'feel myself'. Inside the gloves there was no sensation in my fingers. And all the while, my chin, inside the parka hood, was sinking slowly lower as the clothes became heavier.

It might work to keep still in the Mediterranean or even in the North Sea but not here. I felt a rising panic. I *must* get out now or never. I smashed at the ice with one arm, while the other threshed wildly to keep my head above water.

The seconds seemed like minutes and the minutes like hours. The precarious platform of ice rind was too strong to smash with one arm. Only with the weight of my chest could I crack it, a few inches at a time, and my strength was draining quickly.

My arm slapped down on a solid chunk, some inches thick,

suspended in the skein like a layer of clay in quicksand. I levered my chest on to it. It held. Then my thighs, and finally my knees.

For a second I lay gasping on this island of safety but once out of the water the cold and the wind zeroed in. It was −39°C that morning with a seven knot breeze.

Moving my stomach and wriggling legs and arms like a turtle in soft sand, I edged to the nearest floe with the nilas bending and pulsating under me as though it were alive. But it held. Standing up I watched the water dribble out of boots, trousers and sleeves. When I moved I heard my trousers crackle as they froze. The shivering began and I could not control it. I tried press-ups but five had always been my limit at the best of times.

I slumped over to my skidoo and the air movement was bitter on my face and legs. It would be foolish to walk back to the others. My skidoo had stalled. I could not start it again without removing my thick outer mitts. This I could not do although I struggled with them. The leather had gone rigid and shrunk.

For fifteen to twenty minutes I plodded round and round my skidoo with a sodden heavy jog, flapping my arms in wheeling windmills and shouting all the while.

Then Ol arrived.

"I've fixed her," he said. "What's the next bit like?"

"Unsafe," I told him. "I went in."

"Is there a way round?" he asked, then, "Good Gawd, so you did!"

After that, all was action. I got on the back of his skidoo and we went back slowly to where Charlie was stopped with an over-turned sledge. Quickly they erected the tent, started the cooker, cut my boots and wolfskin off with a knife, and between them found bits and pieces of spare clothes enough to replace my wet ones. Soon the wet items were strung dripping above, while tea brewed and Ol rubbed the blood back into my fingers and toes.

I assured the others as well as myself that future ice-testing forays would be conducted with greater care. The rule of 'white ice being thick and grey ice thin' would no longer be enough; we would use an axe or a prod on all dubious places.

Twelve hours later my clothes were damp but wearable. My Mountain Equipment duvet sufficed instead of the torn wolfskin.

I was lucky to be alive: few survive a dip in the Arctic. I'd learnt a lesson but the Arctic is no place to learn lessons because all too often, by the time you've learned them, it is too late to take advantage of the hard-won knowledge. Geoff's hands were another case in point. But my survival was one of the only pieces of luck we were to have on this trip. Mid-March had seen record low temperatures, now we were to have record warm ones with the sea-ice breaking up a month earlier than usual. Once the temperature of the water went above −23°C, the whole character of the sea-ice would alter, the top layer become slushy, trapping and spinning the tracks of skidoos.

Oliver and Charlie seemed oblivious to what warmer weather meant. I felt depressed that we might not make the Pole: it would be the first time I had failed to make my objective on any expedition I had undertaken. In a black mood I pushed harder to go north faster, so that at least we could get as near to the Pole as possible. In the tent I lay wrapped in my own thoughts, worrying over the future, whilst fully aware that I was wasting my time.

Our kit was now constantly damp or frozen up depending on whether it was inside or outside the tent and we were averaging only four hours of sleep a night despite taking Valium tablets from time to time. Oliver's fingers gave him hell for they had gone black at the tips, layers of skin had peeled off all but the little fingers, and they throbbed unceasingly. Three of my fingers were also frostnipped, my nose and one ear had suffered and I could only sleep on one side or on my back.

But this attempt on the North Pole was only a training exercise, we would have to cover the ground again *and* the whole of Antarctica. Had we the stamina?

For three years in our London office and for four months in the same tent on the Greenland icecap, relations between the three of us had remained idyllic. Now the strains of the Arctic began to tell. Polar extremes harry a man all day and every night, fraying his temper and sapping his desire to stay calm. Every weakness is aggravated and every characteristic exaggerated. There were moments when tempers flared, the atmosphere crackled with irritation: small things began to niggle, old habits pin-pricked until one of us simmered with silent annoyance. Day by day I felt myself becoming increasingly needled by Oliver, for no good reason. Sometimes I found his unbashable optimism difficult to put up with, for when things were going well, I always steeled myself for a downturn.

Oliver on the other hand was always elated by the slightest bit of progress and, noticing my determined pessimism, would try to cheer me up to his own ebullient level. Without the safety valves provided by our diaries some of this tension might have boiled over into unforgivable words.

We had come to the Arctic to test ourselves as well as the equipment and it was indeed proving a genuine trial. Could we stand each other for six more years? If I did not like the others, they need not be selected for the main expedition. If they did not like me, they need not stay.

Any day now we feared an accident. Every day involved a succession of knife-edge decisions. Was the ice safe to cross on? How and where? One wrong decision and we could lose a man together with all his kit. There were leads that moved fast and evenly, humming like bees or hissing with a sibilant whisper that warned of too-new slush. Others ground together with the sound of chomping horse teeth, spewing green blocks from between their closing jaws.

Success hung in the balance. We worked hard, spoke little, slept rarely, lost a great deal of weight and strength and lived in a dream world. It was a long time since we had seen land. There was no night, no day. The sun circled at roughly the same height above the horizon now with a ghostly light. Every new view might be different but it was always of ice, snow, water, sky.

We must go north. Every minute spent gaining northerly ground was satisfaction, every delay frustration. We travelled for twelve hours, camped for six. Twice we managed over twenty miles in twenty-four hours.

At 86°N we knew we had beaten Bjorn Staib, the Swedish explorer of 1963. At 86° 14′ we passed Nansen's farthest north. At 86° 34′ we passed the record set by the Italian, Lieutenant Cagni.

On 7th May at 87° 11.5′N, some 167 miles from the North Pole, we finally came to a halt in a region of swirling mush. What we needed were float-shoes buoyant enough to let us walk over the porridge. But it was too late for wishful thinking, we had no such objects and we were now too late in the year for it to refreeze. Had we crossed earlier, we might have made it. For nine days we waited, hoping for a freak freeze-up. Instead the temperature rose. If we didn't look out we would be in another just-too-late situation, a position where no ice-floes were long enough or strong enough to allow our Twin Otter to land and rescue us.

If we took a risk now and flunked it, then our reputation in Whitehall, with the Foreign Office and our future sponsors might suffer to such an extent that we would not be allowed another chance. I thought of Shackleton who had been within easy reach of the South Pole some years before Amundsen claimed it. Like us, Shackleton had been at 87° of latitude. But, running out of food, he had decided to save his men and turn back. The ice-floes were breaking up for us: we too must turn back.

On 16th May the Twin Otter came down, we loaded all our equipment and headed for Alert. Two messages greeted me on arrival, one from Wally Herbert: "You beat the farthest north of Simpson, Staib and even Nansen and should feel rightly proud of your achievement. Warmest congratulations. Wally." And the other informed us that HRH the Prince of Wales had agreed to become Patron of the main circumpolar expedition.

Few people had definitely reached the North Pole. We had got nearer than most of the failed attempts, but we had failed nonetheless. Would we make it next time? More worryingly, would others now lend us their support after such a dismal ending? Although we had actually logged over 900 miles of Arctic travel, we had only completed a mere 263 miles towards the Pole itself, ignoring detours. Not impressive stuff for convincing sceptics of our potential.

There was no doubt however in any of our own minds but that the trip had proved exceptionally useful. It had taught us much about our own likely behaviour under extreme conditions and about each other. We knew what to guard against in future in ourselves and had learnt to recognise each other's tolerance level.

We would have to make a very careful re-assessment of all clothing, camping gear and equipment in the light of what we now knew, and in many cases, such as the need for some sort of buoyant float-shoe for slush, we might have to invent a prototype. The Bombardier skidoos had proved better than the groundhogs we'd used in Greenland but they were still rather cumbersome: would they grapple with the mountainous terrain we'd have to expect in Antarctica? Could they be modified or should we look again at the various other snowmobiles available throughout the world, now that we had a much clearer idea of what we wanted? There was a full year to reach satisfactory answers to all these questions.

Food had proved nourishing if uninspiring but we'd do better to eat fewer Mars bars on longer trips, if we were to keep our teeth.

Frostbite and extreme cold still posed problems, particularly for hands. But at least we knew now what we were in for.

We'd tried to reach the North Pole in freak weather conditions. It should be easier next time round, but even if it wasn't, our failure had burnt in my mind the need to start for the Poles as early as possible. Timing was the most crucial factor and I determined not to repeat on the main journey the mistakes which had caused our failure during the northern training.

3

Battle with Bureaucracy

1978-9

Think sideways.

EDWARD DE BONO

If I had to choose two men all over again for companions, there is not a shadow of doubt in my mind but that Oliver and Charlie would be my choice. Why, I can't really say. After all, they were almost as cantankerous as myself. But they were solid, without frills or pretence, and above all, reliable when it counted.

Geoff's hands were unlikely ever to withstand extreme cold again. Faced with another year of office work before any chance of further travel and no certainty of inclusion in the ice team, he decided to leave, as did Mary. They had shown signs of romantic attachment over the past two years about which they had been much teased, but they always denied it hotly.

With Mary gone, Ginnie would need a new person to help her with back-up radio support at base camp. Ideally it should be someone who could double as emergency reserve for the ice team as Geoff had now left, so a man would be preferable, but being of a jealous nature, I did not want someone tall, dark and handsome.

For the main journey – which we had now agreed to call simply the Transglobe expedition – we realised that we would need much more solid organisation back in England, for Ginnie had found our

London volunteers difficult to contact from the Arctic when she needed them. We would have to have a full-time executive secretary, as well as part-time helpers.

Also, much as I had always hated the idea, it seemed inevitable that committees of experts would have to be set up to encourage the different sides of the venture and, after our departure, to keep it rolling.

Through George Greenfield, I approached Sir Vivian Fuchs. He agreed to be a member, but not the Chairman, of our main committee. He approached Rear-Admiral Sir Edmund Irving for that post, retired Hydrographer of the Royal Navy and past President of the Royal Geographical Society. Sir Edmund kindly accepted and over the months ten other eminent individuals joined too.

For Mary's successor and for office help, I advertised whenever free newspaper space was available. A young civil engineer, Simon Grimes, was hooked in this way. "Whilst drunk and eating chips at one a.m. in a friend's flat," he wrote in his diary, "my eye caught an advert: 'Wanted, sixth person to join . . .' With impending unemployment and no better ideas, it seemed like a good idea at the time. Interested in polar regions, have itchy feet and am mad enough."

Simon was a Cumbrian, an experienced climber, a member of past expeditions to Norway, Greenland and Ghana. After getting his degree he had been a trainee engineer on road construction sites, then outdoor pursuits instructor at Brathay Hall. This led somehow to office cleaning and then us.

Neat and self-assured, I sat him down for the 'black talk'. ". . . and I must be honest. I'm not the easiest of people . . ." I paused. "If you're looking for a democratic outfit, you're in the wrong place. I believe the leader should lead."

Simon grinned. "You don't need to give me all that guff. I've been warned you're a ruthless bastard."

That shut me up. Simon moved into the office soon afterwards and began to learn the ropes when I gave him all the food and polar hut responsibilities which had been Mary's. Not surprisingly he didn't find it easy to merge into our well-integrated team for we had been together for some time. He found our way of doing things odd but eventually he knuckled down and we got used to his gruff self-assertiveness. He would not join the SAS because he was a Quaker and would only join a non-fighting unit. He ended up with 144

Parachute Field Ambulance Regiment, a tough-looking bunch whose training turned out to be just as aggressive as SAS exercises. On Welsh training weekends I found Simon as fit as the best of us, if not fitter, so I hoped he would soon be fully accepted.

At this time too Joan Cox and her daughter Janet also joined us: both stayed till the end and, between them, typed this book.

Poul Andersson, a Danish sea cadet who had sailed in Antarctic waters, joined us that Christmas. He had no money so we got him an evening job with the Youth Hostel Association and he slept on the office floor alongside Oliver. He set up an old table beside Charlie's and called it the Marine Desk. At twenty-one, he was several years younger than the rest of us with a wonderful quiet sense of humour: everyone liked Poul.

Early in 1978 two rural characters from Suffolk appeared in jeans and moth-bitten tweed coats. The taller one with salty blue eyes and fuzzy black beard impressed me at once; possibly a subliminal reaction to the many films I had seen of heroic destroyer captains who, minus their sea caps and Guernsey sweaters, resembled Anton Bowring.

He had a Russian grandmother, six years of sea-going experience on iron ore carriers, shrimp boats to Chittagong and more recently Greenland sea-ice protection vessels. His mucker, Mick Hart, was a fellow seaman.

Poul made tea in tin mugs and the interview began.

"There's no pay with us, you know," I said.

"No, that's fine. I'm interested in any form of seafaring job, even cook." Mick, it seemed, was also not fussy. What, they asked, would their duties be and when would they begin?

"Right now," I hesitated – I did not want to lose these two – "right now, we have not actually got the ship we want. In fact we have no ship at all yet. Poul here has been looking into alternatives, haven't you, Poul?" He nodded wisely over his tin mug.

Both visitors looked unconcerned so I took the plunge.

"Really your first job can be to obtain the ship, along with Poul, and you can start right away at the Marine Desk here."

The Marine Desk was toppling under the weight of a heap of Arctic Pilot books. Anton eyed it and the general confusion around the office with enthusiasm, then asked:

"How much is the expedition prepared to pay? I mean what type of vessel are we after?"

I noticed the *we*. This was most encouraging.

"An icebreaker. It mustn't cost anything. That's one of our rules. It applies to the phone and the stationery too. This is because we have no funds."

The talk took quite a while. Next day we borrowed a second desk from the nearby office of the RAF Escaping Society whose staff were absent.

Anton wrote in his diary at the time:

When I heard of the expedition I wrote to Mr Ran Fiennes, some obscure gent I'd never heard of, to ask for a position on his ship: I was thinking in terms of being a deck-hand. His reply implied that the expedition hadn't quite left the country so, with a friend, I went for an interview.

They were pretty well organised but they had no ship. So Ran said Yes. Very happy to have you on the ship but first you must find one and a crew for it. Also all the stores and equipment you think it will need, free berths and port facilities at all likely ports of call on the route etc.

He said all this must not cost a penny. Not a penny. If I was prepared to take this on, then Yes he was happy to take me on and immediately.

A little later Anton wrote:

It all seemed like a nice idea at the time. The more I got involved in it, the more I was beset. It is like a germ, this expedition, or a disease.

Anton, Poul and Mick somehow slotted themselves around the Marine Desk next to Charlie, who had the only phone in the room. There was much yattering and needling between them. As the Marine Desk grew into the Marine Office, Charlie was squashed further and further up against the wall.

Charlie worked well when watched. He was the biggest of us and the most powerfully built. He was, however, idle by nature and took an evil delight in avoiding any task which could possibly be done by someone else. If, on the other hand, there was an important task which could not wait and there was categorically no one but him available, he would set to with a will and enjoy it.

His evasions and plottings were always aimed at one end – to avoid hard, or even gentle, work. When there was no escape he would knuckle down to it. But he knew that I knew that once my back was turned he would take a quick 'smoke break' which would become a 'well-earned five minutes' that in turn would develop into a 'brief siesta' which might well last through the afternoon. Thus there was continual war between us until the real travel began and Charlie was on the move. Then he was transformed, his sullen moods became rare, and he worked as hard as the next man.

It had been his frustrated love of travel, of a fight against the elements, that had brought about his black moods at Thule. Cooped up with two girls, both of whom he felt were nagging him unnecessarily, he had thought of us up on the icecap and felt he was missing out. That and his natural idleness, which the girls resented, had kindled sparks of hostility.

I once noticed two enormous sheets of paper on Charlie's desk completely covered with several hours' work of elaborate doodling. On asking him what he was busy with he replied evenly, "A great many things," took one of my cigarettes and settled down to write a letter to the chairman of a potential sponsor company. The letter began, "Dear Sir Arthur". Five hours later I found the letter still on his desk and this time it said, "Dear Sir Arthur. We would be extremely grateful . . ."

For a long time afterwards whenever someone caught him staring into space they would call out "Dear Sir Arthur". This would have the desired effect of bringing him back to earth.

Oliver, intelligent, full of charm and immediately attractive to all but a very few females, possessed a most generous nature. Unfortunately for him he could not indulge this happy trait because he was penniless. By night he slept in our storehouse within the barracks; by day he ate the left-over food from our training journey. In the evenings Charlie and he worked as barmen at the Admiral Codrington pub close to the barracks. This earned each of them enough money for cigarettes as well as a good square meal each evening.

Life in the little office was bedlam. Simon and Ollie, Ginnie and I shared one phone, Charlie and the mariners had the other. Typing was done by two very kind volunteers who managed to keep up with the flow of correspondence. There were over seven hundred sponsor companies by then: food and equipment were pouring in to the barracks.

I was now hunting for a full-time executive secretary, someone who would handle every complex side of the venture when we had all left the country. There might be a dozen part-time volunteers helping him but they would come and go. He would provide the permanent pivot in London. I found a company willing to pay a salary for such a job of £3,000 all inclusive per annum. No expenses. Not very tempting for the sort of lively executive we needed but it would have to do.

In September 1977 Ant Preston wrote in. He had been a National Service RAF pilot officer, then for twenty years, some spent in Africa, he had done PR and export work. Now he wanted something different, something lively. He began at once on a month's two-way approval. He was a gentle quiet man with a wry sense of humour and endless patience: his idealism and loyalty, which were to be sorely tested, were to prove critical when the troubled times came.

On 15th December our Patron HRH the Prince of Wales asked me to show him the film of our Arctic journeys and to introduce the team to him at Buckingham Palace. Prince Charles flew back that evening from the United States; despite jetlag, he was charming to us and enthusiastic about the endeavour. If I ran into any problems, he assured me, I must not hesitate to approach him, he would help us if he could.

Two major lacks were still an icebreaker and an aeroplane. The ship might set a sponsor back £350,000 and would need a crew of professional seamen who must agree to give up their careers for at least three years. As army or RAF support now seemed to be out and chartering would be too expensive, we would have to persuade someone to help us obtain a Twin Otter for polar resupply which might cost over a million pounds. Ship, aircraft and crews must also be fully insured. Insurers might feel that there was an element of undue risk to our venture, so that also had to be taken into account, with such extras as fuel, spare parts and servicing.

When, by my self-imposed deadline of Christmas 1977, there was still neither aircraft nor ship, I broke the news to the others and to our sponsors, that yet another year's delay would be necessary. We would now leave England on 1st September 1979. Everyone took this philosophically: the work carried on.

In the new year, Anton Bowring dispelled my long standing hope that we would be able to mount our own completely self-contained Antarctic crossing: with our own icebreaker and Twin Otter plane I had fondly imagined that we would be able to cross without help or support from any government.

"Poul and I have now checked up on all ice-class ships on the market," Anton reported. "Most are far beyond sponsorable price. But a few of the older steel-hulled ships just might do the job *and* are on offer at a reasonable cost. These are the types we're concentrating on. But you tell me we must be able to carry 1,500 forty-five-gallon fuel drums to Antarctica, plus 100 tons of mixed dry cargo. Well, any ship we can afford to get and to run will be likely to have space for only two-thirds of the fuel."

This meant getting some 500 drums from Cape Town to South Africa's Antarctic coastal camp at Sanae by other means. There were no other means save the South African ship that annually replenishes Sanae from Cape Town. So South African governmental approval remained critical.

Next problem. We might easily fail to cross the whole of Antarctica in one short summer season, the only period when travel would be possible. If this happened we would have to camp by the coast for the whole of a second winter before carrying on again in the spring from where we'd left off the previous year. The only practical camp for such a contingency was Scott Base which belonged to New Zealand. So the New Zealanders also remained on my critical list.

Lastly, even with our ship to bring fuel supplies in to both sides of Antarctica, the ice crossing distance was so vast and our aircraft so small, we would need a minimum of twenty-three fuel drums at the South Pole itself, roughly our half-way point and the only manned spot along the whole route: a dozen or so American scientists work there all year round. Only the Americans could provide us with fuel at the South Pole. Technically this need not be a problem, since they stored considerable reserves there. However the US State Department, like our Foreign Office, dreaded private expeditions into Antarctica, and they did not need to be brilliant to appreciate that, without assurance of fuel at the South Pole, we would be foolish to set out at all. In a nutshell I *must* get these three governments to promise this specific support or my plans were paper tigers.

I met New Zealand's top Antarctic administrator and polar expert, Bob Thomson, when he visited London. He seemed friendly but made four points clear. In his experience *no* model of snowmobile was capable of crossing the Antarctic continent let alone hauling a sledge over it. A Twin Otter would lack the necessary range. There was no scientific value to our trip and, lastly, "direct radio communication is known to be difficult if not impossible at most times between Antarctica and the UK."

The South Africans and Americans appeared to concur with this bleak summary. All three countries put the ball in the court of our government by saying they would only consider our proposals if we had British governmental support.

Whitehall does have advisory committees on most things from nuclear weapons to garbage disposal but not on private polar expeditions. They could only rely on Britain's polar specialists. Sir Vivian Fuchs and our new Foreign Office friend were our key figures now, since both knew our hopes, and our limitations, and both were influential in those polar circles which could provide or withhold the required backing.

Indeed, Sir Vivian himself had suffered at first from their instinctive mistrust of anything that was not exclusively scientific and the consequent blocking tactics of the polar mandarins. This was why he had suggested to the RGS Expeditions Committee that they might set up a small group to look at my proposals. Since he himself was now on our own Committee he would not participate.

At the same time Sir Vivian warned me that neither he, nor the other members of my own Transglobe executive committee, were convinced that I would succeed in covering all my needs by gifts in kind. They all felt that I should also be trying to raise cash funds.

In October 1978, a year after our return from the Arctic, the RGS Expeditions Committee approved of Transglobe officially, but we still had to get governmental backing. So our Chairman wrote to the relevant person in the Foreign Office to ask how we should set about getting governmental endorsement.

The Foreign Office reply was helpful: "The answer lies in finding an expert body that will give us independent advice about the expedition and whose judgement and status will be recognised by the foreign Antarctic authorities concerned. It seems to us that the Royal Society's British National Committee on Antarctic Research is the appropriate body." The Royal Society in turn suggested that the advice of the British Antarctic Survey be sought to help them in the vetting process.

In November the Royal Society's list of criticisms arrived. The Bombardier skidoos were thought to be underpowered for the weight to be towed at high altitudes and a number of basic points regarding the Twin Otter were assessed as inadequate. We were, ran the summary, likely to need more assistance than might reasonably be expected from existing Antarctic resources. An accident to our Twin Otter could have the most dire consequences.

So, with ten months to go, we remained unblessed.

Both Ollie and Charlie would abscond from time to time, Ollie on 'bird-watching' sprees to Windsor Great Park and Charlie 'on business'. It was seldom necessary with any of the team to check up on them once I had given each a list of 'items required' at the beginning of each month. But from time to time things did go embarrassingly wrong in our dealings with sponsors.

We tried to keep quiet that we often applied to two competing companies at the same time. For instance we might want a hundred pots of jam yet one company would only offer us fifty, so we would approach a rival for fifty more. Or we might need windproof jackets from two competing manufacturers which appeared to be remarkably similar, although they were actually subtly different in certain small ways particularly useful to us, each suiting a different type of climate.

Unfortunately Charlie, in a vague moment one day, mixed the photographs of us using sponsored products in Greenland, sending a slide of Bostik glue to Ciba Geigy, makers of Araldite, and a similar slide of us using Araldite to Bostik. Their feathers were, not surprisingly, somewhat ruffled but they good-naturedly both still continued to sponsor us.

Oliver was about to send off one of our standard circular letters which stated "in return for your sponsorship we will send you colour photos of your products in use against polar and tropical backgrounds and in extreme conditions, together with bi-monthly reports on the equipment concerned" to a firm from whom we were asking for three years' free supply of monthly items for the various female members of the expedition team, when one of our volunteer secretaries noticed the untoward context and censored the letter just in time.

Oliver's wife Rebecca lived in Paris most of the time, where she worked for the Chase Manhattan bank. Whenever she could afford it, she bought a weekend ticket for Oliver so that he could join her but she was becoming increasingly unhappy and feared for his safety, trying to dissuade him from continuing with the expedition.

That Christmas Ginnie and I wanted only to sleep. We passed the

holiday at home quietly with Poul Andersson who could not afford
to go back to Denmark. He didn't seem well, but we thought
nothing of it at the time for we were all tired. Poul had fallen in
love with a pretty blonde Danish girl but he never missed a day at the
barracks.

We still lacked cash. The only person at the time authorised to sign
Transglobe cheques was myself, so I refrained from so doing. This
way of course everything took much longer. Money moves people:
its absence leaves them apathetic. But life was not all grey. His
Majesty the Sultan Qaboos of Oman was kindly disposed to us and,
during a visit to London, he hosted a reception for us at Les
Ambassadeurs restaurant in Park Lane to which my Omani friend,
Dr Omar Zawawi, invited executives from the various UK companies who had work contracts in Oman, many of whom responded
most generously and helped to put our bank balance back into the
black.

Then a director of the Chubb Fire Company suggested to their
chairman Lord Hayter, that they purchase a second-hand Twin
Otter, allow the expedition to use it for polar crossings and recoup
their initial outlay by chartering it out to other companies in between
times. Transglobe had the use of an aircraft at last.

Ant Preston, a keen aerobatic flyer in his spare time, took on all
aircraft details including the obtaining from sponsors of a set of
retractable skis, second propeller, charts, all spare parts and 1001
assorted items, the absence of which in Antarctica or the Arctic could
ground the Twin Otter and cut off the ice group.

There were only a few Twin Otter pilots in the world with
Antarctic experience. One of the best was Giles Kershaw. By 1978 he
had five seasons of Antarctic flying to his credit. He agreed to fly for
us for no wages but, as his flight engineer, he wanted one Sergeant
Gerry Nicholson of the Royal Engineers with whom he had worked
down south. Gerry, a quiet good-natured man from Sussex, was a
regular soldier. Mike Wingate Gray and the SAS lobbied the army for
six months and Gerry was eventually released to us for the duration
of Transglobe.

Inch by inch we were creeping nearer our goal. Prince Charles,
whose diary gets booked up over a year in advance, kindly agreed to
launch the expedition from Greenwich on 2nd September 1979, so
we had nine months to go.

Tarmac International lent us an office with three free phones in

Baker Street as the pace hotted up. I held a meeting every month back at the Duke of York's Barracks for the heat was on now. I chased everyone more than before.

Simon over the last month had failed to progress with the rations lists which I'd asked for. Why? He had had to move his flat: it took up time. But, shouted someone, he still appeared to have time to wander round second-hand bookshops buying up bargains for subsequent sale. Much muttering but eventual promises that the ration lists would be finished in a week.

"Charlie. Yet another month's gone by and you still haven't got the jockey underpants supply."

"The bloke's been on leave."

"Well, try his boss."

"He's in Japan selling underpants."

"Phone the first one at his home. We've got to have the underpants."

"Never mind my underpants, what about more important things? Ginnie hasn't got the radios yet."

A powerful kick from Ginnie landed on Charlie's back.

"Sneak. Mind your own items."

"What *about* the radios, Ginnie?" I had to try to chase her in public though, of all of them, she was the most difficult to pin down and the most fiery when chased.

"Never you mind. They'll be ready and packed with all serial numbers at the customs well before we leave."

Turning to Ollie, the golden boy whose sponsor-getting talents were unsurpassed, I gave him a typed list.

"Seventy more items this month, Ol. The only ones *you* seem to have outstanding are Chinese bamboo poles, skin callipers and the three-year lighter flints supply." I knew Ollie had been disappearing for days at a time, usually when the weather was good, but since he always finished his lists in good time, what did it matter?

Ant Preston gave a succinct run-down on aircraft supplies. "Gerry Nicholson, our engineer," he added, "will join us in the Tarmac office next week full-time."

Anton Bowring followed with news of the latest ships he and Poul were looking at.

When all administrative matters were thrashed out, usually in two or three hours, we changed into running gear. There is a cinders track inside the barracks and this everyone must jog round twenty times. If they did not stop at all and were not too far behind the main group at the end, they must be reasonably fit.

Two of our volunteers with stop-watches shouted out the number of circuits each man had done as he passed.

During one run Poul was sick and went deadly white. I didn't worry over much, since Ollie and Simon had also been sick during the runs. Charlie and Anton invariably arrived last. Ginnie and Bothie, her long-haired Yorkshire terrier, lolloped along tripping the others up and generally being a nuisance. Ginnie was a hopeless case anyway, being far too unfit to jog more than two circuits without stopping to lie down on the grass verge.

David Mason joined up as our ice team reserve and roving trouble shooter to sort out cargo problems in Antarctica, the Arctic and all points between. As a Welsh Guards captain he had received a bravery medal in Arabia: a proud and strong personality. We clashed on the occasion of our first press conference and exhibition at Farnborough one wintry day that February. It was over a simple matter of where to place road signs to direct our guests.

I explained to David that I wasn't interested in arguing the pros and cons. There were probably several ways of doing it but I was an awkward cuss and, on Transglobe matters, my way would do. Or words to that effect.

We had no more problems between us for the next four years, while David took over whole sides of the expedition and, with quiet efficiency, kept our complex resupply going free of transport costs between both polar regions, Africa, America, Canada, New Zealand, Australia and Europe.

At the Farnborough event Anton finally got his ship. His father Peter was then Chairman of Britain's largest insurance brokers, C. T. Bowring. Anton had once worked for them but only lasted as a landlubber for a couple of months. Peter, realising the danger that any dealings with Anton would smack of nepotism and might hinder rather than help our chances, kept a low profile when Anton began to woo the company. Proud of their connection with Captain Scott, whose ship the *Terra Nova* they had provided, Bowrings saw excellent publicity in owning the polar vessel we would use.

Anton had worked extremely hard, hunting for a suitable vessel. As he wrote in his own diary at the time: "It was *entirely* up to me to find the ship and a buyer before September 1979 if the expedition was to set out at all. I had a huge task and was not at all confident of success. On seeking professional advice I became even more confident of failure. I don't think Ran ever understood this or the moments of anguish I went through."

Despite his misgivings, however, Anton had finally run to earth an all-welded hull vessel with a strengthened bow and frame suitable for icebreaking. As the *Kista Dan*, she had been built in 1952 in Aalborg, Denmark, by J. Lauritzen to transport lead from newly opened mines in north-west Greenland to Europe. 1100 tons with two holds and sixty-four metres long, she had a twenty-seven-year-old Burmeister and Wain six-cylinder diesel engine which would give 1200 brake horsepower and, when she was in a good mood with a following sea, a speed of ten knots. Later she had been used for sealing and to make *Hell Below Zero*, the film based on Hammond Innes' novel *The White South*. Then she'd been sold to the Canadians, renamed the *Martin Karlsen* and used as a survey vessel.

Unfortunately she cost twice as much as C. T. Bowring were prepared to pay. However Peter Bowring was engaged at the time in momentous negotiations with the huge New York insurance brokers Marsh and McLennan and they agreed to pay for the other half as a symbol of their joint cooperation.

At our Farnborough press conference, Peter Bowring announced the news of the purchase of this smelly old Canadian sealing vessel and Prince Charles flew the Twin Otter (which Chubb had recently painted with a Chubb Transglobe livery) on to the icy apron beside our exhibition hangar.

The writer Anthony Holden arrived with Prince Charles that day because he was collecting material for a biography of the Prince. He wrote:

In the space of seventy-five minutes the Prince of Wales shakes some three hundred hands and talks to perhaps half their owners. The expedition, at least, is something which gets his adrenalin going again. It is the kind of thing he would like to have done himself if he were not a Prince. He examines the tents, the water shoes, the prefabricated Tri-Wall huts, the skis, the snow-cats, the canoes, the maps and the tins of baked beans as closely as if he were going on the expedition.

He is supporting the expedition, he says, "because it is a mad and splendidly British enterprise". He will hope, he goes on in a fit of enthusiasm, to drop in on it "somewhere in the world in the next three years – if it can be arranged". His staff shoot each other morose glances.

The Prince left us; the hangar soon emptied of people. Ginnie's dream was nudging towards reality.

The office was still under-staffed. I appealed on Radio London and twelve applicants phoned in. Within a week all had dropped out but two. One, Dorothy, was a great help with fast accurate typing. But she had a fiery temper. One day she stomped up to my desk, Afghan coat and blonde hair swinging, and glared at me. I forget what I'd done but I clearly remember her words.

"You are an evil toad and you stink of tom cat." After coffee she calmed down but Ollie, Charlie and Ant Preston, who overheard, were wont to repeat the epithet for months afterwards and to wrinkle their noses when I entered the room.

On certain obligatory weekends the Territorial Army still claimed our time. One such occasion was a spring exercise in Norfolk when the temperature hit $-16°$C. In twos, we were to move secretly across country for fifty miles at night, without being spotted by patrolling Gurkhas. Charlie found an excuse to miss it: he said one of his fingers had been sprained when it got stuck in a pocket of a billiard table, so I paired off with Oliver.

We split up to cross a river. I got wet to the waist. Oliver found a sheet of ice over a deep pool and slipped over dryshod. We moved as fast as possible and reached the final rendezvous an hour before it closed on the Sunday morning: nobody else made it.

This made us feel our polar training had had some use after all. Until I took my boots off and found one black and frostbitten little toe. I had survived Greenland and the Arctic Ocean but not Norfolk in spring.

Back in the office a body blow awaited me. ICI Petrochemicals, after "careful consideration", had decided to withdraw their support with fuel supplies. I had only myself to blame. Back in 1975 my fuel estimates, the basis for ICI's original agreement, were based on a small fishing boat. Once Anton decided which ship we must get, he gave me estimates far beyond my original ones. Gerry, the Twin Otter engineer, did likewise and these new shockers decided ICI to fade out of the picture sooner rather than later.

For me a nightmare hunt began. What good is a ship and aircraft with no fuel? All British avenues were exhausted. I got on to the French, Germans and Italians, even the Japanese. All said No thanks. Philips Petroleum took four months to say No. Six other major US companies obviously considered my request too ludicrous to deserve a reply.

So I did what I had promised myself not to do and asked Prince Charles. He saw me in his sitting room in the Palace and listened intently. There was a twinkle in his eye and he said he would do his best. A week later the Prince's office telephoned. I was to phone one Dr Armand Hammer in Los Angeles.

Before I did so Ginnie found a brochure about the Doctor.

"Good God," she exclaimed, "he's an old friend of Joe Stalin . . . *and* Lenin."

"But the Palace intimated he hobnobs with President Carter."

"Yes, it says here he's been in with most of the US Presidents. He started the Russian–American grain deals."

Her voice rose several octaves.

"He owns a major oil company called Occidental. Wonderful! Clever Prince Charles." She looked puzzled. "But how come Prince Charles knows him?"

"Perhaps the Doctor's an ace polo player?" I suggested.

"Rubbish," she snorted, "it says he's over eighty."

I phoned the Doctor that night, my bandaged black toe sticking out of a slipper end.

"He may be over eighty, but he sounds razor sharp," I told Ginnie afterwards. "It's not his company Occidental who will help: they don't retail gasoline, so they can't. Somehow he's persuaded one of his competitors, Mobil Oil, to agree."

"I thought Mobil refused last month," Ginnie said.

"They did, but that was Mobil Europe not Mobil USA and that was before the Doctor spoke to their boss man."

We were talking of well over a million US dollars' worth of fuel. Mobil Oil's support with fuel for all sides of the venture was a great relief. I thanked God and Prince Charles, Dr Hammer and the Mobil board with sincerity.

The Doctor wrote to me. Was there any other way he could help?

There was. I had asked both Britain's TV companies to send a film team to cover the journey. Both had declined. Could Dr Hammer find an American-based company? Within a month he had found that no US company was interested: the journey was simply too long for them. So the Doctor formed his own film company and started hiring a team to join us.

With five months to go Anton's search for the crew intensified. Since the Department of Trade would not allow our ship to sea without a full professional crew, Anton could not simply sign on enthusiastic volunteers. Yet why *should* professional seamen, at a time of unemployment, when merchant navies were contracting, want to give up their careers and future prospects?

Certainly not for the glamour. If there was to be any of that, the land group were the more likely to reap it. The ship would enter the polar circles at both ends of the world true enough, but only for a few months. Most of the three-year voyage would involve calling at ports quite likely to be visited by any merchant seamen. We worked out it would cost Transglobe £420,000 at standard salaries to pay a crew. That Anton found volunteers to man the ship for nothing but a statutory Queen's shilling per month was I think remarkable. He advertised in free newspaper space and on the radio. One of his earliest finds was Ken Cameron, an engineer. Anton was exuberant. "If I can get a Scotsman for nothing, I'll get the lot."

In Ken's words:

> *I was on a half million ton tanker half way from the Persian Gulf and ready for a change. I saw the Transglobe advert in the* Telegraph *and wrote to the box number. Poul Andersson sent me impressive details in a blue folder. Expecting a well-monied and efficient organisation, I visited the Duke of York's Barracks and asked for the Transglobe Marine Office. I had put on my best suit and was prepared for a stiff and high-powered interview. When I reached the office I found the curtains drawn, Charlie asleep on the floor and Poul Andersson of the Marine Desk just emerging from his sleeping bag under a table.*

Anton soon formed an interviewing committee which sat in the salubrious chambers of Trinity House by the Thames. Presiding was Captain Tom Woodfield, Elder Brother of Trinity House and retired skipper of an Antarctic vessel. I joined them to ensure marine Transglobers did not escape the 'black talk'.

A convinced and active trade unionist and shop steward of many years, Terry Kenchington, applied as Bosun. Cyrus Balaporia, an Indian from Bombay with several years P & O Line service as a ship's officer, appeared at about the same time, both individualists and experienced seamen. Then came two New Zealander engineers, longtime friends, bored with standard voyages, who were hoping to start up a garage in England when they heard about us.

In Jimmy Young's words:

We went to see this Transglobe outfit. It seemed they were desperate for one engineer. Mark Williams and I reckoned we would call their tune a bit and said they could have both of us or neither. We considered ourselves macho, sporty types, so it came as a bit of a shock later to find out the Transglobe people had decided we were a couple of pooftahs looking for a three year marine love-in. My main reason for joining was . . . well, what a journey! I couldn't stand the thought of someone else doing it, knowing that I could have done it.

A couple of natural comics joined up that spring, Eddie Pike – ship's carpenter – and Martin Weymouth, deck-hand. Martin had shoulder-length frizzy golden hair. He came from Leighton Buzzard and was at once nicknamed 'Buzzard'. After a while it was difficult to remember his real name and I found myself introducing him to Prince Charles as Buzzard.

Colonel Paul Clark who, as Air Attaché at the American Embassy in London, had been so helpful to us over our Greenland application, resigned his commission with the USAF on hearing that he was to be posted to the missile defence headquarters inside Boulder Mountain, Colorado and decided that he would prefer to join us as a deck-hand.

Anton now had a crew, except for a skipper, so the Bowring Steamship Company lent us one of theirs, Captain Les Davis from Carlisle, in order that Anton could fetch the boat from Canada, which he hoped to accomplish free of any charge: he did it for £32.

The voyage from Canada was rough and helped knock the volunteers into a tight-knit group, so tight indeed that subsequent crew were to find integration difficult: in some cases impossible. Anton wrote of the voyage:

Having worked for eighteen months with only Poul Andersson, I found it difficult to share the fruits of our labours with the newly recruited crew members all of whom naturally wanted to display and use their own skills which were far superior to our own. So, during the voyage, Poul and I often sat together in a cabin moaning about our apparent redundancy whilst our team of professionals seemed to do everything.

Anton was given a free berth in Millwall Docks by the Port of London Authority, the same used twenty years before by Vivian Fuchs' team before they set off on their Trans-Antarctic expedition. Ginnie, plus champagne bottle, officially re-named the ship the *Benjamin Bowring* in memory of the company's founder who was himself a bit of an adventurer and we called her the *Benjy B*. She was full of atmosphere and became much loved by us all.

Once berthed and christened, work began in earnest to get her ready in time. At weekends, with help from local cadets, there were up to thirty people on board scraping, cleaning and painting.

Some weeks later Poul offered to help Ken and the engineers in the cramped confines of the engine room. Using a heavy hammer at an awkward angle, he began to feel a pain in his chest but, as was his way, he finished the job. Anton, when Poul complained of recurring pains, took him to hospital. Within twenty-four hours Poul had a massive heart attack. Within a week he was dead. At twenty-two years old. Poul was a friend to us all; especially Ginnie and Anton.

That March our pilot Giles Kershaw and I went to Cambridge for a meeting with the executives of the British Antarctic Survey to try to sort out the remaining criticisms of our Antarctic plans. Our lack of a second plane in case the first crashed was paramount.

It was finally agreed we would get an insurance policy to cover any mishaps to a BAS plane, should one be called upon to rescue our ice group. We had also to undertake that the whole expedition would be aborted if, at any time, we did ask for BAS help.

This seemed hard but as Giles said: "You can see their point of view. A few years back an *official* French scientific group needed help and the Americans put three Hercules out of action attempting to rescue them. Unofficial private expeditions, if ill-equipped or ill-conceived, are a menace in areas like Antarctica where there is no room for error."

Sir Vivian Fuchs had put together a legitimate scientific programme for us which in the main consisted of magnetospheric and glaciological research work. But we had other tasks involving meteorology, high frequency propagation, cardiology and blood analysis.

On 9th April, nearly six years after my first approach to his predecessor, our Foreign Office friend wrote to the relevant representatives in New Zealand, South Africa and the USA. He stressed that "nothing in this letter is to be taken as implying that the British Government sponsors or is in any way responsible for this expedition". Nonetheless the government's appointed vetting bodies had judged us scientifically and logistically and they were now prepared to recommend that I be allowed to come for an interview. British Airways offered to sponsor my flights to South Africa and America. Not enough time remained to get to New Zealand as well.

I flew to Pretoria and the South Africans agreed to assist with fuel transport from the Cape to Sanae base. In Washington I met a representative of the State Department and the US overall Antarctic decision maker, Dr Todd of the National Science Foundation.

The Doctor was guarded. The Japanese explorer Naomi Uemura had, he said, also appealed for NSF blessing for a journey to Antarctica. This had been turned down only the previous month. Knowing what good connections Uemura had with the *National Geographic* organisation, I realised the implications. But Dr Todd did not give me an outright no. Indeed he seemed friendly: my request would be considered.

I returned to Britain and, with only eight weeks until our D-Day, received Dr Todd's decision. The US could not assist us in any way because all their resources were already fully committed and none could be diverted from the US programme.

I replied that we would set out soon and, with luck, would be at the South Pole by 24th January 1981. I cut down my South Pole fuel request from forty to twenty-three drums and mentioned that the lack of this small amount might stretch our lines of communication dangerously. Dr Todd stood firm. Sir Vivian thought, "The situation is uncomfortable but can be solved in the time available." I think we all accepted that only direct intervention by the British Government to the US State Department could now alter things.

So we carried on as planned. If, when we were ready to begin the crossing attempt, the US still refused fuel at the Pole, then Giles would somehow have to establish fuel depots on the way across and in the middle of nowhere. Sir Vivian estimated that, for Giles to take twenty-three drums to the Pole himself, he would have to use up 800 extra drums' worth of fuel en route: far more than we would have available.

On previous expeditions I had repaid sponsors by holding exhibitions of their products. On a hovercraft trip up the Nile, shows in

Khartoum and Kampala produced export orders worth twelve
million pounds. I decided to hold eight exhibitions at centres along
the Transglobe route with the help of local British commercial
attachés. As a rehearsal we set one up a few weeks before departure
at the World Trade Centre in London. It took nineteen of us three
days to erect and HRH the Duke of Kent, Vice-Chairman of the
Overseas Trade Board, opened it to the public in early June.

To help our sponsors, we needed as much media coverage as we
could get. George Greenfield now arranged for me to meet the
American Atlantic Richfield owner of the *Observer* and some of their
executives to explain my plans. That lunchtime I made the Transglobe expedition sound as exciting, exotic and hairy as I possibly
could. The next day I had to present the same plans to a group of top
London insurance brokers to encourage them to sponsor us with free
policies. This time the expedition sounded about as risky as a
Tupperware tea party. Thanks to the elasticity of the English language, the *Observer* gave us an excellent contract for the right to
Transglobe feature stories and the London insurance market covered
all sides of the Transglobe comprehensively at no cost.

Anton Bowring was worried. With two weeks to go, he had no
volunteer skipper with or without ice experience whom he considered acceptable. Bowrings were prepared to let Les Davis skipper
for us again but we could not meet his salary. At an emergency ship
meeting, Tom Woodfield of Trinity House said a friend of his, a
retired Admiral, was prepared to take the *Benjy B* at least on the first
leg to Antarctica.

Anton's diary:

*I first met Admiral Otto Steiner (who, despite his name, had
helped sink German ships in the last war) when I entered Tom
Woodfield's office. The Admiral was sitting at a desk. He looked
around at me with a monocle in position and his bearded face
somewhat regal. We shook hands and he said, "So you are the
young commissar!"*

*Not quite understanding the application of the word I thought
this was flattery, looked bashful and muttered, "No, I'm really
just the office boy."*

*The other committee members gathered to discuss a list of
anxieties about the ship and crew which Otto had produced. His
main concerns included oilskins, personal insurance, Master's*

reports and, above all, the clap. I began to get anxious about him as he seemed out of touch with the requirements of a Merchant Navy skipper. I could see problems arising from having a Royal Navy Master and a wholly Merchant Navy crew. Anyway whilst the committee bravely tried to put the Admiral's mind at rest that the crew would not all get the clap and what to do if, by chance, they did – I wondered just how my carefully selected and good natured crew members would take to the barking discipline of a much older man . . .

After the meeting I made haste to the barracks where I saw Ran and explained my misgivings about the new appointment and my fear that all our plans would be ruined if the crew left because they couldn't get on with the Skipper . . .

My own panic may have been a bit over-reactionary but I was concerned in ensuring the ship's personnel were harmonious . . . At the same time I had my own position to worry about. Ran wanted me to be wholly responsible for the ship and marine side of the venture, except for the Master's role on board. But, at the committee meeting, it was agreed I should be the Purser with the responsibility of being a sort of secretary to the Master . . .

However Ran and the crew seemed to be reasonably satisfied with the Admiral so my anxieties were halved. For the last few days before departure he took up residence on board and got the ship into order. I kept a fairly low profile and remained in the office where I had much work to do if we were to leave on time.

Back in the barracks we toiled till midnight most nights. It was hot and dusty through July and August. I packed, numbered and listed over a thousand cardboard boxes bound for eighteen different bases around the world over the next three years. Ollie had special responsibility for mechanical gear, Ginnie radio gear and Simon food. Only Charlie represented the team back in the office during the last two months and I phoned him daily with new action lists, items to obtain, kit to modify, extra food to order. Now that the chips were truly on the table he worked as hard as anyone and I inwardly forgave him all his previous reticence in the field of labour. Ollie herded us all in a Land Rover for dental checks and assorted injections.

By night with two others I drove endless vanloads down to the docks and dumped them on the quay beside the *Benjy B*.

My mother lived alone in the country. I went to say goodbye. She was and is the best of all possible mothers. I took away a pair of warm socks she had knitted.

The day before we left, 1st September, there appeared in the editorial column of the *New York Times* under the heading 'Glory', "The British aren't so weary as they're sometimes said to be. The Transglobe Expedition, seven years in the planning, is scheduled to leave Greenwich, England, tomorrow on a journey of such daring that it makes one wonder how the sun ever set on the Empire."

Before departure I was meant to introduce Prince Charles to our advisers and sponsors in the Great Hall of the Queen's House within the grounds of the National Maritime Museum at Greenwich. But I overslept and arrived late. Down at the quay by the *Benjy B* Ant Preston marshalled the crowds with a loudspeaker. Overhead I saw a red helicopter; the royal taxi. I ran up the street and saw it land on a lawn behind a tall iron fence. Prince Charles got out and headed for the Great Hall. I scaled the railings, disentangled my coat from the spikes and, hoping his armed detective wouldn't get the wrong idea, headed across the lawn at the double.

His Royal Highness was wearing a black tie. He was in Court mourning because the IRA had killed his great uncle and friend, Lord Mountbatten, a few days before. Prince Charles had cancelled all engagements but the launching of Transglobe, for which he made an exception because he believed the Earl would wish him to help an enterprise of the sort he too had always taken an interest in.

Many of our families, friends and helpers joined the thousands of well-wishers who came to see us off. Geoff and Mary were there side by side.

"When's the wedding?" I asked Geoff. "Wedding?" he exclaimed. "What wedding?"

The only times I had seen Mary cry in the Arctic were when furious with me. Now it was otherwise. A month later they became engaged; the first but by no means the last of our expedition love stories.

Prince Charles took the *Benjy B* away from Greenwich Pier and the gay bunting of the *Cutty Sark*. If ships have hearts that once proud schooner may have sighed to see us go.

Of the expedition Prince Charles said:

One of the expedition's achievements has already been the creation of a unique spirit of co-operation among industrial undertakings in Britain and overseas.

This co-operation during the seven important years of planning and preparation has made it possible for the expedition to fulfil its every need from the goods and services provided by more than 600 sponsors. Transglobe is certainly one of the most ambitious undertakings of its kind ever attempted and the scope of its requirements is monumental . . .

Although so much has changed in the world since explorers first attempted to reach the Poles at the beginning of the century, the challenges of nature and the environment are still very much the same . . .

Above all, the human risks are still the same. They're all there today, the frostbite, the loss of body fat because of the cold and the protracted bouts of shivering, especially at night, the unsuspected crevasses and traps for the unwary, the thin ice . . .

Even though a decade has passed since man first set foot on the moon, polar exploration and research remain as important as ever . . .

As this great journey unfolds and people from many nations become involved with the Transglobe Expedition, I am confident that this ambitious and courageous undertaking will do much to provide interest and inspiration to old and young alike throughout the world.

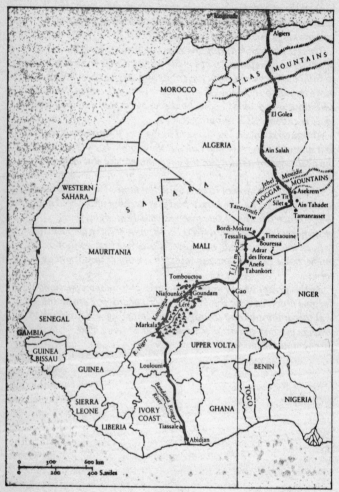

North West Africa: Algiers to Abidjan

4

Desert, Jungle and the
Roaring Forties

SEPTEMBER–DECEMBER 1979

The sun's rim dips; the stars rush out:
At one stride comes the dark.

SAMUEL TAYLOR COLERIDGE

Although the BBC television news showed the *Benjamin Bowring*, skippered by Prince Charles, heading down the Thames with all the Transglobe expedition members on board, seemingly hellbent for Antarctica, most of us were only going as far as Tilbury and the ship itself had much to be done to it before the Board of Trade inspectors would allow her to leave.

Charlie, Ollie, Simon, Ginnie and I were driving overland through France and Spain, across the Mediterranean to Algeria, into the Sahara Desert, then straight on south to Abidjan on the Ivory Coast with two Land Rovers, a Range Rover and three trailers. We hoped to stop in Paris and Barcelona for trade shows and expected to meet up with the *Benjy B* in Barcelona, Algiers and Abidjan.

We left the barracks in sheeting rain. Ollie and Charlie came to a sudden halt in Parliament Square when one of their trailer wheels went walkabout without warning and a split pin in the retaining hub was found to be missing. Our hopes of catching the midnight ferry from Folkestone to Dunkirk were dashed. What a beginning . . .

The British commercial attaché had arranged for our Paris export exhibition to be held in the heart of Montmartre on the first floor of a lovely old house with a circular marble staircase, ornate ceilings and extravagant chandeliers. But the passers-by stumped along in an urban trance, ignoring the furry dummy we had stuck on the pavement to advertise our presence; some even risked death by detouring on to the road to avoid the dummy. Despite minimal attendance, more items disappeared off our stands, including a large quilted sleeping bag, than at all our subsequent seven shows put together.

Depressed, we re-packed the exhibition into some 400 crates and loaded these on to four railcars bound for Barcelona. Then we drove south through France.

Charlie left us and headed in the Range Rover for St Tropez, as he'd decided to meet a recent girlfriend there for a few days' holiday. When we met up with him again at Perpignan near the Spanish border, he announced his intention to marry Twink, a most shapely and attractive girl who was also an executive of one of our sponsors, Berlei. The wedding, he said, would take place in Sydney after we had crossed Antarctica. However, I noticed that thoughts of impending marriage did not dull his perception on the beach that afternoon when a lively little English girl with bared supercargo parked herself beside us. Simon also developed a squint.

One night a rainstorm washed Ollie downhill on his groundsheet and lilo and jammed him under the sump of his Land Rover. Being a remarkable sleeper, he did not wake but looked rough next morning. The next night, determined to keep off the ground, he strung a hammock from the rear of his vehicle to the tow bar of his detached trailer. Charlie, not to be outdone, curled his bulk up inside the trailer. Whenever he turned over the tow bar tipped up and Ollie shot down to the far end of his hammock. Woken, he would worm his weight back up again which sent the trailer down with a bump and Charlie briefly into orbit. Both were grumpy at breakfast which raised the humour and the spirits of the rest of us, such was the way of our land team.

Barcelona had suffered severe storms before we arrived, ten people had been killed and the roof of the hall where our exhibition was to be held had partially collapsed, so our display was cancelled. In many ways this was a great relief, though very bad luck on our valiant sponsors, because it meant that we would not have to load the ship in a rush.

The *Benjy B* was in Barcelona's prime berth, right opposite the port's main bar so I expected to find everyone wreathed in smiles when I arrived, instead I was met with moans and groans. The atmosphere was tense, the Admiral seemed hurt, Anton dismayed by all that had happened, the Canadian first officer looked utterly bemused and Terry, the bosun, appeared apoplectic.

Troubles had evidently arisen the moment we'd left England. We, in the land group, had all signed legal contracts with the Transglobe expedition in London some time before but the lawyers did not produce copies for the crew until the last minute, when they had objected strongly to the clauses they had been asked to commit themselves to. After some arguing, a newly worded contract based on that used by Sir Vivian Fuchs for his own expedition in the 1950s had proved acceptable to all, including the Admiral. But then a new difficulty had arisen: who should control the ship's purse strings?

I had intended that Anton was to have full financial authority but the committee had decided otherwise. Anton had been afraid that the Admiral would spend more money than we had, in an attempt to get the boat up to his high standard. My stinginess had been understood by Anton, who accepted that if we hadn't the money we would just do without, whereas the Admiral felt that the ship needed re-wiring and general smartening up.

It began to sink in that I would do well to forget previous journeys when my hand was the only one at the expedition tiller and recognise that when I was not there, a different hierarchy had to be observed. The *Benjy B* was not a normal ship: her crew were unpaid volunteers, many from the Merchant Navy, and her Master was an Admiral from the Royal Navy accustomed to discipline. It would take some while for them to create a modus vivendi acceptable to all. Meanwhile I did what little I could to smoothe things over.

The Admiral had clearly been very long-suffering and remarkably non-dictatorial but was dismayed when the bosun had laid down a system of deck watches which involved one man being 'on' for a week at a time. The Admiral had then found no one on watch in the vicinity of the bridge when a gyro alarm went off. Had he not noticed it himself, the gyro may well have burnt out.

Terry loved the ship, was totally loyal to the expedition and was willing to work extremely hard but, he also had great experience as a shop floor convener and was not used to having his warps, winches and responsibilities interfered with.

Anton, as always, counselled patience and understanding. He felt the crew of purely unpaid travellers would respond, given time, to the dictates of common sense. They were a fine group of individuals, if their many different nationalities, backgrounds and opinions would make them initially resistant to instant harmony. But he felt they would integrate. "We must work at it," Anton said.

I would soon be off the ship for three months driving across Africa so I realised I had to patch up differences right away. Luckily the Admiral had a forgiving nature and Terry calmed down. I then held a meeting on deck for everybody, during which I talked of future plans, outlined the likely problems we would all have to face in living together during the years ahead and suggested some guidelines. These I admitted might not work; only time would tell.

With that over, we nosed out of Barcelona at night and headed for Africa in a dead calm beneath a cloudless sky. Jill, the cook, served baked mackerel.

I *hate* fish. All fish. But knowing that normal people like it I had jumped at the chance when a sponsor offered us five tons of fresh mackerel. One freezer was full of the stuff. By the time the crew reached Barcelona they'd had a surfeit of it and also of ravioli, another commodity I somehow seemed to have over-ordered.

I took half one bite and drowned it with tomato sauce and pepper. But the evil salty tang came through. Struggling, I noticed a silence in the saloon. Some fifteen pairs of eyes were on me.

I attacked the mackerel at once with relish and switched on an appreciative smile.

"Nice, isn't it?" said Eddie Pike.

I nodded.

"Shame you'll miss it in Africa but, never mind, we'll save you a few hundredweight."

Cyrus, the Indian Officer, sprinkling his with Tabasco sauce, offered to pack a freezer box of mackerel to take on the Land Rovers.

"Help you to get on with the locals — instead of coloured beads," suggested Terry.

"More likely start a revolution," muttered Jill.

Dave Peck, the second mate, seemed to be making all the running with our pretty cook, though I noticed other eyes cast in her direction. But there were plenty of ports to call at for the competition. Probably too many, I reflected, for the Admiral's peace of mind – remembering his dread of the clap.

The next meal was ravioli.

On the second day we came to Algiers where a clutch of officers came aboard. All had gold pips or stripes on their uniformed shoulders. Customs, port officials, police, sanitation and other unguessable authorities.

The Admiral came into his own with white uniform, monocle and conquistador beard; he fascinated our acquisitive visitors and quite put them off what was doubtless their normal custom of demanding goods for favours; or almost did. An hour later with voluminous wads of forms signed and stamped, Otto saw the port junta off his ship with a mere half dozen bottles of whisky and some rather passé boxes of teabags.

"You'd better disembark before their brethren come for a second visit," said the Admiral and without more ado Terry and his deck crew winched the vehicles on to the quay, whilst Jill parcelled up a delicious joint, uncontaminated by mackerel or ravioli. Ken Cameron ambled up to inform the skipper that the variable pitch control for the propeller was jammed in reverse. So we stood on the quayside and watched the *Benjy B* depart backwards into the clammy darkness: we would not see her again until we'd crossed the Sahara.

A British Attaché arrived to take Ginnie, Simon and Charlie away for the night but he warned us that light fingers were everywhere, so Ollie and I decided to sleep in the vehicles. To ensure greater security for all three cars and the trailers, Ollie spun a web of cotton around our line-up and attached tins at intervals. I slept in the cab of the front Land Rover but Ollie decided he could only guard the rear from 'outside', so he set up his lilo and mosquito net in the gutter.

Around dawn the cacophony was indescribable: it sounded like the local foxhounds arriving in full cry. I shot out of the cab, cut my ear on one of Ollie's tins and was almost garrotted by a cotton line. Ollie struggled out of his sleeping bag and mosquito net wide-eyed.

"Christ," he exclaimed. "The hounds of the Baskervilles at full moon."

No dogs to be seen. Instead an impressive mosque overlooked the harbour security fence, from which issued the muezzin's dawn chorus to the faithful. The local verger must have set his loudspeakers on full volume. An appalling noise, unlike any I had ever heard in Arabia, beat the humid air. Even the mosquitoes fled.

"Just as well," said Oliver, pointing.

A wave of black sludge advanced along the gutter in which he had slept, complete with fish bones, half a bowler hat and the remains of a cat.

For two full days I struggled with customs formalities and an alarming complex of bureaucrats. I got nowhere fast until I met the Chief of the Port Authority himself. For the sum of 1,000 dinars, some $250, he cleared the way with three phone calls. This left me with exactly £80-worth of dinars for the rest of our stay in Algeria.

Our last night in the capital was spent in the British Ambassador's house. He was a charming bachelor with a subtle sense of humour. As Simon wrote in his diary: "One of the nicest houses I've seen. Airy French style, slight Moorish influence, old English furniture and books, with oriental rugs and carpets. Beautiful garden with tennis court and pool. Had breakfast served on a tray by my window looking down the Embassy gardens to the port of Algiers."

Ginnie set up her thirty-foot antenna in the Embassy garden and spoke to HRH The Duke of Kent at a communications exhibition in Bayswater, London. Then we drove south on good tarmac with heavy oil tankers for company. Flat-topped mesa straggled away through the roadside haze. Forty-three degrees C at noon. I travelled with Simon, followed by Ginnie alone and the others behind in the Range Rover. There was as much a sense of exploration as on a motorway trip out of London. But it was good to be free in wide open land.

At dusk we stopped beside the rolling sand dunes of El Golea, immediately christened 'el gonorrhoea' by Ollie. A few miles to the south lay Khanem where Ollie was commissioned to catch sand lizards or skinks for the Natural History Museum. While we made camp, Ollie went off to set his traps, baiting them with corned beef.

The sun rose huge and orange next day and all the traps were empty. Clouds of large flies which tickled and little flies which bit attended us all day as the sweat ran down in rivulets. We wore next to nothing. Ollie recorded 50°C in the afternoon. We could not decide whether it was less unpleasant inside or outside the tents.

After two skinkless days Ollie decided we must be more aggressive. Perhaps this particular sandbowl was bad news for skinks. So we trooped out into the dunes with water bags, compass and skink traps.

Two hours of dune-trudging later, Ollie had picked up no spoor, although he assured us that the five-inch lizards did leave identifiable tracks, and decided to call it a day.

"Are you sure you can track them?" I pressed him.

"Of course I can. I have all my notes and my training from Mr Arnold."

"Yes, but that was on the museum lawns at South Kensington."

"Don't fuss." Ol's confidence was undented. "These things always require perseverance. Skinks don't grow on trees, you know."

"Just as well," muttered a hot and weary Charlie, "there don't seem to be too many trees in el gonorrhoea."

Everyone was a bit touchy by dusk when, almost to order, the mosquitoes began their familiar whine.

The food naturally had a fair amount of sand additive. Simon was the cook and much resented the fact that his private knife, fork and spoon had disappeared. It could only be one of us. But everyone denied the theft. "I don't see why people have to lie," said Simon and went off into the dark in a huff.

Next day I joined him in our Land Rover to hunt skink-catchers. In fly-blown El Golea they speak French and/or Arabic. Simon spoke French and I spoke Arabic.

"What do we request?" I asked him.

"*Un homme qui peut attraper les poissons-de-sable,*" said Simon without thinking. "What about in Arabic?"

"Ah." I did not want to be outdone. "The Latin form is *Scincus scincus cucullatus.*"

"These Arabs may not learn Latin at school," he said evenly as we passed by a row of mud and brick hovels.

I was ready for him.

"The colloquial term for lizard is *dhub* or *zelgaag*. Since skinks are lizards that should do."

Much investigation led us to the mud home of one Hamou, the local 'guide'. Inside there was a freezer full of Coca-Cola beside a colour TV set. Hamou assured us he was *the* skink-catcher of the region but he must warn us it was a dangerous and therefore expensive business. Did we realise that sand vipers and scorpions, which lived under the same sand where skinks must be sought, were in abundance? During the last year alone, he assured us, 128 people in town had been treated for scorpion stings and three of them had died. Sand vipers were deadly poisonous.

"Twice," he added, "when hunting skinks, I have plunged my hand into the sand and brought out sand vipers gorging on skinks."

I was glad Ollie was not present.

That afternoon, with Ollie watching closely and three bedu boys to help him, Hamou led us into high dune country, not a mile from our camp and within minutes had captured two prime skinks. By evening he had a third and we took him home to enjoy the tinned fruit and tomato purée with which we paid him.

For two days Ollie applied Hamou's tactics and added to his collection of pickled lizards. Each time he popped a new catch into his formaldehyde bottle he sighed and swore he would never again become involved in anything so cruel. Later Ollie received a letter from the Natural History Museum, thanking him for his work: "Previously, the nearest known localities for the two widespread forms of sand skink were some hundred kilometres apart . . . your specimens narrow the gap to twenty-five kilometres and, as they show no tendency to resemble the other form known from El Golea, it is likely we are dealing with two full species and not just subspecies. One cannot be a hundred per cent sure but your specimens make it much more likely. Thank you for helping to solve the sand skink mystery."

Pleased to leave the el gonorrhoea sauna, we went south to Ain Salah, which means 'salty well', where we replenished our water supply with salty water. Warm winds from the western dunes fanned our camp that night in the Jebel Moujdir. Pretty Walt Disney mice called jerboas hopped about and overhead a lammer falcon wheeled on dusk patrol.

Then on to Tamanrasset, self-styled tourist centre of the Hoggar Mountains. South of the ugly sprawling town we drove off the gravel track at the Ain Tahadet, to Jo-jo spring, as generations of hippies have dubbed it. The proprietor, who looked more Italian than Arab, was introduced to us as Spaghetti by a German tourist already camped there.

"Three dinars for each jerry can of my water," said Spaghetti in passable French. We filled all our cans and paid with Marmite and honey. Below the spring was a dry wadi which the German told us had been a roaring vent fifty metres across only a week before. So we camped beside it instead of in it.

Our next step must be south west across the dry wastes of the Tanezrouft, for our second task was bat-collecting on either side of the Mali border. Papers for such a journey must be signed by the Wali of Tamanrasset and the Police Chief which took several hours. I then visited the hotel with Charlie who discovered to his horror that one beer cost the equivalent of £1.50, and a shot of gin £2.50.

Finally, I located a desert guide who spoke French. "Due west to Bordj-Moktar. The track has not been crossed for five years. Much bad sand, no piste." My Michelin map indicated a good piste to Bordj-Moktar but perhaps the guide was more up to date: after all sand does shift about.

"Best you go Gao by way of Timeiaouine," said the guide. "Then I will take you."

I explained we had only food to pay him with. This disgusted him; obviously an urbanised bedu who dealt only in dinar. "You go without a guide. It is possible. You may not get lost." These encouraging words seemed to absolve him of all feelings of responsibility. I then asked where we might find colonies of bats.

He sat up at that and frowned.

"*Les chauves-souris?*" He pondered awhile. "Ah, those are west. Maybe you look in the wells of Silet."

I was dismissed.

Ginnie and Simon both wished to see the local hermitage of the remarkable French monk Père Charlie de Foucauld. We had a day to spare whilst Ollie and Charles practised their bat-hunting techniques in local caves, so we drove for fifty miles along an excellent rocky track into the Hoggar peaks. At 8,000 feet we came to the pass of Asekrem and walked up a well-worn mountain path to a little rock chapel which had as its sole guardian an elderly French friar, Petit Frère, to whom, as was customary, we carried water and food. The friar, of Father de Foucauld's order, had lived there twenty years. On the plateau above the chapel was a set of meteorological instruments with which he kept meticulous daily records. The view from that lonely chapel was an experience to be savoured. A cool breeze plucked at mountain flowers, rare and tiny, whilst beyond the silent hanging void, great mountains soared to spires and pinnacles of dizzy height. The rock road took us back to Tamanrasset through another pass and dusk fell about us with sudden indigo gloom.

Back at camp Simon lit a fire of roots to cook over for we were hungry. Charlie gave a shout, "Come and have some curry, it's still warm." Ginnie and Simon prepared to wait for their own stew but I went over to the others and Ollie spooned out some curry.

"How was the bat hunting?" I asked.

"Not a sausage all day. There was a storm in the afternoon which knocked the tents down."

I thanked him for putting ours up again and took a heaped mouthful of curry.

Without a doubt it was the hottest I have ever tasted either side of Shiraz. My eyes and tongue bulged out.

"Water," I croaked.

Thoughtfully and with no hesitation Charlie passed me a glass of water which I gulped down in great swallows. The world seemed to come to an end. I was in hell: red hot sandpaper rasping my throat as I gasped for air.

"Hey, Charlie," said Ollie, "that was my gin and tonic and we're on the last bottle."

I threatened vengeance through watering eyes but my words were drowned by their cries of mirth.

From Tamanrasset we drove west on worsening tracks to a place called Tit. Here there was a fork not shown on my map. There was no sign *at* the fork but I found one 300 yards from the current track. Abalesa and Silet lay to the left. The vehicles rattled like peas on a drum as the track leapt from scarred black basalt steps to sand-filled ruts. Stormclouds, dark and massive, massed behind in the unseen Hoggar Mountains. Over wadis green with *gai'sh*, *kfeeter* and the ubiquitous *ghadaf* dwarf palm, we sped, rousing clouds of dust; dust so fine it reflected the very sheen of the sun, an orb of spectral orange. Dusty as ghouls, we emerged to slake our thirst at the well of Silet.

Simon, master-of-water, flung our roped canvas bucket down the stone rimmed hole and drew up a gallon or so. This he poured into a jerry can through a filter.

"Little bastards," he muttered, blowing at the filter's gauze.

I peered over his shoulder, not difficult for Simon is Ginnie's height. A dozen miniature hook-tailed tadpoles writhed in alarm as the warm air struck their horrid little forms.

"Hook worms, liver worms, toe worms, every sort and kind of disease carrier and those are just the visible ones." Simon seemed delighted. "Imagine what a drop of that water would look like under the microscope. The locals here must be eaten alive from within."

I watched Simon apply sterilisation and purification tablets to our bottles once he had pumped the water into them through lime candles: even then I doubt I would have drunk any but for my thirst.

One of the vehicle starters gave up the ghost. For five hours at 40°C Simon struggled to fix it. He burnt his fingers on the hot metal but to no avail. Ollie, disapproving of Simon's methods, ended up shouting at him in exasperation and finally vented his ire in his diary, something we had all learned to do in Greenland. That night he recorded: "S. very set in his ways. He never wants to listen."

Ollie, despite the lassitude we all experienced, decided Silet looked good for bats. I went with him to interpret. We found the village elder who spoke French of sorts. At the mention of bats he showed alarm. "Not in this village. We have no bats. But outside in the wells . . . maybe many."

He tried to explain the location of the wells but without a local map it was useless. Reluctantly he agreed to come, and four miles from Silet showed us some gravel pits where shafts had been sunk between twenty and fifty feet deep. We lowered Ollie down on a rope where the elder indicated. We tried four but found nothing other than pigeon feathers and the foul odour of dead animals. In one well there was water and slime. We watched fascinated as a thin green viper over five feet long surfaced and raised its head to stare at us. Then, as Ollie approached, it submerged with frightening speed.

Allah willed that we should find no bats here but to the west, across the wasteland, we would see countless bats in the wells of Tim-Missao: of that the elder was certain.

We gave him at least a year's supply of tomato purée for his pains. Weeks later I discovered from a Frenchman that bats are thought to be sons of the Devil whose main desire is to steal the souls of young Saharan villagers. No one wished to annoy the local bats by giving their presence away to foreign bat-catchers so the best policy was to keep us moving on to ever-new bat-pastures well away from wherever we were at the time.

For three days Simon rationed our water as we edged south and west over featureless wastes. Violent dust storms raged, blotting out the trail. For hour upon hour we drove through yellow gloom with our lights on, following a compass course, trying to keep to old blurred tracks. It was often necessary to get out and verify we were on a known path: sometimes we seemed to be meandering about on our own.

On 15th October, in a shallow wadi far from any track, we

happened upon three lonely saddles. Close to burial mounds of black rock, the three camel saddles lay in the dust; beside each was a neat pile of utensils, of cast iron cooking pots, carved wood spoons, metal fire tongs and heavy clay gourds. Why? We wondered in silence.

I went off on foot with Ginnie to reconnoitre, to pick up the long-ago piste of twin camel trails. These led south and west and by evening we had re-joined clearly defined vehicle tracks from the north. The wind stirred sandstorms all night which lashed our tents like driven sleet.

Crossing wadis the vehicles bogged down in the soft loose sand. Once we came upon a scene from some surrealist film. Two juggernauts overladen with goods and people appeared fleetingly between surges of the storm. They had sunk in up to their axles, as we had. A giant of a man, turbaned and robed in white, gestured king-like as figures swarmed down from the loads to push and pull in unison. Blue-clad Touaregs from Mali and dusky desert nomads bent in two long lines under the will of the great bearded Moses, their robes whipping and billowing in the screaming dustclouds as we watched from our cosy cabs.

We made camp only one hundred miles north of the Mali border, sticky with dust and our own salt, tired and thirsty. Next day we came to Timeiaouine where we found a guide who took us across the unmarked border soon after dusk: then he left us without a word.

Somewhere north of the path that runs from Bouressa to Tessalit, we reached a more attractive land with no wind, no sand and a pleasant dry heat. Sometimes our 'track' disappeared altogether over stone but never for long. We climbed through high gravel hills, strewn with boulders, the northern rim of the Adrar des Iforas, where camel and goat herds roamed, under the watchful eyes of wiry Touaregs. At night, moths beat at our mosquito nets and the sky was littered with brilliant stars. It felt good to be alive and loose.

Trailer springs fractured, tow bolts snapped and tyres punctured but nothing serious impeded our progress south from the Adrar and down the lovely vale of Tilemsi where, for much of the time, there is water. Our camps became more interesting, filled with scorpions, spiders and the nocturnal music of frogs, crickets and nightjars. Insects of fascinating shapes and hues, rabbits, foxes, lizards and gazelle now appeared. The Sahara was behind us. Some parts were as green as an English spring garden and spattered with indigo where tents of nomads sprawled by herds of grazing camel.

In the low bush land south of Anefis a trailer chassis fractured. Simon assembled our welding kit but his results were not satisfactory. At dusk a Tamachek with wife and child came into our camp. He wanted medical treatment. Doc Ollie satisfied his needs, in return for which service he did a superb job on our trailer, for he turned out to be a skilled welder by trade.

At Tabankort we met four Frenchmen nursing a group of tanned French girls who wore as little as possible. They had somehow lost their trucks. Thereafter, every policeman from Tessalit to Gao stopped us, looked hard at our Land Rover and asked if we had seen the "having gone absent lorries".

Camel skeletons, some still furnished with rags of dried and hairy skin, lay about the trail especially where zones of sand caused mini deserts. In one such arid place a wizened nomad waited. He made no gesture but we stopped. He offered us camel milk from a brass bowl and when we had drunk, he proffered his empty goatskin for water. Another, searching the sands for a lost camel, was obviously parched. He drank deeply; his dust-caked eyes closed tight. I could only guess how wonderful that feeling of relief must be to him; the feel of the water in his throat, a satisfaction which urban peoples, in their comparative sufficiency, can rarely savour.

At Gao we reached the wide, fast-flowing Niger River and followed its westerly curve for four hundred miles to Tombouctou. This was a paradise for Ollie, always a keen ornithologist, and we stopped many times for him to identify this or that species from his birdbook. From the Camargue to our camp at the Torro Bravo, from Algiers to Tombouctou he noted everything with feathers. His entries included the Egyptian vulture, the shirka, the mouse-bird and the bee-eater, the bru-bru shrike, the cut-throat weaver, the white rumped blackchat and the hoopoe.

The bird I remember most vividly was a Tombouctou chicken. We arrived in that town, famous for epitomising the backend of beyond, at dusk and discovered a 'restaurant'. The set menu for that evening (and every evening) was "Sardeen, beer and dead hen". The beer was cold if you drank it quickly and the sardines, if you got them down before the indigenous flies did, were excellent. Our chef, a man with indescribably dirty hands and dish-dash, entered the dark room with a proud air of "now for the *pièce de résistance*".

The *pièce* was, in fact, one of the scrawny chickens harmlessly cleaning up our crumbs and it put up a great deal of verbal resistance when cookie grabbed it by the neck and plucked it nude. Only then was the pitifully squawking bird put out of its misery by having its neck wrung. Our appetites dispersed more quickly than the feathers.

On the northern side of the town stinking dunes piled themselves up against lanes of flyblown kraals, where children with distended bellies lolled in the shimmer of noon. The town's southern flanks sported concrete tenements and tarmac rimmed by dry forest. Tombouctou is indeed the end of the desert. Not far to the south flood plains and vast shallow expanses of Niger water spanned the horizon. We planned to spend four days bird-watching in the lakes of Goundam before crossing the Niger River south of Niafounké and heading through Upper Volta to the Ivory Coast.

Camping in the Forest of Tombouctou is not to be recommended. We woke wet from a clammy sleep to the maddening call of thousands of doves and multi-coloured hoopoes in the pango-pango trees about our tents. Whether that was what the trees really were called, I don't know, but Simon, the only one to have travelled to West Africa before, called them that, so we all followed suit. The sand around us was soft and it was hard to get the vehicles and trailers going whenever we stopped, while if we inadvertently touched the rough dry grass, we found ourselves beset by marble-sized burrs which clung to our clothing and made us itch. There was little improvement on the piste to Goundam where we often got bogged down, struggling to free ourselves by means of our 300-foot tow-rope. Progress was slow and we were passed by many hundreds of donkeys with outsize ears which tripped along in dusty cavalcades followed, rather than led, by little barefoot donkeymen in sampan hats, with skirts hoiked up round their muscular thighs. They shouted happily when we finally managed to free ourselves and roared past them, trying to keep up speed so as not to sink in yet again.

Goundam turned out to be a pleasant village of hilly bumps round which snakes a Niger tributary, fringed by gardens and palms. We drove on for about four more miles to camp in a peaceful spot. From here Ollie journeyed upstream in our fold-away boat to a great reed-covered lake rich in bird life. Close by, in some ruins, he found his bats at long last.

In London, he, Charlie and Simon had been injected against rabies in readiness for bat-bites: nonetheless they wore leather gloves for the hunt. With bird-catching nets stretched across all exit points, they roused the dormant bats and trapped six, none bigger than a sparrow. Ollie's initial delight at this long delayed success soon turned to gloom when he had to pickle the little dears. Charlie made an especially hot curry to cheer him up. Then he located a Senegal fire finch and forgot all about his pickling traumas. That night a powerful wind whipped the river and dismantled Simon's mosquito net while he slept. He was bitten all over and was a miserable sight next day.

I was sorry to leave the river camp, a happy place of chattering fire finches, hovering hawks and lunging kingfishers. Skulls and carcasses of cows littered the brush around us; probably the site of an abandoned charnel house, but there was no smell and we ignored them. As the others zoologised, Ginnie washed clothes on the river bank and I began the detailed plans for unloading in Antarctica. By the time we reached Cape Town some two hundred pages of kit lists must be checked and allotted priority groupings.

Leaving the river, we passed a troupe of long-tailed monkeys on a water melon hunt. Secluded pools flashed with bird colour. Simon was by then incubating malaria but didn't know it. In Niafounké we learnt that the floods were so extensive ferries were unable to cross the swollen river and our route south was barred. To skirt the flood waters, we would have to make a 700-kilometre detour through wild nomad country before we could get back on our original road south. It was a rough area and at Léré the lieutenant of police who checked our papers told us that we were the first foreigners to pass in four months.

My memories of our journey south of the Niger are fractured. A camp with a new moon outlining giant ant hills and cicadas that chirped through the silver night. A once great forest of dead and dying trees where no birds sang and too many cattle had for too long churned the undergrowth into pig-pen mire. A pueblo village where it seemed every inhabitant came out at our approach and followed us jogging and clapping along their only street, until the last child and yapping dog dropped away beneath a dusty halo. A nomad encampment where negroid Arabic-speaking Mauritanians sang at sunset, the men with spears, shields and knobkerries, the women with proud banana-end breasts and rings of coloured beads. Soft orange light etched the scene on my mind, dug-out canoes beached high among the reeds, groups of smiling girls stomping and chanting in time as they flayed heaps of millet to flour dust. And lowing herds of African long-horns jostling behind thorn corrals, each with a series of long branded scars on its flanks.

Simon's diary for that night has an echo of isolation. "Cheerful atmosphere; the North Pole gang feminiscing of Alert."

For three days we drove south-east through damp forests and the irrigated rice lands of Kouruma until we reached tarmac again by the thundering Niger barrage at Markala with its Coca-Cola sign scenery. Wild Africa is shrinking day by day.

Now our camps were in forest not savannah, under coconut palms and baobab trees. One moonless night I heard Ginnie moaning outside our camp area. She was lying on her back. There were ants on her legs but she ignored them. For some years she had experienced slowly worsening stomach pains, tests had indicated a spastic colon but all the normal pills she tried gave no relief. I gave her pain-killers and by morning she felt well enough to drive.

Simon's eyes were badly bloodshot from the dust and irritation of the past few weeks, made worse by his contact lenses. In Loulouni, close to the Ivory Coast border, he bought yams and guavas and cooked a delicious meal over a log fire. We dined in an elephant grass clearing whilst lightning forked and thunder burst in the rain forests all around.

Beside the guava market, Simon told us, he had found a sign in French saying "Trade-in Western clothes for sale" and under it the English translation – "Dead White Man Here."

At the Mali border I took our five passports to a big black officer who not only spoke English but came from Goundam. He was proud when he heard that we had stayed in his city but extremely baffled when he spotted the word 'Traveller' in Charlie's passport. "But dis man cannot have traveller for job. No man can make money from travel!" He went out to the Range Rover to inspect Charlie in silence. Then he burst into laughter and proclaimed, "So it is indeed a lazy man we have here." An irate Charlie, suspecting me of putting the officer up to it, made threatening gestures from his cab. In exchange for much tomato purée, we filled our cans with fresh water and drove on south to the Ivorian frontier of Ouangolodougou.

On 4th November we reached Tiassale and stopped in a restaurant for beer and biscuits. We were a bit high from the weeks without baths. I hoped to find a camp beside the Bandama Rouge River where we could swim as well as snail hunt, for Ollie still had one last task left to perform in Africa, to collect bilharzia-bearing water snails from stagnant pools in this jungle area.

Seeking access for our vehicles through the forest to the riverside, I found a smart bungalow overlooking the river. Parking outside, I walked gingerly over a well-trimmed lawn, flanked with exotic flowerbeds. A kitchen boy with an apron appeared and I asked to see *le propriétaire*. The kitchen boy fetched a houseboy with secateurs. He called a uniformed butler who produced a spectacled and thick-set secretary. Was there anywhere my vehicle could reach the riverside I asked. "*Monsieur le Président est à l'église*." He shrugged. An hour later Monsieur le Président, who turned out to be the local judge, arrived in a Mercedes with a white wife and kindly sent his houseboy, Jean, an Upper Voltan, to guide me. After an hour's drive through the forest our muddy track emerged by the river bank where two dug-out canoes were beached beneath giant jungle trees.

That night we set up camp in a space cleared of bamboo and undergrowth. Charlie found a nine-inch black scorpion which Ollie promptly pickled "in case it's interesting to the museum".

Simon cooked over a slow log fire of mahogany and procured a chicken from Jean whose village was only a mile down-river. Using a Land Rover starting handle for a spit, he fried the bird with yams. Together with stewed onions and aubergine, dinner was a feast. As well as being my co-driver, Simon had purchased all our fresh food from London to this, our last African camp. I now asked him how much we owed him, knowing his barter system had not always worked. "A pound each should cover it," he replied.

Ollie led us on a snail-hunting foray into the nearby forest. Fifty yards from the camp we came across an apparently endless file of black ants some half an inch long. They packed a shocking bite, as Ollie discovered when a couple became lodged between his shirt-tail and pants.

Simon spotted a snake curled up in a rotten bamboo cane. On its neck a death's head symbol was elegantly fashioned. Ollie and Charlie refused to get friendly with it for the sake of my camera but Simon prodded it gently and initiated a disappearing trick of un-believable speed. There were black and yellow spiders of great beauty and everywhere dappled light falling in laser beams from the black canopy so far above us. Tree boles were massive, the vegetation underfoot deep and rich with decayed matter. Butterflies, moths and dragonflies graced the speckled gloom till dark when gyrating fire-flies took over.

Happy with his slimy plunder Ollie took us back to camp. Ginnie, clad only in dusk, was bathing on the sandspit, her towel and soap at the ready on the end of a mahogany canoe. As I joined her by the twilit river a native, silent as the current, arrived in a second dug-out and beached on the spit.

Ginnie whipped round and grabbed her towel, all two-foot square, and faced the visitor. He stared back entranced and not at all embarrassed. My camera and flash sadly were not at hand so I could not record Ginnie's expression of outrage. In a while the fisherman grinned and went into the jungle.

After two long bird-watching patrols Ollie was satisfied and we left the forest. Three hours' drive to the south brought us to the coast and the capital city of Abidjan, a place of skyscrapers on hills rich with foliage, fashionable hotels and suicidal orange taxis.

Anton came to meet us in the northern suburbs and told us that the *Benjy B* was already at berth in the harbour with Ken Cameron and his helpers sweltering away in the engine room at 40°C. Anton guided us to a villa owned by a British building company where two of our crew were in bed with malaria, nursed by Jill the cook. Simon with swollen glands, malaria and heat exhaustion, soon joined them.

Everyone else began to unload the exhibition crates from the holds. Trucks shuttled them to a marble-floored glass-walled hall in the city centre and within two days, despite intense humidity, the crew had the exhibition ready for its official opening by the Minister of Mines.

Ginnie's stomach was giving her jabbing pains: she wanted to rest. I had a great deal of paper work to do and, down in the sultry crowded cargo hold, must move and number boxes whilst the ship was static. But the local functionaries and exhibition supporters held nightly parties for us so, after days yattering to visitors at the exhibition, it was necessary to change shirts and yatter away again to the local VIPs. In order to get the more important arrangements made, I kept two evenings clear. This was a bad mistake. Ollie, who went to the functions on those evenings, was told by the British Ambassador's wife that my absence was "disgraceful and rude".

On 20th November the *Benjy B* moved out of Abidjan's wide lagoon into the Atlantic. We were at once in heavy swell. Eddie and Dave were still weak from malaria but back on duty. Simon, nauseated and vomiting intermittently, felt alternatively hot and cold. Paul Clark, appointed ship's doctor, looked after him.

Next day, just off the Greenwich meridian, we crossed the Equator. Admiral Otto, dressed as King Neptune with pitchfork and crown, presided over the Crossing the Line ceremonies. The golden-haired Buzzard, with two footballs under his T-shirt, was Neptune's bride, Aphrodite. Terry, the bosun, with a fire hose and tins of green detergent thoroughly soused those crew members unlucky enough not to have crossed the line previously.

Sperm whales were seen and flying fish died on the hot decks, while up in the fo'c'sle sorting out cargo, the cloying odour of bad mackerel clung to my shirt and hair. I saw no ghosts in the fo'c'sle, despite tales from Terry of the Danish seaman thought to haunt that part of the ship.

We moved into the Benguela Current and the weather closed in. Down in Number Two hold our forklift truck broke loose and slammed down on its side, crushing a generator and other cargo. Battery acid ran free and poured down through the floor slats on to the Antarctic cargo below. The weather deteriorated still further and now the whole clammy ship smelled of mackerel, 'Ran's mackerel' I was hurt to hear them called. It seemed that the forward freezer, where our polar wolfskins were stored with the mackerel, had ceased to function so the fish had gone bad and would now have to be thrown out, after they had impregnated our polar gear with their smell for ever. Genial, bulky David Hicks, the steward who had never been heard to complain about anything to anyone at any time, seemed to enjoy the experience, but Anton was not so happy: "slipping about as the ship heaved and rolling in a mess of bloody fish bits; grabbing at sloppy bundles of putrescent mackerel . . . not my idea of heaven."

They moved it all, but for days an evil cloying odour wafted about the ship. Months later, when least expected, it came at you suddenly from the bilges so that 'mackerel' became a swear word on the *Benjy B*.

The wind stayed around Force 7 for days. Sometimes the watch officers kept headway at a mere three knots in the plunging seas. The order went out for safety lines on deck as waves crashed over the bows. Lockers sprang open, gear smashed and the Canadian officer's pet lizard escaped so all hands were turned to on a lizard hunt as the

Benjy B rolled thirty-seven degrees and more. But even Ollie's expertise with skinks was of no avail for the lizard was never seen again.

Poring over paperwork in our stuffy cabin made me feel sea-sick so I worked up in the hospital, an isolated two-bunk cabin near the stern. I noted in my diary:

> *Down below at nights our porthole leaks: each time we roll to port it submerges with a buffeting crash, a stream of sea water running down to soak the bench and the carpeting. Last night Charlie screamed as a specially violent wave knocked us sideways. A heavy glass ashtray full of dogends and ash careened off his bedside table on to his face. Ken Cameron, being Chief Engineer, has a double bunk. Each time the ship rolls beyond thirty degrees he shoots out sideways like a cuckoo on a platform: a moment later he returns up against the wall with a noise like a butter pat falling on the kitchen floor. All night as we plunge and heave, I hear strange noises. Our cabin is just above my stores hold and I lie wondering what such and such a crash, thud or metallic grind might mean. Has a vital steel sledge come loose? Or a box of delicate radio gear? What is that smell of gasoline: has an ice spear punctured a fuel drum?*
>
> *The imagination tends to run riot for landlubbers like me. I try to remember that our old sister ship the* Magga Dan *was once rolled through a giant wave trough at seventy-eight degrees, taking the sea into her funnel, yet still she recovered.*

One night Ken woke me, his face ashen. He had discovered an error which, left uncorrected just a few minutes more, might well have caused the engines to seize up and so put us all in the soup. He soon calmed down, being a phlegmatic northern Scot. But I was glad not to be the guilty party.

In her early days, as the *Kista Dan*, the ship had made sufficient headway to face the South Atlantic with supreme confidence. Now, as the *Benjamin Bowring*, her engines were twenty-seven years old and her pistons somewhat scaled. In itself this was neither dangerous nor remarkable but, bearing in mind her ice resistant shape was not designed to cleave smoothly through heavy seas, the loss of power caused by scaling was a factor which could not be ignored when planning a heavy-laden voyage through the biggest seas in the world. With no landmasses to intervene and break them up, the huge waves of the Southern Ocean surge right round the world, increasing in size and power. Sometimes freak waves reach colossal proportions and come smashing down on ships with tremendous power, hurling tons of water on to the superstructure. Ships like the *Benjy B* are no safer from such freak waves than Shackleton's or Scott's wooden ships were. Icebergs and growlers can be avoided thanks to radar, but not rogue waves.

Our old engines which, on our way to Cape Town were slowed down by mere Force 7 headwinds to less than three knots, might well not produce enough power to keep steerage in the foaming conditions of an all too common Force 10 gale south of latitude 45°S.

The moment of truth, given such conditions, would come if the skipper deemed it was safer to turn tail. The action of turning the ship between waves would temporarily put her in imminent danger of broaching, should a vertical force of water hit her hull, broadside on. Even after a safe turn, the danger of pooping would remain so long as gale conditions prevailed.

Slowly we edged south down the west coast of Africa towards the Roaring Forties, but luckily for us the seas grew less boisterous. Of the crew I wrote: "Things may well alter but, touch wood, I've not heard a cross word nor a grumble between any of those on board, except two of the officers who rub each other up a touch. They are a great bunch but obviously have a hard job with this old ship. It is as well they seem almost to love her."

On 3rd December, a bit dazed and most happy to see land, we reached Saldanha Bay a few hours north of Cape Town. Flocks of seagulls, countless thousands of them, rose and fell over shoals of fish. Colonies of jackass penguins squawked and squinted from their rocky homes along the shore line. Terry and the Buzzard ran to the chain locker. The anchor rattled away at a touch to attach us to the South African seabed.

With three days to spare before the ship must sail for Cape Town, Dave Peck decided to photograph his inflatable Fyffes banana, the trade symbol of our fresh vegetables sponsor from Covent Garden in London. Fyffes, like most of our sponsors, expected periodic photographs of their products being used or displayed against unusual backgrounds.

Wearing jeans and a thick leather belt, Dave posed with his three foot yellow banana for photos on deck. A sudden wind tore the banana away. For a while it soared into the air but, caught in a downdraught, soon plunged into the sea and floated off.

Dave, a resourceful man, and not second mate for nothing, immediately launched one of the ship's lifeboats and, with the radio officer, set out to rescue the banana.

Since a Force 5 wind was blowing the banana reached the shore first. Dave's diary describes the chase:

> *I spotted the ship's banana in low scrub and so swam ashore. Three sunbathing locals were puzzled. Their expressions changed to amazement when I plucked the biggest banana they had ever seen from a bush behind them and swam back through the surf.*
>
> *Pleased with the success of the rescue mission I stepped into the bottom of the boat aft of the engine. I am not clear what happened then but I slipped and my jeans wrapped themselves around the revolving propeller shaft. As it rotated away from me my leg was pulled over it and the jeans began to force my leg under its far side. The jeans ripped apart then and, in seconds, my gym shoe, jeans and two-inch leather belt were ripped off and shredded. Nick pulled my body clear but as he lifted my right leg, it folded up forwards just below the knee. The foot was limp, the ankle bloated and the skin between knee and ankle appeared to have collapsed inwards like a popped balloon. There was a hole two inches below the knee through which dark arterial blood was pumping.*
>
> *I squeezed the femoral pressure point and the flow eased.*
>
> *The boat bucked about and, while Nick steered to the Benjy B, I fired off red flares. A launch came from the local jetty. I was naked save for my left gym shoe. Back on our ship, Simon gave me a morphine jab. Later I went to Cape Town hospital for an operation. The leg was shattered in many places but the banana was safe.*

Dave Peck had to leave us for six months while he had several operations to re-set his leg. Anton's old Marine Desk friend, Mick Hart, was summoned from Suffolk to take Dave's place.

On 8th December the *Benjy B* came into Cape Town harbour under the gaunt block of Table Mountain. Although I had lived not far to the west, in the Constantia hills, for ten years as a child and twenty-five of my cousins still lived in the Cape, I hadn't been here for a long time and hardly remembered it.

There was no time for cousinly visiting however, the exhibition must be set up at once and with nineteen of us working full-time, we got it all ready in twenty-four hours.

A press conference followed. Ginnie was asked by a feminist reporter whether her role as base camp leader and radio operator proved that the sexes are equal, even in the most extreme physical conditions. Her reply:

> *I'm not going on this journey to prove a woman can do anything a man can, as some people seem to think. There's a role for women and a role for men and they should complement each other, not create a feeling of competition. I'm not a women's libber, nor out to prove myself in a man's field. I came because I love my husband and he's here, not back at home. I have helped with the planning and organisation from the start, but I'm not brave. If I thought about it in depth at a personal emotional level, I probably wouldn't be here now.*

Ollie's wife, Rebecca, came out from England. They were very happy together. Ollie told me, "It's like a second honeymoon." I hoped that she had come to accept his remaining with us for the next three years.

On the first day of the exhibition there were 5,000 visitors, a far cry from Paris. At times the lanes between exhibits were jammed solid. Outside our quayside hall, two of the ship's engineers, Mark, from New Zealand and Howard Willson, from the east end of London, gave hourly demonstrations: Mark in a Dunlop inflatable with skids beneath its hull rammed and jumped over a raft, representing an Arctic ice floe, to demonstrate one of the problems we envisaged and how we hoped to deal with it. Howie, in a wet-suit, walked about in the harbour on water-shoes. About five foot long, they looked more like miniature canoes than shoes. By the fourth day, 22,000 visitors had passed through the show, with one day set aside for those with a purely commercial interest.

Sir Vivian Fuchs visited for a week and I was able to obtain last-minute advice from the only man in the world to have led a trans-Antarctic expedition.

Charlie, being fairly dark-skinned, had long suffered mickey-taking as to his origins and I was the main offender. He got his revenge in Cape Town when the Mayor presented us with Cape Town's own flag. The Alderman, a cousin of mine and a genealogist, announced to the gathered throng that he and I shared the distinction of being close cousins of Karl Marx.

Until Cape Town the filming of our journey had been done by Anton Bowring and me but now Dr Hammer sent a highly paid, four-man professional camera crew to take over. Bad relations between photographers and the others have actually stopped expeditions from time to time and had, from my point of view, ruined one of my own previous ventures, so I was determined to get on well with Dr Hammer's men and sorry when things began on a bad footing.

They heard about a scheduled radio talk I was due to have with HRH Prince Charles. Since our radios were packed up Ginnie had asked the South Africans if she could use a transceiver in a government base. They agreed on condition nobody else attended as no filming was allowed at the base. This upset the new film team. Unfortunately I exacerbated things further by feeling unable to guarantee them the exclusive use of a skidoo, sledge and tent in Antarctica.

Their sound man, Tony Dutton, later wrote:

> *Our first real contact with Ran Fiennes was not a happy one, and indeed left us confused and rather angry. We could see no real justification for what seemed to be the obsessive secrecy of the radio call with Prince Charles, and the refusal to commit tents or skidoo to us nearly caused us to abandon the shoot. I now count myself fortunate at not having been involved in the acrimonious discussion which followed and I was able to spend time getting to know the team members. This contact gave me, not explanations, but a growing insight into what made the expedition the remarkable cohesive force, the family, it undoubtedly became.*

Bad relations between expeditions and the media trying to cover them are almost traditional. Back in 1921 during the famous Everest Reconnaissance expedition Hinks wrote to Howard-Bury, "We are having a devil of a time over these sharks who want photographs. No one regrets more sincerely than I that any dealings with the press were ever instituted at all. I was always against it."

David Mason now flew out to join us, bringing with him Ginnie's terrier, Bothie, and on a burning hot day, carrying his polar gear and dressed in baggy World War One shorts, a faded drill shirt and a battered trilby, came Anto Birkbeck. I had planned for Anto and

Simon to winter alone together wherever we unloaded the *Benjy B* so that they could look after all our equipment and fuel, see it did not disappear under snowdrifts and maintain an airstrip. I was aware that neither had any experience of living under Antarctic conditions but felt that the two of them could manage. Ginnie, Oliver, Charlie, Bothie and I would spend the winter in another camp about three hundred miles further inland. We wanted to be all ready to make a start for the South Pole as soon as the weather got warm enough.

On 22nd December we left South Africa for Sanae: on board were twenty-nine men and women, one dog and a number of mice. The Mayor and crowds of well-wishers saw us off. David Peck was also there, ashen faced but out of hospital, although his leg was entirely cased in plaster, having been fractured in eighty-eight separate places.

Ollie wrote: "I found great difficulty in not crying as I waved goodbye to civilisation. The sea was rough and I think most of us felt miserable and a bit frightened of the future."

I know what he meant. It would have been different if just one of us had some knowledge of what we were shortly to face.

At seven p.m. we passed Cape Agulhas, the last land for 2,400 miles, and set a course south towards the pack-ice.

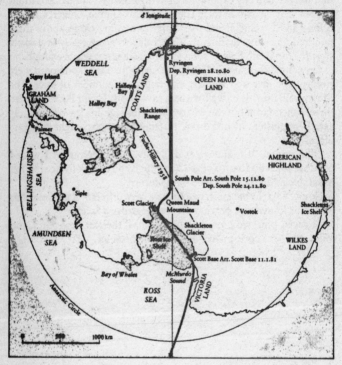

Antarctica

5

A Foot in the Antarctic Door

JANUARY–FEBRUARY 1980

*We must select the illusion which appeals to our temperament
and embrace it with passion, if we want to be happy.*

CYRIL CONNOLLY

As we punched into the heavy sea, Admiral Otto Steiner addressed us
all.

*Initially we anticipate Force 8 gales, gusting to Force 9: west of
the Agulhas Basin are found some of the worst seas anywhere. It
will be rough, but worse still in the Roaring Forties which we
enter on Christmas Day.*

*The direct route to Sanae is 2,400 miles but we must add a
dog-leg in order to approach it from the east. Last year the South
African icebreaker, Agulhas, tried a direct approach and was
forced back with damage by dense Weddell Sea ice. Don't forget;
it was in the Weddell Sea, sixty or so years ago, that Shackleton's
ship was crushed and sunk.*

*Our first icebergs can be expected after 45°S and from the end
of December there'll be permanent daylight. We will not make
way in whiteout conditions and all bergs will be passed to the
windward: growlers lurk to their leeward.*

We have sufficient food for twenty-nine men for five months and I am pleased everyone including the ice team, the scientists and the film crew have agreed to take their turn at watches and, in the event of an ice build-up on deck, work with shovels and axes.

Otto also laid down a number of rules stressing the dangers of the southern seas in a ship heavily laden with high octane fuel. Only one of the crew, Buzzard Weymouth, had sailed in Antarctic waters before. Quite apart from individual icebergs, some up to fifty miles long and 200 feet high, pack-ice creates a formidable barrier around the frozen continent. The annual freeze-up spawns the pack which grows in depth at a rate of two to three feet per year and extends outwards from Antarctica for as much as 1,000 miles. Average summers tend to break the pack into a mass of fractured floes which form a wide protective belt off the coast but often leave a narrow navigable shore lead.

Although the main pack is from two to nine feet thick, there is a short period during December and January, the summer months, when icebreakers and ice-strengthened vessels like ours can shove and manoeuvre their way through it. But not every summer: sometimes it is impenetrable and sometimes, although a vessel may find loose pack on entering, she may be beset as she tries to escape due to an early freeze-up or simply a local wind change that contracts the pack and any object caught in its clutches.

Aware of the dangers we all wished for speed. But the old *Benjy B* cruised at a mere nine knots with favourable conditions. It was as well to be patient. Some of those on board had more immediate worries. Simon wrote: "Queasy all day. Slept a lot. Not sure if the Stugeron pills are helping."

Bothie soon proved that dogs that are house-trained are not automatically ship-trained. Uncertain where to go, he spread his blessings all over the ship and usually in dark shadowy gangways. If he had been a planter of anti-personnel mines he could hardly have been more effective. Not a day passed but some new victim trod fair and square on his latest trap. Anyone who left their cabin door open was fair game until the day he discovered the lawn. It looked like any lawn and was situated on the boat deck at the stern. Further north, in warmer climes, this green mat with 'grass stems' of rubber was used for sunbathing off watch. Bothie took it over in the Roaring Forties and the Filthy Fifties. His favourite folk on board were the London engineer Howard and Terry the bosun.

Our resident scientists, both from Cape Town University, were involved in oceanography. Not knowing their names, I had in my chauvinist way stuck a label on their prospective cabin door stating SCIENTIFIC GENTLEMEN. It turned out that one of them, Lesley Rickett, was a slim blonde girl and a good friend of the other, Dr Chris McQuaid, who was not a South African at all but Northern Irish. I apologised for shoving them in the same cabin but neither objected.

The *Observer* sent freelance photographer Bryn Campbell who had been with me on a previous five-month expedition in British Columbia eight years before. Bryn had the knack of getting on with most people, unless they interfered with his job. This was, from my past experience, a rare ability for an expedition photographer.

Giles Kershaw and Gerry Nicholson had had six seventy-five-gallon fuel tanks installed inside the fuselage of Transglobe's Twin Otter to enable them to increase their flying range from five hours to nineteen. They then proceeded to make their way towards us in a series of carefully worked out hops. First they flew from England via Iceland and Ottawa to Toronto where they had a set of retractable skis fitted. The Chubb Group, owners of the plane, kindly agreed to purchase these at a cost of over £50,000. From Canada the Twin Otter had hopped to Miami, the South Caicos Islands and on to Trinidad.

Giles took off early in the morning from Trinidad to avoid cloud build-up over the jungle and then covered the whole of Venezuela and North Brazil in one long day's journey to Manaos on the banks of the Amazon, in Gerry's words:

> *Very impressive and a little worrying. After piranha and chips, up at 6.30 a.m. and on to Ascencion in Paraguay. The longest leg of the whole flight; 1,330 miles in nine hours. Then to Mar Del Plata for Christmas in shirt sleeves. Down the coast to Commodoro Riviera, also in Argentina, our stepping off point for Port Stanley in the Falkland Islands. We spent an extra day for our clearance to be checked: there is a dispute there at the moment about who should own the islands: Britain or Argentina.*

Gerry also wrote that they had found the price of fuel at their various stops varied from fifty cents a gallon in some USA airports to $2.50 in Paraguay.

While Gerry and Giles were celebrating their Christmas in shirt sleeves, we were preparing to celebrate ours well into the Roaring Forties with the ship tossing and rolling in grey-black seas. A Christmas tree, lashed by the crew to the mast, was torn away by powerful gusts. In the jumbled chaos of the galley, little Jill and big Dave Hicks strove to prepare Christmas fare for the hungry masses, whilst walls of green water curled over the down-plunged prow, then buried the bows and fo'c'sle with shuddering blows felt by everyone on board.

At all times, five were on watch, either on the bridge or on radar look-out for growlers, semi-submerged bergs such as had sunk the *Titanic*, whilst other people were down below sleeping or wandering around; this left fourteen or so to fit snugly round the little saloon table for meals. Now for Christmas we would be bursting at the seams with twenty-four all gathered together at once whilst Mick Hart, guitar and song master, led the revelry. Dave Hicks, the steward, served Irish coffee and mince pies. Tangerines, nuts and the occasional meatball flew from table to table. Plates and cups surged like flotsam in an eddy from side to side along the polished formica. Brief speeches were drowned by catcalls and laughter. Bothie yapped and cleaned up gifts of turkey in his seventh heaven.

Amidships and close by the skipper's cabin Anton had hung a brass inclinometer, the same simple instrument Captain Scott carried on *Discovery* and our only relic from that earlier southern voyage. Cyrus was at the helm that day as a giant roller forced the *Benjy B* to keel to forty-seven degrees both ways. Christmas goodies bit the dust, Bothie slid on his side a good six yards and the Admiral nearly swallowed his pipe. Everyone together shouted "Cyrus!" For the next three years, whenever the *Benjy B* took a wave more violent than most, whenever somebody spilled their coffee at an imagined pitch or toss, poor Cyrus's name was mouthed like a swear word, whether he was in fact at the wheel or snoring in his pit.

It seemed to me the ship could not take such treatment for long. She would surely be shaken to pieces. Would her thirty-year-old hull survive the twin strains of the enormous weight of our fuel and cargo within and the hideous battering from without? As a poor and infrequent sailor, secretly in need of reassurance from an old salt, I sought Anton.

"Sit down," he said, "have a dram."

I refused, deeply regretting the quantities of Christmas food and booze I'd already put down.

"Everything OK?" I asked.

"How do you mean?"

"The ship. The hull . . . you know."

"Ah," Anton's black eyes glinted. "That is not a thing anyone would predict. Perhaps. Perhaps not. This is not *rough*, you know. We'll be lucky if we get away with no worse than this." Then he told me the story of another British expedition which had set sail for Antarctica the previous year via Rio de Janeiro in a converted war-time tug, the *En Avant*, eight years older than the *Benjy B*. Her hull had been strengthened to cope with ice and she had set out in the southern summer, as we had, bound for the Falkland Islands and never to be seen again. Her crew included the well-known polar sailor and mountaineer, Major Bill Tilman, then in his eightieth year. "It is my bet they were knocked down by a wave in heavy weather," concluded Anton, making me feel worse than before.

I went below and held a Christmas church service. Ten people turned up and we sat through it for standing was not sensible. I held quite a few Sunday services whilst on board but attendance was poor. Once the only other person was Simon, the Quaker.

The next few days were if anything worse but I got used to it and began to work again down in Number Two hold. The mackerel odour was very faint now. In the lower half of the hold movement was restricted to a crawl, torch-in-mouth, between the tops of boxes and the rusty slats of the ceiling. Despite various odd noises and much creaking, every item seemed secure. Terry and his men had done a thorough lashing job.

With the exercise my appetite returned. Everyone, even Simon, was eating three full meals a day, and somehow Jill coped in the twelve-foot square galley with its thirty-year-old cooker.

To watch her baste a turkey as the scalding hot fat slurped from side to side was fascinating. The galley floor was generally slippery with spilled liquids and grease. Just to move about, let alone handle great tureens of steaming soup for twenty-nine hungry mouths, required balance and dexterity.

Jill said: "It's not much fun cooking when you feel sea-sick but you've just got to keep going because everyone goes on eating."

She developed defences against the non-stop rolling. Like using more saucepans only half-filled, rather than fewer fuller ones. And jamming them in series on the hotplates so none could move.

Did she find it satisfying?

I don't think I'd do it again. Everyone's tastes are so different. Some hate garlic or onions. Others won't touch fish. Some get unhappy if they don't get their specific favourite items each breakfast at the right time. And, of course, they expect it. If I do bother to do something different, I guarantee that half of them will either dislike it or simply not notice.

We crossed the 50th parallel late on 28th December and the first iceberg passed abeam. Up on the bridge at one a.m. the graveyard watch stood silently. Ahead little could be seen but the glint of wild foam. One man hunched over the radar console, his features long and gaunt in its reflected orange light. Now and again he would pass some brief information to the figure behind the oaken wheel. Our course was 220° magnetic.

Ollie, in a dark donkey jacket, was often to be found out on the bridge wing, binoculars at the ready. His bird sightings list grew. . . . black-browed and grey-headed albatross, orion, skua, giant petrel, prion and many more.

Each day, with Terry operating the winch gear, the 'gentlemen scientists' trawled for plankton. With bathythermographs they obtained depth to temperature profiles. Using these side by side with salinity measurements they identified large-scale water movements. Their aim was to study current patterns and the interaction of the water bodies at sub-tropical and Antarctic convergences.

The behaviour and condition of these currents influence the existence of tiny phytoplankton and thus their predators, the zoo-plankton, including krill. Chris McQuaid showed me a jar of sea water solid with tiny crustaceans after only a ten-minute trawl.

"This," he said, waving his hand at the great grey expanse, "is the most productive ocean in the world. For a scientist its richness and diversity are irresistible. Krill may well prove to be an important source of food, so abundant that it can be harvested in thousands of tons. Already commercial krill fisheries have been established by several countries."

He dabbed a finger in the jar of slimy sea-life. "Unfortunately there are plenty of examples in recent history of what happens when commercial interests go on a spree and ignore the simple laws of nature. Here we have a source of protein which is valuable and, by modern methods, quite easy to harvest. It may take only a few years to be culled to the point of scarcity, even extinction."

He warmed to his subject.

"Krill is the central link in the vast and complex food webs that form the ecology of the Southern Ocean. Remove too many krill and you endanger whales, seals, seabirds and fish. In order to cull a new source of food for man and exploit it profitably, commercial interests may cause havoc."

Chris's Irish brogue grew stronger with emphasis. "Unless we, the researchers, know all the facts we cannot present a convincing argument for control. But our resources are limited in manpower, money and opportunity, unlike those of the krill fishermen whose backers feed on their own profit and mankind's necessity. That's why the voyage of the *Benjy B* is such a Godsend."

As 1980 approached, pack-ice closed about the ship and battle was joined. The hull juddered each time we struck a solid chunk and our bows rode high to mount the ice. With luck our laden weight would split the obstruction and sunder it in two. More often than not this happened. When it didn't the skipper simply repeated the ram until he eventually won. The wind still blew, a lot colder now; but the sea was calm beneath its weighty mantle.

Simon went down with a sore throat, sweating, aching bones and headache. He had been burning the galvanising off pipe fittings with two of the engineers and they were similarly afflicted. The symptoms, according to our reference book and in the absence of a doctor, seemed to fit those of zinc poisoning.

Paul Clark, as medic, tried to help. Simon was not appreciative. "Paul," he wrote, "stared at me with those piercing eyes of his and talked of antidotes which we don't possess. Afraid I was rude to him and told him to forget it since even if we had an antidote it would be too late now to do any good."

Eddie Pike and the Buzzard cornered me in the hospital on New Year's Eve. "This mouse," Eddie proffered a brown china mouse an inch long, "is of the Pike family and having travelled all the way from Greenwich should go back there *via* the Poles. Take him with you."

I took the mouse with care. It was called Mouser Pike.

Buzzard handed over a corked bottle about the same size. The bottle's inmate was a gnome namesake.

"Gnome Buzzard," his owner prodded my chest, "must also go round that way and expects good treatment. None of your rough and tumble for him. Other gnomes, like your world famous Gnome Jerome have been up the Amazon, down the Itchycrutchee Falls and all over the bloody place but *none* of 'em have done the polar route. Gnome Buzzard," more chest prodding, "will be the first."

The deputation went and I packed the items up with my favourite compass and pocket knife. That night there was much festivity. The film crew recorded the start of the Hogmanay celebrations but by midnight the director and cameraman were even more elated than their subjects and quite incapable of further artistry.

Tony Dutton, the sound man, was becoming almost a friend of the land team members; an unusual event in my experience of film people but then you can never generalise: it's the exceptions that make the world go round.

For two days we averaged three knots within the pack-ice. Only once did the skipper retreat and search for a new route, rather than batter a way along the selected one.

The crow's nest was big enough for one man to sit in slightly cramped comfort. Ginnie, who hated heights, refused to scale the ladder to the nest; a pity since the view of the pack, especially in the eerie pastels of evening, was worth the climb. Two hours was the normal stint for a crow's nest watch. The occupant used binoculars to ensure his route choice was not simply the next most inviting lead but the general direction of least ice for as far as he could see: he then passed directions down an antique intercom system to the bridge.

Dave Hicks who, being steward, was in charge of the ship's drink supplies, took his own central heating up to the nest with him. His course through the pack was noticeably more zig-zag than other people's. When not passing directions he would hum, whistle, belch and generally carry on a bizarre conversation with himself all of which came through the loudspeaker on the bridge. I am not sure if any of Admiral Otto's bridge watches coincided with Dave's crow's nest performances.

On 4th January we entered the coastal lead and, back at nine knots, moved west with the high cliffs of Antarctica to our south and the rim of the pack to starboard.

Ginnie made radio contact with the South Africans at Sanae base and their leader promised to send flares up from the ice bay at which it would be safest for us to unload: he called it by the Norwegian name Polarbjorn Buchte. His base was only ten miles inland from this bight and the weather, he said, was good. His tone suggested fine weather was not something to be taken for granted.

As many of us as possible now lined the deck scanning the many indents in the ice cliffs but we saw none where the ship might berth, let alone unload, since the cliffs were at least forty feet high. Then around midday we spotted the South African flares in a bay which was about half a mile wide at the mouth. Hemmed in by high cliffs, it tapered V-like for a mile and a half to its apex where the cliffs fell away to a snow ramp which gave access to the interior. We would have to manoeuvre the boat as near as possible, unload fast and then move everything some two miles to the ramp itself.

Although the Antarctic summer was well advanced, the sun high in the sky and the temperature only around freezing point, the winter sea-ice had not yet left the bay and to my ignorant eye its surface looked solid enough, but Sir Vivian Fuchs had warned me not to trust such bay ice as it only needed a strong northerly wind to start new fracturing which would begin along the seaward edge where we were unloading. Sir Vivian's team had lost a great quantity of stores in this way, including 300 drums of fuel, a Ferguson tractor, coal, timber and engineering stores.

As the ship must leave Antarctica as soon as possible in order not to get iced in, we must unload hundreds of drums of fuel, each weighing 450 pounds, and over a hundred tons of mixed cargo fast. I had been planning the details of this all through Africa, in Abidjan and in the South Atlantic and if my paperwork was right, we should be able to finish in eleven days, using *all* crew members, despite their ignorance of snow vehicles and cold weather hazards. To accomplish this we had only one little groundhog from our Greenland trials and five skidoos.

As soon as Giles and Gerry appeared with the Otter, they would have to ferry close on 100,000 pounds of cargo inland some 300 miles to the edge of the Antarctic plateau where we hoped to set up a forward camp at 6,000 feet above sea level, near the abandoned South African base called Borga on the edge of the known world. This base hugged the ice ridge of the Kirwan Escarpment, south from which man had never ventured. The mountain beneath which we would hope to spend the long dark winter was named Ryvingen.

For 900 miles towards the South Pole, a vast tract of unknown ice, over 10,000 feet above sea level, awaited us. As far south as Ryvingen we would simply be travellers: thereafter explorers of one of the earth's last untrodden regions.

It took Sir Vivian Fuchs a hundred days to cross the continent by a shorter route and using closed cab vehicles which cut down the risk of exposure to the men. His team had great difficulties with crevasses. We must obviously count on at least that long a journey. The Antarctic summer, the period when it is *possible* to travel, is but 120 days in all. Amundsen tried to challenge nature by starting his South Pole attempt a month early. He regretted his rashness when extreme cold forced his team back to their base for a further month's wait. Captain Scott failed to return from his own South Pole journey by early February and was caught out in an autumn blizzard that sealed his fate. To be isolated from a base on the polar plateau outside the narrow confines of summer is to invite a speedy demise. We hoped to start for the Pole in October once the temperature had risen to a travellable level.

The Admiral rammed the edge of the bay ice to make a nest for the ship right up alongside, so that a ladder could be lowered straight on to the ice. The *Benjy B* crew lost no time in disembarking to feel Antarctica under their mukluks and to talk to the South African men who had come to greet us. Tall, rangy men with unkempt beards, shoulder-length hippy hair and head bands, they had seen nobody for a year. Looking down from the fo'c'sle with Simon, I noticed two groups had formed: one of hairy South Africans bunched around Jill; the other a group of Transglobers, all armed with cameras, ringed around a single Adèle penguin which stared back at them with an arrogant expression. Simon and I couldn't decide which group was the more mesmerised.

The South Africans were one of several scientific groups from various countries stationed in Antarctica, including a group at the Pole itself. Their leader took me up the snow ramp. A mile beyond it he paced out a relatively flat 600 metres.

"The prevailing wind goes this way. You can tell by the direction of the nearby sastrugi, the ridges of snow, so your Twin Otter could use this as an airstrip and you can lay out your cargo alongside it."

I thanked him and the South Africans left us after a feast on board of all those things they had long since run out of at their base – fresh fruit, vegetables, milk and whisky.

Whilst the crew sank telegraph poles into the bay ice to act as anchors, I took Charlie and 200 flagged bamboos to mark out a route from the ship to our inland cargo site, and on to the site of the hut where Simon and Anto Birkbeck must spend the winter beside the cargo lines. Finally, poles with numbered flags were planted alongside the airstrip to mark off where different priorities of equipment and fuel must be placed. Every single crate, and there were close on 2,000, not including drums, was numbered and allocated a priority for its flight to the Ryvingen inland base. At any time a blizzard could drift snow over the cargo and cover it, so the numbered flags would tell us where to dig for any given item without delay.

Summer was well advanced and the sun high in the sky. With no wind and the temperature around freezing point, we might as well have been at a Swiss resort. That evening the South Africans brought a mobile *breiflei* down to the site of our airstrip. A barbecue would be the English equivalent. Frozen steaks, sausages and bacon sizzled on hot charcoal in a homemade brazier and Transglobers trudged up the bay and the ramp in their party clothes to join in. An unlimited supply of South African wines filled the rear of one snowcat.

By three a.m. everyone was back on board, ready for an early start – except for the Canadian chief officer and Dave Hicks. These two were carried back over the bay ice. The Canadian was dragged up the ladder and put to bed, but Dave Hicks, despite his pot belly, was a big strong man, and being as limp as a dead carrot, defied all efforts to load him aboard. Finally, they tied a rope round his chest and half-heaved from above, half pushed from below, and his body began to ascend. Something went wrong as he neared the gunwales and he plummeted downwards. There was a sizeable splash on contact with the sea between ice and hull, then he settled belly up, still asleep and bobbing like a beachball. It was only −3°C but the others decided he would be better off in bed. With reinforcements they finally hauled him up and dried him off.

Six hours later and sober as a judge he attended the meeting at which I briefed all on board as to the unloading operation. Ginnie handed out walkie-talkies, Jill produced ration packs and Ollie laid down the safety law for the inland ferry run. This would be a non-stop round-the-clock affair with Eddie Pike, Paul Clark, Charlie and Anton Bowring handling the skidoos and the three engineers alternating between the groundhog and ship's engine watch.

Admiral Otto, Cyrus and two cooks would remain aboard ready

for immediate withdrawal in the event of a storm or invading icebergs: the ship might easily be trapped and crushed if a wary eye was not kept to the north at all times. All the drivers carried sleeping bags and safety gear in case they were temporarily abandoned. David Mason and Mick Hart went inland with tents to help erect Simon and Anto's hut, and to log each item from the boat into its place in the airstrip cargo lines.

Ollie's task was to keep all vehicles fuelled and running at all times and check the drivers did not get over-tired and vulnerable to exposure, while Ginnie maintained non-stop vigil on the VLF walkie-talkie band. Bothie kept one eye on her.

Terry, Buzzard and the chief officer handled the winches and down in the holds, my helpers were Dave Hicks, Chris McQuaid and the radio officer. As each item left the hold I marked it with a serial number to show its priority and position in the cargo lines, so that David and Mick would know exactly where to stow it. The film team and Bryn Campbell could roam at will. Bryn subsequently roamed a bit too far on a skidoo in a whiteout and gave himself a nasty shock when he discovered how easy it was to become disorientated and lost.

A light wind sprang up and the temperature dropped to −20°C which was several degrees below what most of those involved had ever experienced even briefly, so they wore polar mitts, parkas and mukluks.

Every six hours the cooks brought coffee and sandwiches down into the hold. Even with the block-buster biceps of Dave Hicks to help, I began to feel the worse for wear after thirty-six hours and my back shot nasty warning pains at me. Gradually the mountain of stores subsided. At the end of day two about a quarter of the cargo was logged in at the airstrip by David Mason.

The third day saw a turn in the weather. The temperature shot up fifteen degrees, the northern horizon grew dark, the ship moved slowly against the ice as an increasing swell shifted her, and her anchor stakes started to work loose. The winch engine over-heated and needed repairs. Unloading had to cease.

Once I stopped, I realised just how exhausted I was after seventy hours' unceasing work; fully clothed, I fell fast asleep in my bunk. Meanwhile Ollie abandoned his fuel and servicing point on shore and clambered back on board to radio through to hold all vehicles and drivers at the airstrip until the weather improved. The South

Africans had kindly left us a box-hut some six foot square, stocked with rations, close to the snow ramp so Mick and Simon were able to huddle together with the skidoo drivers inside.

The Admiral had no wish to abandon the anchorage but by midnight the wind had risen to over fifty knots and spray surged high as mounting waves crashed against the rim of the bay ice. Great icebergs began to shift ominously to our north and soon two of our mooring stakes snapped. The other two followed in a little while and we were adrift. The Admiral had no choice but to head north to ride out the storm a safe distance from the coast.

Ten drums remained near the ice front and also Ken Cameron's motor bike which he had unloaded for personal reasons.

Soon after the *Benjy B* stopped to hover offshore, bows to the storm, Ginnie woke me. Up on the bridge we watched whole segments of the Buchte ice ride out to sea. On one I counted eight drums of Twin Otter fuel, 320 precious gallons. They floated past and on into the wind-whipped whiteout. We never saw Ken's motor bike again. I reflected that if some southern sailing skipper, after dinner and a dram, were to spot an ice floe bearing a gleaming Honda past his ship, he would probably go teetotal for life.

The weather cleared as quickly as it had deteriorated and the sun shone from a cloudless sky when the Twin Otter arrived in style, roaring over the *Benjy B*. After a faultless display of mast-hopping, Giles landed beside our airstrip, not on it. We were to discover he took particular delight in virgin landing sites untouched by axe and shovel.

For the first time all elements of Transglobe were together. In a short while the ship must leave and the aircrew had less than a month in which to ferry enough fuel and kit to the inland Ryvingen site for our eight months' sojourn there. Then they must flee Antarctica before winter closed in.

With a prefabricated hut erected at Sanae and everything but the fuel drums positioned between hut and airstrip, Giles flew Ginnie and me inland over many black mountains and the glinting scars of crevasse fields. To the east the impressive power of a moving river of ice, the Jutulstraumen Glacier, flowed north in a chaos of broken blocks.

Beyond the peaks of Giaeverryggen and the Borga massif, Giles descended close by Huldreslotte, the mountain where the old South African camp lay buried. The horned peak of Ryvingen reared from the snow fields eleven miles east of Huldreslotte and below it Giles settled the Twin Otter on a soft gradient.

With a tent, survival kit and half a plane-load of flagged poles he left us and flew off. Giles was never one to linger: he knew the value of fine weather better than anyone after five seasons flying in Antarctica for the British Antarctic Survey.

As Antarctica is by far the coldest place on earth with temperatures likely to plummet in winter to −84°C, it was essential that our winter base be sheltered from the blast of icy winds. For it is the wind that affects humans most by scouring the skin of those vestiges of warmth trapped by pores and hairs. Minus 40° in still air is quite comfortable but −20° with a sixty-knot wind is lethal. The lie of the sastrugi told me that the prevailing wind blew from the south so we must seek shelter on the northern leeward side of the mountain. But Ginnie was determined to maintain good radio contact with England, despite the warning of Bob Thomson, New Zealand's senior Antarctic administrator, that British Antarctic bases are seldom able to talk directly with Britain. She also wanted high frequency and very high frequency contact to the south, back north to the ice group at Sanae and the Twin Otter crew during the coming crossing attempt, so she didn't care for my initial choice of site. After a heated discussion in our tent – hundreds of miles from the nearest person, we could vent our opinions as loudly as we liked – we agreed to compromise.

First we marked out the antennae sites with poles, west of the mountain's wind shadow, where there was a clear line south towards the Pole. Then we paced a cable distance back east and flagged the site for Ginnie's radio hut. We left a fifty-metre gap between it and the generator hut and another twenty-five metres between that one and the hut we would live in. Finally we paced 800 metres east up the hill and sited the very low frequency research hut, putting its antenna site a further 800 metres beyond. The VLF recording equipment had to be this distance from our generators because of its sensitivity.

The next day Simon and Anto were flown in by Giles together with all the materials needed to erect our cardboard radio hut which was put together in twelve hours. Giles now flew ferry flights each of a round 500 miles with hardly a break, backwards and forwards, bringing in fuel drums, cargo and all the walls to make our thirty-six-foot long main living area.

Leaving David, Simon and Anto to dig trenches, erect huts and place in position cargo and fuel drums, Ginnie and I flew back to

Sanae to find that the ship had now been completely unloaded and was ready to sail. The only mishap had been to Howard Willson who had broken three ribs when moving some hut sections. But every crate and drum was in position on shore and all was ready for a farewell party.

The next day, 17th January, we sat on our rucksacks by the fractured edge of the bay-ice and watched our friends sail away, the mournful hoots of the *Benjy B* reaching back to the bay long after she had disappeared.

Rick the cameraman cried openly; truly an artist. He wanted to reproduce the emotion of the moment on film. For that he needed sound but poor Tony Dutton, the sound man, managed to let the wind catch his tapes. They blew around like confetti followed by dark looks from the rest of the crew.

The weather had changed up at Ryvingen, intermittent gusts of wind lashed at the one finished hut. The walls were made of standard corrugated cardboard as used for everyday packaging. It provides excellent insulation. The team had to work without pause during lulls, afraid that the next blow would undo any half-finished work. Once they completed the digging of a foundation trench, three feet deep, twelve feet wide and twenty-four feet long, only to have it filled in again by a new storm. Fortunately the huts were incredibly light to move about and simple to erect and Simon and Anto worked well together, a good omen perhaps for their coming winter confinement down at Sanae.

Simon wrote in his diary:

On 18th January we began the main hut, the longest, and worked through the night and the next day in bitter cold, stiff mitts and icy balaclavas. There was a fire in the radio hut because the stove was left on too high a setting. David discovered it just in time; a warning to us all. Blowing snow and misty all day. No ferry flights. The camp looks habitable and occupied. Nice to have started it from scratch. I think Ran credits Anto and myself with the bulk of it. The surrounding nunataks, especially Ryvingen which overhangs us, never cease to catch the eye. The ever-changing sun and clouds bring a new view every day. Sanae will seem dull and sordid after the clear crisp air up here.

Giles had flown the film crew up so that they could film the huts being assembled but they were to leave Antarctica on the icebreaker due any day now with the new South African base team and our last 600 fuel drums. No other ship would call for a year or more so it was essential that they be down at Sanae on time, but a spell of mist now kept Giles and Gerry grounded at Sanae.

Giles risked a rare break in the fog to come to collect them but bright sunshine changed to minimal visibility in fifteen minutes flat. Bryn Campbell of the *Observer* who, with David Mason, was also going out on the boat, wrote: "We could hear the Twin Otter overhead but a landing seemed almost impossible. The camp is surrounded by rocky peaks and 600-foot crags. Suddenly we saw the aircraft lights appear in the gloom. Giles made a perfect landing." The cargo was removed and the film crew whisked off into the blinding glare of the whiteout to catch their boat.

That was Giles' fortieth flight but half the Ryvingen-bound cargo still remained at Sanae, so he had many more to do.

Gerry worked on the plane when Giles had his rare cat-naps. Gerry: "As usual down south the engineer only gets the aircraft to service when the weather is too bad to fly, but do we complain? Of course we do but it makes little difference."

He had escaped death with Giles in Antarctica during a previous season's work for the British Antarctic Survey. "We were over the peninsula when one engine stopped. There was ice build-up in the fuel systems and, about forty miles from our base, the other stopped, too, and we had to glide the Twin Otter down on the ice shelf somewhere, strip the systems apart and hang the bits out to dry in our tent."

He gave a nervous chuckle. "Water freezes quite quickly down here so you need to be *meticulous* with the amount of fuel you put in when filling up. As for contamination, you just keep checking and checking and checking. Filters and water detection kit, you know."

He looked at his fingers as though surprised they were all there. "Some of the time you tend to get a lot of fuel on your hands and, well, fuel and cold don't mix, as far as hands are concerned. You need to wear gloves, yet for fiddly jobs, you can't. You tend to, well I do anyway, get very irritable when you're servicing. There's no shelter here; no hangar. It's all done outside. I shove handwarmers in an outsize pair of mittens and sort of push my hands into those to recover their blood supply every few minutes. Then carry on with the job."

Gerry is a master of understatement; a good many memories of fine pain were doubtless concealed in his words.

On 25th January the ice team consisting of myself, Ollie and Charlie left Sanae. Our skidoos were identical to those we used in the Arctic in 1977 except the carburettors were improved. The journey to Ryvingen would zig-zag between mountain ranges and crevasse fields. Although the magnetic compass was usable, for the local error was a mere 18°, it had to be used with care for the alcohol was cold and thick which made the needle sluggish. I soon developed the habit of double-checking its final lie and tapping it gently in case it had yet to settle true.

Each skidoo towed a laden sledge which carried 1200 pounds in all, more than we would need for the 370 kilometre journey, for I planned to use the run as a rehearsal for next year's crossing attempt.

Thirty-foot double ropes linked each skidoo to its sledge. In

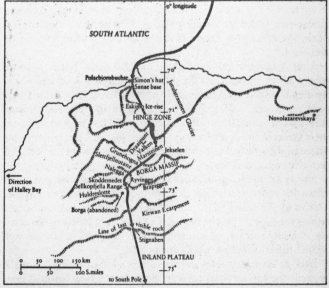

Sanae and Ryvingen

principle any one unit could plunge into a crevasse but would soon be arrested by the halted weight attached to it. Of course, going downhill or on slippery ice the principle might not work too well if the skidoo were to fall through first. There would be no benefit to a driver whose skidoo dangled in an abyss anchored by its sledge if he himself carried on downwards. So we each wore a mountaineer's harness with a line attached either to the skidoo or to the sledge depending on personal preference. Ollie and I believed the latter to be safer, Charlie the former.

To begin with there was only a flat and featureless whiteness; a good firm surface and the machines ran well over the ice shelf. Difficult to accept that all this ice *floated* on the ocean. Somewhere not far south we must cross the dreaded Hinge Zone where this floating shelf became the Antarctic ice sheet: then we would, for the first time, be truly on the Antarctic continent with rock beneath the ice under our feet.

This ice sheet covers all the land of Antarctica save for a few 'dry' valleys. Its 5,500,000 square miles dwarf the United States. Seen from outer space it "radiates light like a great white lantern across the bottom of the world", according to astronauts. These impressive characteristics did not occupy my thoughts as we approached the rim of the sheet, only the nature of the Hinge Line, its location and its crevasses.

After a number of over-flights Giles Kershaw spotted a route inland which crossed onto the sheet at a seemingly unbroken place. By then I had discussed the journey with the South African boss who gave me a series of compass bearings used by previous snowcat forays from Sanae. If snowcats found it safe, I mused, it should bear mere skidoos. So I opted for his route and ignored Giles's subsequent findings. This turned out to be a bad mistake but not one that we ourselves were to suffer from.

Ninety kilometres from Sanae whiteout conditions clamped down as we descended gently from the wide mound called Eskimo Ice-rise. The South Africans had warned me of big crevasses on the northern side of the ice-rise. Not having seen any yet, I felt it best not to carry on without visibility, so we camped until two days later there was again brilliant sunshine in a clear blue sky.

Back at Sanae crevasses were opening and Bryn wrote: "At night we hear the bay ice breaking with the noise of a tank battle. A long fissure spreads from the western cliffs, still very narrow but hundreds of feet deep. Across the top of the bay, a pencil thin line breathes in and out. We agreed not to wander around on our own!"

That day we set out to cross the Hinge Line using the South African route. A year later a group of twelve South African scientists did likewise. They lost two machines for ever and a young scientist fell ninety feet and broke his neck. In 1981 at a British base further round the coast two scientists were killed in crevasses using skidoos like ours. In 1982 three scientists from another British base disappeared along the coastal ice on a local patrol. The little expeditions of the 'eighties are studded with tragedies, as were those longer journeys of Mawson and Scott. Radios and aircraft do not, as modern armchair scoffers would have us believe, provide some magic safety screen.

I lined up the bearings of a succession of features, at first mere floating mirages, weird and distended, but growing to distinctive shapes as we approached. All had Afrikaans names – Draaipunt, Valken and Dassiekop, head of the rabbit – and each was isolated by many miles of moving ice.

Crevasses in this zone average six to nine metres wide and four to five kilometres long from north to south. Summer was well advanced: we could expect the drifted snow cover hiding the crevasses to be rotten and weak. But our skidoos, unladen, weighed only 700 pounds and their rubber tracks spread the ground pressure to a mere .028 pounds per square inch, less than the foot of a dog or a man. The narrow runners of the heavy sledges were a different kettle of fish: they would break through more easily. To prevent this, speed seemed the best answer. Warily, we edged east towards the black mound of Marsteinen.

With no warning the Hinge was before us and beside us. A glint of under-shadow, a few yards ahead, green and sinister in its suddenness.

I accelerated, felt a lurch beneath me, then solid ice once more. More green lines left and right now. Head for the white. Forget what's happening to the sledge. Worry only about the skidoo and yourself. Four or five within a hundred yards . . . sweating as you tug the steering bars left, and left again, spot a new chasm and veer right flinging the body weight sideways and forward to give more cutting edge to the steering ski. Then a patch of firmness.

I stopped and looked back, breathing hard.

My sledge had opened up craters. The worst place for the others to go would be in my tracks. They realised this soon enough.

Watching is worse than doing it yourself, I thought, any moment expecting to see one of the little jinking machines and its muffled human cargo disappear.

They stopped before reaching me. I had crossed to the solid place over a spit of snow. I saw that my sledge had broken the spit and a two-foot wide green scar now cut the others off from further progress. It seemed narrow enough to jump. Remembering my duty as cameraman I unloaded a 16 mm Bolex ciné camera and moved to the edge of the crevasse. Ollie and Charlie watched from their side but did not stop me. It was a foolish action: eleven months later a young man was to die in the same area through moving unroped over this spider's web of hidden cliffs.

Only luck stopped me plunging the height of St Paul's Cathedral. I was at first quite unaware of any danger, for I could see that the far lip of the crevasse was a sheer drop. Had I stopped to think, memories of crevasse photographs and diagrams would have warned me that my own side of the divide was likely to be no clean cut right angle but a tapering overhang liable to imminent subsidence under pressure.

The monopod of the Bolex probably saved me. I placed it a yard from the edge and it sank unopposed through half a dozen inches of granular snow crust into thin air. My blood froze. I found myself shouting at the others, "Why didn't you warn me, you bums?"

Their reply was a good deal of laughter muffled only by their facemasks. Quite how much they appreciated the peril of my predicament I never did find out. With the feeling I remembered so well from Arabia, treading where anti-personnel mines were suspected, I retreated as though barefoot on hot bricks. Once, one leg went down to the calf; I remained rigid then picked it up and placed it with slow pressure elsewhere. Sweating, I got back to firmer cover and cursed myself as well as the others under my breath. I filmed their wild charge over the rift but from a safe distance which ensured a boring film and a live cameraman.

That morning kept the adrenalin pumping and the eyes behind our goggles shifting rapidly as we advanced over the most broken of icefields.

With a sense of relief I swung south east up the last steep climb to Marsteinen nunatak. We were over the Hinge Zone, the first known obstacle behind us.

By sticking with care to the old South African route and travelling for fourteen hours, we reached the black and orange cliffs of Nalegga with their ridgeline needles; high sentinels of the horizon.

All day the temperature remained around −28°C and with little wind, pleasant for travel. As new scenery unpeeled to the south and west, great ranges hovered in mirage, pulsating images of levitated cathedrals and castles in the air. Jekselen, Grunehogna, Slettfjell-nutana and many an unnamed pinnacle. Deep windscoops like immense polished amphitheatres fell away to our flanks and hillocks of blue mirror-ice crowned fields of sastrugi in the katabatic wind lanes. Rocks of crazy shape lounged lone and menacing like druid megaliths, spawn of long-ago rockfalls on their willy-nilly way with the iceflow to the north and the sea.

We camped under the shadow of Nalegga. Morale was high for the sledges handled with ease. The unspoken feeling was one of relief. Antarctica, it seemed, was an easy touch compared to the Arctic.

The first main climb was behind us for the ice sheet was 5,000 feet above sea level at this point. A series of chunky nunataks guided us south and east out of the Sellkopffjella range: then wide open snowfields between flanking escarpments to the rocks of Skod-demedet, our penultimate goal. As we rounded its southern wall the distant bulk of Ryvingen Mountain rose peak then shoulders into view, until the whole impressive feature reared above the snows of the eastern horizon. With binoculars we could see the little smudge of shadow at its base, our home for the coming winter.

Ginnie and Simon were hard at work: the huts were finished but a great deal remained to be done before the long months of darkness began. Simon had been taught to erect radio masts. Using Charlie and me as his labour gang, he mounted the ten-inch triangular sections one by one until he was eighty feet up tightening the last bolt. Ginnie then made up antennae which we hoisted to the top.

Simon joined one of Giles' ferry flights down to Sanae so that he and Anto could settle in to their own winter camp. They were surprised to find the film crew, Bryn and David, still there as the South African ship had delayed her departure back to Cape Town. On 1st February, the day he returned to Sanae, Simon wrote:

A great feeling of elation when we took off from Ryvingen but this subsided on getting back to our hut at Sanae. Damp, windy and despondent: met by David Mason in a black mood and a silent Gerry. David painted a grey picture of what I would find

and, for once, was not far wrong. Whole place in a shambles,
squalid and depressing. The cargo lines broken up by odd ragged
bits of kit scattered about and sticking up out of the ice. The hut,
which the cameraman once described as "your cosy little home"
in a filthy condition. Dark and smelly inside, all the film crew on
their bunks from which they apparently rarely stir, apart from
Tony who is embarrassed by it all. Just outside it's like a
battlefield; burnt pots mark the site of our loo, with muck, loo
paper and slops all around the entrance. Anto is in a silent rage. I
try to remain cheerful. If I lose my temper, the film crew will be
out in a tent.

Two days later the crew, Bryn and David Mason left with the
South African icebreaker. So Simon and Anto began to clear up.
Simon: "When I lifted the stove I found a deep charred hole beneath.
The drip valve and flue sections were also damaged. Very angry. If I
see them again, they won't be welcome."

Giles and Gerry finished the last of seventy-eight ferry flights on
10th February. After a hot meal with us, they took off on their long
flight back to England and soon disappeared into the gathering dusk
above the southern ice sheet. Next day the weather clamped down;
whiteout and nil visibility. From now on Ginnie, Charlie, Ollie,
Bothie and I were alone. Should anyone be ill during the next eight
months there could be no evacuation, no rescue in *any* shape or form
and no medical assistance.

We must daily handle batteries but must beware of acid in the eye.
Extreme cold burns, fuel burns, deep electrical burns, appendix
rumbles, serious tooth trouble, all such hazards must be avoided.

Temperatures would plunge to $-50°$ and below. Winds would
exceed ninety miles per hour. The absolute wind chill factor would
reach $-84°C$. For 240 days we must live with caution.

6

The Long Dark Winter

FEBRUARY–OCTOBER 1980

Silence is a great peacemaker.

H. W. LONGFELLOW

We were now encamped at Ryvingen on the icecap itself for the winter. As soon as it got warm again we would try to cross the whole continent of Antarctica which is bigger than Europe, than the US and Mexico combined, than India and China together and far larger than Australia. Ninety-nine per cent of this huge tract is buried unseen beneath an ice sheet in places over four kilometres thick, which crushes the landmass downwards by some 2,000 feet, although there are mountain peaks which rise to over 16,000 feet.

Three hundred and fifty million years ago there was life of sorts here, worms and scorpions, then the temperature dropped and ice closed over. Eighty million years later the ice receded, leaving a marshy terrain with meandering rivers and peatbeds that later became coal seams. Two hundred and twenty-five million years ago there were forests of horsetail and shrub-like ferns roamed by reptiles that grazed on the luxuriant foliage and provided meat for smaller fish-eating reptiles. Two hundred million years ago Australasia, India and Antarctica were all joined up but ten million years later they began to drift apart and the Antarctic was riven with volcanic eruptions for fifty million years.

Because it is so cold the air holds little moisture: the very coldness and remoteness make exploitation of minerals unrealistically costly. Neither Sir Vivian Fuchs nor Dr Armand Hammer felt there was much chance of oil or mining companies showing more than superficial interest in the foreseeable future. This is excellent since Antarctica is surely the last untainted wilderness which man has yet to despoil.

We were quickly impressed by the power of the wind. The long lines of fuel, equipment, food and skidoos were soon hidden by drifts. Marker flags blew away and I decided everything but the fuel must come inside. The huts were too cramped already to use for storage, so I excavated tunnels. Hut doors, unprotected by foyers, were quickly blocked up by drifts and leaked at the edges where a spray of super-fine snow blasted through: to stop this, sticky tape was applied to all cracks and only one door per hut was used, not for direct access to the elements but into ice tunnels.

Ginnie's radio hut foyer was a circular yard with high walls of drifted snow. I covered this over with a parachute. This was never satisfactory for long because snow weighed the material down and tore it. I had to replace the chutes once every two or three months. Ginnie refused my offers of a snow tunnel foyer on the grounds it would be claustrophobic in her daily work place. This was to prove extremely fortunate. Her remote VLF hut however had a small ice foyer which could only be entered via an empty forty-five-gallon drum with top and bottom sawn off and a removable hatch: a short ladder leaned against the drum's bottom but access was awkward, especially carrying heavy twelve-volt acid batteries.

Ollie built a thirty-foot long tunnel down to his garage door. This turned corners, was narrow, low and furnished with metal struts which caught you on the cranium unless you eeled downwards with great caution. The Pharaohs would have paid Ollie a princely sum as a pyramid entry-system engineer. The tunnels leading to the only door of our main hut had three escape hatches, two of which were ice staircases with canvas trapdoors and one a high drum with a step ladder dangling from it.

It was sensible to learn how to negotiate these tunnels in the dark and in a hurry. We all knew the fate of eight Russians the previous year whose hut had caught fire. Their bodies were found in an egress tunnel and all had died from asphyxiation. They presumably failed to find their escape hatches in the dark.

I remembered a three-week BBC sponsored expedition through London's underground sewers when our navigator, a seventy-year-old sewer officer named Alf, led us down brickwork tunnels of magnificent Gothic arches. All walls were peppered gorgonzola-wise with pipes which periodically gushed effluent into the main artery. Alf knew every bend: once a pipe by a tunnel Y-junction produced a brief but pretty waterfall and Alf stopped to glance at his watch.

"Eleven thirty sharp," he announced, "that'll be the French Ambassador."

He had been down there on and off since the Second World War and many a time his intimate knowledge of the network allowed him to escape alive from sudden flash floods. After three or four months we too were able to move through the tunnels and locate our hatches in the dark. But fire remained an ever-present fear.

The main tunnels took me two months to excavate. They included a lavatory cubicle which stayed around −31°F throughout the winter. It was good to get away from the others and to meditate for a while; a fairly short while since although your backside freezes far more slowly than your extremities, it still does freeze if you expose it for long enough. By the end of March the tunnels were two hundred yards long and every item we possessed was in them. By pouring kerosene into a small hole in the middle of the tunnel system and igniting it with burning rags I ended up after three days with a thirty foot deep slop pit down which to throw dirty washing-up water.

Cleaner washing water, I threw over the snow platforms, steps, and walkways in the tunnels to turn them to ice: we called the result 'permaslop'.

One day, running short of nails, we decided to visit the old South African base below Huldreslotte Mountain, some eleven miles west of our camp. Bothie could not be left alone, Ginnie said, so she put him in a rucksack. I had an old photo of the buried entrance shaft to the base but an hour's fruitless digging revealed only a box hut. We retrieved some nails, mostly bent, and as it was late in the day, headed back east.

On the way Charlie took a steep hill at a sharp angle, his sledge overtook his skidoo and overturned. Rolling it back he noticed on each side that five out of eight upright steel bars, the supports between runners and platform, had fractured. I checked mine and found it similarly broken. Ollie's was not. Further inspection revealed that the platforms themselves were slightly buckled. The unpleasant truth dawned slowly that the crossing journey was now at risk. I had two spare wooden sledges with me at Ryvingen, purely as camp workhorses, but no spare steel sledges because after their success during our Arctic training, I considered them unbreakable.

My error was in thinking that the 12′ 9″ Antarctic models, being exactly similar in every respect but length to the 8′ 6″ Arctic models, would prove equally tough. In normal circumstances perhaps they would have, but I had foolishly allowed the ship's unloading team to use them for transporting fuel drums inland, often three at a time. There were bigger wooden sledges for that purpose but I had thought to speed things up. There being no point in crying over spilled milk, I resolved to repair the bars later in the winter.

With the tunnels finished we began to train in the valleys around the camp which seemed to be crevasse-free. First Ollie unpacked his ice drill and excavated core samples from the surface to a depth of ten metres. He would have to do this at each degree of latitude during our crossing. Then, since neither he nor Charlie were practised in cross-country skiing, I laid out a half-mile ski-track circuit, and after some initial instruction, they trained on it daily and later around the Ryvingen plateau. In early March we started towing pulk man-haul sledges for increasing distances. If we successfully crossed Antarctica the day would come in the Arctic when we must pull our own sledges over mountains where no skidoo could go. Our last chance to master the art was here in Ryvingen before the sun disappeared.

On many expeditions where there is no way out, due to lack of transport, forced togetherness breeds dissension and even hatred between individuals or groups. Although the four of us had worked together on and off for four years, the relationships between us were undergoing constant changes. New sets of physical circumstances induced different reactions. For instance a personal fear of crevasses might simmer for many months in one person and not in the others. Sometimes minor injuries affected our moods. For a while Ollie could not lift his left arm above shoulder level without shooting pains. One morning, after a bad night, when approached by Ginnie to start up a generator, he reacted with unaccustomed spleen asking her why Charlie, who had less to do, could not do it.

In our little living hut Charlie and Ollie shared one end, and Ginnie and I the other. In the centre was our communal cooking and eating area, with the exit door that led into the tunnels. Two doors separated the two ends of the hut, so each pair could converse without being overheard.

Ollie felt, "Charlie is similar to myself. I am much closer to Charlie than Ran. Ran leads the expedition and as a leader has to be slightly offset. Charlie is like myself, likes enjoying himself." Ginnie and I, since the tantrums of honeymoon and early marriage, had grown into an easy relationship which gave us both the invaluable knowledge that we each had one totally loyal ally who would never be disparaging behind our respective backs. Charlie and Ollie were good enough friends to trust one another likewise, and this produced two units that understood and respected each other's strength and peculiarities. Thus was avoided the unspoken fear of betrayal which makes for suspicion and aggressive isolation: important in such close confines, where any slight shift in the atmosphere was felt without a word being spoken.

When I felt positive antagonism towards Charlie or Ollie for some petty reason I could either wax virulent to Ginnie or else spit out vicious prose in my diary. The next day or even hour I might feel quite different about the earlier object of my dislike and wonder how on earth I could have put such abuse on paper. Ollie and Charlie doubtless used the same vent-holes for their frustrations and spleen.

Apprehension of what lay ahead may well have affected us without our knowing it. The strain was there and every now and again it burst to the surface. During that winter word was spread amongst some of Ollie's and Charlie's acquaintances in London that we were engaging in hostilities, even knife fights, in our cardboard camp. Luckily, far from physical punch-ups, we actually experienced less verbal hostility than most marriages contend with in a similar timespan but less cramped conditions.

Down at the Sanae camp, our two friends had their own moods to cope with. Simon's diary:

> *Working silently in a temper. Every movement Anto makes is a desperate irritation when I'm mad. I suppose because there's nothing else to vent my feelings on. Grit my teeth and work on in angry silence. Good mood and good relations return if nothing said. . . We visit the South Africans on the skidoos. Anto would not keep level despite the bad visibility. Infuriated but I kept quiet . . . he was very cold with painful hands and groggy on arrival. I left him in their power-shed to dry. One topic which is*

taboo here is apartheid. There is a mixture of two types: the extreme 'left-wing' British commies (as the others call them) and the extreme right-wing Dutch farmer types . . . I wouldn't choose to winter in isolation with one person again. Anto and I were perhaps saved by the social security of visiting South Africans. I believe, as with two people climbing together for four months, for example, they get on each other's nerves and may feel like coming to blows.

Bothie's presence was more of a help than a hindrance. He continued to leave his signature where it was not wanted and, as camp cleaner, it was my daily job to remove these frozen offerings. To teach him that 'outside' did not mean the tunnels but the open air outside the tunnels proved beyond me, and Barbara Woodhouse was not available for advice.

Ginnie did not want him in her radio shack while there were bare electric wires all over the place. Later, when the shed was ready, she took him there daily, except during blizzards when she was hard put, with both hands free for the safety line, to reach the hut. Bothie could not, in such conditions, be allowed out unless on a lead. He would quickly have got disorientated and died within minutes, as we would but for the safety lines from hut to hut.

Much of the time Bothie had to be left in the warmth of the main hut. Ollie, with meteorological reports to make every six hours (the job of three men in most polar bases) and three generators to maintain, was usually at work in the garage. My own time was largely spent in the tunnels and around the camp with shovel and hand sledge so Charlie, whose main job was cooking, was often alone but for Bothie. In his diary he complained that Ginnie had brought the dog all the way out and now he, Charlie, had to look after him. But I think he quite liked the dog's companionship: certainly they spent many hours playing together, mainly with rubber balls which Bothie was adept at catching and 'throwing' back.

Despite a lack of exotic materials Charlie somehow kept the food tasty and interesting. When we ran out of dried vegetables the two of us went back to the South African camp and this time located the main hut. After digging down to the main entrance we entered a dark passage festooned with cascades of ice flowers. The main living room with bedsteads and cast-iron stove was caving in from above and below. Floor sections heaved up at odd angles and the roofing was buckled and contorted. Not a safe place to sleep. But the last inhabitants had left quantities of foodstuffs which enabled Charlie to tick off two-thirds of his shopping list.

We made the food sortie none too soon for the weather closed in along with the fast fading sunlight. By 2nd May the temperature had dropped to $-41.6°$ with a thirty-knot wind. The wind chill factor, in other words the temperature experienced by our skin, was $-110°F$.

Oliver had set up an anemometer which recorded wind speed and direction. The mast was beside the garage and cables ran beneath the snow to read-out instruments in Ollie's end of our shack. Knife-cold katabatic winds poured off the polar plateau, gaining velocity as the land dropped through 5,000 feet till they slammed against the very first obstruction, our little cardboard camp beside Ryvingen Mountain. We were partially protected from the south-east winds but not from the south-westerlies. With the latter, our cardboard life became a distinct problem. I found it difficult to do any job over and above keeping the camp running safely which was a full time occupation. Ollie had a similar struggle with his generators as the carbon monoxide exhaust fumes blew back into his hut. Try as he did to rectify this, nothing worked.

The gusts hit us with no warning. One minute Ollie's anemometer would read absolute zero and there would be a deathly silence. The next, the hut shuddered as though from a bomb blast as an eighty mile per hour wind from the high icefields struck us.

Visiting the VLF hut one morning I was knocked flat by a gust although a second earlier there was not a zephyr of wind. A minute later, trying to rise, I was struck on the back by the plastic windshield from my parked skidoo. Ripped off from the cowling, I never found it again. An empty forty-five gallon drum which Ginnie had placed at the base of the eighty-foot mast disappeared altogether and the camp haulage sledge which weighed 300 pounds was blown sixty yards and deposited upside-down. Ginnie's parachute 'porch' tore apart and two tons of snow blocked her doorway.

I had erected the pyramid tent we would use for the crossing and found two guy ropes broken and one of the four ten-foot metal legs buckled. The tent is the finest available and is used by the British Antarctic Survey as well as other governments operating scientific field parties in the South. The BAS had warned me that katabatic winds can tear away even a three-man pyramid tent; over the past few years they have lost field survey teams through this fact alone.

Safety lines were vital in these conditions, even between huts fifty yards from each other. One morning I left Charlie at the main tunnel entrance, some hundred yards from the living hut. I wanted to film him shovelling snow through a hatchway to fill the melt tank inside, our only source of water. He left the entrance a minute before me while I prepared my Bolex camera.

Once clear of the tunnel the whole world was the wind. Only by concentrating every faculty could I move against it in the right direction. Whiteout conditions were complete. I lost the safety line and was at once totally lost, totally confused. There was no point in opening my eyes to windward for sharp spicules of blown snow blew horizontally at eighty knots. I tripped over and felt a fuel drum. By the angle at which it and those beside it were stacked, I knew the direction of the hut some thirty paces away. I aimed at the middle of the hut and with relief walked right into it at a point where the snow had not yet drifted right over the roof. Carefully I edged along the hut until I bumped into Charlie. He had only just reached the snow hatchway after a similar experience. Had either of us walked a touch further left or right and missed the fuel drums we might well have wandered about disorientated for as long as it took to freeze.

At other times spirals of snow, some forty feet high like sand devils, whirled across our plateau, struck the camp briefly then raced on to disappear down valleys. These spirals sometimes united into great moving fronts of whiteness that bore down upon us to claw at the huts, shriek hideously through the radio masts and suck away any item left unanchored on the surface.

When it was black and moonless these plateau storms were unnerving. Even inside the hut conversation died when the heavy roar shook our fragile walls and the floor panels creaked as though about to take off. Even the tiniest hole or crack was sought out by the fine powder snow. A keyhole left untaped would permit a pencil-thin jet which, given time, could fill a room to its own level. So we taped every leak in every hut and every tunnel.

I spent long hours every day shovelling entrances and porches clear, ensuring escape hatches were free and burning rubbish in pits from which it could not blow away. Not a day passed but I found myself redoing the manual work of the previous day. Snow kept blocking entrances, burying fuel drums and lines and safety ropes. Because the drums, for safety, were stored well away from the huts I daily had to dig out and roll the required number to the sites from which we would drain them.

My first tunnel slop-pit was close to the entrance and beneath a drum escape hatch. One evening a bad storm half blocked the entrance. Ol emerged through the howling gloom and found me shovelling at the entry hole. He made off towards the drum hatch intending to climb down from it on the dangling ladder. Just in time I remembered there was a kerosene fire raging inside the ten foot deep slop-pit immediately below the drum hatch. I rushed out into the blizzard, hurried along the relevant safety line and reached Ollie just as he had lowered himself half into the drum. In his duvet jacket he would have fried like an unplucked chicken.

The worst risk we faced was from fires. Our stoves worked simply on a gravity drip-feed system. The amount of heat radiated depended on the amount of kerosene you allowed to flow into the 'burning bowl' at the stove's base. Any sudden downdraught entering the stove's metal chimney could put out the flame. Within minutes the hut's temperature would be down in the minus twenties and work, especially in the radio shack, became difficult to put it mildly.

I spent hours modifying chimney stacks and vents with little success. One forty-five-gallon drum screwed into a stove's drip-feed pipe gave it fuel for eleven days. The drum tops, where the type of fuel was specified, became iced over as they lay in the fuel lines. Each week I dug three or four out, diesel and petrol for Ollie's shack; kerosene for the radio and main huts. In poor conditions with no light I made the occasional error and once screwed a gasoline drum into Ginnie's kerosene drip-feed system. The results were spectacular but luckily Ginnie was inside at the time and applied a fire extinguisher before the whole hut went up in a ball of flame.

We also used smaller wick heaters but these had their own hazards – not fire but soot. If the wick was not trimmed correctly or left burning after the fuel ran out, black soot was deposited in layers over every item in the hut, greasy soot which smeared and contaminated. When south westerly winds prevailed at the same time that Ginnie needed Ollie's biggest generator, a ten-kva diesel, to power her one-kilowatt radio, his worst problems began. With wind from that quarter he could not open either door for the garage would fill with snow. The diesel generator put out a great deal of heat and had to be watched whilst operating as it was faulty. With temperatures of −45°C outside, Ollie would sit naked in his shack with sweat pouring off him counting every minute till Ginnie's call was over and he could stop the generator.

After supper, Ollie went straight to bed for at midnight he would be up again for a met. check. Ginnie, Charlie and I played cards at the kitchen table every night by candlelight, as we switched off the generator at nine p.m.

After cards Ginnie and I went to bed in one end of the hut. We all slept on boards along the apex of the roof. At night we turned our stove low to save fuel. At floor level the temperature dropped to −15°C, and at bed level, eight feet up, about 2°C. Down at the other end Ollie had to keep the temperature well up since he had to get up at midnight and six a.m. On nights the wind blew our stoves out it was quite nippy in bed.

On their separate bed platforms Ollie and Charlie had room for clothes, books and a mug of coffee. Ginnie and I had no spare room but we did have the advantage of each other's company. The other two never openly objected to their lack of female companions but it may, I suppose, have become an unspoken source of friction had not the four of us worked together as a group for so long beforehand. The long nights with the roar of the wind so close and the lingering smell of tallow in the dark are now a memory which we treasure.

I talk of night or day but in reality there was only moonlight or pitch darkness. None of us appeared to mind this any more than, in summer, the equal oddity of permanent daylight. Then in April many nights were lit by a carnival of aurora, ribbons of iridescent green or white that snaked in subtle patterns from horizon to horizon. On moonless nights the stars were close and brilliant. At −41°C with no wind, navigation practice was a pleasure. Normally I shot Nunki, the lead star of Sagittarius which trailed behind the seahorse shape of Scorpio. Also Syrius or Canopis and Spica, an old favourite from the northern hemisphere.

Before the last few hours of sunlight left the plateau we set out for a peak named Bråpiggen. The journey was to be the last of our ski-training runs some eight kilometres either way. We carried between us a seventy-pound rucksack and two pulk sledges with 200-pound loads. Eight hours should see us back in camp. There was no wind as we left. Our breath rose in personal haloes lit through by orange autumn sun.

At the foot of Bråpiggen we stopped to eat chocolate, shift rope traces from bruised shoulders and generally savour the personal pleasure of a hard struggle well won. Four hours only but in very sharp conditions. I noticed Ollie lagged far behind but thought nothing of it for Charlie was usually more able to plod faster when carrying or towing heavy weights. We all wore cross-country skis with sealskin strips for uphill grip. On the return journey the leather thongs began to work loose and our hands were too numb with the cold to readjust them tightly. So progress slowed. A snow scurry I had noticed at the base of Ryvingen developed into a local wind-storm. The sledges by now felt millstone heavy.

We wore winter-gear, not polar-gear, because sledge-pulling causes sweat in clothes that are windproof and do not breathe easily. I felt frostnip cracking at my wrists, neck and hips where gaps between garments allowed the wind to rip away my body heat. Windburn blisters would, I knew, grow in these places.

With four miles to go I entered the storm belt and at once lost sight of the others. Although I could see nothing at all ahead, not even the tips of my skis, the disembodied peak of Ryvingen, dyed pink from the sun, remained visible above the surface storm. A steep brow lay ahead. At its base I bumped into Charlie: one of his cheeks was blistered and his hands were numb. Together we hauled my sledge with its tent, stove and safety gear, to the ridge of the rise as dusk fell. Another hour or so would see us both as rigid as deep-frozen meat: Ollie, who carried a tent and cooker, would have to look after himself. During our winter Welsh mountain training we moved always as individuals and learnt not to rely on others. This is not accepted mountain behaviour but it is the way the SAS work. By the time we saw the beam of a powerful lantern Ginnie had placed by the tunnel entrance, neither of us was talking clearly. Ginnie looked worried but she said nothing and gave us hot soup.

Ollie appeared forty-five minutes later, his face bloated with frostnip. Realising his danger he had abandoned his sledge at the foot of Bråpiggen and struggled back with lifeless hands. The last hour of dark groping had worried him as much as it did the rest of us. The following day in clear windless weather I collected Ollie's sledge with a skidoo. For a week or two we wandered about with blisters like boxers, feeling tender. Ollie and Charlie, who had most unpleasant ones, took Bactrim broad-spectrum antibiotics for a week, then their sores stopped weeping and settled down.

The experience made it obvious that not all clothes acceptable for use on skidoos were ideal for man-hauling. My own home-made balaclava had a small mouth-hole which was adequate for skidoo use. Ski-ing in the storm I breathed hungrily and, unable to suck in enough air through the small frozen hole, I had to tear the balaclava's face flap down and so got frostnipped lips. Also, despite my wind-proof neck extension, the action of ski-ing caused movement and allowed wind to enter above the jacket top. A seven by one-inch band of frostnip, red and tender, rose below my Adam's apple. Goggles misted quickly. As navigator I needed to see clearly, so I removed them but the liquid in my windward eye started to congeal so I closed it and the eyelashes quickly became sealed with ice.

The ski-training run had proved useful for we still had plenty of time to alter our facemasks to cope with man-hauling in such conditions. In a week the polar darkness closed in for good and we made no more sorties.

After weeks of work laying cables, cutting antennae and trying them out at different frequencies, Ginnie achieved clear communications with Cove Radio Station and with Portishead Marine Radio Station on the Severn estuary. They were able to connect her with any telephone subscriber in the world in a period when the ionosphere suited a given frequency. Since no one who knew our whereabouts would expect us to telephone them we decided to use this to our advantage for April Fool's Day.

I phoned Andrew Croft using a German accent (the operator kindly announced a long-distance call from Hamburg) and greeted him as an ex-Wehrmacht Colonel who had been involved in the same work but on the other side during the Second World War. I invited him to lunch at London's Savoy Hotel on 1st April. He accepted. George Greenfield and the foreign editor of the *Observer* were both phoned from Kabul in Afghanistan by a Scottish journalist with a scoop about the Russian campaign there. They separately agreed to meet him at the Savoy. Ant Preston was offered an attractive job by a London magnate and Ollie, as a Greek shipowner, invited two others along, Geoff Newman, who didn't fall for it, and our aircraft committee chairman, Peter Martin, who did.

At 12.30 p.m. on April Fool's Day the various guests turned up in the lobby of the Savoy to meet their unknown hosts. They ended up well and truly fooled but mollified by lunch together, as the guests of Ollie's elder brother, who happened to be the managing director of the hotel. Back in Ryvingen with home-made raisin beer, we drank a toast to the longest-distance April Fools in history.

All communications at Ryvingen involved basic co-operation between Ollie providing the power from his little generators and Ginnie with her transceivers and know-how. Sometimes the generators were being serviced just when needed, due to lack of warning by Ginnie. Sometimes a power line would crack in the cold or a generator fail during an important schedule. Ginnie and Ollie would sometimes become temporarily cool towards each other on these occasions.

To avoid the possibility of a breakdown during some scheduled high frequency experiments with Cove Radio Station, Ginnie hauled a small generator down to her hut and set it going in the snow lobby outside her hut door. A slight wind blew the carbon monoxide fumes into the hut unnoticed. By chance, I called Ginnie up on a walkie-talkie from the main hut and, receiving no reply, rushed along the tunnels and down to her shack. I found her staggering about trying to carry out the fairly complex signals tests but making no sense at all. I dragged her out through the parachute covered lobby into the fresh air. Then up to the main hut to recover. Back in the radio shack I heard Cove Radio calling. They were worried; not knowing what had happened. I told them just before the frequency became unusable.

The next day Ginnie received a signal from the Chief at Cove:

Very distressed about yesterday's occurrence, especially that it should have occurred whilst working on our behalf . . . I will not presume to advise on general safety precautions but . . . even in a temperate climate and comfortable environment the operation of electrical radio equipment is considered a hazardous operation. In your location the hazards are considerably increased. It is suggested two people are always present when servicing takes place and ready to cut the mains power in an emergency . . . Remember it can take as little as 30 mA to kill. Never wear rings or watches when apparatus is live . . . Beware of snow on boots melting on floor . . . Your 1-kilowatt transmitter can produce very serious radio frequency burns. Also static charges will build up to several thousand volts in an aerial. Toxic berillium is employed in some components . . .

Four days later with all her sets switched off and no mains power, Ginnie touched the co-ax cable leading to her 400 watt set. She was stunned by a violent shock that travelled up her right arm and, as she put it later that morning, "felt like an explosion in my lungs". It was probably just static built up in her V-type antenna by the caress of wind-blown snow.

Ginnie's technical expertise was nil, but necessity, and a few visits to Racal, the manufacturers of all her radio gear, plus an above average helping of common sense and determination, allowed her to cope when things went wrong. The principal high frequency work involved her sending special transmissions to RAE Cove with which they could measure signal strengths, fading patterns and circuit reliability by means of special data transmission. This all added to their knowledge of ionospheric characteristics. Ginnie's biggest, 1-kilowatt, transmitter was a heavy sophisticated set which is usually handled with care at normal room temperatures. Naturally, the extreme conditions and rough handling caused problems. When these occurred Ginnie made contact on the smaller 400-watt set but this was once inoperative too. She then set up a tiny 20-watt transceiver and managed to obtain clear communications to Cove for just long enough to describe the malfunction with the 400-watt set. Cove talked her over with a diode replacement. With the medium set working, she then learnt that two of the 1-kilowatt's resistors had blown.

There was no suitable spare so she raided my spare parts box for the Belling cooker and pinched a spare hot plate ring. This she cut up. She then sat it on the floor on an asbestos mat and wired it up to the transmitter's guts. Everything then worked perfectly and the home-made resistor glowed red-hot on its mat. She was modest about her ability but the Chief at Cove was not. He described her as an "amazing communicator".

As winter set in, coatings of ice built up on the various antennae increasing their diameter from one-eighth of an inch to well over one inch and their weight correspondingly. This broke many terminals loose and the eighty- to ninety-knot winds tore two-foot metal screws from their snow beds, allowing the antennae to blow free, wrap themselves around the mast and its guys and in places become buried in new snow drifts. With a torch in her mouth, Ginnie struggled around in the blizzards unravelling wires, soldering con-nections and digging up ice-caked antennae with care for they broke easily. She took two days to excavate a twenty-foot long, four-foot deep trench in which to bury cable since more snow blew in as she dug. I helped her whenever I could but much of the time she never asked, just got on with it.

To improve the transmission of her main V-antenna she cut sixteen twenty-one-foot copper radials and laid them out at the two ends of the V, connected by resistors to create a false earth. Quite how effective or useless the ice sheet itself was for an earth remained open to debate.

Ginnie was often over-tired. Her work involved long hours outside in the dark after storms and she began to get nervous. In late May Ollie mentioned casually that he heard footsteps following him from the generator hut to the tunnel entrance. This he summed up as his imagination. Not long afterwards I noted in my diary, "Last night Ginnie's stomach pains were bad and she went down the tunnel to the loo with a torch. When she came back shivering, she said, 'There's something there.' I remonstrated but she insisted. 'I don't mean a danger but . . . a *strong* presence.' 'Nobody ever lived here before,' I said. 'Giles has stories of Hitler's air force dropping metal swastikas on the rock features to claim the terrain but even that is probably baloney.' "

For a while there were no further 'happenings' but during a June storm she again felt something. "*It* came round behind the radio shack and followed me back down the tunnel." She had seen and heard nothing.

Down at Sanae all was quiet. Simon:

This morning we failed to start the skidoo despite two hours' work in a growing wind storm. The South Africans contacted the American radio operator at South Pole base and mentioned the proposed Transglobe crossing. It seems none of the Americans there knew anything about us. Now they do! No idea what political repercussions there will be but it strikes Anto and me as amusing. The shit is stirred and we are in a temporarily safe backwater . . . The enormity of what we are all trying to do still hasn't sunk in.

Ginnie widened her network of radio contacts. One was Signy Island, a small British base on the tail of Antarctica, the peninsula which stretches further north than the rest of the continent and is derisively described as 'the banana belt' by people in more southerly, supposedly colder, bases. The Signy inmates were not happy. They had just learned that their relief ship could not reach them due to ice conditions and they would have to spend a *third* year in situ.

Ginnie also wrote up a little broadsheet called the *Ryvingen Observer* which summarised the BBC World News. On 6th May bodies of US airmen were flown out of Iran following an abortive attempt to rescue the hostages. Tito's funeral was discussed. One hundred demonstrating Afghans were shot by helicopters over Kabul. SAS soldiers killed half a dozen terrorists at the Iranian Embassy in London. The food in British motorway cafés was summed up as greasy and tasteless.

Early in June my back began to pain me as though bruised at the base of the spine. Very few positions were easy other than lying down. Ollie as medic was naturally concerned. At breakfast one morning he told me his usual weekly fuel needs but added, "Since your back's bad you can hardly roll drums around. Let me collect the drums for you."

"Rubbish," I snapped. "I'm quite capable of moving the drums myself."

As I left the room I regretted my senseless pride and rudeness. It was to Ollie's credit that he did not blow a gasket at my behaviour. In his diary that night he simply wrote: "Ran's back is bad so I offered to help him with fuel. He is so stubborn he won't accept any help over his drums. As far as I am concerned he can look after his own medical and dental problems from now on."

There were, of course, good and bad days as the endless roar of the wind, the lash of the driven snow and, above all, the uninterrupted polar night ensnared us all in our pettiness, making mountains out of the smallest molehills. Gradually our focus became more introverted, more tied up with our separate egos and reactions to the most mundane matters. The denizens of the parish of Ryvingen became about as parochial as the spinsters of Piddletrenthyde on the Floss.

Mixed excerpts from my diary:

My lumbago troubles were worse today: can't even bend without pain in the leg . . . Slightly late for breakfast. As the eggs have gone off I added horseradish and salt to them. Ugghh! The fried bread is full of the filthy taste of the bad fat we nicked from the old Borga base. Still, the cup of tea and Charlie's bread is great, even though the margarine is ten years old.

Ollie cut Charlie's hair today. He also poured warm oil down his own ears to clean them out. He thinks he's going deaf. At supper he wears a red pile suit which is streaked with oil smears. Bothie gets randy and clasps Ollie's legs. Ollie tries to shake him off but Charlie guffaws and encourages the tyke.

Tonight Charlie began the Hobbit books for the third time round. His cheese and ham flans are excellent but Ollie's home fermented apple flake beer is disgusting.

Some evenings we waged war over the radio with Simon and Anto and separately with the South Africans. Quiz rules were difficult to enforce since you couldn't see what cheating the opposition got up to, such as referring to dictionaries.

Simon's diary:

The South Africans have challenged Ryvingen to a straight quiz. This could be funny to listen to as they don't know how good Ran is at bluffing. One has to be pretty alert and ready to parry his innocent assumptions, the basic one being that he is right . . . Later entry: The South Africans take no truck from Ran and call his bluff frequently.

My diary again:

Ginnie says Ol has been behaving oddly of late and is easily irritable. I took some piping to his garage this morning to crush it in his vice. When I came out I felt light-headed and a touch sick. The CO fumes are strong down there on days like today when the wind's from 110°. I went down again an hour ago to see if Ol was OK. He seemed fine. But perhaps the continued inhalations are affecting his 'mood'. If so, it should clear up when we depart . . .

Today Ollie passed out in the garage but luckily came to and groped his way out. He has a filthy headache. As a result of the shock he has given us all a tour of the garage and generator workings so we can cope if he should come to grief. We have tried everything to improve the situation but nothing works . . .

This evening I ran into Ol staggering down the tunnel. His face was pale and he slurred his words. He told me he'd sat down for a bit in the garage to have a smoke and noticed that his hands were twitching. Getting up with difficulty, for his legs felt leaden, he nearly collapsed in the garage tunnel.

> *Ginnie is cross and says Ol is rude and pompous. She feels he
> does not appreciate how hard she tries to make contact with
> Portishead radio to get telephone contact with Rebecca for him.*

That same day Ollie wrote: "Everyone, except Charles, is very bad
tempered so I'll just stop talking."

Some three hundred miles away down at Sanae, Simon and Anto
co-existed, marking time until Giles and Gerry returned with the
Antarctic spring and there was more work for them.

> *Anto's presence, his teeth chomping as he eats, his silent
> book-bound presence, exasperates me at times, the symptoms of
> cabin fever . . . His current maddening trick is to put pans of
> water on and, being deaf which he admits, to leave them boiling.
> He's got the idea though, because I slam them on to the floor if I
> have to cross the hut and take them off . . .*

Having the South African base only ten miles away was one great
safety valve and they visited it about once a month. Another was
uniting in pouring scorn on the organisation and method of the rest
of us at Ryvingen. To read Simon's diary you would wonder how on
earth the Ryvingen gang ever managed to reach Antarctica, let alone
cross it.

> *I told Ollie on the radio how to make up a honey-whisky-lemon
> drink for Ginnie's birthday, but he says they only have honey
> left. Lack of self-control, lack of care in stock-taking, lack of
> interest or lack of competence? Whatever it is the mind
> boggles . . .*
>
> *Spoke to Ol and told him the various things we've done to the
> skidoo here which he said only needed a new drive axle. It's like
> talking to a brick wall . . .*
>
> *Am reading a polar book by Paul-Emile Victor. He
> summarises Nansen's equipment as chosen and designed for
> "lightness, simplicity and efficiency". Shackleton I respect, but
> Nansen is a man after my own heart. Our ice group could learn a
> lot from him, but I'm sure they won't . . .*
>
> *Where a lot of people have a relatively simple job to do, the
> military command structure works well. As with our ship
> off-loading operation. Several South Africans commented how
> smoothly it went compared to their operation, where 'polar
> experts' seemed to be in the majority. But for longer operations,*

like a polar wintering base, I don't know if the same style is right.
The South African base boss swung to the opposite extreme,
popular democracy, which works very well.

The dark days flew by. I began to cherish our crude but peaceful existence with its beguiling simplicity. Also I experienced subtle tremors of apprehension when, on moonlit days, the bald white scars of the Penck escarpment rose livid through the silvered distance to the south. With each month that slipped past my stomach turned as it once used to during school holidays when the next dread term-time approached.

In Antarctica Christmas is no great feast day. Instead Midwinter Day, 21st July, is celebrated fiercely in each and every lonely base camp by the 750 men and handful of women from a dozen nations who form the transitory population of the whole vast continent.

Radio messages of fraternal greetings zing back and forth, the state of the ionosphere permitting, between the multinational scientists all of whom feel the same joy that the longest night is over and the sun is on its way back. Most bases were ignorant of our existence but those with wide-eared radio operators knew and sent us greetings: the Japanese, the South Africans, the British and the Soviets based at Novolazarevskaya, some 300 miles east along the coast from Sanae.

Ollie laid the table with our SAS flag, fashioned serviettes from meteorological report paper and produced a secret bottle of bubbly white wine with which we toasted our patron and the crew of the *Benjy B*. We gave each other presents and harmony ruled at Ryvingen.

The mini euphoria of Midwinter soon dispersed. Reality was after all another three months of darkness and blizzard even if the sun was slowly climbing our way unseen. Raging snow storms ripped through the camp one after another, week after week. Continued shovelling kept the entrances free and, in Ol's case, the generators operating. Then the diesel generator, our main work-horse, seized and Ol found a hole the size of a silver dollar in the crankcase. This was beyond his means of repair so he moved it to one side to make more room. Charlie and I helped him tug the heavy machine over the plywood floorboards. He felt uneasy of a sudden and went outside.

Hearing his shout I followed. Ol shone a torch *under* the hut. A cavern some fifteen feet deep and wide as one third of the hut itself gaped at us. The exhaust pipe from the diesel had for months eaten away at the snow and now the garage foundations were somewhat shaky. Perhaps it was as well the diesel machine would no longer vibrate and wriggle about but, with less power at his disposal, Ollie's servicing work on the smaller machines doubled. He began to look tired and blotchy. Again we all tried to think of a solution for the ever-present dangers of Ollie's generator hut but nature defeated every attempted modification.

The next day I groped my way along the safety line to Ginnie's VLF hut with a man-haul sledge. My hips hurt most of the day although my back was back to normal. Opening the hatch cover of the drum entrance, I dangled both feet down to feel for the ladder's top. Carrying a fully charged 12-volt battery, I had no spare hand so, when the ladder slipped, I failed to steady myself. I fell only seven feet into the ice lobby but acid spilled over my gloves, clothes and boots and the battery fractured. There was no acid in my eyes, so I was thankful.

Ginnie joined me in the hut for soon her VLF work would begin and there was much preparation yet to be done. The hut's heater caught fire on ignition and in extinguishing the flames Ginnie's hand was burnt. Only surface burns but a nuisance in a place where things heal slowly. She had also placed her Zippo lighter in the hip pocket of her trousers and, laying cables that afternoon, she forgot to remove it until she received a cold burn on her thigh in the shape of the Zippo.

That night I could not sleep and at dawn felt queasy, almost seasick. A sharp, ragged pain from that part of my stomach where I consider my appendix hangs out. This did not go away so I eased myself down the home-made ladder from our bed platform. Once erect, I felt faint and nauseous. I stumbled to Ollie's area and woke him. He looked down. "Probably fumes from the heaters; get some fresh air." He should know. I went out into the tunnel. Hot and sick, I lay down on the ice floor in my longjohns and tried to breathe deeply. Then the cold got to me and I moved back into our room.

I may have blacked out for an instant. I don't know but I found myself on the floor, head spinning and I called for Ginnie. She had only been asleep for three hours after night VLF work but she woke and dragged me to a cardboard 'couch' we'd made. The pain came suddenly and surprised me in its intensity. Rather like a knife-grinding session deep in my gut. It was a worse pain than I can remember at any time and stretched around from the stomach to the small of my back. With it there was numbness and tingling in both hands and up the arms to the elbows.

Ollie took my temperature and felt my appendix with an uncommonly cold hand. By midday the pain had gone and by evening I felt normal. Ollie, I reflected, must have been as relieved as I was that he had no appendix to cut out. It was two years since he had watched an appendectomy. A year later a New Zealand doctor, listening to my description of the pains, diagnosed a chronic case of indigestion. Whatever it was I am glad it never recurred.

Next morning Charlie threw a wobbler. Bothie had yet again used his clothes; this time right inside one of Charlie's fur boots. I removed the mess, smacked Bothie with a ruler and agreed that he should thereafter sleep in my end of the hut locked away from Charlie's boots by two doors. But we were all tender-nerved by that time. Everybody felt the atmosphere crackling, so nobody spoke.

It reminded me of Thor Heyerdahl's words: "The most insidious danger on any expedition where men have to rub shoulders for weeks is a mental sickness which might be called 'expedition fever' – a psychological condition which makes even the most peaceful person irritable, angry, furious, absolutely desperate, because his perceptive capacity gradually shrinks until he sees only his companions' faults, while their good qualities are no longer recorded by his grey matter."

That Sunday I asked Ollie for some Loctite glue, a special type for bonding steel to rubber. At midday he brought me a bottle of the stuff.

"Know how to use it?" he asked.

"Yes," I replied.

"Are you sure?"

"Yes, of course."

Instantly Ollie exploded. His voice came sharp and hard. "You always scorn my advice." That was the sum total of the eruption but it penetrated deep for Ollie was quiet the rest of the day and that was not like him. Normally an hour was the longest a mood stayed with him. Long afterwards we would joke about the nadir of our relationship, calling it the Loctite episode, but at the time our emotions were very real and very raw.

In his controversial biography, *Scott and Amundsen*, Roland Huntford wrote, "In polar expeditions, as in most tight-knit groups, there is usually a process of selecting a natural or psychological leader. It is a conflict akin to a fight for domination within a wolf pack or a dog team; a more or less overt challenge to the established, formal leadership. How he deals with this threat to his authority is one of the tests through which most commanders have to go and upon the outcome of which depends the cohesion of the group."

I never consciously engaged in such a struggle with Ollie or Charlie but on none of my previous expeditions, nor during my army days, had I held any brief for split command. As a great believer in the thin end of the wedge, I steer clear of asking for advice or suggestions from those within my current 'group', since this must surely encourage them to proffer further advice when it isn't wanted.

At the end of July Ollie went ski-ing in the moonlight. Five minutes out from the huts he discovered his trouser zip was undone. His hands were too cold to handle the metal tab effectively so he left it undone. On returning he found his family jewels were frozen assets and hastily used a saucepan full of warm water to improve the situation. He was lucky. That day was our coldest. The wind held steady around forty-two knots, the temperature at −45°C. The chill factor was therefore −131°F at which temperature any exposed flesh freezes in under fifteen seconds. Ollie semi-exposed his for a good fifteen minutes.

At this time the crew of the *Benjy B* were earning enough money through charter work to keep the ship a going concern. The only charter available was passenger and cargo work between the coral islands of Tuvalu near Western Samoa; a hot and humid region. So Anton Bowring and the rest of our 'family' sweated and nursed their prickly heat in the damp oven of the *Benjy B* whilst we shivered to their south.

Back in London David Mason, Ant Preston and a group of volunteers tried to get things ready for the second half of the expedition. Every week Ginnie sent back lists of equipment needed at one or more of our Arctic bases. Each time I thought the lists were closed, new items occurred to me . . . poor David.

That July he wrote a short account of his experience as the man at the hub of it all.

I think I can pinpoint the time when my hair started going grey to when Ran blithely turned the job of organising all stores over to me in July 1979. To comprehend part of the problem, think about just one ration box wanted for just one remote base – Byron Bay in the North West Passage. The contents were a fairly complex ice team-type of ration rather than base camp, desert, jungle or ship-type. The calorific totals and packaging methods altered each time.

The twelve man-days-worth of rations for Byron Bay amounted to exactly 0.0005% of the total food to be consumed during the expedition yet rations were a small fraction of the weight of the thousands of other items to be obtained, checked, packed and transported on time at no cost. The failure of this one box of rations to arrive at remote Byron Bay on time might have serious consequences for the team.

The Duke of York's barracks where I worked is used by a number of Territorial units who use different buildings within the complex. Ran and Ginnie had worked there since 1972 and were allowed a small office which no one else wanted. But as more and more equipment arrived they ran out of space and had to go around asking different regiments if they could use 'small corners' of their garages and stores. Over the months they obtained concessions for several 'small corners' which I will call A, B, C, D, E and F.

In a while these areas proved insufficient, so Ran staked a claim on a bit of what he called waste ground (it was in fact a car park) in the barracks where he erected a tin hut which he had scrounged.

From then on a running battle raged between Ran and the real owners of the stores and garages. The Quartermaster of A would find, on his monthly inspection, that the 'small corner' had become so large that his inward opening doors wouldn't open properly. In an apoplectic rage he would send for Ran who, knowing this was going to happen, had gone away on an astro-navigation course for a week. At the end of the week he would return and at once move the contents of A to B in order to appease the Quartermaster of A. The stores would then be undisturbed till the Quartermaster of B made his own monthly inspection. There would then be a similar performance (Ran away, this time on a skidoo maintenance course). All moves were made by night with a wood barrow normally used by the men who kept the barracks tidy. These men were regularly driven berserk with frustration at having no barrow as Ran had left it in the wrong place and often with a puncture through overloading.

By the time I took over the barrow and the system it had developed a fault owing to one Quartermaster doing spot checks instead of monthly ones. I am thus kept permanently on the hop.

In March 1980 when I returned from Sanae I found a sponsor for a forty-foot long storage container. I arranged transport from a second sponsor and an unloading crane from a third. Everything went well until after crane and lorry departed. Then I received a phone call from one irate barracks officer demanding the replacement of part of the barrack's main gate and from another reporting the telephone wires had been pulled down. (I asked him how, in that case, he was speaking to me – but that did not help.) A third officer wanted to know who was going to remove the enormous container from what was left of his car park. I told him I would try to find out.

Within a month great quantities of stores had arrived and bulked out even my container. So I loaded the roof of the container and covered it with a giant polythene tarpaulin. The officer who rang to complain about the container now phoned to complain about the tarpaulin on top of it. I said nothing as I reckon I am on fairly safe ground as he no longer complains about the container itself. He must have got used to it. He originally complained about the tin hut but he has certainly got used to that. He will surely get used to the polythene.

Part of the container is to be used for packing the rations and to this end I have run an electric light on a long wire to it; this fuses all the lights in that part of the barracks whenever it rains.

I have discovered an almost extinct FANY unit, ladies, normally called fannies, who operate from somewhere in the barracks and have done so I believe since the First World War. Their uniform looks as though it hasn't changed since then, but they are a delightful crowd and have taken over all my ration packing work.

Whilst David handled the barracks work, Ant Preston slaved away in the office with three or four volunteers doing excellent work at our nerve centre.

The Committee, especially the Chairman, Sir Vivian Fuchs and our Foreign Office friend were still trying to gain American approval for our twenty-three vital fuel drums at the South Pole. As yet they'd had no success. Ant Preston warned me that Giles Kershaw would now be able to fly the Twin Otter in the Arctic for only one of the two seasons we expected to be up there, so we must find another pilot. For three weeks Ginnie chased radio frequencies hour after hour to make telephone contact with the only three Arctic Ocean pilots whom we knew had sufficient experience to do the job up north. Karl Z'berg, the pilot who had flown for us back in 1977 when we failed to reach the North Pole, was available and said he would fly for us for $100 per day. I agreed, since there was no option, and contacted my old friend from the Omani army to ask whether he and Dr Omar Zawawi might meet this unforeseen wage bill. They kindly agreed.

There were two other temporary 'nasties' that occurred through the winter but the worst news involved a problem no radio call could solve.

On 26th July Charlie warned me that he thought Ollie's wife, Rebecca, was putting considerable pressure on Oliver to get him to leave the expedition once we had crossed Antarctica. Charlie told me he thought that Ol would leave the expedition rather than his wife.

"But that choice won't have to be faced," I expostulated. "Ollie had always told Rebecca he will only do one more sector of the expedition. He told her that back in '76 regarding Greenland, yet he's still with us. She always lets him carry on when the time comes. There'll be no problem."

But Charlie knew Ol better than I did and he was not convinced. A few days later I talked to Ol about it, suggesting we ought at least to warn the Committee of the faint possibility of his disappearance. But Ollie was adamant. "It's none of their business," he pointed out. "It is a personal matter and anyway nothing may come of it."

So we left it until September hoping it would go away. But it didn't. Poor Rebecca became so ill she had to enter hospital. Ollie managed a radio call to her there and assured her he would leave Transglobe after Antarctica. We began to discuss the situation if he *did* leave. I was determined that no untried replacement be thrust upon us. Charlie was of a like mind but not as determined to resist any pressure the Committee might exert should they feel three was a minimum safety factor.

Using a press-proof code Ginnie devised, we informed London of our intention to carry on as two if Ollie did leave. The Committee's reaction was understandable. They were very much opposed to this reduction in the team for what would be the most hazardous leg of the expedition. But whatever might happen in the Arctic, we had

Ollie with us for the more immediate crossing attempt, so tomorrow would have to look after itself.

On 5th August, a memorably cold day, the sun re-appeared for four minutes precisely. Down at Sanae, Simon reported hundred mile an hour winds and foul conditions, but the irrepressible Ol produced some 'beer' he had fermented from old vegetables of an indeterminate type and we toasted the sun.

Over the last three months Ginnie's work doubled because her VLF programme, after initial experiments during the first half of the winter, started again in earnest. She had to record at precisely the same time as two other Antarctic coastal stations involved in the same programme. It is perhaps worth explaining the experiment which is known as the International Whistler Programme.

Our participation was formulated by the Department of Space Physics at the University of Sheffield who designed mobile equipment consisting of a twin-loop antenna, preamplifier, tape recorder, goniometer, oscillator, earphones and battery supply unit. This allowed Ginnie to record ELF and VFL signals originating from thunderstorms in the Arctic and to fix the direction from which they came. By operating simultaneously with other recording stations she could obtain recordings which should enable Sheffield to fix the point at which the signals penetrate the lower point of the ionosphere. The most interesting and complex movements affecting the signals occur near the boundary between the co-rotating part of the earth's magnetosphere which has high electron density (causing great delay of the signal) and less dense areas. The mean position of this boundary region is strategically placed, relative to recording bases at Halley Bay (British), Siple (American), Sanae (South African) and the inland Transglobe station.

Despite training up in Sheffield, Ginnie was hard put to set up the antennae and equipment correctly by herself. Initially Charlie and I followed her instructions and mounted the forty-foot steel mast one mile from the main hut. The three of us laid four numbered cables, frozen stiff and therefore very fragile and easily damaged, between the VLF shack and this mast. Ginnie connected all the cables to a buried preamplifier and we began to raise the complex antenna on a pulley. As it neared the top of the mast the cast iron pulley at the mast-head supplied by Sheffield snapped and the entire antenna assembly collapsed. Owing to the extreme cold this sudden movement damaged much of the cable.

Working with a lantern and a small heater in a tent for two days Ginnie repaired the broken cables. Unwilling to collapse the forty-foot mast (only two and a half inches in diameter) for fear of breaking it we decided to climb it and lashed a series of six-foot ladders to it. Precariously we managed to scale these as the mast wobbled and curved in the dark and replaced the pulley with a stainless steel karabiner and fibre glass pulley.

Once the antenna was up another day was spent checking its calibration. Ginnie discovered that the oscillation in her time code generator had failed due to the cold. This meant abandoning the project or else completing it manually. Manual operation involved her pressing a recording button every four minutes for twenty-four hour periods without a break. Night after night she sat in the little hut buffeted by the wind. Her careful training in Sheffield ensured that she could recognise and record in the log-book the types of 'whistler' that she monitored; these went under such names as gibbons, chorus and tweeks. Only in exceptional circumstances, such as an HF radio experiment due to RAE Cove, would she allow me to try my luck with the VLF work. Wrapped in blankets she kept awake with flasks of black coffee. There was no fixed heater in the VLF hut, so I kept a mobile kerosene burner going for her. The fumes gave her headaches but that was better than working in an ice-box.

Some nights I took a sleeping bag up to the hut and slept there to keep her company. I have weird memories of that little cardboard room vibrating in the storm, the wind a solid roar all about us pierced only by the unearthly sound of the whistlers. Sometimes the whistlers stopped and there was utter silence. Then, *exactly* like the frenetic dawn chorus of the Borneo jungle, a mad jumble of electronic chirps, shrieks and animal cries issued from the speaker.

By October Ginnie was dog-tired and hallucinating. She began to make silly errors and once I found her asleep on the cold floorboards with a livid red weal between swollen eye and cheek. The last of her candles was flickering and almost out. She had been outside checking the antenna and had forgotten to close the visor of her face mask. Her journeys to the VLF hut were often in pitch darkness and blizzard with no possible means of navigating the half-mile stretch from our tunnel hole except hand-over-hand along the safety line. From time to time she heard crying in the darkness and someone whispering indistinguishable words from close behind her. If I was not sleeping up there, I went with her to the hut and collected her again the next morning.

By early October we had several hours of sunlight each day. All winter the moonlit summit of Ryvingen had irritated me. I felt a powerful urge to climb it. The others did not share this so I tried alone. I failed to get beyond the scree walls on my first go, then on my second and last attempt by way of a steep 900-foot ice wall, I broke a crampon half-way up and came down inch by inch in a muck sweat and shaking with fear. I am terrified of heights and never tried again.

A neighbouring peak was unnamed on our map so Ollie agreed to record its height with his aneroid barometer. There was one remaining pair of crampons so we each wore a crampon on our right mukluk. Ollie feared heights even more than I did so our attempt to scale the peak (which he intended to call 'Prince Charles Mountain') was a dismal failure. Sitting on a rocky shoulder of the mountain some 700 feet up, unnaturally close together, chatting in tenor voices, we tried to avert our gaze from the horrific white void below.

"Look," said Ol, "a hole on the ski slope." Sure enough a wide blue fissure gaped at us from the very middle of our old ski and sledge training slope where we had so often fallen heavily and unroped.

"When did that happen?"

"I don't know," Ol replied, "but there have been explosions around and about these last few days."

We descended using ropes, ice axes and finally our backsides. On return I drank some of Ollie's beer for the first time. He relieved his nerves by writing me a ditty:

> *Holes like that on yonder hill*
> *Really make me feel quite ill,*
> *Reminding me of Charlie's mouth,*
> *I hope there are none to the South.*

As the sun climbed higher day by day sudden explosions sounded in the valleys and rebounded as echoes from the mountain walls about the camp. Avalanches or imploding crevasses? We did not know.

"I wish you were not leaving me," Ginnie said.

We expected to set out during the second half of October, once we knew Giles and Gerry had safely flown the Twin Otter back from England and crossed to the Antarctic mainland from the Falklands.

On 17th October Ginnie contacted Buckingham Palace but a minute after Prince Charles started to speak to us the communications closed down. All I heard was that he had entered a steeplechase and was placed fourth out of five riders. He had completed the course and received £40. The Palace organised a second call on 20th October which came through clearly and Prince Charles wished us God-speed for the crossing attempt.

A week before our departure date the temperature was −50°C. To the south, high winds raised snowstorms that obscured our intended route up the wall of the Penck escarpment. With four days to go, Ginnie received from London a copy of a news release from New Zealand criticising our intended crossing as under-equipped and our skidoos as under-powered. Apparently there was a sweepstake all set up in the offices of the New Zealand Antarctic Division in Christchurch.

A map of the Southern Continent was pinned with flags along our proposed route with such comments as "First crevasse accident"; "First skidoo breakdown"; and "Pulled out by US Rescue Hercules." Their Scott Base field commander, Roger Clark, was a lone voice saying that, although he admitted our aircraft was a weak link, he thought we'd make it. Others laughed, knowing Roger was a British expatriate. The general view was "Too far, too high and too cold."

These sombre predictions could not easily be laughed away as we sat in our cardboard hut contemplating the immediate future. They were after all the voice of those who knew Antarctica.

Wally Herbert, whose travels included pioneer Antarctic journeys as well as his unique crossing of the Arctic Ocean, made an interesting comment:

I have personally found I have a great deal of doubt about astrology but there is one aspect of it that has long fascinated me. If you take the top thirty polar explorers over the last 200 years and check their sun signs you will find they all tend to fall into a set pattern. For instance, the astrologist tells us that every human being on earth is born either as a leader at heart or as an organiser or as a communicator; it depends on which of the astrological signs you are born under. Now, in the case of these top thirty polar explorers, a total of eighteen were born under the sun signs which made them, according to the astrologers, organisers, a total of ten were leaders and the other two were communicators. These two, as it happens, were Captain Scott of the Antarctic and Dr Cook of the Arctic. What do we say? Both failed. In the case of Scott, he failed to get back having reached his objective. In the case of Cook, he perhaps reached his objective but failed to convince the public that he had done so.

Now the astounding thing is that Ran is also by this definition a communicator. So it is really up to him. It is perhaps a challenge to him he would love to take on, to prove astrology wrong and to succeed but he will be doing it against all the massive evidence of history.

Whether we succeeded or not, we had weathered the eight months' polar winter and remained friends. We had had our moments of aggravation, some tiffs and arguments, but as Charlie said, "We had worked closely in preparation for the trip. We knew each other's moods and when to lay off. Therefore the strains were negligible."

On 28th October Giles Kershaw landed heavily on our home-made strip. He brought us mail from the outside world and he had also stopped to pick up Simon at Sanae on the way through. We slept for four hours and then at 2045 hours on 29th October 1980 said goodbye to Ginnie, Simon and Bothie and left Ryvingen for ever. The temperature was −50°C and the wind a steady twenty knots as Charlie, Ollie and I set out for the South Pole.

7

The Last Unexplored Region
on Earth

OCTOBER–DECEMBER 1980

*I suppose the one quality in an astronaut more powerful than any
other is curiosity.
They have to get some place nobody's ever been before.*

JOHN GLENN

Charlie and Ollie wear five layers of clothing, topped by Eskimo
wolfskin parkas which still smell of bad mackerel. I too have five
underlayers, but my outer one consists of a large duvet jacket of duck
down; perhaps not quite as warm as theirs but much easier to move
about in and see out of. It smells of damp dog. Despite three-layer
footwear, mitts, caps, goggles and facemasks, the coldness cuts
through as though we were naked. Fingers are soon numb but still
alive enough to hurt, which is good. Toes and nose likewise.

I lead, pulling my two heavily laden sledges, clinging to a straight
course of 187° magnetic, making across the Penck Glacier for the
high wall of ice called the Kirwan Escarpment. For sixty-four
kilometres we cross blue-white steppe interspersed with ice dunes;
each time we crest the top of a dune, we see the black pointer rock of
Stignaben, the last feature for a thousand miles and more.

Nearing the escarpment, I notice that it is grey, not white, and realise that this means sheet ice, honed to marble consistency by centuries of wind. Still darker veins lace the great slopes: gravity cracks. I look back once, the others are black specks on the rolling dunes of the Penck. To the east, streamers of blown snow crest the escarpment but right now beside the Stignaben cliffs visibility is good and I spot the curve of a slight re-entrant. With adrenalin pumping away all feeling of coldness, I tug the hand throttle to full bore and begin the climb.

Will the rubber tracks grip on this incline of ice? There was nothing like it in Greenland or the Arctic Ocean. If they don't, we're in trouble. I try to *will* the skidoo upwards, to force every ounce of power from the little engine. Twelve hundred pounds weigh down my two bouncing, leaping sledges, a hell of a load for a 640 cc engine at 7,000 feet above sea level. Twice I wince inwardly as the tracks fail to grip. Flinging my weight forwards, then rocking to and fro, I pray aloud. An uneven patch saves the situation, allowing renewed grip and another surge of speed which carries the skidoo – just – up the next too smooth section.

The climb seems to go on for ever. Then at last an easing of the gradient, two final rises and, wonderful moment, the ridgeline. Fifteen hundred feet above our winter camp and forty miles from it I stop and climb off. Such moments of pure elation are fleeting and rare. I savour the feeling. To the north the peaks of the Borga massif seem now like mere pimples in the vast snow sea, Ryvingen itself just a shadow along our back-bearing. Within the hour the others are up and chatting happily. We may yet prove our detractors wrong.

The immediate vicinity of the escarpment is no place to linger, so we take a last look at the distant mountains then press on south. By dusk there is nothing to see in any direction but endless fields of snow. Now I have only clouds to navigate by: soon they too will be gone.

30th October is unpleasant. A thirty-knot wind stirs the snow and soon sets up pea-souper conditions. We climb gradually: the true plateau is still 4,000 feet above us. Hard ice bumps, not visible in the gloom, upset our skidoos. As they roll over, the riders must jump well clear to ensure their legs are not crushed between the ice and the 700-pound machines. Charlie's goggles split this morning and allow the bitter wind to nip the bridge of his nose. He cannot see at all well and needs to concentrate hard to spot my tracks. We must not lose each other.

When we packed up our three-man tent Ollie told me he felt very tired. This was unusual from someone who never complains about his sufferings. After four hours' travel he staggered off his skidoo and lurched over un-roped. His speech was slurred.

"I'm getting exposure. Must stop a bit."

He was shivering. As medic he knew exactly what symptoms to expect. In these conditions it would take us two hours to make camp so Charlie and I merely unpacked the vehicle tarpaulin and, struggling against the wind, secured it around a sledge in such a way as to provide a small windproof shelter. We boiled water from snow and gave Ollie two mugs of tea and some chocolate. He is physically the toughest of us all, so if he is already shivering on day two, despite full polar gear and a wolfskin, then we will have to be very careful indeed. The main problem on open vehicles is the wind. Still there is no point in wishing for closed cabs for they would use up too much fuel: more than the Twin Otter could ferry in. We must carry on day by day, mile by mile and *be careful*.

Ollie looks grey but says he feels better. We don our facemasks again, tie up hoods and reluctantly emerge into the elements. It has got worse. Now I can see hardly a shadow, no cloud, nothing but my skidoo. Even my sledge is a mere blur in the howling murk. After eighteen miles of frozen creeping, the last vestiges of perspective go and we make camp.

Ol's diary for the day. "Very bad weather. I think we should have stayed in the tent."

I saw his point, but Greenland in 1976 had taught us we could travel in whiteout and high winds. Every hour of progress, however slow and painful, might help tip the scales in favour of eventual success. We have a very long way to go, 2,200 miles across Antarctica, and only four months of travellable conditions to do it in. It is so easy when the winds roar and, outside, your eyes sting with the hissing spicules of flying ice, to stay tentbound. When you look out of the tent and cannot see the nearest sledge, let alone the sun's source, it is easy to say to yourself how pointless to try to travel in the certain knowledge that twelve hours of frustration may at best produce a mile or two of progress.

Poor Charlie has spilled his full pint-mug of coffee over his sleeping gear. His only comfort is the sight of Ollie's fingers and mine which are badly split at the tips and down from the cuticles. For some reason we have always been more susceptible to this than Charlie.

I check the map and tell the others we are now at 9,000 feet above sea level. The skidoos are pulling the loads effectively. If this is still true another 2,000 feet up, we will not have to worry about the altitude power loss predicted for us by the New Zealanders.

To set against this, I notice that Ollie's steel sledge uprights have now also cracked, so we have between us three as yet undamaged wooden sledges and three possibly dicey steel ones. During the winter I had drilled the broken tubes until they accommodated metal rods down their middles. These I secured with splint pins. As yet these splints seem to be preventing further damage. But we are only two days out.

With the sun up full-time, ultra violet rays gnaw at the snow-bridges over crevasses, so the sooner we cross them the less rotten each will be, the less likely we will end up plunging to a speedy demise. To avoid the harsh glare of driving into the sun I have opted for travelling during the twelve-hour period which, on the Greenwich timescale, is called night. However, following the scare Ollie's condition has given me, I switch to 'day-time' travel when it is slightly warmer, as the sun is higher. Ginnie, Simon and the aircrew have to switch too but the changeover gives us all twelve hours extra rest. The change had the side-effect of making navigation, especially around midday when the sun is dead ahead, a real problem. It is more difficult to spot some imperfection or oddity in the snowfields ahead at which to aim my compass.

Since I like to take sun altitude shots at midday not midnight, yet do not wish to interrupt our travel hours by a prolonged halt, the new schedule means less position-fixing shots. I decide to use the mileometers for approximate latitude progress and the theodolite only when we stop for Oliver to drill for ice core samples which he must do at every degree of latitude. I was glad to discover that, when I did stop for a noonday sunshot on 31st October, it gave us a position of 74°32′ S, 02°26′ W, only one degree out from the intended course despite the conditions. That day we broke camp at 0530 and travelled until 1730 despite the intense cold.

Especially uncomfortable are fingers and toes, nose, forehead and cheeks. Charlie is still having trouble with his vision and now also has a swollen knee to contend with after a heavy over-turn this morning. I have painful piles and the back of my left hand is swollen egg-like. I caught it between the chassis and sastrugi when my skidoo went over: nonetheless there are no serious injuries and Ollie's aneroid barometers confirm we are climbing steadily.

On average I stop every ten minutes for a bearing, still 187° magnetic, against the clouds. As they are moving slowly and thus maintaining their silhouettes for quite a while, this seems to work well enough. But the midday glare is so harsh I experience liver spots on my retina and when I squeeze my eyes tight shut I 'see' a deep red colour full of floating black dots.

The snow has become deeper and softer which makes me think we are in a shallow valley. Perhaps this is an illusion, although Charlie too commented that, "Everywhere is uphill." I looked all around and saw what he meant. The terrain does indeed appear to rise away from us on every side.

At mid-day, after a compass halt, I try to move off but can't. Ollie checks my skidoo over.

"The drive axle's gone."

"Can you fix it?"

"I can, yes, but in these conditions it may lose us a day. As we are only ninety-six miles from base could we not get Giles in? It seems flat enough here. He could bring in a reserve skidoo."

My natural reaction is to refuse. It seems pointless carrying a spare drive axle if, when a replacement is due, the job is not done in the field. And again the aviation fuel we possess at Sanae and Ryvingen is strictly limited. We will need every drop we have, a few unscheduled flights could scupper the whole trip. We have allowed twenty per cent additional fuel for unforeseen emergencies but this is plainly no emergency.

While I debate what action to take, we unload and erect the tent, for we will need its shelter anyway, whether we change the axle or wait for the plane to arrive. Then we light the cooker to warm up the radio for an hour until it is usable and call up Ginnie. Giles is ready in Ryvingen and happy to come as he would anyway like to check on our position before we get too far away. That decides it. Within three hours the Twin Otter appears and we swap skidoos. Before he goes Giles confirms our position, warns us to conserve fuel and suggests that we build snow block cairns every time we make camp so that he can, if necessary, trace our route visually, given clear conditions, because the sun will glint on the vertical snow piles in terrain where everything else is horizontal. He explains that he is flying blind most of the time, being too far away from the Omega beacon transmitters for his direction-finding kit to give him his position. A fairly small error in navigation could mean the loss of aircraft or crossing team. Giles' greatest fear is the ignominy of a forced landing in the middle of nowhere which might mean having to ask assistance from the only two other aircraft sources in Antarctica: both hundreds of miles away.

As we settle down for the night, I notice that the temperature is −53°C. This excessive coldness makes Oliver suspect that we are now more than 10,000 feet above sea level. The trouble is that we never seem to get acclimatised to the cold; its numbing reality never leaves us. Stumbling about in the tent, trying to get into my sleeping bag, I tell Oliver that in future drive shafts will have to be changed in situ.

"Well," he replies, squinting badly, a sure sign that he is over-tired, "I only carry one spare and the way you stop and start every few minutes for a compass check, we are going to break a good many drive shafts. They've got plastic teeth, don't forget. Each time you pull away with a jerk-start to drag your sledges out of the soft snow, you put tremendous strain on to those teeth, not to mention the torque elsewhere. You've got to stop less often or we'll get nowhere fast."

I can see his point but can't resist making mine. "We'll get nowhere even faster if we get lost. I need to keep checking. It's not as if there are any features to use."

He does not reply: we both know that I would have to work out some other means of navigating which entails less halts.

As we head further south away from the mountains and away from the sea there are no storms and no clouds, only surface winds and mists. Without clouds the land becomes utterly featureless. At times when whiteouts hide the sun, all I can do is aim my compass at imperfections in the snow up ahead. What I need, when the sun shines, is a sun compass such as I used in the army in Arabia. These are simple to make: the next day I scratch a series of lines around my plastic windscreen: it is useless at protecting me from the wind so it might as well be given some purpose in life. Then I make another set of scratches on the flat fibreglass cowling just in front of the handlebars.

To check on the accuracy of my new compass and to get some life back into our frozen limbs, I stop for five minutes every hour. Charlie keeps at least one mile behind me and Ollie a mile behind him, so when I stop to take a compass bearing on the two specks back along the trail, I have an immediate check on our angle of advance during the last hour. If this has been two degrees too far west, I overcompensate by two degrees to the east the following hour.

For four days and nights the temperature hovers around the −50s creating weird and wonderful light effects, haloes, sun pillars, mock suns and parhelia but we are in no state to appreciate them. There are no more broken driveshafts but three upright bars go missing from Ollie's sledge. Further cracks in the welding of Charlie's and mine are spotted most evenings.

At one halt Ollie is smoking a cigarette whilst we stamp about in small circles attempting to force the blood back into our toes. With no warning, a deep belly-rumble sounds from somewhere *under* our feet: a sinister reminder that nowhere out here in these seemingly innocent snowfields should we move about unroped and off our guard.

So early in the season there is still a fair covering of drift hiding the presence of crevasses so that even if an open fissure lies dead ahead I doubt that I would see it in time: it is quite possible that all three of us would drive straight down it. After all, I spend my time staring up at distant clouds or down at the scratches on my cowling; Charlie's vision is hardly good enough to follow my tracks, let alone spot holes and Ollie, well, he is half asleep most of the time, trying to forget the torment of his feet and his hands.

Each day is a repeat of the last. Up at 5.30, work fast to get warm. One mug of coffee each from the flask but no food. I exit first followed by Ollie and start to pull the tent pegs out. This unsettles showers of hoar frost inside so Charlie curses me silently. Sometimes not so silently.

Outside we each pack our particular items of responsibility. Nobody talks. Just before we are ready to go we do up each other's facemasks and check there are no chinks at all for our number one enemy, the wind, to seek out and bite through. Once goggles, facemasks and hood of wolfskin or duck down are in place, vision is restricted to dead ahead and the only hole is a penny-sized breather vent over the mouth.

To fix safety harness around crotch and hips involves taking outer mitts off and so must be done in a few seconds. If you don't get it right first time, and it has to be done by touch since you can't see below your voluminous jacket, then mitts go on again and minutes are wasted banging arms up and down violently to force the blood back into freezing fingers. When the harness is on you clip it to a twenty-foot coil behind your skidoo seat. Then the task of starting the engine at a temperature which engines do not like. Make one wrong move or an out of sequence action and long delays are caused. Try to engage gear too soon and your drive belt will shatter into fragments of brittle rubber. Turn the ignition key a touch too hard and it will break off in the lock. Get the choke setting wrong or out for too long and the plugs will foul up. Changing plugs at −50° with any sort of wind makes your fingers cold again and that makes the first hour en route purgatory.

My first compass check is done with care. If the sun is visible, even though only as an approximate light source in a wan white sky, I absorb myself in its positioning and the angle of existing shadows, however faint they are, vis-à-vis our desired azimuth for the day.

Then we set out at one mile intervals. Sometimes the whole day might pass without a word spoken between us. For ten unspeakably long hours we head south. By 5th November the snow surface is still reasonable so there is little to divert the mind from the nag of feet and hands and face. As you travel you are forever kicking one foot or the other against the chassis or booting the air hard to keep the blood down in those faraway toes.

Without your right hand on the throttle grip the skidoo stops just as a car does if you take your foot off the accelerator. So when you want to swing your freezing throttle hand about in windmill motions you have to use your left hand across your chest on the right handlebar where the throttle grip is. To steer like this is not too effective and, on a rough surface, unfeasible. When it is rough going therefore your throttle hand, especially the thumb, goes through a good deal of unpleasantness.

I am lucky. Fifty per cent of my mind is at all times concentrating on the exact direction of our heading, either against the clouds or, when as from 6th November onwards there were none, the shadow play on my cowling scratches.

The other two have no such diversions. Only their private thoughts and the bitter vicious cold. That we have managed to cover half the distance from coast to Pole on open vehicles at such temperatures speaks well for the clothing and footwear which protects us.

When at length the ten hours are over we are more than ready for sleep. But there is much to be done. Ollie tends to the skidoos and covers them in an orange tarpaulin. Then, if we have crossed a degree of latitude since his last site, he drills for ice core samples. I build an eight-foot snow cairn as a marker, erect the tent and lay out all our bedding gear. Then I start the cooker and shout for Charlie who brings in his radio gear. He begins to prepare the day's only meal by melting snow blocks. If we are at a drill site, I take sun shots to establish the sun's altitude then retire to the tent to compute our position. Charlie melts the ice core samples in a steel pot then carefully bottles the results for Ollie to label. Before each man enters the tent he brushes as much ice and snow off as possible. If you want to make yourself unpopular quickly, bring snow into the tent.

Wet clothes and footwear are hung around the tent roof on string lines where they soon begin to steam. Life while the cooker is on is heavenly. The evening meal takes an hour and a half to rehydrate. When ready the food pot is placed on Ollie's sleeping bag for he traditionally sleeps in the middle. Then Charlie makes a noise of a certain sort which indicates the chef's go-ahead. As one, three spoons dip into the pot. Each spoon is precisely the same size and should not be dipped more regularly than the other two. I am exceptionally greedy and, since both the others know this, any attempt to get more than my fair share is normally a failure. But I keep trying. The meal consists of rice or dehydrated vegetables mixed with one of four varieties of dehydrated meat. This meat is in reality soya beans but we conveniently forget that fact. We do not wash our pot because the residue is either scraped clean or left to be mixed with the following day's menu.

After a cup of hot chocolate, the evening radio schedule, which includes a full weather report for the World Meteorological Organisation, and the taking of urine samples for use with our calorific intake programme, we sleep by 10.30 p.m. trying not to think of tomorrow's travel.

Despite having 6,500 calories per man per day Ollie loses twenty-six pounds during the journey. Charlie loses sixteen pounds and I lose three.

On 6th November we come to 77° 30'S and converge with the Greenwich meridian. Two hundred miles into unknown terrain, with 800 still to go to the South Pole, we stop for Ollie to complete one of three special extra assignments. He drills a core sample but does not melt it down, instead it is simply bagged and sent back to laboratories in Copenhagen. How it gets there, on sponsored freight all the way, is a nightmare to be faced by Giles, Simon and David Mason in that order.

While we have been travelling twice as fast as my schedule predicted, Anto alone at Sanae, Ginnie and Simon at Ryvingen and Gerry and Giles between the two camps, have been endlessly loading the plane with fuel drums to increase the dump at Ryvingen. Our rapid progress has caused Giles a major problem for we need more fuel every 300 nautical miles. Although we can travel in extremely bad weather, Giles and Gerry cannot and they are increasingly concerned lest we stretch our lines of resupply too thin before they are ready.

Simon and Ginnie are alone at Ryvingen for most of the time. Their relationship is a mixture of mutual respect alternating with periods of hostility. Simon does most of the physical work, whilst Ginnie battles with London by radio. For 7th November Simon wrote in his diary:

> *Left in peace. Ginnie and Bothie and me running the smallest base in Antarctica for the aircrew is with Anto. Had an acrimonious exchange with her today about protecting kit from snowdrifts down at Sanae – but this didn't leave ill feelings . . . Hectic work while Giles is airborne, for we must keep the radios and generators working into the small hours. Peaceful here when only Ginnie, Bothie and myself remain. Ginnie very relaxed and friendly, a total contrast to back in London although, like me, she's not much good before mid-day. She carries a lot of responsibility for admin, kicking London and keeping worries off Ran's shoulders.*

Meanwhile we edge south. The surface has begun to change. At first mere outcrops of isolated hummocks like African anthills but gradually more and more of these are connected in ribbons across our front which makes crossing them a boneshaking process. At noon on 8th November Charlie hands me three steel struts he has retrieved en route. Checking my front sledge I find six uprights are gone and one runner is no longer held rigid. Any form of repair is out of the question. You don't mend hand-welded steel tubes out on the ice. We must just hope the sledges last out and these bumps disappear. Perhaps it is just a local phenomenon. By evening we have covered fifty miles. In ten days we have covered 444 nautical miles from Ryvingen and our camp tonight is half-way from the coast to the Pole but the major suspected crevasse fields are still ahead.

Two chunks of tooth filling came away yesterday and now the evening meal and morning coffee, previously the best times of the day, are purgatory for they set my mouth aching like hell, although Ollie gives me oil of cloves to apply to the cavities.

Since Giles's Omega system does not work this far south we must hope that snow cairns lead him to within beacon range of our location tomorrow night. By then we will need fuel although we have food rations for three weeks yet. However we will be near maximum range for the Otter from Ryvingen, so he must find us at the first attempt.

As we progress further and further south, the time will come when we are out of range for him and he will have to stop on the way to us to refuel at a dump he has had to build up in advance. This means using up more fuel in the process. The best way round this would have been if the Americans allowed him to use some of their aviation fuel at their South Pole depot, then he would be able to use this as a flight base as we got nearer the Pole. But tonight's radio call told us that the US authorities, as expected, have confirmed their 'no help' stance.

Giles has always believed it would be possible to complete the whole crossing of Antarctica without outside fuel support, despite official opinions to the contrary, so now I have told Ginnie to go ahead with Giles's plans for this contingency. Meanwhile we will carry on to 80° and wait there until we hear details of their flight plans.

Today, 9th November, saw the worst terrain yet. To reach this camp at 80° 04′ involved us in a tortuous journey over ever worsening ridges of sastrugi. They average eighteen inches to two feet high and are often perpendicular so we cannot mount them. This means a zig-zag course, precious fuel used in detours and many stops for Ol to replace broken springs and buckled bogey wheels. Still we *are* at 80° a month ahead of schedule.

Tonight Ginnie passed us Giles's beat the fuel shortage plan. He will bring enough aviation fuel to this camp at 80° 04′ to enable him to set up a further fuel depot at 85°. Once *this* camp is stocked to that level we will set out to 85°, whilst Giles, Gerry *and* Anto Birkbeck remain camped here with the Twin Otter.

When we get to 85° Giles will ferry all the fuel from 80° to 85°.

Then he and the others will stay there until we reach the Pole. This 'one leg on the ground' principle is necessary because Giles would never be able to find a fuel cache out here unless someone with a radio beacon is left there too.

To add to our problems, a warning from the London Committee has reached us ". . . to emphasise the dangers of arriving prematurely at South Pole, without adequate resources to proceed immediately from that vicinity, we have been informed quite firmly that you will be *evacuated* by the Americans at the expedition's expense."

So we lie hugger-mugger in the little tent, whilst Giles flies in with fuel drums whenever the weather allows. Every day we delay is for me an almost physical hurt. The terrain shows every sign of deteriorating to the south, as do our skidoos and sledges. But my main concern is the southern crevasse fields. Every day we delay, the snow bridges which might see us safely over the danger zones become weaker and more rotten.

Nobody knows what lies ahead because nobody has been here before. But unmanned balloons have traversed above and analysis of their instrumental data indicates that great coastal glaciers are fed from this part of the ice sheet. At around 81°–82°S to either side of the Greenwich meridian the presence of a high valley is suspected. This is thought to drain ice from the plateau down to the giant Recovery Glacier. Huge crevasse systems as far inland as 83°S, 15°E suggest a deeply penetrating ice 'stream'.

Before leaving England we enquired about the crevasse dangers and Dr Doke at the British Antarctic Survey replied: "Previous traverses into the area have been turned back by crevassing, so it seems possible that a lot of the way between say 79°S and 83°S may be badly crevassed." The uncertainty of the hazards ahead makes waiting difficult. For days the weather is filthy and Giles cannot fly. Communications are also difficult, at times impossible.

Simon visited the lonely VLF hut at Ryvingen by himself at this period. He wrote:

No sign of Ginnie's ghost, a presence which she and Bothie felt during the winter, despite ragging from R, C and O. A youngish man, I gather. Scandinavian? Not malevolent, just there. Bothie was sometimes scared but that may just have been ice movement. But I believe Ginnie. The long solo nights in the hut must have enhanced her perception. Her experiments are over, but I went up

*to the VLF hut today to scavenge wood for sledge repairs. It is an
empty hut with an aura. I sealed it up as I knew I would not want
to go back up there. The graffiti on the wall, written by Ginnie in
three different pens, presumably in stages, was apt and rather
scaring in a way.*

> *As whistlers' and gibbons' cries*
> *Screech in the ears*
> *The ghost of Ryvingen*
> *bursts into tears.*

> *"Why have you come to disturb me*
> *after these many years?*
> *I will haunt and will taunt you*
> *and drive you away."*

With the wood from the hut Simon strengthened a camp sledge
and Giles brought this out to replace Ollie's steel sledge which had
begun to look decidedly dicey.

It was difficult to maintain good relations between the three of us.
We were cramped up, damp, dirty, often cold and above all frustrated. The days passed so slowly. The sound of the wind gnawed
into your brain: it never stopped. An intended joke meant as banter
at the expense of someone feeling low could cause the blood to rise
very quickly. At such times the offender had to recognise the danger
signals in time and back away at once if the atmosphere was to
remain healthy. This was neither the time nor place to maintain,
openly at least, any rigid viewpoint or stance if we three strong
individualists were to bear each other's company.

After seventeen days Giles completed his tenth flight to our camp.
To stock up the fuel cache to the minimum needed for the next phase
he had, in dubious weather, to fly 12,000 nautical miles in ninety-
two hours which used up 6,000 precious gallons of aviation fuel.
Only twenty-five drums now remained at Ryvingen. It was difficult
to appreciate fully the risks Giles took, especially on take off from
Ryvingen. As he said: "I had to take off in the mountains from that
terrible surface of hard, criss-crossed sastrugi and carrying an enormous weight. I couldn't spread the load over more flights because we
didn't have the fuel."

There had been one advantage to the long delay. Ollie had
completed three deep drills and had calibrated his aneroid baro-

meters. Dr Gordon Robin, the Director of the Scott Polar Research Institute, for whom Ollie's work was carried out, had explained the reasons for drilling out the core samples:

> *We are interested in how the Antarctic ice sheet works. We want to know whether there is a faster outflow of ice than the snow falling on top. There are many things you can't learn from flying over the ice sheet and this is where the Transglobe expedition comes in. What the snowfall is. What the temperature is and various other records of climate. The ice sheet stores an incredible record of past climate. People have drilled down to 2,000 metres into the ice sheet: that tells a history of climate over a hundred thousand years or more through the study of two types of oxygen atom. To understand this you need to know what the snowfall on the top surface was like at first. So we asked Transglobe to collect a sample at every degree of latitude on the whole crossing down to about two metres, melt it down and bring a sample back from each spot so we can see how the ratio of oxygen of one sort to the other varies.*
>
> *Additionally we need to know the accumulation of snow. This is difficult to measure for a small rapidly moving group but they will try to take very detailed samples down to about ten metres. We will eventually get these samples back and put them in a sort of nuclear counter device. This will tell us exactly where the 1955 deposit from the H bomb explosion was at that time in the ice sheet and by measuring how deep that is you can work out how much snowfall has fallen during the following twenty-five years.*

The day we left the 80° cache, the Americans gave permission for Giles to refuel from South Pole stocks. This was the result of direct contact between the Foreign Office and the State Department which in turn followed seven years of approaches, proposals and dis- appointments. The delay in receiving the permission had cost us seventeen tent-bound days.

Now the polar summer was with us and life was positively comfortable in terms of temperature for we were well into the −30°s. But the sastrugi did not improve. Day by day they increased in size and number. By the end of November, entering the theoretical crevasse fields draining to the Recovery Glacier, we noticed long rounded spur features descending from higher ground to the east.

But my mind was not on crevasses. The sastrugi ridges now

resembled a ploughed field with the ridges running directly across our line of advance. For 200 miles these ridges averaged two to three feet high. But the four-inch raised blade at the front of our skidoo skis could only mount a sheer-sided obstacle twelve inches high, so we had to hack paths through these ridges with our ice axes. Then we had to manoeuvre the skidoos over each ridge, followed by each of our sledges. If we pulled the sledges on our standard fifty-foot tow ropes, they just became caught up between ice furrows and jammed, so we changed to five-foot tow ropes which, in the event of a crevasse fall, would probably have meant the sledges would have quickly followed the skidoo downwards into the abyss. Often, we could not pull the sledges through the tracks we had cut, but had to manipulate them, and their heavy loads, through one by one.

Progress was painfully slow and involved much work, many overturns and a great deal of fuel wasted on detours. Once, for twenty-nine miles with hardly a break, the sastrugi walls stood three to five feet high and our progress was tortoise slow, leaving us with a series of broken springs, and sheared off steel sledge struts. I did not dare to glance at my sun-compass. Only by keeping total concentration on the maze of ice walls ahead was any progress possible without frequent overturning of skidoo and sledges.

On the last day of November we entered a series of rolling valleys quite free of sastrugi and began to feel elated, although none of us dared hope the ridges were all behind us. I stopped as usual at the end of an hour and, without noticing any irregularity, on a slight incline to the south. I leaned back enjoying the sensation of resting my back muscles against my bedding bag. In a little while Charlie drew up beside me. He stood up astride his seat, stretched and said "Well!" which was what he normally said at halts.

Intending, no doubt, to check his sledge for any new damage, he stepped off his skidoo which was no more than four yards away from mine. As though a trapdoor had opened up beneath him, he was suddenly foreshortened, disappearing right up to his thighs. One hand never left his handlebar and, as he fell, he hung on for dear life. Slowly he withdrew his hips and legs and pulled himself back onto his seat.

"Gawd," he breathed, looking down at the blue green hole into which he had so nearly disappeared.

Seen from the security of my skidoo seat, the incident was hilarious and there was no way, on seeing his wide dilated pupils, that I could stop myself breaking into hysterical laughter. Charlie watched me in silence. He looked at the thin rotten ice around the periphery of the hole and then at my skidoo.

As my laughter died a bit he said evenly, "You think that funny? In a minute or so it'll be a whole lot funnier because there must be a good two inches of snow bridge, maybe less, right under you at this moment. Any movement you make in pulling your starter cord is going to send you on a long drop to nowhere. And is Charlie Burton going to shed tears? No. He is not. He is going to laugh himself sick."

The realisation that he was absolutely correct, that I *was* in imminent danger of collapsing the fragile skin of granular snow sitting over God knows how deep an abyss, froze the smile off my face. Gingerly I started up and engaged gear. With sweat breaking out on my brow, hardly daring to breathe, I pulled away. Nothing happened. The air hissed out between my teeth. The others crossed safely and we carried on.

That night we camped at 82° 50' and a degree or so to the east of the Greenwich meridian. This placed us at the northern limits of a suspected crevasse field, some sixty miles in depth and forty miles wide. I prodded the surface carefully before erecting the tent.

We now heard that Giles, in landing at Ryvingen, had run into a bank of sastrugi. The Twin Otter had bounced over the ridges but the tail of the aircraft rudder was damaged. As Giles wrote:

> It didn't hurt the aircraft nearly so much as it hurt me. I lay awake all night thinking. Since my first flight, aged sixteen, I had never scratched an aeroplane. Of all my flights, seven seasons and 4,000 flying hours in Antarctica, never mind all the other hours in other countries, it had to happen here. If things had been a bit different, if there'd been a cargo on board, the whole tail might easily have been a write-off. No, I really didn't get much sleep that night.

Gerry repaired the damage overnight and they returned to the 80° depot. With the Twin Otter, its crew and Anto sitting it out at the 80° cache and all fuel rationed, I knew we must reach 85° before requesting any flight. But the first few days of December saw us in worse conditions than I had thought existed in Antarctica. Bogey wheels, ski attachments and springs snapped and buckled. Ollie ran out of certain spare parts and had to improvise. In places the iron-hard ridges were separated by ditches less than the length of a skidoo in width and negotiation of the successive walls involved axe work and man-handling as on Arctic Ocean pack-ice. Our progress slowed to a painful creep.

With breaks of one or two kilometres between them, these forbidding sastrugi fields carried on for 300 miles, sometimes almost impassable, sometimes mere serried waves of ice bric-à-brac. With increasing frequency whiteout conditions clamped down. To negotiate even the lesser sastrugi belts without a clear idea of where the bumps were, would be asking for trouble so we always stopped until the light improved. Cannoning off a wall of ice in a medium-size sastrugi belt, I felt resistance and found that a sledge box had dropped through a hole in the steel mesh platform of my lead sledge. So much of the sledge's tubing had snapped and broken off that there were now whole areas with no tubing at all. Using canvas straps, I plugged the hole, hitched up the loose boxes and carried on.

The principal criticism of our steel sledges was always their rigidity: their lack of 'give' when crossing rough ice. Now I noticed that so many connector tubes were missing that the twelve-foot long runners were in fact bending and snaking to conform with the ice surface below. So long as a few upright tubes held the runners to the platform, they might yet make the journey.

But my second sledge was of oak and hickory, an adaptation of an Eskimo design. On 4th December, in the centre of a particularly rough ridge belt, one of its oaken runners split right along its four-inch thick length. There was nothing to be done but abandon it, together with its load. We shared out the vital fuel cans between us but left behind the crevasse ladders, tent heater and all non-critical gear. Then we limped on. Life had become a succession of monstrous sastrugi fields. The Pole seemed unattainable. It was better to forget everything but the next horizon. My toothache was now persistent and more than a mere nuisance.

The ski leaf spring of Charlie's skidoo broke and Ollie had no spare. With tape and wire he effected a temporary repair but this would last only hours. Some twenty-eight miles short of 85° the ski became inoperable so we scouted about for an airstrip. A four-hour search revealed a narrow sastrugi-free lane just long enough for a runway after a lot of axe work. We set up camp at this bald vein amidst the sastrugi fields on 5th December.

Five days previously a group of twelve South Africans had set out on a sixty-mile journey from a geological field base back to Sanae. Led by their boss, Hannes, a tough Afrikaaner with previous field experience in the region, they were home-bound by the same route over the Hinge Zone that we had ourselves used to reach Ryvingen.

One of their heavy snow tractors plunged sixty feet into a crevasse and was jammed still further down by its one-ton fuel sledge. The three men in the cab were rescued with only a few bruises but neither tractor nor sledge could be retrieved.

There were now only two cramped cabs for nine people. The democratic leadership system, so much admired by Simon during the previous winter, was still active. Three of the group decided it would be best to return quickly to Sanae which was about a day's ride over flattish terrain. The weather was fine so they set out on a skidoo with no tent and minimal rations.

The remainder carried on with extreme caution and camped on the edges of the Hinge Zone. At some stage Jed Bell, a young scientist whom we had often spoken to by radio during the winter, fell ninety feet down a hole and broke his neck.

The five survivors, after recovering his body, made radio contact with Sanae. They learnt that the three-man skidoo group had not materialised. Worried, Hannes himself set out on the second skidoo to find them and soon picked up their tracks. He failed to notice the spare fuel can he carried scuff up against the skidoo's chassis and start leaking. He ran out of fuel and lost radio contact with Sanae.

Meanwhile the weather closed in on the three-man skidoo group. They mistook the faint hump of one ice-rise named Blaskimen for another called Eskimo. Close by the seafront, they weaved their way between crevasses along the tide crack but, uncertain whether they were east or west of Sanae base, decided to stay put. Within hours the two sleeping bags they owned between them were soaking wet. They had but eight packets of dried biscuits and no cooker to melt snow. So they began to dehydrate as they shivered away the days.

Those left at Sanae were now shocked and leaderless. They could not call up search and rescue aircraft because there was no such apparatus available. The British base 450 miles away had no operational aircraft at the time. The American ski-equipped Hercules were over 2,000 miles away at McMurdo Base and would be unlikely to be able to land anywhere in or near the search area.

The Transglobe Twin Otter was the nearest, but Pretoria seemed embarrassed officially to request our aid in searching for their employees.

Within hours of our arrival at the 85° cache, Giles left the 80° camp manned by Gerry and Anto and brought us our first fuel load. A second flight would be necessary to bring in more fuel before we could press on so Giles flew back to 80°. On his way there he received a radio message from Ginnie saying that Pretoria *might* shortly ask for our Twin Otter to carry out a search and rescue flight near the coast. At 80° Giles was some 700 miles from the likely search area and 600 miles from the South Pole. His total flying range was about a thousand miles without refuelling.

Should anything happen to the Twin Otter at this stage with our own lines of communication so stretched, our fuel at bare minimum without catering for any problems of our own and two major crevasse fields still between us and the Pole, we could quickly end up in a trickier situation than our South African friends. Their débâcle had, after all, occurred within ninety miles of their permanent base camp.

Not having anticipated the need to turn off his engines, wait or restart again before returning to us on his second fuel flight, Giles had left his only portable generator with us at 85° during the first flight, in order to lighten the Otter and conserve fuel. This left him with nothing at 80° with which to power the aircraft's vital engine heater and battery and now he had unexpectedly to wait at 80° for two hours for confirmation of the rescue mission. When he heard nothing he opted to start the aircraft engines at once before they became too cold and to fly down to Ryvingen where there was a generator and he would be closer for possible rescue work.

Gerry and Anto climbed out of the little tent at 80° to see Giles off. Anto wrote in his diary:

Giles had a good charge reading, 15 per cent rpm (well above the requisite 12.5 per cent), active ignition . . . the lot. But she wouldn't start. Our hearts sank. We took the battery into the tent and warmed it up over a Primus. Then we covered the starboard engine with a parachute and applied a Primus to it until the engine oil temperature rose to 20°C.

Again Giles tried. Again 15 per cent rpm, yet still the engines would not fire. Now we resorted to the spare battery. Gerry had assumed this was an exchange unit, so had not checked its charge. The truth was not long in coming. It had never been charged. We were stuck at 80° south. The very middle of nowhere.

It was an evening of despondency as the full realisation of the disaster hit home. Four men might die. Also the critics would now have their predictions confirmed. We would have to be rescued. A restless night followed as we tried to keep the primuses going to warm the battery. We also had to keep our little solar panel lined up with the sun to get the full benefit of its trickle charge.

Next morning: *There is just enough charge left in the main battery to merit another attempt at starting off it. Again we used a draped parachute and the primuses to warm the engine to 20°C and then again attempted to start up.*

As before the propeller turned, over and over, but wouldn't fire. Giles could only keep his ignition on and watch the battery life drain away. Suddenly she fired!

We broke into a carnival and rushed to dismantle the camp. We contacted Ginnie and she said the South Africans did not require us now because Hannes, the boss, had at that point just reported picking up the tracks of the three missing men.

Our final take-off from 80° was hair-raising, due to the heavy load, high altitude and short strip.

We lurched heavily to beyond the air strip we had cleared and clipped the first sastrugi as we lifted off. But we made it.

Late on 6th December Giles brought in the remainder of our fuel which we hoped would be enough to see us to within sixty miles of the South Pole for, without too many detours, we could make 300 miles with full sledge-loads and with no replenishment. Giles, worried about his engines, flew straight off for the Pole hoping to pick up its radio beacon when a hundred miles out. When he reached the Pole another message came in from Ginnie. Hannes was himself now missing. The other three had been out with no shelter for six days and their outlook was grim. Giles flew direct to the fifty-square-mile coastal zone where he felt the lost men must be. As the straight line distance from the Pole to Sanae is 1,300 miles, and the Twin Otter's range is about a thousand, Giles reached the search zone on his 'last drop'.

By the uncanny nose he had developed after seven seasons down south, Giles picked up some tracks several miles south west of Sanae base camp and soon afterwards overflew the black huddle of the lost group. He landed close by. All three men were still alive. A blizzard had blown snow into their clothing and sleeping bags which had been melted by their remaining body heat and then turned to ice as they became colder. One of them was the base doctor and he had rationed the biscuit packets carefully. The men were soaked through and utterly dehydrated. The doctor lost twenty-six pounds, the other two sixteen pounds each. Giles flew them back to Sanae, refuelled and, an hour later, located and brought in Hannes as well.

Up at Ryvingen Ginnie received the good news. Simon wrote: "Ginnie gave up the radio shack for the first time in twenty-nine hours and went for a wash."

Two days of hard slow toil saw us out of the last sastrugi field. By 85° 30′ the dreaded dragon's teeth bands had disappeared and the surface began to improve. The weather deteriorated and twice we struck camp in total whiteout conditions. For three days I followed an easterly deflection to avoid the crevasse zone 110 miles before the Pole and then, on 13th December, began the final run in along 201° magnetic. For the last eighty miles we were enveloped in mist.

Two of our sledges were falling to bits, their structure bearing no resemblance to the sleek greyhounds of a month before. Yet the runners were undamaged and the platforms, attached now by only four corner uprights out of sixteen, still supported the full loads with a little help from makeshift cross-straps.

On 14th December after nine hours' travel through the mist, I stopped with sixty-one miles on the mileometer. This must be the South Pole. There was nothing to be seen. When Ollie came up he was excited. "We passed the huts about a mile back on the left." Elated, Charlie and I followed him back. He stopped and pointed. Sure enough three black shapes could be seen in the gloom.

Closer inspection revealed merely a group of flags some six inches high; probably ice markers. Initial disappointment soon turned to anticipation. After all these were the first local 'features' of any sort we had seen since leaving Ryvingen, a thousand miles to the north. And where there are flags there are likely to be people. We quartered the area for an hour or so but found nothing. We camped and contacted the South Pole operator.

"You are three and a half miles from us. We have you on the radar. Come on in."

He gave us a bearing and, an hour later, a dark silhouette loomed through the thick mist directly ahead.

At 0435 hours on 15th December, some seven weeks ahead of our schedule, we arrived at the bottom end of the earth.

8

Pole to Erebus

DECEMBER 1980–JANUARY 1981

Nature is often hidden, sometimes overcome, seldom extinguished.

FRANCIS BACON

The American base at the South Pole, unlike any other in Antarctica, is protected from the elements by a metal dome. This is just big enough to house eight prefabricated and centrally heated huts and, in winter when the temperature plunges to −110°F, its outer doors are closed. The dome is designed for the wintering of a dozen scientists and six or seven administrative workers.

The base commander, Tom Plyler, was an ex-Marine lieutenant with Vietnam experience. A strict disciplinarian, his methods of running things were precisely the opposite to those of Hannes back at Sanae. Mine were I suppose somewhere in between or perhaps they just chopped and changed according to the people I was involved with at the time.

Not willing to set out for the second half of the journey, which included a potentially unpleasant descent of the Scott Glacier, until Ginnie had set up a radio base at the Pole, I asked Tom if we could stay at his place for a week or so. Washington had by now notified him of our impending arrival and agreed that we should have the twenty-three drums of aviation fuel. Anything else was up to Tom's discretion. We erected two pyramid tents about a hundred yards

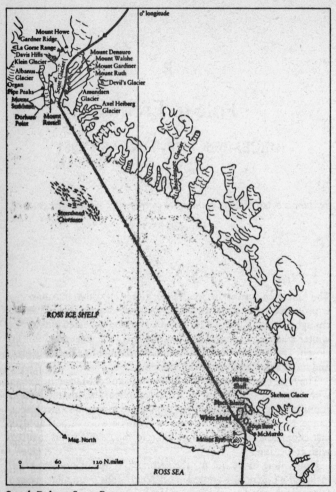

Mount Howe
Gardner Ridge
La Gorse Range
Davis Hills
Klein Glacier
Albanus Glacier
Organ Pipe Peaks
Mount Ruth
Salisbury
Durham Point
Mount Russell
Scott Glacier

0° longitude

Mount Deneuro
Mount Walshe
Mount Gardiner
Mount Ruth
Devil's Glacier
Amundsen Glacier
Axel Heiberg Glacier

Steershead Crevasses

ROSS ICE SHELF

Minna Bluff
Black Island
White Island
Mount Byrd
Mag. North
Scott Base
McMurdo
Skelton Glacier

0   60   120 N.miles

ROSS SEA

South Pole to Scott Base

away from the dome and accepted his kind offer to eat with the Pole folk in their canteen in exchange for dish-washing and general clean-up duties. This released some of the base staff for much needed work elsewhere. Tom also let me visit the base doctor who had dental equipment and, although he had never before worked on a real live mouth, he did a wonderful job on my cavities and put an end to my incessant toothache.

A year before there had been a couple of worrying incidents. Down at the McMurdo base, nerve-centre for all US Antarctic outstations, helicopter and Hercules crews had helped recover 224 bodies from the remains of a Air New Zealand DC10 which crashed into Mount Erebus, the volcano overlooking McMurdo, whilst on a tourist sightseeing overflight.

Of more personal concern, the discovery was made by chance that the dome's sewer outlet was not far enough away. For a number of years the effluent, sinking into the ice, had opened up a cavern beneath the dome over a hundred feet deep, the bottom thirty feet of which consisted of chemicals and sewage. As a result the dome was slowly tilting one way and stress on its nuts and bolts had already caused some to shear off. Given further strain and extreme temperatures the situation could easily become serious. The wintering scientists would not enjoy the twin threats of being crushed by falling girders or of suddenly descending into a lake of sewage.

Tom held a karate black belt. I had never before been particularly impressed by the activity but, in a little makeshift gymnasium at the base, he gave me a demonstration. Fortunately his blows, a vicious blur of palm, fist and foot, fell short of my nose, crotch and knees by a hair's breadth – as intended.

"Do you rassle?" Tom asked, as I let out my breath.

"Rassle? Is that something to do with cattle?"

"Negative. Arm-rassling, Turkish rassling; we use these judo mats."

"Ahh, wrestling. *No*, I never have. Except with my wife to get the car keys."

"Well," said Tom, "you're a good size, so come along tonight after you've done the evening dishes."

It was an interesting experience. I did manage to extract a howl of pain from Tom with a standard British Army lock which put his forearm out of commission for the evening but not before he had almost squeezed the guts out of me with a Californian scissors and my neck was all but dislocated by the ex-college rassling champion who acted as local instructor.

In the interests of further skidoo travel I refrained from any more rassling sessions and restricted my activities to the stainless steel sinks in the canteen.

Underneath the dome's ice floor snaked a long tunnel carrying pipes and electric conduits. Over the years a good deal of ice had formed from past leaks and clogged up the footways. I accompanied Tom and two 'field-hands', one an ex B52 bomber pilot, on an ice-chipping detail armed with axes and empty sacks to fill with ice debris. On the way down Tom showed me a vertical vent shaft.

"One of our cooks tried to clear snow from that vent. A column of it broke off and crushed him dead."

Luckily all our ice chipping took place in a horizontal shaft but I was beginning to think life in the polar dome was more hazardous than out on the ice sheet. At least you could fall down crevasses out there and not drown in your own sewage.

"We have to watch germs here," Tom warned me.

"But surely the cold kills all germs."

"It does outside, but some of our scientists spend their entire Antarctic year in centrally heated huts either up here or down at McMurdo. You say your wife will be bringing a dog here. It will have to stay outside in your tents, for there is a firm rule: No pets at the Pole. It would not be worth my while to even consider making an exception."

"He'll be fine in our tents. He's very long-haired."

"Good," said Tom "and another thing. Be careful of cold germs. They are really virulent up here and we can't afford, especially during the summer season, to lose a scientist's working hours. It is said in Washington to cost one million dollars to keep just one scientist here for a year."

He explained one of the cold prevention methods. When a new arrival enters McMurdo he is given special iodine impregnated handkerchiefs in sets of three: one to blow the nose, one to wipe the nose and one to wipe the hands. At one dollar per handkerchief it costs three dollars to blow your nose.

Ice sheet neighbours to the Pole Station are the Russians 720 miles away at Vostok. They hold the world's record temperature, $-128°C$. Some of the US scientists, about to fly there by Hercules for an exchange visit, took orders for a 'shopping list'. They had an agreed barter system and prevailing rates were:

1 bottle USSR vodka = 1 bottle of US vodka
1 Russian leather hat or leather boots = 1 cassette radio
1 complete leather outfit = 1 pair jeans or a calculator.

Not having vodka, jeans or calculators, we missed out on the deal.

Back at Ryvingen Ginnie and Simon packed up the valuable instruments and gear we would need in the northern hemisphere, then gave them to Giles to fly down to Sanae where Anto boxed and listed them together with kit from his own base.

Later that spring the South African ship would come to replace Hannes and the others at Sanae. David Mason was due on the ship too in order to help Anto pack and load. The two of them would then return to London with the gear and, in a few short months, have it serviced, repaired, re-packed and sent to await us at various Arctic outposts.

On completing the last cargo flight down to Sanae Giles decided to take Anto and Gerry on a joy-ride to the Russian base of Novola-zarevskaya, some 300 miles east along the coastline, which had never previously been visited by non-Soviets. They flew in unannounced and unexpected with plenty of South African wine and Cadbury's chocolates to the great delight of the inmates, all of whom were Russians except for four East Germans who acted as interpreters.

A banquet was at once set up and a twelve-hour drinking session began. Unlimited quantities of Russian champagne, vodka and a liquid similar to brandy smelling like rocket fuel flowed copiously. Sipping was frowned upon although there were short intermissions during which fearsome-looking Soviet gherkins were swallowed.

The interpreters were kept busy with speeches of goodwill which stressed the non-political status of Antarctica and non-stop toasts were drunk to everybody in Britain, the USSR, Antarctica and everyone else in sight. Gerry became particularly animated on the rocket fuel, but Giles explained that he was the pilot and that he never drank before flying. This seemed to amaze the Russians who declared they could not understand anyone flying in Antarctica *without* drinking.

Anto, too polite to admit that he seldom drank, kept accepting top-ups of rocket fuel and pouring every second tumbler full into his canvas mukluks. Each time he got up there was a distinct sloshing sound but this was drowned by the general revelry. The next day he suffered from something uncannily akin to trenchfoot.

When the party finally broke up, the base commander, Igor Antonovitch, took Giles to one side and thanked him profusely for the visit.

"You are the first foreigner to call here. Now our Novolazarevskaya is truly an international airport. We are most grateful."

With aid from the Russians, Giles and Anto managed to load Gerry on to the Twin Otter then the three of them, all in Russian bearskin hats, flew back to Sanae. Anto left them there for he was to leave Antarctica on the South African icebreaker.

On 21st December Ginnie bade a sad farewell to the cardboard camp at Ryvingen, her home for eleven months. Soon it would disappear beneath the snow for ever.

Jamming herself in the fuselage with Simon and Bothie she must have wondered if Giles would ever take off for the load was well over the recommended maximum figure. Giles never tried to do anything he was not absolutely certain *could* be done. The take-off was a nail-biting affair but it worked and brought us the last cargo we needed at the South Pole. The mathematics of what Giles had achieved were startling. Every pound of cargo that he flew from the coast to the South Pole used up thirteen pounds of fuel. My requirements list for the Pole, mainly fuel and rations, totalled 7,500 pounds and to get it there cost us 230 drums of fuel from Sanae.

Gerry is a keen cricketer and brought his bat and ball to the Pole. To celebrate their arrival we played a cricket match outside the dome. Bothie, who specialises in ball games, became hysterical and local camera enthusiasts had a field day. Gerry offered the bat to an American scientist who inspected it and asked: "Gee great, but what is it?"

"A cricket bat," said Gerry.

"Thanks, buddy, but back home we kill crickets with aerosols."

Gerry was unable to decide whether or not the Michael was being extracted so he kept the bat anyway.

With our base group all at the Pole I wanted to press on. The second half of our journey involved some 180 miles to the edge of the high plateau, a 140-mile descent down a mountain-girt valley, the Scott Glacier, and 600 miles over the Ross Ice Shelf to the sea at McMurdo Sound.

For five years I had tried to gain information about our descent route, the Scott Glacier. Even the Scott Polar Research Institute had no details. It seemed no one had experience of its nature; certainly not in the last decade and, like the rapids on rivers, crevasse hazards change over the years. The aerial map of the glacier indicates extensive crevassing at its crest, some 9,000 feet up, crevassing in belts along its course and crevassing at its foot, some 500 feet above sea level. It looked generally unhealthy: to be treated with great caution. I planned to take ten days over its descent. If we are cautious enough, I decided, we should be all right.

One private worry was the question of actually locating the glacier's crest some 180 miles from the Pole. It is one thing using sun and compass for 1,200 miles to reach the South Pole, but quite another to pinpoint mountain or glacier features travelling *from* the Pole when moving obliquely across the direction of the South Magnetic Pole. Ollie commented: "I was staggered that we had managed to navigate so accurately that when we got to the Pole and despite the whiteout, we were only three and a half miles away from it. If we'd had clear visibility we would have easily seen it. But I was slightly worried about the next stage. From South Pole to Scott Base would be more difficult and a lot more hazardous."

I made up my mind to leave the Pole as soon as Ginnie's radio arrangements were made, since each day we lingered increased the dangers ahead. Summer was already well advanced. Crevasse bridges, already weakened, would soon be rotten, and in places, non-existent.

Inside the dome colourful preparations were going on for Christmas was but three days away. Charlie and Ollie were enjoying themselves and had made many friends. It was good to be with Ginnie again and undeniably tempting to stay just two more days to enjoy a proper Christmas. Ginnie did not try to stop me although, like the rest of us, she was nervous of the Scott Glacier.

"Besides," she said with a weak smile, "the Christmas dishwashing is probably well worth avoiding."

So we made ready to set out the next day, 23rd December. I thought with a twinge of sympathy of Captain Scott. He had left the Pole, sixty-nine years ago on 17th January, too late in the summer to be sure of a safe journey back. "All the daydreams must go," he had written. "It will be a wearisome return."

Next morning, with unexpected radio calls and messages to write, I was late in getting my kit packed. As a result, I committed a cardinal navigator's error, I failed to rehearse in my mind, my navigational intentions for the day, to obtain a mental picture of direction through sun and wrist-watch. I had no excuse as the sun was clear and visibility unlimited.

Tom Plyler and a chilly band of amateur photographers were stomping up and down by the international flags which mark the exact spot of the geographical South Pole. I lashed my kit down quickly, kissed Ginnie and set out due north. *Every* direction was due north and I aimed for the airstrip, forgetting that we had actually *arrived* via the airstrip seven days previously.

Soon realising my predicament, I determined to put a bold front on it and complete a wide left hand circle on to the correct bearing once out of sight of the dome, hoping none of the polar scientists would notice. With luck they would have rushed back to the warm dome to unfreeze their camera fingers as soon as we were out of photographic range.

I had forgotten Giles. Catching a lift on a snowtrack, he rushed after us with the news that we were heading back to Sanae. Having flown in and out of the Pole so many times in all weathers, there was no way Giles was going to be taken in.

I thanked him but kept to my circular correction. Some three miles out I stopped and checked the charts. About 180 miles away a single jagged peak, Mount Howe, marked the upper rim of Scott Glacier. This my mathematics suggested was on 261° magnetic, so my true 'meridian of advance' should be 147°W and this should lie directly beneath the sun at 2100 hours, 44 minutes Greenwich time.

But the sun in fact passed over what my compass indicated to be this meridian almost an hour too early. So I must be heading along 132°W. I put all this to Ollie and Charlie who were quite happy to follow in more or less any direction just as they had en route for the Pole. Not even Ollie who is mathematically brilliant could see any discrepancy, so I continued to follow 261° magnetic. Whatever error I might be making would be to the left and west of Mount Howe so if, when we reached the edge of the plateau, the mountain was not visible, a sharp right turn would in theory take us straight to it. Uneasily and with frequent accusing glances at the sun, as though it were personally to blame for my uncertainties, I carried on along 261°.

At five p.m. on Christmas Day I stopped on a small rise and noticed a black speck dead ahead, the summit of Mount Howe: the first natural feature for over 1,000 miles and as good a Christmas present as anyone could wish for.

That night Ollie completed a latitude ice core drill and changed the carburettor jets on the skidoos in readiness for the descent of the glacier. The next day there was an air of nervousness – about us all. I could *feel* this, as I suspect the others could, despite our habitual silence on the move.

Our aerial map showed the crevasse fields plainly, a regular rash of them dotted all over the glacial valley like smallpox scars. There was little point in plotting a careful zig-zag course which, on the map, avoided the chasm belts, since there were bound to be countless unmapped crevasses, just as lethal, which the photogrammetric interpreter had decided were unworthy of his map, if indeed they had showed up on the air photograph in the first place. Better to steer for an obvious feature on a simple downhill route and to keep checking its bearing in readiness for sudden whiteouts.

A series of great east-west swells or ogives heralded the first ice disturbance. We held our breath as we passed over huge bridged crevasses but there was no need to worry: these monsters had solid enough lids to take light weights. It was the narrower fissures, from four to twenty feet wide, yet potentially as deep, that were the more likely killers. And these we came to around noon.

That day we learnt that sweat comes easily at −30°C when fear sits in your stomach and creeps down your back.

Oliver counted forty crevasses crossed in twenty minutes. He travelled last and still had two sledges whereas my second sledge had long since been abandoned broken, and Charlie's finally gave up the ghost at the Pole.

Each time I crossed a relatively weak snow bridge my sledge broke through and made my route impassable for the others. Charlie, knowing this, naturally veered off my tracks each time a green scar showed up what he called a 'bomb crater'. He then caused further cave-ins beside my own craters and left Ollie with a good deal less choice, especially at those crevasses with only a narrow causeway of remaining snow. Often weird ice hummocks or boils went side by side with the more cut-up zones and served as sinister markers. But not always: some of the most rotten slopes had the most innocent appearance.

By evening a mist crept dark and sinuous from low lacunas to the east. The La Gorse mountain range to which we were headed on 244°

magnetic disappeared. Soon I could see nothing at all and being in the very middle of a belt of boils and cracks to the east of Mount Early felt it best to stop and camp. I prodded round about with an ice axe, then Charlie let me out on a long rope until I had cleared a short airstrip and tent-spot. Cracks like veins ran everywhere: each of us on occasions stumbled into them, usually merely to knee-depth. We called them 'ankle-crackers' and there were several across the airstrip. Since the mist stayed wrapped about us all night Giles never came.

In the morning a steady wind cut down off the plateau, averaging thirty knots. Keen to find a safer spot for Giles to bring us fuel, I decided to move on despite the total lack of visibility. In retrospect this was not sensible. To move through a highly volatile zone unable to spot the hazards ahead or underfoot could be described as stupid. My motivation was purely a desire for progress: it was well known that these glaciers can be misty for days, even weeks, on end. To wait for good visibility might write off much precious time. When my decisions appeared to be wrong, Charlie provided an excellent weather vane. He showed his disapproval without a word through his mood; by what he did *not* say. He would tell Ollie his feelings, not me, but he knew that I knew he disapproved.

Ollie's diary: "Charlie very shirty as he thought we should have stayed in the tent and not travelled in the whiteout through the crevasse field. Ran wanted to get to a better airstrip."

By chance, the whiteout cleared an hour or so after we set out. This was just as well for our nightmare trail led down through a long blue corridor which twisted and fell then ended in a cul-de-sac caused by a twenty-foot ice bubble. We were surrounded by seemingly bottomless cracks, so we retraced our way back up the corridor to an offshoot and tried again. A maze of sunken lanes beset with hidden traps finally released us, shaken but unhurt, a mere five miles from Gardner Ridge. Through binoculars the snow slopes south of this rock ridge seemed gentle and solid.

By early afternoon we had reached its foot and made camp beside a potential airstrip. The view to the east and north was impressive. Dizzy cliffs shrouded in frozen gloom but capped with that golden light only seen in far polar places where the air is pure as the vast white fields which have drowned all lower land.

Great dikes of pegmatite, of fine-grained igneous rock, reflected the sun's fire in ochre splendour. The upper sediments of sandstone and shale were interspersed with seams of lignite coal and many fossil stems and leaves of ancient plants. Lower down, in the shadowed moraines, were fossil tree sections up to eighteen inches in diameter, evidence of warmer times. Rare sparse lichens, the southernmost living plants in the world, clung to the polar granite.

This wild forgotten place, witness to millennia, seemed to stress that our transitory aims were but a fleeting episode in eternity. My thoughts wandered and I let them. It was good to relax after the pent-up strain of the upper icefall. But another 6,000 feet of nastiness lay ahead.

Giles arrived with Ginnie from the South Pole. We took twenty-four full jerry cans in exchange for empty ones. Then they flew down the glacier to spot trouble zones. Giles was casual yet precise in his description of the obstacles and in his route advice and I marked every detail of the crevasse zones he gave me over the radio on to my map. I learnt later that, not wishing to worry Ginnie nor to discourage us, he had decided not to paint too lurid a picture of what he saw.

As the glacier narrowed, flowing down between successive mountain ranges, tributary rivers of ice poured into it from flanking valleys. The junction points where these met were zones of greatly disturbed ice which, for us, were areas of extreme hazard. Likewise, wherever the ice was confined by sheer rock faces and squeezed through narrow passes, there would be trouble. One such defile, five miles long, was in Giles's opinion impassable. He suggested a detour up a side valley and back via a hump-back pass which he simply said "looks possible".

After this recce flight the aircrew and base group left the South Pole for the long flight down to Scott Base at McMurdo Sound, the last of Ginnie's Antarctic bases.

Early on 28th December, in a whiteout with wind gusting to forty knots, we skirted the east side of Gardner Ridge and followed the Klein Glacier for a dozen miles to the mist-blurred outline of the Davis Hills. Here the Scott and Klein Glaciers clash with a silent but ferocious force, creating a jumble of gleaming chaos for some miles. "It doesn't know whether it's coming or going," was Ollie's immediate reaction to the impressive vista of nature showing off. We sneaked gingerly along a finger of good ice beside a gravel spit, until a region of hummocks and splits to our immediate east met up with the monoclinal pressure ridges and chasm belts from the main Scott Glacier flow.

By way of an excuse to delay the moment of truth, I stopped a few yards short of the first snowbridge, an eight-foot stretch of yellow sagging snow, and took out my carefully marked up map. My leather mitts were old and shiny with use. The wind, powerful all morning, sliced through the gully and tore the map away. Briefly it caught against a hummock and I leapt after it. My safety rope jerked taut and I fell flat on my back. The precious map scuttered away like an autumn leaf. I tried to start up in a hurry which, with skidoos, is usually a mistake. The plugs fouled. The map was gone. Giles's topographical commentary was now only in my head. Luckily however I always take a spare map and navigation kit packed on another sledge. Charlie produced it and I found Giles's suggested route which ran along a curly spine, the impact line between the two converging ice lanes. This we followed, grateful that we were neither to the left nor to the right, because the deep shadows of great caverns marked each flank like the random stripes of a tiger.

The crevasse field ended in a mile or so. Then gradually our route veered north north east and the Scott Glacier fell away before us to reveal a breath-taking panorama of mountain and glacier, ice field and sky. The world seemed to start at our feet, dropping 600 metres to the far horizon where our highway disappeared between the cliffs of Mount Walshe and the Organ Pipe Peaks. Still keeping to the centre of the glacier we made good time for thirty miles until, close to Mount Denaro, a rash of rotten snowbridges collapsed beneath us. Everyone suffered shocks. As usual Ollie at the back was worst off. I spared him no time for sympathy, for soon I must locate the valley which gave access to Giles's detour.

Four miles short of the defile between Mount Gardiner and Mount Russell I stopped to check on Giles's comments with binoculars. The ice between the forbidding cliffs ahead was in shadow but nonetheless I could see a line of uneven disturbances. I was reminded of rapids-spotting from upriver in British Columbia, only there no detour had been possible, whereas we hoped to cheat the icy jaws ahead by a sideways jink into the mountains.

No sooner had we veered to the western flank of the glacier than Charlie's sledge collapsed a wide snow bridge. I saw Ollie struggling to help extricate the dangling load but was not going back over one step of the perilous route unless needed so I sat and watched until they were again en route. We climbed over 1,000 feet to a high wild pass where the wind bit through our clothes and whipped up spirals of snow from the granite fortress of Mount Ruth and its senior twin Mount Gardiner. To the west we could see a ragged company of primordial peaks spearing the sky, mere reminders of the vastness of their ice-buried bulk. Around them curled serpentine rivers of ice bearing names from the 'heroic age' of polar exploration; the Amundsen, Axel Heiberg and Devil's Glaciers.

From the pass we climbed still higher to the north until at the extremity of the detour, we arrived at the crown of a steep valley leading back down to the Scott Glacier. Charlie, careful never to sound excited about anything, described the subsequent downhill journey:

> *The descent was hair-raising, too steep for sledges which ran down ahead of the skidoos sometimes wrenching them sideways and even backwards over wide droopy snowbridges. Some of the bridges had fracture lines on both sides and were obviously ready to drop at the first excuse, like over-ripe apples. How we made the bottom, God only knows. We camped on blue ice.*

I had not wanted to stop but a wall of pressure hummocks and crevasse scars blocked off the bottom end of the valley from one cliff-face to the other. We had travelled some fourteen hours and covered five days' worth of scheduled progress. The only way out of the valley was forwards to rejoin the Scott Glacier. If we were going to sleep somewhere solid it had to be here on the deep blue polished ice above the pressure wall. The spoil of many rockfalls lay all about embedded in the ice and the wind shrieked down the natural air funnel all night but we were tired and slept well.

Next morning there was no talk over coffee. All were apprehensive. The wind had gone and it was warmer than at any time for a year. From the flat lip of our blue ice campsite another steep slope saw us once more sliding downwards, sledges out of control, brakes fully applied. Below the last incline I headed for the northern foot of Mount Gardiner, hoping for an exit lane around the pressure wall. There was none. The Mount Ruth side looked impossible so we nudged at the wall itself and ran along a narrow corridor at its foot. In one place, rotten as a worm-eaten plank, the wall was split and a branch corridor led through to the main flow beyond.

One by one we passed cautiously over the sagging divide and then the fun and games began. What a day! At the end of it Ol wrote:

"Thank God it's over and done with, as it was quite the nastiest and most dangerous experience of my life."

Much of the surface was glare ice, smooth as glass and difficult for the rubber tracks to grip. With so little steering traction it was difficult to make sudden changes of course between crevasses. On one occasion Ollie's two sledges both fell into separate crevasses bringing his skidoo to an abrupt halt just short of a third. One disturbed region averaged a crevasse every two yards and two-thirds of these were quite unbridged: the rest were too rotten to support more than one sledge crossing at speed.

Charlie's diary:

The descent was a nightmare which I don't care to recall. Some people will think it must have been easy simply because we descended so quickly. All I can say is let them try. Ran and Ol were as frightened as I was, even if they don't admit it. That's why Ran kept going hour after hour without stopping. He zigzagged in every direction trying to avoid the worst areas. He didn't have much success and on one of the upper ledges, we found ourselves right in the middle of a major pressure zone. Great ice bubbles and blue domes reared above us as we slithered along a maze of cracked corridors, totally trapped. My sledge took an eight-foot wide fissure diagonally and broke through the bridge. My skidoo's rubber tracks clawed at the blue ice, slipped sideways and the sledge began to disappear. I was lucky. A patch of grainy white ice gave the tracks just enough forward purchase to heave forward again. The sledge wallowed up and over the forward lip of the crevasse . . .

I could mention a hundred or more such incidents during the descent. Each of us could – but what's the point? Nobody who wasn't there, who hasn't felt the deadly lurch of snow giving way under his seat, hasn't seen the line upon line of white or blue telltale shadows in a major crevasse field and been forced to carry on going over more and more for hour after hour, can imagine the sweaty apprehension we experienced.

Perhaps if we had got there earlier or there had been heavier snow the previous winter, it would have been better.

At one point it was necessary to cross from the west to the east side of the glacier because the former had become impossible. This involved moving parallel with the crack lines and, unless extremely quick and wary, ending up with both skidoo and sledge travelling along the top of a delicate snowbridge. In such circumstances there would be no escape from a cave-in. We completed this crossing along an imaginary line drawn between Cox Peaks and the western end of Organ Pipe Peaks. The last concentrated nightmare, south west of Mount Zanuck, was a series of swollen ice waves similar to swell in the Southern Ocean. In between each rounded crest were furrows pocked with treacherous seams. Ollie had a particularly bad time here. After that there were many isolated crevasses up to twenty yards wide but with room between them to collect our thoughts.

The hours crept by but so did the features, weird isolated boulders borne by the flow many miles from the original rockfalls that spawned them, the powerful in-flow of Albanus Glacier, the sastrugi slopes below Mount Stahlman and finally the outcrops of rock which led to Durham Point beyond which there was nothing but ice and the Pacific. We had arrived on the Ross Shelf.

Dog tired we camped, a mere 500 feet above sea level, and there spent a day repairing, repacking and in Ol's case drilling.

On the last day of 1980 we moved due north for fifty miles and away from the crevasses that shift about the foot of the glaciers. The surface was excellent once on the move but its slushy texture made it hard to tug out the sledges from a standing start. The snow thrown up by our skidoo skis landed on our clothes: the sun then melted it for the temperature was +1°C.

There was no longer any need for facemasks or sweaters. Life was comfortable, easy and carefree. Following the northerly push I switched half-left on to 183° magnetic, a heading which we kept to for nine days and which I was confident would miss the great complex of disturbance called the Steershead Crevasses. Gradually the mountains to the left tapered away until, as on the plateau, there was nothing but ice and us.

Once a whiteout stopped us for eight hours and Giles flew out from Scott Base for we were low on fuel. Giles: "Today Simon and I flew our last long resupply to Ran. We almost didn't make it as we encountered seventy-knot headwinds and it took over five hours to fly the 417 miles out. However it only took two hours to get back the same distance so we couldn't complain."

On the fifth day out we completed seventy-nine nautical miles in ten hours. The glare was intense and I navigated by storm clouds to the west. When we finally camped, Ollie fell asleep whilst drilling and Charlie whilst cooking the stew.

On the seventh day we crossed the 180° meridian which, at this point, is also the International Date Line. We increased our mileage for the day to ninety-one nautical miles and used only a gallon for each eight miles.

On the ninth day despite a semi-whiteout we drove one hundred nautical miles and likewise on the tenth when, at noon, a high white mushroom cloud first became visible on the horizon ahead and to the right: the steam cloud of Mount Erebus. Beneath this 13,000-foot volcano nestled our goal, Scott Base.

By dusk two other features, made famous through the expeditions of Scott and Shackleton, appeared faraway but distinct, Mina Bluff and Black Island.

On 10th January after eighty-one nautical miles and some unpleasant crevasses, large and small, we camped at the tip of White Island. Two hours out from Scott Base, Charlie's skidoo developed piston trouble. Ollie had carried a spare engine all the way from Ryvingen, now he put it to good use, and completed the engine change by midnight.

Next day at six p.m. Roger Clark, the New Zealand Commander of Scott Base, came out to meet us with a sledge drawn by huskies. He led us over the sea-ice, scattering docile seals and screaming skuas, to Pram Point where the wooden huts of his base huddle by the edge of the sea. Above on the rocks some sixty New Zealanders looked down at us and a lone kilted piper struck up the haunting tune, 'Amazing Grace'.

Ginnie came down with Bothie on a lead to prevent his quick demise at the jaws of the huskies.

In sixty-seven days we had crossed Antarctica but as yet the expedition was halfway in neither time nor distance.

9

Up the Other Side of the World

FEBRUARY–JUNE 1981

If the Creator had a purpose in equipping us with a neck,
he surely meant us to stick it out.

ARTHUR KOESTLER

Many kind folk around the world sent messages to say they were pleased we had made it, our Patron, HRH Prince Charles, and President Reagan among them. A note from our SAS Regiment simply stated: "Just in case you are not getting your copy of the *Red Star* regularly. With best wishes." Enclosed was a cutting from the relevant Soviet newspaper *Krasnaya Zvezda* commenting on our journey.

Ant Preston kept a careful watch on polar expeditions from various countries, especially Pole-bound ones. A message arrived with details of three Canadians on skis pulling fibreglass sledges. They set out that spring for the North Pole but within five days one had frostbite and they were all evacuated. But much more worrying, the American, Walt Pedersen was now ready to make a bid for the South Pole in early 1982. Determined to become the first man in the world to reach both Poles overland, he had spent twelve years getting his act together. He had been to the North Pole in 1968; now it looked as though he would beat us by four months. There was no way we could speed up our own attempt on the North Pole. The earliest we could possibly hope to reach it would be in April 1982. Mulling over our Antarctic crossing, as I repacked used gear for use in the north, I reflected that virtually nothing we had learnt was applicable to the coming Arctic struggle. The two places were as alike as chalk and cheese.

Scott Base owned some twenty husky dogs. Each summer a dog trainer/driver ensured they were kept fit and regularly used. They were the last such dog team on that side of the continent and were not immunised against diseases likely to be carried by Bothie, despite his long stint in the south, so the trainer, called Doggo by all, made it clear to Ginnie that Bothie should keep well clear of the huskies at all times.

A surprise donation from our friends at the South Pole enabled us to hold a party with the New Zealanders. We expected to stay at Scott Base for a month while we waited for the *Benjy B* to arrive. They let us eat with them and sleep in the base. We shared camp duties and gave them our remaining rations though these were not all in good condition, being three or four years old. Simon joined the three Scott Base instructors whose job was to train the McMurdo Americans in polar survival.

Giles and Gerry had their work in Antarctica officially recognised in Britain by the presentation of the military Rory Cape Award to Gerry and the Guild of Air Pilots' Sword of Honour to Giles. Of us all they were the only professionals in terms of experience and skill. They had worked in Antarctica during previous years with many different governmental organisations. Giles had a critical nature: vital to a good polar pilot. He was later asked what he thought about the amateur nature of Transglobe.

> I think probably deep down, early on before we even left London, I really doubted that they would succeed. I think the great thing is that the land team are not professionals at anything. I mean, they have learned how to cook in the case of Charlie; how to be a mechanic in Ol's case; and Ginnie, how to be a radio operator. Ran is a good leader, probably a great leader but he had to learn about navigation. The great thing about these four people is their persistence *in the face of terrible difficulties in getting across; not their individual abilities.*

I think Giles knew that much of our strength, despite our lack of experience, lay in our collective ability. Remove any one of us and the other three became a far less capable entity. Unfortunately, it was now clear that Ollie *would* leave us. He was determined not to give up his marriage and felt that he could no longer stay with us and keep Rebecca.

In England there was a lingering suspicion that he was using Rebecca merely as an excuse, that Ol had some other deeper reasons for leaving. Some suggested he might be frightened of the Arctic Ocean: I knew that, even if this were true, he would never leave because of it, any more than Charlie or I would. I was full of suppressed fear about the Arctic Ocean but this was no reason for giving up, having just completed the Antarctic crossing.

Another suggested motive was a deep rift between Ollie and the rest of us, most likely between him and me. Such rumours, once started, tend to mature over the years, so I would like to scotch this one fast, by quoting Ollie's own words when he was being interviewed at this time, by an American film team at Scott Base who asked him if the team individually had "gotten more happy as the expedition has progressed?"

> *Ollie: I don't think we have got more happy, but we certainly haven't got less happy. Ran and Ginnie tend to keep themselves to themselves. Back in 1976 and 1977 was the time Charlie and I got to know them . . . Since then we have worked with implicit trust between us. No, it hasn't got happier: it's always been happy.*
>
> *Interviewer: Both you and Charlie have a pronounced sense of humour. How do you feel about Ran? Does he have a sense of humour?*
>
> *Ollie: Charlie and I joke a lot the whole time and I think we reflect the lighter aspect of the expedition. Ran has more worries; I think his sense of humour is not as warped as Charlie's and mine. He is, I think, the finest expedition leader one can come across. He plans things to the most minute detail and he's very easy to work with – there is no, if you like, leader/others atmosphere; we are very much like a family. I certainly wouldn't have gone across with anyone else.*
>
> *Interviewer: And now you are going?*
>
> *Ollie: I think two is the best number. With two you have less equipment and two can generally do things quicker than three.*

However a message came from the Executive Committee that a

delegation of three, the Chairman, Sir Edmund Irving, Sir Vivian Fuchs and Mike Wingate Gray, would fly to New Zealand to ascertain that the question of a replacement for Ollie was thoroughly discussed. They were solidly against Charlie and me attempting the Arctic alone.

On 19th January the *Benjamin Bowring* came through on Ginnie's radio. She was seven miles out in heavy pack. Simon climbed up Observation Hill with his camera and the four of us walked out past Captain Scott's wooden shack to Hut Point. It was not difficult to imagine the feelings of the pioneers in the early days when their masted ships appeared on that same horizon. For weeks on end they posted look-outs on Observation Hill to scan the northern limits of McMurdo Sound. As our own little ship entered the bay I wondered whether our friends would all be there after their year of hard grind and charter work in the South Pacific.

The *Benjy B* finally slid between the ice floes below Scott's Hut and strains of 'Land of Hope and Glory' came over the ship loudspeakers. The two sections of the expedition were meeting up after a year and many miles. Not all eyes were dry, nor, in a short while, were many throats. Bryn Campbell of the *Observer* was on board, and so was a new film team. We made a few sorties into the foothills of Mount Erebus with them, and before we left Antarctica for ever the *Benjy B* was anchored off Cape Evans, the site of Captain Scott's main base, so that we could go ashore to see the hut from which Scott and his four chosen companions had made their last journey. The site has been carefully preserved by New Zealanders on visits from Scott Base. It is just as it must have been seventy years back: pony harnesses hung on hooks; Victorian chemical bottles in the 'laboratory' and seal's blubber spread over the lobby floor. On the granite hillock above the hut a rookery of penguins flapped and strutted in their dinner jackets and the two dozen Transglobers strolled about more quietly than was their wont. We felt, I think, a silent affinity with our dead countrymen, their journeys, long done, ours but half complete.

Back in the *Benjy B* we learned that six weeks before, in these very waters, the 2,500 ton German research vessel *Gotland II*, ice strengthened like ourselves, was crushed by encroaching pack-ice. By luck her deck cargo was five helicopters and the pilots were on board. Everyone was flown to a nearby island and later to a coastal summer base. Our skipper, Les Davis, who had now taken over from Admiral Otto Steiner, took note of the Lloyd's report: "The ship was of maximum ice security standard and her officers were experienced in Antarctic conditions." Les knew that the Arctic Ocean pack-ice would be twice as hazardous to any ship as this Antarctic ice, for it is harder and thicker in the north and individual floes are more massive. So his most testing time was yet to come.

We were rolling violently on 23rd February when the cloud-hung mass of Campbell Island was sighted. Soon we entered the protection of its long natural harbour between green hills. After fourteen months without a blade of grass, this remote but fertile land was a wonderful sight and not unlike a Hebridean isle.

A dozen New Zealand scientists worked at a base beside the entry fjord. They made us very welcome. We were the first British registered ship to call since records began in 1945, according to the base leader. He had his men show us the island. First a colony of sea lions playing in a rock-girt bay, then elephant seals wallowing in noisome pits from which they reared their ugly heads to mouth foul-breathed roars. All around were bogs of peat and beds of kelp and on a high hill flanked by cliffs we listened to the hollow clap of beaks where the rare Royal Albatross hens sat on eggs as big as cricket balls.

We left Campbell Island the same day bound for Lyttelton, New Zealand. On our way north to the Arctic, where the ship would leave the ice group off the mouth of the Yukon River in the Bering Sea, we would stop in New Zealand for careening and an exhibition, then for further trade exhibitions in Sydney, Los Angeles and Vancouver. Since we could not count on the Yukon River being ice-free until mid June, nor the North West Passage until late July, there was for once a slower pace to be kept to.

Anton was by now in love with little Jill, our cook, and planning to marry her. His diary told of the bad times as well as the good: "Jill furious in the galley; in tears because of the noise of pots and pans crashing back and forth. Spilled milk and coffee in the duty mess, broken glass in the pantry, filthy table cloths dampened for a non-slip surface and covered with muck."

Most of the New Zealand scientists we had taken on board at Scott Base had completed their work along the coast of Victoria Land, to the north west of McMurdo Sound. This had involved a geophysical survey of land and core sampling from the sea-bed, but our own oceanographers, Chris and Lesley, were still busy with their plankton trawls. They were delighted with the capture of an amphipod further south than ever found before. And two New Zealand zoologists were at most times of day or night to be found on the bridge spotting birds and mammals.

Although the lower Number Two hold was a joy to work in compared with cramped pre-Antarctic days when the cardboard hut sections alone had filled half its space, the surveyors had lashed a control caravan in its centre, so Ash Johnson, a Kiwi passenger helping with cargo listing, and I had to keep a permanent eye against emasculation on sharp corners and garrotting on lashing strops each time a new lurch sent us stumbling over the dim-lit equipment. The stink of mackerel had almost disappeared.

In the evenings groups would collect in the saloon, or squash into somebody's cabin to discuss the experiences of the last eighteen months. We were from such different backgrounds and outlooks, no subject brought out a single unified opinion.

The *Benjy B* crew had now shaken down into a cheerfully exuberant, argumentative but cohesive group who all worked together to make Transglobe a success. There were inevitably stresses and strains for conditions were tough: it was an old boat, there were no wages, the heat in the engine room in the tropics reached 42°C in the coolest corner, strong independent personalities frequently clashed, but on the whole conflicts were amicably resolved. Everyone got on with his or her particular job without being nagged for the standard of self-discipline was high. The skipper and his officers gave orders but then they had to fight for their food on equal terms with all the rest in the mess: no one pulled social rank.

As the ship rolled violently, plates and cups went back and forth. A wooden parrot, hung from the ceiling, gyrated above the saloon table and Bothie played endlessly with rubber balls which needed no throwing since now they rolled about with a life of their own. From time to time a dark wall of water struck the plate glass saloon window, then hissed away down the scuppers. I listened to the tropical memories of the year in Samoa, a part of Transglobe I had missed of necessity but with regret.

Unable to get charter work anywhere else after dropping the ice team at Sanae, Anton had agreed to ten months' cargo work between the coral islands of Samoa.

Based on Apia, Western Samoa, the *Benjy B* had monthly plied a 300-mile passage to the outer Tokelau Isles whose names the crew mispronounced with delight, Fakafao, Atafu and Nuknonu (Nookey-No-No!).

There is no air service to these islands and no harbours once there: their lagoons are ringed by atolls with no entry points big enough for ships. So the *Benjy B* had to lie off, unable to anchor owing to the great depth, and send her cargo and passengers in on small boats which could run the reefs.

"We was like a refugee ship," said Buzzard. "People and pigs everywhere. Couldn't walk without stepping on a chicken or a baby. Friendly people, though."

"Up on deck," Eddie Pike added, "they boiled rice in great cauldrons which they carried about till everyone was full. And down below we had up to twenty-five first-class passengers. Hicksie did the Polynesian steward act with them – he wore nothing but a blue sarong and a flower garland round the neck."

Dave Hicks had become Hicksie to distinguish him from Dave Peck who had re-joined the ship once his leg had recovered from the Great Banana Rescue.

"Hicksie treated them like children," added Buzzard, "and never allowed them any pudding till every scrap of their first course was eaten. He spoke pidgin English based on theirs but not intelligible to them or us."

There was much general guffawing about the table at this.

"It wasn't all fun," added Nigel Cox, the Irish radio operator. "Just a scratch on the leg meant several days on antibiotics. And dirt everywhere. We were infested with roaches, and mice and flies crawled all over, especially on open scratches. But it was an experience. Those islands were truly beautiful. I wonder if they'll remember us or even the *Benjy B*." He mused a while, then added, "I'd like Transglobe to be remembered as a group of people who gave up money, promotion and three years of their lives on a venture which they wanted to succeed, a common cause they all believed in."

As February passed by the weather slowly improved and by the time we reached the green hills of New Zealand life was back on a more even keel. It was raining as we entered Lyttelton harbour to put the ship into dry dock for inspection and careening. Fortunately, there were no expensive surprises and we were able to sail north to Auckland on 23rd March and our meeting with Sir Edmund Irving, Sir Vivian Fuchs and Mike Wingate Gray to discuss the thorny issue caused by Oliver's imminent departure. The Committee was determined Ollie should be replaced. I was equally determined that he should only be replaced if I found two of us alone could not cope. Charlie was not particularly adamant about the matter either way but, *if* there was to be no showdown, he was inclined to favour two. Ollie himself spoke strongly in favour of our being allowed to do as we saw best, since we had as much Arctic Ocean experience as did our Committee advisers.

I thanked Sir Edmund for passing on the views of those back home and tried to make my own points sound as reasonable. I quoted Wally Herbert, the only man to cross the Arctic Ocean before. During his crossing he wrote: "As a two-man party we would travel harder, faster and more efficiently than as a three-man unit."

"But not more *safely*," Sir Edmund pointed out.

I could not argue this point except in a roundabout fashion.

"Naomi Uemura," I said, "a five-foot tall Japanese, reached the North Pole alone and unscathed. I can see no reason why two hulking great Brits can't do likewise *and* carry on down the other side of the Arctic."

There was silence at this so I pressed on.

"The two of us have spent six years together including travel in Greenland, the Arctic Ocean and Antarctica. We know each other's limitations and strong points. We have worked out a mutually acceptable modus vivendi. However well we may know some third person in normal circumstances, he may turn out very different given the unique strains of Arctic Ocean travel. Quite apart from character interaction between us and such a third man, his very presence could easily undermine our own mutual compatibility."

Mike Wingate Gray, changing tactics, asked Charlie what *he* thought about another man. Charlie, as slippery as an eel and as difficult to pin down when he doesn't want to be, answered only part of the question.

"For the *wintering* at Alert I think I would prefer no one else but the three of us, including Ginnie. I do know another member of the team whom I could put up with but I don't think he would fit in with Ginnie and Ran. Equally I know that Ran has someone in mind who wouldn't suit me. So we are in a predicament where it would be better to keep just the three of us."

The trouble was that I had not trained a third person in ice travel since Geoff left us. There were two possible candidates who would be available at a pinch but neither was experienced at Arctic Ocean travel. I therefore resolved to put my side of the situation to Prince Charles when he visited the *Benjy B* in Sydney during his coming Australian visit and at the same time to hedge my bets by alerting the two possible reserves that they *might* be needed.

The fact that Prince Charles was prepared to take the risk of becoming involved in such discussions of expedition politics filled me with admiration. It would have been so easy for him to have suggested we sort out our own problems. Because he *did* act as final arbiter for the expedition, we were able to sort out such matters in a friendly manner by passing the buck upwards to someone whose judgement we all respected.

The meeting in Auckland was frank and friendly but it ended inconclusively. More meetings followed in London. Andrew Croft wrote: "The fact that you have no one adequately trained to be the third man has forced the Committee to compromise with you against their better judgement."

And five months later Sir Vivian Fuchs made it quite clear that if I did set out with no third man the blame, should things go wrong, would be entirely mine. In retrospect, I think he was correct in emphasising this when he did.

Captain Scott once gave a glimpse of his feelings about Committees in a letter to his friend, Nansen. "Whilst I have been trying to carry out the equipment [tests] on the precepts you taught me in Norway, a committee of thirty-two scientific men have been quarrelling as to where the expedition is to go and what it is to do. Too many cooks spoil the broth and too many men on the committee are the devil."

I, however, could not forget that without the backing of our Committee we would not have set foot in Antarctica, that their time, advice and support was given free and in goodwill and that, were they to agree to everything the field leader proposed, there would be no point in their existence.

The Auckland exhibition was opened by the Right Honourable Robert Muldoon, Prime Minister of New Zealand. In his speech he likened the Transglobers to old English merchant adventurers whose exploits struck responsive chords with New Zealanders. He forecast revitalised trade for British goods and was complimentary about the equipment he inspected at the exhibition.

Our hall was really the passenger terminal in Auckland's central harbour. The *Benjy B* was moored right alongside, an added attraction for our visitors. One thousand five hundred came on each of the first two days, on the third 8,000 flooded in and the last day was indecently crammed with 12,500, a long queue stretching down the terminal steps and out of the building.

Paul Clark left his job as deck-hand and took on the task of obtaining and selling Transglobe merchandise. At the beginning of the Auckland show he borrowed 6,000 dollars from one of the local sponsors. With this he bought T-shirts printed with the Transglobe logo and sold enough during the show to pay back the debt as well as to buy more stock for the next exhibition in Sydney.

The lithe and garlanded Maori girls of the Queen Victoria School sang us away from the quay, their grass skirts and their fine young voices at one with the blue sky and the sun on the sea. They wished us love and luck as they waved: *"Arohatinani."*

The passage to Australia was calm and warm. I had crated off for the Arctic a great deal of Antarctic equipment in two containers. The work for the Yukon River and North West Passage journeys could be done on the long voyage from Sydney to Los Angeles so, apart from fifty-two 'thank you' letters to Christchurch and Auckland, I tried to relax and get rid of my Antarctic pallor.

It is worth mentioning a bit about the exhibitions since they worked well and, as far as I know, had no precedent.

On a previous journey by hovercraft up the White Nile we held impromptu demonstrations of our equipment and machines in Khartoum and Kampala. Over ten million pounds' worth of export orders resulted, so we decided to set up similar but better organised shows during Transglobe with the aim of encouraging sales and establishing new import agencies.

For four years in London one of our volunteer staff had worked to set up eight exhibitions in Paris, Barcelona, Abidjan and Cape Town followed, after Antarctica, by Auckland, Sydney, Los Angeles and Vancouver. Everything had to be free of charge, from hire of hall, transport, trolleys, electrician, advertising, security and insurance to ship's berth, dockers' services, fresh water and ship's telephone. One or two major local companies sponsored each event and some 200 of our sponsor companies promoted themselves at the shows, free of any charges save for the cost of brochures in the correct language and of course their mobile display cabinet. Many of these were made of the same cardboard as our polar huts and were all stacked in the Number One hold between exhibitions. The theme of the exhibition was Reliability. We were not just plausible salesmen spouting about manufactured goods. Our lives had depended upon this equipment in extreme conditions. It was on show because it was the best.

Everyone on board had to lend a hand in getting the 300 200-pound display crates out of the hold and setting up. But it was worth it. We gained many export orders and set up many agencies for our sponsors large and small. In Sydney alone we instigated one order for two million dollars for Gestetner Duplicators and gained new business for our binoculars sponsor with the Australian Forces. Local British commercial attachés ensured that any local representatives of our exhibitors were fully involved. One day was set aside for commercially minded visitors; the next, buses would disgorge school groups to be given tours by a limping Dave Peck, Howard and Cyrus.

Paul Clark set up his merchandising stands and Eddie, with the Buzzard in attendance, wired up non-stop audio visual projectors and a film show of the Antarctic crossing introduced by HRH Prince Charles. Once every hour through the day Mark Williams, our ship's engineer, gave impressive demonstrations in one of our inflatable boats, now armed with wooden skids for ramming ice-floes. Since these were scarce, we asked the local harbour master to make an imitation ice-floe from a wooden pontoon, painted white and greased, and to float it just off the quayside. Once Dave Peck had marshalled the crowds with a loudspeaker, Mark proceeded to ram the heavy pontoon at speed and, to the amazement of all, initially his own too, fly over the top of the 'ice-floe' and land with a splash on the far side.

Howard Willson then gave lessons in water-walking in the fibreglass 'shoes' we'd had made for Arctic use.

Since there was great demand to see Bothie who was not allowed off the ship for quarantine reasons, Dave Peck always announced his presence at the bows of the *Benjy B*. Terry would then appear on cue with a barking Bothie in his arms.

During the evenings there were always local functions to attend, interviews with press and representatives from trade journals; on one occasion even a major ball where all the crew were hired tuxedos by the organisers.

In Sydney the *Benjy B* was moored to the harbour's passenger terminal, directly opposite the city's Opera House. On 14th April HRH Prince Charles visited us. On the boat deck we gave him three cheers and a miniature silver globe marked with our route by way of congratulations on his engagement to Lady Diana Spencer. Bothie joined the cheering with an aggressive yapping session which he stopped only when Prince Charles patted and spoke to him.

In the skipper's cabin I explained to our Patron the likely Arctic problems. He appreciated that things were unlikely to go as well as they had in the Antarctic and he noted my point about not accepting a replacement for Ollie. Afterwards he toured the exhibition, as did Dr Armand Hammer who kindly re-affirmed his support for our venture and said he would send further film teams to the Arctic to ensure the documentary film had no gaps in it.

The sponsors of our Sydney show estimated that some 31,000 visitors had passed through our doors and in all we reckoned that about 112,000 people came to our six exhibitions in France, the Ivory Coast, South Africa, New Zealand, Australia, America and Canada, which created a great deal of business for our sponsors. Exactly what the export figures finally were has not yet been quantified but everyone seemed delighted, in particular the various local British Consuls who were well pleased by our efforts to display the latest British technical inventions and specialised equipment to advantage.

When the last visitor had gone, the packing up carried on into the night. Everything had to be taken down, crated, returned to the *Benjy B* and restacked back in the hold: a tiring rigmarole but one we learned to do with speed and efficiency.

Whilst in Sydney, Charlie married Twink whom he had last seen when we were driving through France. The next day Anton married Jill. They would all honeymoon on the way to Los Angeles; the *Benjy B* was becoming quite a family ship.

To help Jill with cooking and cleaning, a pretty young New Zealander named Annie had joined us. The Buzzard had met her in the Wellington bank where she worked, fallen in love with her and ensured that she was smitten by his golden locks and lively ways. He secretly assured me that his designs were of a permanent nature "little buzzards and all that" and attributed his luck to Gnome Buzzard.

Paul Clark stayed behind to organise merchandise after-sales and Ollie to tidy up the aftermath of the exhibition. After that he would return to London and Rebecca. He promised to check up on the running of administration in the barracks. Ginnie was to fly back to England to go through her Antarctic tapes with the analysts at Sheffield University Space Physics department but she would re-join us in America.

On 17th April we left Sydney for Los Angeles. From there we would sail up to Vancouver to give another exhibition, and then follow the coastline north to the mouth of the Yukon River in Alaska. There we would disembark from the *Benjy B* and travel by rubber dinghy up the Yukon as far as we could into Canada. With luck we might get near to Dawson City. We would then truck the boats and all our gear by road from Dawson City to Inuvik, near the mouth of the Mackenzie River. From there we would set out in our dinghies through the North West Passage to Ellesmere Island at the northern tip of which is the remote weather station of Alert. There we would spend the dark winter months prior to setting out for the North Pole.

On the way across the Pacific Ocean from Australia to Los Angeles, I worked in my old hold in the *Benjy B*, now comparatively empty, to prepare the kit needed for the two rubber boat trips. It was sweltering hot down in the bowels of the ship as we wallowed along. One blazing day near the Equator, the skipper took pity on us all, stopped the ship and let us all, including Bothie, slip overboard for a swim in the cool Pacific swell.

President Reagan had kindly agreed to open our Los Angeles exhibition if his commitments made it possible.

Nigel showed me a copy of telex traffic between our London office and an American telex operator.

Telex operator: "I get no reply. Who is 440074?"

Ant Preston: "It is the White House."

"I know that but it is too broad."

"I want to send a telex to Ronald Reagan."

"U can't send a telex to Ronald Reagan. U have to give an office or department."

"One moment. Yes, the President's office."

"The number is ex-directory."

As it turned out the President was shot and wounded and so could not attend the exhibition. Instead he sent us a message:

My warmest congratulations to you all on your magnificent achievement of completing the 2,200 mile crossing of Antarctica on open snowmobiles. Now that you are half-way through your polar circumnavigation of the earth, we welcome you to the United States and pray that your luck and skill during the next half of your trip, which promises to be even more harsh and hazardous, will keep you from harm's way. You are attempting something which has never been done before which takes tremendous courage and dedication. The "can do" your expedition so perfectly exemplifies is still alive in the free world. We wish you Godspeed and clear sailing.

The charming black mayor of Los Angeles met the *Benjy B* on our arrival and officially gave us the key to the city. It was eight inches long and imitation copper. The Los Angeles exhibition went smoothly, although the site was in old deserted dockland and difficult for visitors to find. The local British Consul General reported back to London later that:

The Transglobe team gave a positive impression of a young dynamic Britain making use of new advanced technologies, displaying initiative and enterprise – qualities which Americans, particularly in the west United States, greatly admire. There is no doubt that the image of contemporary Britain was given a very good boost from which business prospects of participating firms can only be enhanced and benefit the export drive.

Once again the exhibition was laboriously taken down, packed away and put in the holds. Ginnie rejoined us and we all headed north for Canada in the *Benjy B*. But the atmosphere on board was unsettled. The excitement of the Antarctic success had faded. For the crew, the future looked dreary for soon they would drop off Charlie and me and be left to face another period of charter work or laying up whilst we struggled across the Arctic. For the land group, a journey of great uncertainty lay ahead and filled us with apprehension.

It was a time of squabbles and muted ill feeling. A chance visitor might have noticed nothing, for all seemed fine on the face of it, but in reality the uncertainties were causing upsets. I talked little with Charlie, for Twink naturally took up most of his time, but honeymooning on a crowded small boat must have been a great strain for both of them and for Anton and Jill. They had little privacy and were constantly being interrupted: nerves became frayed and tensions increased.

Charlie and I had worked together now for seven years. During all that time I had been married and so I had become accustomed to grappling with the two entirely different kinds of relationship: that between husband and wife and that between two explorers. But Charlie was having to make his adjustments in the midst of an expedition on a crowded boat. It was enough to make anyone feel fraught. I trusted Charlie with my life but that did not mean I knew him well. This was no bad thing: the fact that we had never been close friends meant that we need never fear losing a valued relationship through too much enforced proximity. For success in our venture there was no need for the various individuals to be friends, just equable companions. Marriage is something else again.

Back in London Oliver wrote to say that life was not going well there either.

> *The skidoos David brought back from Ryvingen have just sat in the barracks unprotected. None of the work I asked Simon to do was done in the Antarctic. You should ensure that Charlie does take the heads off and checks the pistons before use. The set-up back here is very depressing. The barracks are a shambles and I don't feel the office or committees are really pulling their weight . . . London is cripplingly expensive, even if you do nothing. I intend working for six months and seeing how the land lies then. At the moment Rebecca seems to be even encouraging me to do the North Pole, so if all goes well I could come out to Alert in the winter: that is, if the Committee allow it, which at present seems unlikely. All the best and keep your chin up. You are better off than I am here. I only wish I was with you. Luv Oliver.*

I wrote back wishing him well at finding a job and expressing my hope that he would soon be back with us.

As I worked at getting the rubber dinghies ready for our trip up the Yukon River and through the North West Passage, I became increasingly nervous about their vulnerability. As we might sink if the open Dunlop inflatable boats were punctured by ice-floes, I had had foam pumped into them as extra protection, but the company who had completed this work had rather overdone the injection of foam leaving very little room for air to be pumped in around the foam. Each inflatable was some eighty pounds heavier, at least double the weight I had expected to add, through this safety precaution.

Mark Williams, the ship's engineer who had done the pontoon

ramming demonstrations at the exhibitions, advised me that the boats responded with greater power when fitted with longshaft outboards. But the outboard company's representative in Sydney had said that short shafted engines would be best. My own memories of my 3,000-mile journey down the rugged rivers of British Columbia in 1970 suggested that long shafters worked well with heavily laden boats, so I took them but hedged my bets by packing one short shafter as a spare.

The boats were thirteen and a half feet long and would be heavily laden, doubly so as we would only be using two boats to carry all our gear, whereas we had originally presumed that Oliver would be sharing some of the load in a third boat. To power us we had forty horsepower outboards but now Charlie was worried that these engines would not be strong enough. I had asked him to carry all the spare parts in his boat since he was mechanic but he now suggested they should be spread evenly between us in case of a capsize. "Rubbish," I said, "nobody will capsize and if they do everything is lashed in so nothing will be lost."

We held a successful exhibition in Vancouver, leaving on 19th June, to start a race against time. We must get to the mouth of the Yukon by 27th June, as I had worked out it would take us sixteen days to cover the 1,100 miles of the river and six days to drive up the newly opened dust road from Dawson City to Inuvik. We should be on our way through the North West Passage by the third week of July.

Ginnie and Bothie drove north from Vancouver by way of the Alaska Highway to Dawson City to set up a radio base. Simon stayed in Vancouver to tie up loose ends before joining Ginnie.

Less than a dozen expeditions have ever successfully navigated the North West Passage in either direction. Those few all used craft with some protection from the elements and took an average of three years to get through because the pack-ice which besets the narrow coastal sea-lane makes navigation impossible, except for a few weeks, most years. The ice could not be expected to break up, even if 1981 was a good ice year, until mid-July. It was likely to re-form again over the sea by early September which gave us a maximum of six weeks to navigate 3,000 miles of ice-strewn mist-covered ocean, if all went well.

As we edged past the Aleutian Islands and up the Bering Sea, I prowled about restlessly on board, champing with frustration. We had got to be at the mouth of the Yukon by the 27th, yet we seemed to be beset by endless head winds which slowed us down to a miserable crawl for days on end. By 29th June we were still 112 miles away from our objective, bouncing about in a Force 6 from the north and pitching around in twelve fathoms of shallow water. At one point we had to stop for thirty minutes to fix a fuel leak which added to my impatience.

Research in England had intimated that the ship should be able to approach to within nine miles of the Yukon River mouth without running aground on shallows caused by silt, but as we got nearer, we realised this information was unreliable. By the evening of 30th June the echo sounder showed that there was only eight to ten feet of water under us as we steamed inshore with a ten knot wind whipping across our faces. Fourteen miles offshore Eddie checked with the lead line, as we anchored at eight p.m. There was only six feet of water beneath us.

I was anxious to be away as soon as possible, so the next day we launched the two rubber dinghies, although we were still fourteen miles from the mouth and despite a twenty knot wind which was lashing up a nasty sea.

The dinghies slammed up and down in the lee of the *Benjy B* as we loaded them. Bryn Campbell from the *Observer* was to come with us up the Yukon and, like Charlie and I, wore a rubberised foul-weather suit.

After bidding farewell to the crew we cast off from the ship and set out through choppy seas for a shoreline we could not even glimpse from the surging wave tops. Very soon the *Benjy B* was a faraway speck yet the low, featureless Yukon flats were nowhere to be seen.

After an hour's buffeting, I noticed the swirl of white breakers ahead and I thought back to the very first day of a Canadian river expedition ten years before. Bryn Campbell had been on board my boat then and within an hour of our setting out was very nearly drowned after being knocked overboard by a branch and caught in a swirling log jam.

History I knew has a habit of recurring.

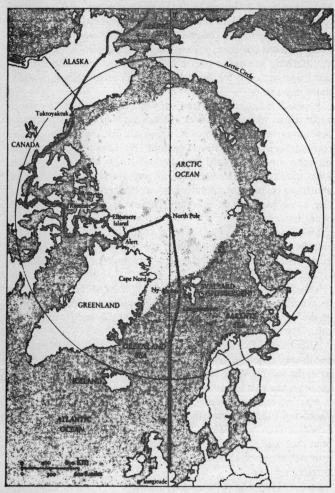

The Arctic

10

Alaska – Race Against Time

JUNE–JULY 1981

No. There's the land. Have you seen it?
It's the cussedest land that I know,
From the big dizzy mountains that screen it,
to the deep deathless valleys below.

'YUKON', ROBERT SERVICE

Bryn began the journey in my boat but navigation and compass work was difficult with the two of us on board. I manoeuvred close to Charlie and Bryn edged across to join him. Bryn wrote of the next few minutes:

The waves began to break over us, hitting us hard from behind. Often we were completely awash and I marvelled at our buoyancy – a stubborn muscular resilience you could actually feel. But as we watched Ran's boat pounded by the sea and disappear into the ten-foot deep troughs, we had all too vivid an image of how vulnerable we were. I turned to talk to Charlie and saw him lifted bodily by a surge of water and thrown clean over my head. As the boat capsized, I tugged my feet free of the fuel lines and jumped as far away from the propeller as I could. Then the hull crashed down beside me.

Some distance ahead of Charlie and Bryn I was beginning to

suspect that the evil conditions were not purely the result of the current squall. The surface turbulence could be caused by the sea-floor conditions over which the water moved. The combination of Yukon flood water from prolonged rains and the annual thaw, the probably uneven silt banks beneath and the eastward set of the Bering Sea against these banks, could have combined to produce a local cauldron.

A wave of silt-laden seawater crashed down on my boat from behind. Another surged in from the side. For a long moment I could see nothing but foam and spray. I rubbed my eyes which stung from the salt and at the top of a new breaker glanced backwards. A momentary flash of orange movement, then nothing as I slammed down into a furrow. The next upswing was a big one and allowed me a clear view of the turmoil behind. Charlie's boat was upside down 500 yards back. There was no sign of either occupant.

It was a while before I could even begin to turn round. The secret of survival in these shallow riotous waters was to remain totally alert and keep the bows at all times into the next breaker. I remembered the thrill of great whirlpools and the curling tubes of hydraulic waves below mid-rapids boulders. In these same boats we had come safely through far worse conditions on the rivers of British Columbia. It was a matter of aim and balance. After another big one, I whipped the tiller round and the game little boat sped through 180° in time to face the next attack head on.

Now the wind was more ahead than behind and this was safer. On each upsurge I crept closer to the upturned inflatable, my mouth dry with apprehension for still I could see no bodies. Then an orange clad Charlie dragged himself slowly on to the boat's bottom. I had asked the manufacturers to sew hand-holds along the hull for this sort of incident but in wet mitts it was difficult to keep a grip on them. Soon I saw that Charlie had grasped Bryn's hood and was helping him up. I breathed out with relief.

A wave deposited me close to the others. Almost too close for my propeller sliced the water beside their rubber hull. I needed more control. Unlashing my cargo tarpaulin I began to chuck full jerry cans overboard. With six gone and some 300 pounds lighter, there was more response to the tiller but, since everything had to be done with one hand, time had passed by. The others looked blue with cold. Using the hull handgrips they were trying to right the boat with their weight. It did not work.

I coiled up a safety line and tried to come alongside. Both craft were flung about violently. Twice I was almost washed over them, then I flung the wet rope.

"Got it," Charlie shouted. "Keep it slack while I fix it."

With the boats secured, I left my engine on idle and jumped across. Together we heaved to right the boat but she continued to wallow with little response. A wall of water rushed by tearing the rope from its fixture point on Charlie's boat. My boat was adrift and rapidly moving away from us. Stunned and breathless from our exertion I watched with my mouth open.

Charlie's voice interrupted my mental void. "What a bloody silly time and place to get drowned." He was about to leap off our little patch of safety.

Released from my reveries I jumped clumsily as far as I could towards my boat, by now some twenty yards away. Each new wave increased the gap. My survival suit made any movement heavy. I felt futile but an edge of desperation and a burst of effort saw me beside the hull and clear of the propeller. Clambering on board, I prepared a second rope. Our luck was good: there was a brief lull between waves, no more than a minute, but enough for Charlie to attach the line to the centre of one side. Staying on my boat I reversed away until the line was taut with elasticity. Charlie and Bryn bent their backs and, on the next upsurge, their boat flipped over like a reluctant limpet prised by a fisherman's blade.

Naturally Charlie's outboard defied all attempts to re-start it so I made fast a long line and began to take the others in tow. If my own outboard had stalled, our lives would probably have been lost and the expedition brought to an abrupt halt. True, we carried in Charlie's boat a spare engine which had not broken free and, although wet, had not ingested water. But the chances were slim.

However, the one engine plodded on and tortoise-like we returned to the *Benjy B*, our only haven of safety. In her lee the seas were calmer and the crew soon had us all safely aboard. We said hello again to the friends who, three short hours before, had waved us off for a likely three years' absence. Dave Hicks brought mugs of hot tea.

Charlie had lost nothing but his rifle. Bryn was unusually silent. The incident had made a considerable impression on him, though he said little at the time. His main camera and favourite lens were lost but, more serious, his inner equanimity had, not surprisingly, been

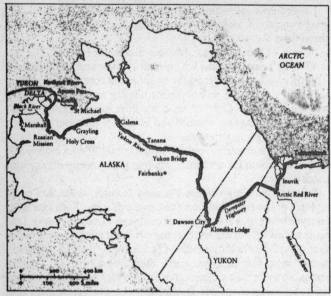

From the Yukon mouth to Tuktoyaktuk

ruffled. He looked defensively tense when, a few hours later, I made him a proposition.

"Bryn, would you mind handling a third boat yourself up the Yukon River?"

There was no outburst but he was obviously unhappy at the prospect. His personal objective was purely to cover the river journey photographically as well as he possibly could. He did not see how this would be possible if, like us, he was having to look after a boat, with one hand at all times on the tiller. It was indisputable that there would be times when he could get better photos through being in a third boat. But, *most* of the time, he was convinced his photographic scope would be diminished.

He could plainly see that my motives were selfish. All I wanted was to succeed in getting from A to B as quickly as possible and catch up on the precious time that we had lost. I knew we could ascend the Yukon with three inflatables. All my load plans had been prepared for it. Weight is critical to small inflatables: a few pounds can mean the difference between their 'planing', almost gliding, and their failure to 'get off the hump' and thus dragging through the water using too much fuel. With only two boats, three heavy people and all their necessary equipment we would probably double the time needed for the Yukon. This I could not afford to allow simply to maintain a long-standing friendship with Bryn, a man whom I greatly admired.

So, despite his obvious dislike of the idea, I pressed him and he kindly made no open complaints. But his mood towards me underwent a change. Luckily he shared two great loves in life with Charlie, Rugby and cards, and the two had during the expedition become great friends.

As I had despatched Oliver's craft back to England for David to have airlifted with other cargo for Alert, I had to borrow an ancient inflatable patched all over from past wounds, from Anton who kindly donated it to us for use as a third boat. Now we needed to find a less hazardous approach route to the Yukon's mouth.

The skipper took the *Benjy B* south some thirty miles to the Black River which is connected to the Yukon. Again we nudged inshore as close as Les dared. Nine miles offshore, with twenty-four feet of water beneath the hull we waited for good weather; but it worsened, with ugly skies and driving waves. We knew the breakers closer to land would be as bad as before since a Force 5 gale was blowing from the north west. Overnight this increased to Force 7. Soon the ship began to strike the sea floor when pitching in the heavy swell, so Les weighed anchor and we moved to deeper water.

That night we made radio contact with an Alaskan barging company who advised us to try another mouth of the Yukon much further north. On my maps this northern mouth did not appear to connect with the main river but to merge instead with inland swamps. Our radio contact assured us this was not so; we should head for this mouth called the Apoon Pass to the north of Norton Sound.

Together with the skipper, Anton and I pored over the charts. How to close with the Apoon Pass? A glance at the soundings off its mouth indicated the best course would be to go sixty miles east of the pass and anchor off Whale Islet, in thirty-two feet of water. The inflatables would have but four miles of protected water to negotiate to the harbour of St Michael village, the original Russian settlement in Alaska. There we could seek advice about the coastal journey to enter the Apoon.

With 120 miles to go, off a dangerous lee-shore, one of the tie bolts which hold the ship's engine in place sheared. This had happened before and Ken Cameron had only one spare bolt left. This he fitted as we floated slowly towards the Alaskan coast. After eight hours of toil down below, the engineers were satisfied although anxious lest another bolt sheared with no replacement available. Early on 3rd July we reached Whale Islet and, after brief farewells – for the second time round is seldom so emotional – we again went overboard.

St Michael was a sunny windswept place of sodden turf with a few desultory wooden houses connected by duckboards. Once it had been a thriving Russian hamlet, indeed most of the Eskimos had Russian sounding names, but then the capitalist Czars had sold Alaska to the Americans; now the village had the air of a ghost town. Wyatt Earp had retired here when his gun-toting days were over, to become the keeper of the local beer saloon. The local fuel agent suggested that we follow the coastline west to the Apoon Pass and then travel up river as far as the village of Kotlik. He offered to guide us in his own fibreglass boat, a Boston whaler. This was four or five feet longer than the inflatables and about the same width. Like them it was open but its great advantage was a more robust transom which would take two outboards and so allowed twice the thrust. The disadvantage was its weight, which made it impossible for two men to beach, let alone portage, over shallows or rocks.

The coastal journey was slow, wet and cold for, west of the sheltering promontory of St Michael, we met the full surge of the Bering Sea. Despite the shortness of the journey, some seventy miles, we took from midnight on 3rd July until well into the next day to reach Kotlik and, on arrival, we were soaked through, stiff and cold. In itself this mattered not at all but it did not augur well for the future: here the water and the air were comparatively warm but up in the North West Passage both would be near freezing. I made up my mind to change from inflatables to a Boston whaler, such as our guide to Kotlik owned, after the Yukon journey. It was a question of intuition more than persuasion through the weight of evidence. We would get wet in either type of boat. The amount of fuel used for distance travelled was fairly similar. The amount of cargo space was about the same. The two main factors I juggled with were the better speed of the whaler compared with the portability of the inflatables. The whaler won by a short head.

Our two new inflatables would be fine for the Yukon but Anton's old boat was not fit for further use without major repairs, so I left it with the Kotlik state trooper, a policeman with sheriff-like powers. In return I obtained an old and dented aluminium dinghy with a flattish bottom and so light I could lift it with one hand. On flat river water it was adequate but if we were to run into rapids . . . the state trooper clicked his teeth together: "Not so good. A couple of waves and she'll go straight down." The thought of Bryn losing the rest of his camera gear turned me cold; he would eat me alive. So I gave Bryn my inflatable and put my own gear in the aluminium river boat.

The state trooper had a radio telephone, so I asked him if I could use it to contact Ginnie, who was staying at the Klondike Lodge just east of Dawson City. The Lodge was a small truck-repair, garage-cum-hotel, where, in exchange for food and the use of a bedroom, Ginnie made beds, washed up and waited at table in the tea-room. Late that evening I made contact with her and asked her to obtain an open Boston whaler with two outboards to power it and to get everything, in twenty days' time, to Inuvik where the northern road runs out and the Mackenzie River begins. As we couldn't afford to buy all this extra equipment, she would also have to obtain full covering sponsorship for the boat, the engines and the cost of transportation to northern Canada. Ginnie didn't sound in the least perturbed by this complex order. She said that her Land Rover and trailer were in good repair but that Bothie was suffering from mosquitoes that favoured his nose and ears.

That night the state trooper kindly allowed us to sleep in the Kotlik jail. There were three little cells, dark but protected from rain and mosquitoes, and we laid our bags out gratefully. Unfortunately a drunken Eskimo ran amok and Charlie was thrown out of his cell. This was acceptable since by squeezing up we still had sleeping room. But, an hour later, another Eskimo threatened to shoot our state trooper who naturally conducted a pre-emptive strike with his Eskimo deputy and hauled the would-be assassin into the second cell. We were homeless again.

Fortune was with us for the Yukon salmon run happened to be in progress that very week, the annual event which makes more money than anything else for those Eskimos and, further east, Indians who own nets and a boat or a fishwheel trap. So the ramshackle Kotlik fish station was open. A private company which paid cash to the locals for their fresh salmon, prepared and boxed it, then flew it out once a day by small plane, from a strip of muddy grass nearby. The fish folk let us sleep on their floor and fed us waffles and coffee.

We rose early. The rain had stopped and I went to thank the state trooper.

"Be careful," he said, "most of the year there are no rapids for a thousand miles upstream from here. But this is the time of the summer winds. I have seen waves as big as houses out on the river. No river man will operate on certain stretches during the winds. You get the wrong conditions, man, and you'll sure as hell drown."

"But you say there are no rapids," I protested.

"Sure I do. This is something different but just as bad for a boat. Mebbe worse. Lookit: the winds power down the river canyon and strike the water. All you need is a strong south wind hitting a north-south canyon with the water running *into* the wind."

He drew a diagram in the dust of his hut floor. I noticed his wife was an attractive Eskimo girl.

"The down flowing ripples get whipped up till you've got line after line of standing waves real close together. You get caught in that lot, fellah, and you'll get to Dawson like I'll see heaven."

I thanked him but a last thought struck me. "When you say waves as big as houses. How big's that?"

"Twelve feet high, friend. Twelve feet high."

We left around midday and the three boats moved well despite full loads of fuel. Past the deserted hamlets of Naguchik and Hamilton to the Nunachik Pass. Deep forest closed in on either bank until, by an encampment called Kravaksarak, we joined a major arm of the Yukon, the Kwikpak. This in turn, after five hours, led to a place of many forested islands and the river, brown and immensely powerful so soon after the break-up spate, widened to two miles or more. It would be easy to go wrong in the maze of winding channels but our maps were accurate.

Not long afterwards, a thirty-five-year-old American, Carl McCunn, asked to be left alone in an Alaskan valley to photograph wildlife. When the plane went back to fetch him eight months later, they found they had left him for too long; frostbitten, starving and frightened, he had shot himself with his last rifle bullet. The diary he left behind him began with records of his delight at the wail of the loon and the beauty of the short flowering season but ended in a bizarre scrawl as the cold and the loneliness closed in.

We too found delight in the peace, the wildness of the scenery and the glimpses we gained of foxes, bears and many river birds. We had to watch for sandbanks and floating snags but the miles slid by. We progressed through the twilit night without sleep and covered 150 miles. But on reaching the river settlement of Marshall we were still over a week behind schedule with little hope of gaining time. Every hour lost on the so far balmy river could represent a day of painful progress up north, for we were already operating within the narrow eight week time-corridor of the Arctic summer. One of our out-boards had developed troubles which Charlie had been unable to solve, so I bargained with an Eskimo in Marshall called Simeon. He owned three outboards and said he might sell me one. He was a proud man and wished to show he would not be rushed into a deal. I followed him about the village awaiting his reply. He went shopping in the single store and smiled at me from time to time. He was considering it. I followed him down to the river bank, to an odd low shack like a chicken coop where steam seeped through the rafters, for it was the village sauna. He crawled through the single low entry hole and must have stripped off inside. I could see several pairs of bony legs in a row. I paced about outside swatting at the mosquitoes for twenty minutes. When the old man emerged, his skin shining, he looked at me and nodded. The deal was on.

Next day we set off again but, three hours out, the thin wooden slat on the transom of my aluminium boat split and the engine 'jumped' clear of the boat and sank, breaking its safety cord.

I carried a spare, a light eighteen horsepower model, and clipped this on instead. We progressed but slowly. I gnashed my teeth with frustration and told myself all about Solomon and the lilies of the field but it did no good: I continued to fret.

For a while now the river had been getting gradually narrower but after seemingly endless hours struggling hard against a seven or eight knot current which frequently raced down upon us through rock-girt canyons, the river broadened out as it passed the lonely village of Russian Mission. High above the village, on a forest-clad hill, stood the Balkan silhouette of a Russian Orthodox church. Half an hour past this village, I looked back to see Charlie's boat drifting round in circles in mid-river. His engine had given up the ghost and he was unable to restart it. There was nothing to be done but to turn round and float back on the current to Russian Mission for repairs.

Bryn seemed a touch despondent and said he would like to spend an extra day photographing the village, the church and the graveyard with its Orthodox memorial crosses. Bryn's job was photography and he had not been getting the results so far that he had anticipated. The blame for this he would be quite correct in laying at my door, so I acquiesced, but inwardly I seethed at the loss of time this would entail.

I found myself silently annoyed with Charlie at his apparent inadequacy with the outboards. Yet this, too, I knew to be my fault, since there had been plenty of time during the expedition to have Charlie given extra instruction by local outboard service centres in addition to the basic training we had all received.

I spoke to Ginnie again that night. She had located, through friends in London and New York, a Manhattan concern called Morgan Stanley who had kindly agreed to buy an eighteen-foot Boston whaler for us. Evinrude's boss, whom Ginnie finally located in Hong Kong, agreed to let us have two sixty-horsepower outboards. A new whaler was available in Vancouver and Simon had simple modifications completed in a local boatyard, including an extra skin of fibreglass on the hull. Now Ginnie had quickly to fix free transport for the boat to reach Inuvik.

The *Benjy B* had returned to Vancouver and was berthed in the city harbour. When Anton heard I was planning to use a whaler he was unimpressed. He wrote:

> *I personally think that a Boston whaler is not a clever move. Its use to Ran is going to be very limited as it will only be useful in open icefree water. It weighs 1,500 pounds plus the weight of forty gallons of fuel and two sixty-horse power engines at 260 pounds each. It will be quite impossible to pull across ice. It cannot be flown anywhere in the Twin Otter, so they will have to ditch it before they've got half-way. Also the engines use up eight gallons of fuel per hour. Even if they can do thirty m.p.h., should there be any rough sea, they will be reduced to a crawl or risk breaking its back with all the fuel weight. Nothing to do with me but the inflatables without the polystyrene filling would definitely have been the best bet.*

With the outboards repaired and Bryn looking happier, we set out from Russian Mission on a blustery morning. I noticed with surprise that no boats were out or about, nor was there any other sign of life. This was especially strange since it was the middle of the salmon run, the short annual period when a healthy income could be made on the river.

I received some nasty little shocks during the morning and took quite a bit of water in the aluminium boat. The inflatables could happily fill to the brim with water and carry on floating high, but any water in my dinghy had to be removed at once. Draining was only possible when moving fast enough to tip the bows up, then a clumsy wooden bung could be removed from a hole near the base of the transom. Unless the plug was replaced after draining, this hole could cause the boat to leak rapidly as soon as she slowed down and returned to a level plane. Lose the bung and things could get tricky.

Until noon the confused state of the river made me cautious but not alarmed. I noticed a pall of dust in the sky further upriver but when we reached the area where I thought I had seen it, there was nothing there. Just a trick of the light it seemed.

But some fifteen miles short of Holy Cross we entered a long narrow valley heavily forested on either side where the dust cloud effect was again evident. At the entrance to the valley an Eskimo fishing village nestled on one bank, its river boats drawn well up above the shingle bank. Two men watched us pass. I waved. There was no response but a slight shaking of the head from the older of the two.

The water began to careen about, striking with miniature breakers against the rock walls on the rim of each minor curve. But still I felt no undue threat beyond the normal swell and undulation of the great river's forces. As I nosed further out into the northerly-bearing valley, an unseen surge moved against the right side of my boat and almost tipped me off my plank seat by the tiller.

With little warning, waves unlike any I had seen except in sizeable rapids seemed to grow out of the water like boils erupting from the riverbed. Breaking into a sweat, for I have a healthy fear of rough water, I steered quickly for the nearest bank. This was unfortunately the 'cut' bank, indicating that side of the river where the faster current runs. 'Lee' banks are very often low and dressed with gentle sand slopes for there the water is quiet. Where the river flows down a straight stretch, cut and lee banks may alternate on either side depending on the configuration of the riverbed.

Dust clouds emanated from the cut bank as I made to escape the central turmoil. It was as though a dragon breathed there. As I closed with the bank, a pine tree toppled over and crashed into the river. Then another and, with it, a whole section of the bank itself collapsed. The roar of my outboard drowned all other sounds and the forces of destruction which gnawed at the river's banks operated in silence as far as I was concerned. This added to the sinister, almost slow-motion appearance of the phenomenon, for such it was to me. I could not at the time grasp what was happening. I had, after all, boated up or down thousands of miles of wild rivers in North America and never once experienced this. Also, my private, long-nurtured idea of the Yukon was of a slow wide river as gentle as the Thames.

Above the collapsed bank I saw that the forest, from undergrowth to the very tops of the giant pines, was bent over and alive with movement. A great wind was at work, although in my hooded suit on the boat I could feel nothing.

For a moment I hovered in indecision. The waves in the middle of the river, some 600 yards wide at this point, were totally uninviting yet any minute my boat was liable to disappear under a falling pine, should I remain close in. There was no question of landing. No question of trying to turn broadside on and then head back downstream. My boat climbed and fell like a wild thing; shook as though in a mastiff's jaws, then veered towards the crumbling cut bank in response to unseen suction.

Ahead the river narrowed into a bottleneck, the banks grew steeper and the chaotic waves of the river's spine here extended almost clear across our front. Between standing waves and crumbling bank, I glimpsed a sag in the water. It was fleetingly possible to see the river actually mounting in height the further away it was from the bank. I had often heard that the centre of a river can be several feet higher than at the edges given sufficient flow and force, but never before had I clearly viewed the effect. It was distinctly off-putting.

I pushed with both hands on the tiller and the boat, reluctantly, edged away from the cut bank and began to head obliquely across the river. Perhaps things were better on the far side. But to get there I had to pass through the middle of the river, where the turbulence was greatest and the hydraulic waves so close together that my boat no sooner fell down the face of one than the next raced curling above me. It needed just one brief error on the tiller and I would add critically to the ten inches of silt-laden water already swilling around my feet. I would sink within seconds.

From the corner of my eye I noticed Bryn had seen my dilemma and moved his inflatable as close as the turmoil allowed. When I sink, I thought, Bryn's boat will be my only chance. "As big as houses" I remembered the state trooper's warning. I could see why such an exaggeration might come about. These waves were no more than four or five feet high yet their configuration, violence and closeness would make any local river boat a death trap for its inmates.

Before another wave could swamp my wallowing craft I turned broadside on to the hydraulics, applied full throttle and headed straight into the maelstrom in the centre of the river. Whether sheer luck or the shape of the waves saved me I do not know, but no more water came inboard. Much of the time it was like surf-riding along the forward face of a breaker, then a violent incline and sideways surge as the old wave passed beneath and the next one thrust at the little tin hull.

An edge of exhilaration broke through the sticky fear which till then held me in thrall. For the first time since entering the turbulence I realised there was a chance of getting through and began to experience the old thrill of rapids riding from the days long past when we had tackled far greater waves from the comparative safety of unsinkable inflatables.

How long it took to cross the river was impossible to gauge but gradually the waves grew less fierce and less close and then there was quiet water but for the outwash from the rough stuff. Ahead I could see, between waves and lee bank, a lane of smooth water edged by sand. Bryn and then Charlie emerged from the waves like bucking broncos. Both were smiling for my narrow escape had not gone unnoticed.

There were other stretches where conditions were tricky but never a patch on that first windy valley. That night we stopped in Holy Cross and the keeper of the travellers' lodge, Luke Demientieff, told us we were lucky to be alive. We had been travelling north in the first big southerly blow of the year in winds exceeding seventy knots.

"Even paddle steamers," he said, "would not, in the old days, venture at such a time."

We had covered the worst stretch of the river in the worst possible conditions and, as far as the riverside folk were concerned, we were quite mad.

When I asked him how anyone should know or care that we had passed, Luke said: "It only needs one pair of eyes from one riverside shack to see you go by for the radio phones all along the river to start buzzing. When you passed the old huts at Paimiut and entered the slough by Great Paimiut Island the word was about you were goners." He paused and added with a chuckle, "Still we're pleased you made it to the lodge after all. Business has been poor lately."

For days we progressed up the river across the face of Alaska towards Yukon Territory and the Canadian border. Deserted shacks, long overgrown yet still named on the maps, were often the only sign of life for fifty miles or more. Evocative names such as Debauch Mountain and Old Woman Cabin gave an atmosphere of days long gone. On one short stretch the map mentioned Old Andreafsky, Wilburs Place, Konolunuk and Kwikloaklol, but all we saw was a few empty huts in the trees and a wilderness of wooded hills and tangled creeks. At other times sheer cliffs hung down from racing storm clouds: these were particularly spectacular where the 4,000-foot high mountains of the Kokrines reared to a halt at the very edge of the river.

By travelling long hours we were trying to make up lost time, but always some new mechanical delay seemed to hold us up. At Tanana, I contacted Ginnie and asked her if she could bring the Land Rover and trailer to the only bridge across the Yukon River between the sea and Dawson City by 15th July. If we too could reach there by then, we might yet make it back by road to Dawson City by 16th July which would give us a good chance of entering the North West Passage on time. We had done well over a thousand miles in our rubber boats since 1st July and must now keep this speed up if we were to catch the Beaufort Sea free of ice. Even a week's delay could lose us a year.

It was a long and tiring drive over mountain passes for Ginnie but the pick-up went ahead as planned and we sold the old aluminium boat to a local lad at the Yukon Bridge for two hundred dollars. I was almost sad to see it go. With the inflatables and all our gear loaded, we headed for Dawson City, reporting our arrival in Canada to the Royal Canadian Mounted Police around midnight on the 16th. The head Mountie said that we had been lucky to get through: "The bad winds have caused seven drownings round here during the past three weeks. Mostly canoeists. They just fill up and sink. Many of them don't wear life jackets because they spoil their suntan."

The 700-kilometre route from Dawson City to the north coast had once been patrolled by Mounties with dog sledges. In 1911 one Corporal Dempster had been sent to search for a lost patrol and located their frozen bodies after a journey of great hardship, so the new 1979 highway along the old route now bears his name. The only road on the American continent to be pushed north of the Arctic Circle, its construction for oil workers in a land of permafrost was a notable feat: largely snowed under in winter, it's still inclined to get waterlogged in summer.

My plan to move north at once was foiled by a further four days' delay because the raging winds and local storms had destroyed part of the road. Whilst we waited for it to be re-opened, we completed arrangements for the Boston whaler Simon had been working on to be transported from Vancouver to Inuvik by an old friend, Bob Engel of North West Territorial Airways, who brought it in on board his Hercules C 130.

While we waited, Ginnie, Charlie, Bryn and I visited the sights of the Klondike, scene of one of the world's great goldrushes. Open seams are still worked by hopefuls from all over the world, though they are not as profitable as they were in their heyday. Diamond Tooth Gertie's Saloon, with its blackjack tables, can-can girls and bouncers in cowpoke gear, is still going strong and, outside Dawson, the countryside is stiff with fascinating prospectors' detritus from the gold days.

We were joined by Jackie McConnell, a Scot who had accompanied me down the rivers of British Columbia in a rubber boat ten years before. He'd so loved Canada that he had left the army and emigrated. I had met no one as tenacious nor as easy to get along with as Jackie in all my previous travels; it was good to see him again, although he could only spare the time to stay with us until Tuktoyaktuk, on the coast.

News came at length that the road was re-opened and we set out to drive north to Inuvik. The route wound through a virgin land of rolling forest, tumbling creeks and very little else; there can be few roads left in the world which are so desolate and unspoilt; long may it remain that way. We crossed the Eagle River where, fifty years ago, the Mad Trapper of Rat River had killed a Mountie and been hunted for weeks after by posses of angry vigilantes. A gun battle beside the river finally proved that the Mounties usually get their man.

Long hours of rain had made the road as slippery as an ice rink and we helped one Indian tow his pick-up truck from the glutinous mire in a roadside ditch. Otherwise the hours passed with hardly a vehicle to be seen. Eventually we came to the north-flowing Mackenzie River, which we crossed by ferry early on the second day and then drove on to Inuvik, a small town clinging to the river's eastern bank, about a hundred miles from the sea.

Here we met up with Simon who had flown in with the Boston whaler. The crew of the *Benjy B*, he told us, were making themselves at home in Vancouver, since Anton had not been able to find any charter work as yet. Dave Hicks, always original, had discovered a local nudist camp with no beer vendors. This, he decided, was a crying shame and must be put right. So he purchased beer, obtained ice from an ice machine in a hotel beside the *Benjy B* and spent the summer naked, dispensing ice cold beer cans on the beach. Many of the others found work gardening and house painting. Mark Williams, the engineer, had a motorbike accident and almost lost one arm, so he sadly had to leave the expedition. Terry, the bosun, made friends with the local Irish population who frequented the pubs beside the ship and sang rousing IRA songs late into the night.

Simon now fitted together the engines, steerage linkage and fuel systems to the Boston whaler and explained all the various mechanisms to Charlie, then launched it into the Mackenzie River. Charlie, Ginnie and I then started off for the sea, followed by Jackie McConnell and Bryn in one of the inflatables. Simon took all the base camp equipment along on the river ferry for the Land Rover and trailer could come no further and would be driven back to Vancouver by a friend.

On the afternoon of 24th July we were back on schedule as we entered the harbour of Tuktoyaktuk in the North West Passage; here Jackie and Bryn left us. Although it had been an uncertain gallop to get here on time, filled with vicissitudes, it had been a useful lesson testing us and our boats to their limits; we had gained much useful experience within the confines of comparatively tame countryside which was now to stand us in good stead along a barren and mostly uninhabited coastline.

From Tuktoyaktuk we would be navigating 3,000 miles of icy water to Alert, traversing through a desolate archipelago whose only inhabitants were a few Eskimos and the manned but isolated Distant Early Warning radar posts. For four years I had written to the

Canadian and American forces who man these posts for permission to use these stations as bases. They had at length agreed that they would hold fuel and ration boxes for us, provided we supplied all the fuel and food and got it to the stations. Nordair, the subsidiary of Air Canada who provision the stations, kindly agreed to fly all our stuff in free of charge and had done so during the month of June.

We would not have any form of re-supply between the DEW outposts so we must carry a carefully selected amount of spare parts, exactly the right amount of fuel and enough rations to cover each stage, and any emergencies which might arise.

Back in 1977 Dr George Hobson of the Polar Continental Shelf Project, a Canadian government research department operation in northern Canada, had allowed us to use his huts at Alert for our training journey. Now he gave us facilities at his three main northern bases, Tuktoyaktuk, Resolute and the old camp at Alert. He also agreed to drop off fuel caches in remote spots, providing these were within Twin Otter reach of his bases. In exchange for our later completing certain glaciological research tasks on the Arctic Ocean, Ginnie and Simon would stay at each of these bases in turn and use the Polar Continental Shelf Project's radio frequency. As soon as we moved out of range of the first base, they would move on to the next.

I spent a day checking all spare parts and spare fuel outside the Polar Continental Shelf Project Parcol hut where Ginnie and Simon were to live and operate their radio base. Assured that I had too many spares of everything rather than too few, I handed the lists over to Simon and forgot about them.

From Tuktoyaktuk, I would have to navigate with my magnetic hand compass, my watch and the sun. I knew nothing of the Canadian archipelago, as the Arctic islands off Canada's northern shore are collectively called, save the long history of expeditions attempting to force the North West Passage and, in hundreds of cases, paying with their lives.

Nowadays great icebreakers are able to crash through the sea ice between the islands of the archipelago or even to the north of them but in our boat class, the non icebreakers, only a dozen or less expeditions have navigated the Passage in either direction and those that have, all using boats with some form of protection from the elements, averaged three summer seasons to complete the journey.

The company whose flat-bottomed barges ply between Inuvik,

Tuktoyaktuk and, when the ice allows, Eskimo settlements further east, had an office by the harbour. I went there to pick up advice. A barge skipper with sixteen years of experience in the region agreed to speak to me. His accent was Scandinavian and his voice harsh. I shook his big hairy hand and said: "We are going east along the coast to Spence Bay and then up to Resolute in a small open boat. I wondered if you could give me advice on navigation?"

He looked at me with hard eyes. "You are mad," he said.

"No." I showed him my compass and chart. "I have the latest charts and an excellent compass."

"You're mad, man. Throw it away."

I began to get annoyed but took care not to show it. "What do *you* use to navigate?" I asked. He moved to the window and pointed at a sturdy barge-towing tug. There was pride in his eyes.

"She has everything. She goes in the dark. Radar beacon respondders, MF and DF and we stay out in the deep channels. You," he shook his head dismissively, "you must hug the coastline to escape the storm winds, so you will hit the shoals. There are thousands of shoals." He began to sound as though he were enjoying himself. "Also you cannot cross the hundreds of deep bays for fear of the wind and big waves so you must hug the coastline which is like the graph of a heart beat . . . up, down, in, out . . . like crazy pavement. So you go much further and use much more gas. And most of the time it will be fog. No sun, so you must use your compass. Yes?"

He showed me his chart of Cambridge Bay, a few hundred miles east and along our route. One strong finger indicated the words "Magnetic compass useless in this area". He turned away dismissively. "Too near the Magnetic Pole for your compass, you see. You stay here in Tuk. Have a holiday."

I thanked him.

As I left he shouted, "Maybe you can navigate by the wrecks of the other madmen who've tried. There's plenty of them."

On 26th July we said goodbye to Ginnie and Simon. Bothie was out chasing gophers. Ginnie said she would move north to Resolute as soon as my radio signal began to weaken. In thirty-five days we must not only complete the 3,000 miles of the Passage, which traditionally takes three seasons, but we must also cover an additional 500 miles still further to the north, since our aim was not just to travel the Passage but to complete our circumpolar journey. We must reach somewhere within skiing distance of our Arctic winter quarters before the new ice began to close over the sea and forced us to abandon the whaler. The sun hid in an orange haze as Charlie and I left Tuktoyaktuk in our Boston whaler and turned east into a restless swell.

11

The Passage

JULY–AUGUST 1981

No man really knows about other human beings.
The best he can do is suppose they are like himself.

JOHN STEINBECK

Many have tried to pass through the North West Passage over the last two centuries and hundreds have died in the attempt. The stories of misery and starvation, cannibalism and death, of shipwrecks caused by hidden shoals, violent storms and invading ice are legion. Such tales are apt to encourage the adventure-seeker, until such time as he or she actually sets out along this loneliest of coastlines. John Buchan described the Passage as a "part of the globe having no care for human life, not built to man's scale; a remnant of the Ice Age which long ago withered the world".

This sounds a touch flowery but even the down-to-earth *Encyclopaedia Britannica* is unusually descriptive:

The hostile Arctic makes the North West Passage one of the world's severest maritime challenges. It is 500 miles north of the Arctic Circle and less than 1200 miles from the North Pole . . . Thick pack ice, moving at speeds up to ten miles per day, closes nearly half the passage all the year round. Arctic water can freeze a man to death in two minutes. Frigid polar north easterly winds blow almost constantly and can howl to hurricane force. Temperatures rise above freezing only in July and August . . . Visibility is often obscured by whiteouts of blowing snow . . . Thick fog usually shrouds the channels during the brief summer . . . There are uncharted shoals . . . little is known about the currents and tides . . . Navigation is difficult even with the most modern devices . . . The compass is useless because the magnetic North Pole lies within the Passage . . . The bleak featureless Arctic islands provide few distinguishing landmarks. Arctic blackouts can frustrate all communications for periods from a few hours to nearly a month.

Navigation was the immediate problem as we took the whaler east, for the coastline was flat as a board and invisible whenever shallow water forced us out to sea. The treeless tundra of the Tuktoyaktuk peninsula might just as well not have been there. But the sun was visible so we maintained a due east heading until the glint of the breakers off Cape Dalhousie showed like silver froth on the horizon. We closed to the south with caution for there were many shoals and breakers about.

We were making for the DEW line station near the Nicholson peninsula, but at first I was unable to tell which flat headland was which on my chart, so I set out across the ten mile gap of Liverpool Bay, not quite knowing where we were. Halfway across, a hill stood proud from the otherwise invisible coastline and gave me some indication of where to aim for. Not long before dusk we crept round a low sand spit sticking out like a heron's beak into a sheltered little bay and called up on our radio:

"Cape Nicholson, this is Transglobe, d'you read?"

The answer came back pat, as though our progress into the bay had been monitored. "You must be the English guys. We'll be down right away."

A jeep arrived in minutes with the cheery station commander at the wheel. Yes, our fuel and rations had arrived and were ready for us but, no, he would not let us disappear from his little kingdom without at least a cup of Cape Nicholson coffee. After all, we were the only visitors he had ever had except those who arrived by air. There were nine inhabitants scattered in caravan-shaped huts clustered round the DEW radar dish. Careful not to be electrocuted, I

The North West Passage

climbed a couple of radar masts in order to set up my radio antenna and contact Ginnie.

As I knelt on the tundra below the masts, talking to her, the station boss shouted, "Bear!" and I found myself ten feet up the mast. "Fetch your camera," he yelled at me. "Someone's seen a Barren Ground grizzly bear down by the rubbish dump."

We climbed into the jeep and soon spotted the great tan animal, although it blended remarkably well with the tundra. I urged the driver to get close for the bear was beside the track and a mere two hundred metres ahead. He accelerated but the bear shambled off down the trail. I was amazed. With thirty m.p.h. on the speedometer we failed to catch the huge beast. For a full minute it matched our speed, then moved away from the track and disappeared into dead marshy ground where the jeep could not follow.

Back at the radio I passed Ginnie a message for the Committee in London, a note deliberately discouraging as to our chances of making Alert in the short timespan left to us. This was not because I *believed* we would not make it. My mind was quite open as to our chances. But I did want London to start thinking hard *now* about the realities of our being delayed for a whole year. Seven years before I had chosen Gjoa Haven as a possible wintering base should we fail to make the whole passage in one season, and with this in mind I had packed enough kit for three of us to winter there. Now I wished to acclimatise the key figures in London to the idea that failure to get through the passage in one season did not mean the overall failure of Transglobe. After all, the handful of people who had beaten the Passage in the past nearly all took three seasons to do so. I wanted to prepare the less placid members of the Committee for the possibility of a winter's delay: unwelcome though an extra polar winter at a lonely Eskimo outpost might be, it need not cast doubts on our eventual capacity to succeed. I reminded them of the words of Dr Hattersley-Smith, accepted expert on the Passage: "Whilst I would not doubt that this journey can be done piecemeal, I think it unrealistic to suppose it can be done in *one* season. At least, you would have to have the most phenomenal luck to do it."

Ollie had been used to my outward pessimism hiding my inward determination. He had told the camera crew back in Antàrctica: "Ran treats life from a pessimistic angle which I think is very good, because if you expect the worst and you get it, you aren't disappointed. If you don't, then you feel very pleased. So he always looks at the rate of progress or the way the expedition is running in a pessimistic light and always tends to treat things as if they are going badly, whereas they might, in fact, be going well or on schedule."

Unfortunately my personal policy of openly committing myself to less than I inwardly hoped to achieve had an unfavourable effect on Charlie who found it depressing.

"You are too pessimistic, Ran," Charlie would say.

"You're wrong, Charles. I'm not pessimistic."

"Well, negative, then. You're over-negative."

"What do you mean? When am I negative? *When* have I been negative on this expedition?"

Charlie thought for a bit: "Not in the boat, no. And maybe not from day to day. But you give the others in London a generally negative impression. And that must be bad because you'll make them negative too. You're infectious that way."

The thought of *two* more winters of darkness shut up in the Arctic, without Twink, could not have been a pleasant prospect for Charlie.

A strong easterly wind began to lift the bay swell as Cape Nicholson disappeared behind us. The next DEW station was more sea miles away than could be covered with a maximum fuel load, unless we travelled in straight lines well away from the coast. Somewhere ahead was Franklin Bay with a mouth far too wide to cross and be sure of making an accurate landfall the other side with only a hand compass to steer by. Safer by far to hug the shoreline of the bay, despite its deep incursion to the south and away from our easterly course. To do this we would need two extra drums of fuel which some time ago the Polar Continental Shelf Project's Twin Otter had dropped off on a narrow spit of shingle south of Baillie Island.

For forty miles we bucked and tossed through a rising sea, soaked in spray at every wave crest. With the floor bungs out the whaler drained herself dry as quickly as the waves washed inboard.

A clammy mist hid the land to our east but we eventually heard the crash of waves so guessed where the spit must be. Trying to land from the east, for that was the side where our drums were, was not possible. The boat would have been battered and swamped in minutes, so we edged down the long shingle finger to its tip, hoping that conditions on the lee side would be slightly better. However even there it was still too rough to beach, so Charlie slung out our light anchor. I lowered myself overboard into the surf with two empty jerry cans, a drum opener and a fuel pump. While Charlie kept the boat hovering just beyond the breakers, I waded ashore. He then threw another twelve jerry cans after me which floated in with the surf.

Three hours later I managed, to the accompaniment of much sweating and swearing, to get all fourteen back on board filled with gasoline, the correct amount of oil and not too much blown sand.

Between Baillie Island and Cape Bathurst the narrow channel of Snowgoose Passage rips through shoals and bars. At first we were relieved to get through into Franklin Bay unscathed, but we very soon wished ourselves back again, for now the full force of wind and wave struck the little whaler. The lie of the coast was south-south-west and we had no alternative but to follow it with the waves curling at us from the port beam. We must travel down the line of the wave troughs and hope to avoid a swamping. Any mechanical breakdown would be likely to scupper us for good, since a rampart of unbroken cliffs from forty to ninety feet high formed the shoreline for over forty-five miles ahead. Occasionally the waves crashed on to a narrow shingle beach at the foot of the cliffs but mostly against the black rock itself, to rise in great curtains of spume that were whipped away by the wind.

The sky darkened and the waves grew higher, smashing inboard with increasing regularity. We were both soaked and our teeth chattered in unison. It would be so good to stop and light a fire but this could not be until the cliffs receded. Each time a wave broke over us salt water poured through the face holes in our rubberised survival suits, running down back and chest and legs to collect in slowly rising pools inside our waterproof boots. What clothes we wore beneath the suits were soon sodden. Our eyes stung with the salt and my map grew soggy. Progress became slower as the waves grew in size. We tried moving further away from the cliffs but conditions only worsened. Time and again we were forced to face fifteen-foot walls of water racing up from the east. Often the boat hung almost on its side as these waves surged by in a rush of power.

As the day grew darker I saw fire ahead, glowing through the gloom. For an hour it came no closer then, to our astonishment, we saw that the cliffs themselves were burning and an acrid smell of chemicals was discernible in the wind lulls. Dante's Inferno. Sulphur deposits glowing red and orange, forever on fire. Yellow-grey fingers of smoke curled from deep crevices. All that was missing were devils with pitchforks and screams from the burning damned.

As the cliffs smouldered and smoked above the angry surf and the wind increased, I realised that we must find some shelter where we could ride out this storm. The chart showed a tiny beachside lagoon the other side of a reef of shingle where a river disgorged itself a long way ahead but the chart was nine years old. Would the silt have blocked it up by now? I climbed up on to the prow to scan the ring of breakers to look for a gap in the fury of boiling white water. Spotting a place of lesser violence, I indicated its general direction to Charlie.

"Seen," he yelled above the din of outboards, wind and waves.

For a moment there was chaos as we bucked cork-like in the breakers. Then we were over and into a channel hardly wider than the boat's own width. The propellers bit into the silt almost at once. Charlie cut the motors and I poled in with an oar. The comparative silence was blissful – now only the roar of the pounding sea against the narrow walls of our haven. We could only advance some fifteen yards into the lagoon as it was so shallow and we made camp at once on the shingle. Rain fell in a thin drizzle but we lit a fire of driftwood and climbed thankfully out of our sodden suits. Turned upside down, sea water poured out of the leggings. Our feet were white with the crinkled trenchfoot skin of a soggy corpse.

Not a good spot for communications to Ginnie, but I raised a DEW station somewhere to the east and told the operator we were fine and close to the cliffs of Malloch Hill.

At dawn a mournful mist shrouded our tent and the sodden beach. We climbed with clenched teeth into the wet suits and plodded up and down the shingle for an hour to induce warmth. I estimated a journey of some thirty miles to the far side of Franklin Bay, quite a bit further than from England to France. The wind had abated overnight to a mere breeze and only the swell of the storm remained. We set off on what I believed to be an easterly bearing, but after an hour there was no sign of land in any direction.

"Surely we should head further right?" Charlie shouted in my ear.

"I know what you mean," I screamed back, "but the compass says this way so just keep straight ahead at the dark patch of clouds."

I had a local error of 43° set on the compass and had added five more for the effect of the boat's engines and metal fittings. How great the influence of the magnetic Pole was as yet I did not know but I had, over twenty years, developed an implicit faith in the compass compared with most people's instinctive sense of direction. Nomadic peoples often develop uncanny instincts on their home ranges but, as often as not, folk with urbanised senses make a real hash of direction finding. They feel an 'urge' to head here, there and everywhere, thrilled at the thought of using long-latent natural skills, but they usually end up going round in circles.

Two hours later faint splotches of darkness nicked the misty horizon ahead. Fragments of ice, none larger than a football pitch, lined the eastern flanks of Franklin Bay but only in pockets. This was ice which had grounded on shallows and so would spend the next four weeks slowly melting until winter arrived to re-skin the sea-lanes of the Passage.

If we were where I thought we were, then the foreland which finally emerged through the mist was unnamed on my map anyway. The shoal of what I hoped was Rabbit Island passed to starboard and we nosed with caution between Booth and Fiji Islands and into Cow Cove. A wan sun opened a shaft through the mist to reveal the radar dome and masts of Cape Parry DEW station which glimmered briefly then vanished like a half-suspect dream. We were on course.

The station boss insisted we stay for a meal and a night's sleep. Knowing what lay ahead I hastened to thank him and accept for this would be our last 'safe' stopping place for close on 400 miles. This had been made quite clear in a note from an old adviser, John Boctoce, probably the most knowledgeable man alive as regards travel along the coastline of the Passage. "Do not stop unless it is urgent anywhere between Cape Parry and Lady Franklin Point. There is not a bit of shelter for a boat too heavy to beach." But Cow Cove looked fine to me: I thought that the hills would protect the boat from the prevailing east wind and that the whaler would be all right if we left it with its anchor holding the stern out and a bowline painter tied to a rock on the beach.

We slept well in the warm comfortable base, ignorant and therefore unperturbed that the wind had boxed the compass overnight and was now screaming in from the west. When at last we ambled down to the cove, we found that surging surf was thundering on to our previously sheltered beach. The stern anchor had torn lose under the strain, swinging the whaler abeam to the beach. As the gravel scoured her hull with each new breaking wave, so water poured over her into the kit inside and into the breather holes in the fuel tank.

For two days we dried out equipment. Whilst we waited, we got to know the eleven camp inmates, most of whom put up with the isolation because of high wages and the languid pace of life. One told me: "I think my brain slows down up here. You only need a vocabulary of three hundred words to get by."

Going outside the station, even in the mildest weather, meant putting on layers of warm clothing and taking them off again once back in the hut, so the men mostly stayed indoors when off duty, watching video films, playing darts, pool or chess. There were no women. Each base comprises a large igloo-shaped radar dome and four radar dishes facing north towards the USSR. The whole net-work of thirty-one stations, twenty-one in Canada, six in Alaska and four in Greenland, was installed to give warning of any sneak attack by bombers or missiles over the top of the world. They were built to last ten years, but are still going strong twenty-five years later, despite the deployment of satellites and over-the-horizon radar that can do the same job. The stations we called at were run by Canadians who passed all daily weather information and radar readings to North American Air Defence Command down in Colorado Springs.

On 30th July, in a fog and a twenty-knot westerly wind, we headed east to the narrows of Dolphin and Union Strait. For thirty-six hours without a break we ploughed east and saw very little ice but beach-grounded bergs. Our luck was holding. Being wet we were soon cold but the mists cleared and stayed away all day and night, on through to the next day. We grew very tired and it was necessary from time to time to shout at each other to stave off drowsiness. Often, for hours on end, we would sing to ourselves. Past Clinton Point, Cape Young and a thousand nameless bays, determined not to stop on this barren north-facing coast with no stitch of cover from the elements. The evenings were soft and full of wild beauty which faded from red dusk to purple dawn with no night-time between. But winter was poised on the balls of its feet. Already the sun at midnight caressed the silent surface of the sea.

For 340 miles we stood in the narrow space between helm and fuel cans until at last, dodging between a rash of islets, we crossed the narrow channel to Victoria Island and left the Canadian mainland for the first time. Late on 1st August we came to the DEW site at Lady Franklin Point and thankfully moored the whaler in a well sheltered bay.

How, asked our film team later, did we react to the long cramped hours together?

"Well," Charlie replied, "team members were chosen for their temperament. We do lose our tempers occasionally but very, very seldom and mainly when under pressure. If something goes wrong, say an engine problem and Ran says, for instance, 'Couldn't it be the water separator?' Then I might turn round and say, 'For God's sake, shut up, it can't be the separator because the other engine is running and they both work off the same separator.' When you've been up for thirty hours you really can't put up with that sort of advice. What do I do to keep myself awake? Well, I'm always talking to myself. I'm the sort of person who listens to myself. Not really surprising. It's mainly about mechanical things, because I'm not a mechanic and need to chat the problems through in my head. Also you've got to amuse yourself because you can't hear what Ran is saying unless he yells, or you yell and he can't hear what you're saying so you chatter away to yourself to keep going."

At Lady Franklin everyone seemed asleep for it was well past midnight. I went behind the huts with my radio gear in a sack and, as at Cape Nicholson, scaled two radar masts to hang out my antenna. I picked Ginnie up at once. She and Simon had been watching live television coverage of Prince Charles' wedding. At Tuktoyaktuk a severe storm had piled the 'tide' up to three feet higher than normal. Many Eskimo boats in the bay had sunk or broken up complete with outboard engines and fishing gear, so they'd been worried about us. But I gave Ginnie a fairly optimistic view of our chances, at least as far as Gjoa Haven, under strict instructions that no hint of optimism should leak out to London.

I noticed that the station boss was lurking close behind me. Since I had my earphones on he need not have pussy-footed to get there. He glared at me. I smiled back politely, for he was host and had a right to glare. I decided to close down to Ginnie. Perhaps I was unwittingly on a frequency that interfered with the base radio.

"With whom are you communicating?" he asked.

"With my wife."

"Where is she?"

"In Tuktoyaktuk."

"Do you have permission to use the radio up here?"

"Yes. On 4982 megahertz."

I opened my bag to stack away the headphones and antenna and he moved closer to peer inside. Deciding to seize the bull by the horns I laughed and said: "I am British, you know; not a spy." He gave me a severe and hostile look which clearly indicated that the second half of my observation was a non sequitur.

"Well," I said, "I'll be getting some sleep now. We must push on first thing tomorrow." That did seem to please him.

A hundred and thirty miles to the east one outboard gave up the ghost and failed to respond to any known remedy. We limped back thirty miles to Byron Bay DEW site where we spent three days replacing the crown pinion gear. Then on towards the DEW station at Cambridge Bay. Wild storms lashed our passage over wide bay mouths and past forlorn capes of twisted red lava domes and fluted black pillars of cutaway bedrock. I looked for places of shelter but there were none, not even a shallow cave or leaning boulder. The rain drove down from a forbidding sky. I marvelled silently at our predecessors of a century past who had ventured along this coast under sail and with blank charts. More than a hundred of Sir John Franklin's men had died in this region. Many of the features which did have names reflected the unpleasant memories of those pioneers: Cape Storm, Starvation Harbour and other evocative echoes.

By the time we reached Cambridge Bay on 6th August the wind had steadied. As we entered the inner bay on a sunny if blustery afternoon, I thought of Colin Irwin, a young sailor from Bournemouth, who had managed to sail the entire Passage to this point in a specially constructed yacht. But he got no further for sea-ice closed in from the east. He was patient but the two following summers saw no improvement. He finally married a local Eskimo girl and gave up the attempt.

It would not do to start counting our chickens yet: we were less than halfway to Alert and John Bostoce had warned us to be "out of the Passage by the end of August or you'll be in trouble!" By his reckoning therefore, we had less than twenty days of safe sea travel left.

An American DEW official collected us from the gravel spit where we had anchored the whaler. Charlie began to sort out some wet kit whilst I set up the radio.

"Bring your firearms to the station commander's office," the American requested. "No weapons whilst you're in town."

I took my revolver and Charlie's .357 magnum bear rifle into the well appointed office of the camp boss.

"Clear the guns, please," said the American, "the commanding officer will be back soon." I emptied the six bullets from my revolver and handed them over with some more from my pocket. Then I took Charlie's rifle and checked the built-in magazine. I cocked the unfamiliar bolt and a four inch bullet fell to the floor. A brief look into the chamber. Nothing there. So I pointed the rifle at the floor and squeezed the trigger.

It was a powerful weapon and the noise in that confined space was deafening. Blood spattered over the carpet as did glass from the fluorescent lights, plaster from the ceiling and parquet from the floor.

I had definitely cleared the gun so I handed it to the American.

There were sounds of approaching feet in the corridor. The American poked his head out: "No problem," he shouted, "just trouble with the lighting." This seemed to satisfy whoever had approached as his feet could now be heard departing. The American found a brush and pan and, with commendable speed, whisked all the debris away. There was a gaping black hole, still smoking, in the floor in front of the base commander's desk. This he covered up neatly with a floor mat from another part of the room. The place looked as good as new.

I traced the blood to my chin. There appeared to be a small hole in it to which I applied a handkerchief to stem the impressive dribble of blood. The American seemed to be enjoying himself immensely. "Geeze," he said, "if the Arctic doesn't get you guys I guess you'll do a pretty good job on yourselves. Never a dull moment, eh?" He drove me to the local dispensary where an Eskimo girl sewed me up with curved needle and dental floss.

That evening Charlie, seeing my half naked, half bearded chin collapsed with laughter. However, he did not get the satisfaction of finding out the story behind my discomfiture for at least eighteen months for I had sworn the American to silence.

Unfortunately, the Eskimo nurse did not check inside the hole before sewing it up and to this day my chin swells up periodically as some mobile foreign matter, glass, concrete or parquet perhaps, travels around the jawbone.

At Cambridge Bay, the first Eskimo settlement we'd visited since Tuktoyaktuk, we learnt that ice almost certainly blocked our way east. In a week or two, said local boatmen, it might shift but in their opinion it was more likely to get worse. In fact, one good north wind had been known to fill up the whole of Queen Maud Gulf with ice from Victoria Strait. If this happened it might then stay there until the sea refroze in three or four weeks' time.

I radioed Ginnie: everything was packed up and a Polar Continental Shelf Project Twin Otter was due to fly her and Simon and the radio gear to Resolute Bay, her next intended base many hundreds of sea miles to our north. En route they would be stopping to refuel at Cambridge Bay.

Could they take me, I asked, on a reconnaissance flight to the east of Cambridge Bay? It would not take long and would give me an idea of the amount of ice around. By good luck the Twin Otter pilot flying for PCSP was Karl Z'berg who was booked to fly for us up in the Arctic Ocean the following year. He agreed to help where he could and the next afternoon landed at Cambridge Bay. Ginnie, Simon and Bothie looked well but there was a second dog too. A black labrador puppy even smaller than Bothie.

"What," I asked Ginnie, "is that?"

"This is Tugaluk. Two months old and a good dog."

"*Whose* is she?"

Ginnie thought quickly. "She's a wedding present for Simon."

Simon butted in that he wasn't getting married and even if he had been he wouldn't want Tugaluk.

"You can't keep her, Ginnie, you know that, don't you?"

Ginnie did. But, she explained, the puppy would have been shot if left as a stray in Tuktoyaktuk.

"Anyway," she said with finality, "Bothie has fallen in love with her. He'll probably get over it in Resolute so I'll find a kind owner and leave her there."

The matter was closed. Or so I thought.

I had a discussion with Karl. Charlie and I had not seen him since somewhere near the North Pole four years before when he had piloted the resupply Otter we were chartering from Bradley Air Services.

If the sea to the east of Cambridge Bay was blocked with ice we had but two alternatives. To wait, which I had no wish to do, or to skirt the mainland coast well to the south and, by adding a dogleg of some two hundred extra miles, creep around the ice along its southern and eastern limits. Obviously, if the ice extended right up to the eastern coast of Queen Maud Gulf, even this plan would fail.

Such an extended route along a hazardous coastline with no settlements and no DEW sites would mean at least one extra fuel cache and Karl advised the loading of three fuel drums for the reconnaissance flight. This done we took off at once for it was getting dark. Almost one hundred and fifty sea miles south-east of Cambridge Bay we flew over a nest of shoals and islets one of which looked long, narrow and flat.

"Perry Island," Karl prodded at his chart. "It is said to be OK to land here except after recent heavy rain. If you have to come this far south, it will be on your way." He gave me an enquiring look and I nodded. If we decided to come along this southern route, fuel right here would be ideal. If the ice up north proved penetrable, well then, we'd go that way and someone else could use our fuel cache here if ever they found it. Looking down at the hostile mass of islands I found it hard to believe anyone would want to visit, let alone live in, so desolate a region. Yet until recently there had been a village on one of these islands, complete with a shop and mission post. As Karl circled lower I began to appreciate that this was the very last place to choose for a boat journey. There were literally hundreds of islands, some merely rock platforms half awash, some just below the surface and between them countless shoals punctured the sea. Moreover the Eskimos had informed me that this storm-bound coast was spattered with wrecked small boats. But however hostile, this route would provide the only alternative to a year's delay if the sea further north proved ice-bound.

Karl buzzed the mud island, allowing his heavy rubber wheels to touch down briefly. Then with a surge of power, rose again and, circling, inspected the wheelmarks. How soggy was it? He had every reason to be careful. Too much deep mud would prevent his taking off again from the tiny strip. Six circuits and trial touch-downs later, we landed smoothly and rolled the three drums to the edge of the island. The sun had already disappeared when we left the islet with a perfectly timed lift-off.

Karl skimmed over the shorter northern route: two-thirds of the sea was ivory white with ice, the rest a dusty ink. Jenny Lind Island, our cache point for this route, was already cut off from the west. We need see no more. Either we go by the longer southern route or not at all.

I squeezed out of the cockpit and joined Ginnie in the darkness of the fuselage. We promised each other no more expeditions after this.

Back at Cambridge Bay, Simon and the dogs joined her and Karl and they flew away north to set up the radios at Resolute Bay.

Charlie and I stacked the Boston whaler with our gear and with as much fuel as was sensible and set out to cover the southerly route which I'd just flown over. Beyond the bay, the fog became dense which made navigation by eye impossible, nor was I helped by finding the shoalbanks on my map blotted out by the printed words MAGNETIC COMPASS USELESS IN THIS AREA. White flashes of broken water in the mist and slight changes in the colour of the ocean warned us of underwater rocks. We carried three spare propellers but with 200 miles of shoal water ahead, could not afford to break off any blades too early on.

The wind rose to thirty knots but still dense fog banks covered the islands and the mainland. It became impossible to tell which was which. I knew I must not lose our position against the chart, since it would be extremely difficult to re-locate ourselves once disorientated. We nosed into a calm bay and waited for an hour. Briefly, a headland to the east cleared and we set out again; navigation-wise it was a difficult day. For nine miles the coastline was flat and devoid of a single feature. I bade Charlie hug it like glue or I would be unable to fix our position. We came to corridors filled with countless shoals where the sea boiled between gaunt stacks of dripping rock and we lay-off to plot a route through the obstacles before committing the whaler to running the gauntlet. Hour after hour I strained my eyes to recognise coastal features but there were hundreds of islands of all shapes and sizes and the coastline was so heavily indented with bays, fjords and islets that the mist made it all too easy to mistake a channel for a cul-de-sac. A great deal of luck saw us safely and accurately through 130 sea miles of this nightmare passage but in the evening a storm came from the west and threw great rolling seas over the shoals and against the islands.

Despite a strong desire to locate the three-drum cache, common sense dictated shelter and I sought a long deserted Hudson Bay Company hut on Perry Island some twelve miles short of the cache. We found the hut hidden around the bend of an island fjord and anchored the boat off its horseshoe beach.

For twenty-four hours the storm bottled us up on the island. There was rain and sleet as usual but inside the old wooden shack we were comfortable with sleeping bags on the floor and buckets under the leaky parts of the roof. Our sodden boat-suits did not dry out but we did. I trudged across mossy rock to the south of the island, disturbing on my way a snowy owl with a lemming in its beak, two ptarmigan and a gyrfalcon. Ollie, I thought to myself, would have been ecstatic.

Quite suddenly I happened upon an Eskimo village of six one-room shacks. Seal pelts, bearskins and moose antlers littered the shingle. Broken sledges and rotten fishnets lay about but not a soul answered my calls. I fixed up the radio but Ginnie did not answer. A friendly operator from Gladman Point DEW site some 200 miles to the north east, and our next port of call, picked up my call and wished us good luck.

On 10th August the storm showed no signs of abating and my patience ran out. We dodged between islands to keep away from their exposed shores. Sometimes we hitched up the outboards and waded the boat over rockbeds. At noon we came to the island of our cache but mudbanks extending from it meant leaving the boat 200 yards away and trudging through shallows with the jerry cans. Since the mud was soft and deep our boots sank in and we were often held tight with suction, especially on our way back with full cans.

Two weary hours later we were ready but found that the boat, heavy with fuel, was now stuck in the mud.

As though from heaven, an Eskimo in oilskins came chugging up in a long low river boat. He spoke no English but pointed towards Perry Island. Perhaps he came from the huts I had seen but he and the other inmates were all out on a summer fishing trip. We fixed a line to his stern and after many jerks with the two of us heaving knee-high in mud, we eventually unstuck the whaler. Twice more we became jammed on unseen shallows but each time our Eskimo guardian angel helped us away.

Clear of the mud channel we again came to a maze of rock islets and shoals. The sea had calmed down and we headed east for ten hours, sometimes out of sight of land, save for ever more isolated islands to the east and south. Since the compass was useless and the sun made no appearance I kept my nose glued to the chart.

At dusk the wind again raced down from the north and we plunged off creaming breakers. Twice the whole heavy boat was flung into the night as great black walls of water struck us broadside.

"We'd better do that last bit again," Charlie screamed in my ear. "Remember, we're not allowed to fly. This is a surface voyage." I saw his teeth grinning in the dark, then grabbed at the handrail as another unseen surge sent us keeling madly to starboard. I began to feel nothing could turn us over.

Not long before midnight, in the middle of a timeless, bucking nightmare, a thin moon scudded clear of the racing cloudbanks, not for long, but enough for us to spot an indent in the silhouette of the cliffs ahead. Our current progress was clearly suicidal, so I shoved my beard against Charlie's dripping hood. "We'll go in there till dawn – but watch for rocks."

The indent proved to be a well-sheltered inlet. Charlie steered us in without a bump and I sloshed up the beach with the painter. We erected our tent, peeled off the boat-suits and lit a woodfire. Charlie located some whisky. It is disgusting stuff I have always thought but, when you are very cold indeed, it has distinct advantages. Three hours later the bottle was all but finished. Streaks of livid orange announced the break of a new day and the cold shapes of rock and seashore imposed themselves on our salt-stung weary eyes.

I made waking-up noises and Charlie groaned. By dint of much shouting at the sky and running on the spot I persuaded myself that I was not only alive but could just about face the awful moment of climbing back into the clammy confines of my boat-suit. The fact that sand from the beach clung to its inside did not help, especially in the neighbourhood of my crotch for the insides of my thighs were red raw from the long days of salty chafing.

For a further fourteen hours we weaved our weary way through innumerable gravel islands along a bewildering slalom course with north as its basic ingredient. This was now easy, since I could catch enough glimpses of the sun through the haze to orientate myself. The distant DEW dome of Gladman Point under a low black sky was a wonderful sight and we yearned for warmth and sleep. As the station boss proffered us hot black coffee, he told us that fishing parties from Gjoa Haven had been stranded by the bad weather at various points for the last five days. We could stay until the storms subsided if we liked, he said. It would be safer . . . the Eskimos knew best. If they did not think it safe to travel, we would do well to follow their example.

The bay provided scant shelter given a storm; if we sat tight and waited for safe conditions, we would never get through before the winter ice formed. No, I would press on. It was not a question of deriding local knowledge, but purely a matter of time and distance mathematics. We picked up our fuel supplies and carried on towards Gjoa Haven, seventy miles to the east, which marked the half-way point of our North West Passage journey.

By evening we reached Gjoa Haven and, almost drunk with weariness, secured the whaler between two Eskimo boats. This narrow bay was where Nansen's *Gjoa* had spent a winter during her three-year epic voyage through the Passage, the first in history.

The Eskimos warned us that sea-ice almost certainly blocked the Humboldt Channel and the Wellington Strait to the north. Better to call in at the last settlement before Resolute Bay, a hamlet at the head of Spence Bay Fjord, and take guides.

For once we set out in good weather and no mist, following the coastline of King William Island until, at Matheson Point, I took a bearing off the sun and headed across Rae Strait. For a short while in mid-crossing there was no land anywhere, then inverted mirages of the coast danced over the horizon and we made good time to the great rock-girt arm of Spence Bay, arriving late on 13th August at the isolated Eskimo hamlet.

Our morale was high. From now on we would be travelling north once more. True, time was running short and soon we would meet ice, but already we were further by far than could have been achieved in a year of even average ice conditions.

We moved into a 'guest cabin' for one night and plonked our kit down in the living room. Once we had moved into our rooms I took my spare set of maps out of Charlie's boat bag and settled back to read through the notebook which he used as a diary.

Charlie and I were both wont to read anything we came across but an old saying goes that eavesdroppers never hear good of themselves. The same might be said of those who, on expeditions, read other people's diaries. Since, as official book writer of the expedition, I believed that, as after our polar training, I would be reading the contents of all the expedition diaries, I felt no qualms about reading Charlie's.

But when I actually did so, it upset me. When he came back, I asked him why at one point, he'd said I was lost. Because, he replied, I had said so myself. Yes, I agreed, but I'd only meant it in terms of our exact position vis-à-vis two river mouths, not as regards our overall position.

But, said Charlie, he had not written that I was lost over all. He'd just made a note of what I'd said in his own way. Did I want him to stop keeping a diary? No of course not, I replied. It did seem to me that Charlie's laconic entry could easily be misinterpreted by an outsider, should he read it, even if Charlie and I knew what it meant. But I kept such thoughts private and cursed myself for being so sensitive to criticism. Charlie was quite right: his diary saw the expedition through his eyes and my diary through mine and naturally and inevitably we interpreted events differently and equally our entries could also be read in a variety of ways.

Armitage, in his book on Shackleton, is careful never to use diaries as a basis for fact. He simply sums up the character interplay between Scott, Wilson and Shackleton in general terms: "Hardship is not always ennobling: if it produces self-sacrifice it can equally well produce irritation and hostility. The enforced physical proximity of the three men, while they were pushing themselves to the utmost, must have had an effect on their behaviour to each other and any latent antagonism or rivalry between the two could hardly be concealed all the time."

Any latent antagonism or rivalry between Charlie and me was certainly not apparent when we were on the move. Perhaps because our energies were fully occupied simply coping with getting to the next camp site. Only when we emerged from the lonely wastes to some warm, relaxing outpost did Charlie sometimes seem unnaturally quiet and moody. But then, even after seven years spent in close proximity, Charlie was still a closed book to me. I would do well, I mused, always to remember that he was keeping his own record of what was happening, of my words and behaviour.

Two other boats left Spence Bay ahead of us. We followed in convoy. They too were eighteen feet long and outboard powered. Included in their crew were the Spence Bay Mountie and a local Eskimo hunter with an unrivalled knowledge of the region. An hour or two north of Spence Bay the other boats turned aside and beached. We hovered off shore. What was wrong? "There's a storm coming," the Mountie shouted, "a bad one. Our friends will go no further and advise *you* to stop here or head back to Spence Bay."

The sky was clear and there was no more than a light breeze from the west. I told the Mountie we had better press on and would camp if the storm materialised. He shrugged and waved as we pulled away. Three hours later the wind had indeed risen. Storm clouds poured across the sky and, on the western horizon, a rugged run of ice edged the blackness of the sea.

"Sheep," I shouted to Charlie, pointing at a small cream-coloured animal moving along the beach. As we approached it turned into a polar bear patrolling its patch of the coastline.

For a hundred miles we moved north through increasing signs of ice, thick banks of fog and winds of up to sixty knots. Since the coast we followed was unindented and the waves smashed its shore with mounting fury, there was nowhere we could stop. The next fuel cache was a low sand spit somewhere in Pasley Bay. With luck we would find shelter from the storm within the bay and camp until the winds abated.

After six hours of drenching in ice cold water our eyes were inflamed and our fingers ached with the cold. The moment we reached the mouth of the bay, conditions altered. For the worse. The whole bay writhed with the power of the storm. Serried lines of wind-lashed breakers smashed into every shore. There was no shelter. But we could not go on, nor could we turn back. To turn broadside on to the rushing walls of water, even briefly, would be to invite immediate swamping. I squinted at the chart and noticed a stream which looped its way into the bay dead opposite to the mouth. If we could but cross the two mile reach from mouth to stream we might find shelter.

Off Perry Island we had experienced bigger waves but none so powerful, so steep nor so close together as these. The bows plunged off one six foot wall vertically down its front and into, not over, the next. The boat's floor was quickly awash with cans and kit floating about our feet. The wave tops completely covered the prow and smashed down into the cockpit. Most of the time visibility was nil for as soon as we opened our eyes, a new deluge cascaded over our heads. The water, streaming down the insides of our suits was far colder than it had been further south. Somehow the whaler made it through that interminable crossing. Never did two miles seem longer.

A brief gap in the pounding beach surf revealed the river's mouth. We nosed upstream, delighted at the comparative calm, and the depth, for we had feared shallows. After a mile or so we moored the whaler to a piece of driftwood and struggled ashore to erect the sodden tent. The wind whipped out the tent pegs so, using our remaining full cans as weights, we half fixed up the tent, brewed coffee, ate chocolate, removed our slimy suits and slept, in that order.

Next day there was no wind and the bay was smooth as a millpond. Hard to imagine how so pretty a cove could boil in such fury as it had but six short hours before. We soon found our fuel drums, cached on a nearby spit, and we continued north. For an hour we enjoyed a pallid sun, then fog closed dense and yellow all about the boat and we nosed between chunks of ice and the coastline for a while before deciding to pause until we could see something. Camping on a tiny shingle bar, we watched a herd of beluga or white whales pass through nearby shallows, flashing white and black as they rubbed old skin off their stomachs along the gravel.

Belugas are not hunted commercially but the Eskimos catch them in nets and eat the fat, the meat, even the skin which they say tastes like the white of an egg. Herds of beluga have been seen in Arctic rivers many miles from the ocean which makes sense, since their worst enemies are sharks and polar bears.

When the fog dispersed we kept going along a craggy coast with well defined mountains and bays that made navigation a delight. From time to time lonely bergs, grounded until the recent storm sailed by us without posing a threat until, at the end of the day, we reached the great cliffs of Limestone Island, spattered with the droppings of a million seabirds. Ahead lay Barrow Strait and, on its far side, Resolute, the only settlement on Cornwallis Island, where Ginnie was. But the crossing was forty miles wide and pack-ice stretched across our front from horizon to horizon.

There was little fuel left and our last cache before Resolute was another twelve miles around the island's north coast. So we edged on beneath the cliffs. Carefully, because the sea was full of chunks of half-drowned ice, from marble to man-size. We progressed down an ever-narrowing corridor between the cliffs and the pack. A strong breeze blew from the north. This worried me because the pack could shift south with the wind and close in behind us. Soon we were nudging along channels in the pack with ever decreasing sea room. With ten miles to go to the cache, I decided to turn back until the north wind stopped blowing. We might well reach our cache but the chart showed nowhere near it likely to afford protection from invading ice.

Back the way we had come by some twenty miles there was a deep inlet, Aston Bay, which looked as though it would provide cover unless a west wind blew for long enough to pour the pack back down Peel Sound and trap us in the bay. Charlie did not look happy at the idea of turning back but I long ago learnt that you can't keep all the people happy all the time. I was content to take risks if I had to but was damned if I would when any alternative course remained open.

My mother always told me my father respected his boss, Field Marshal Montgomery. The Field Marshal *never* moved forward if he could avoid it until the cards were stacked where possible in his favour. Neither Nature nor Rommel would be likely to hand out second chances. In a situation like this I usually avoided asking for the opinion of others. Why? Charlie probably nailed my reasoning process correctly. He once said:

> *I think Ran finds it very difficult to talk of the logistic side for the simple reason that I will see something and say: "Well, how about doing it such and such a way?" But that might mess him up from his own thinking as to how he wants to do it. Obviously there is more than one way of playing any ball game so, if he airs his views to me, I will come back and say, "Well, why don't you do this or that?" Then he's got another something churning around in his head, so he'd rather not listen. So he keeps it all to himself and I think it eats him away slightly.*

The fjord down which we retreated was almost ice-free and several miles deep. We eased over a shallow sand bar to the terminal bay in a wide gravel valley. Shale slopes overlooked us and water from the summer melt tinkled its way down to the fjord via several outwash gullies.

Using the tent and an oar for antenna masts, I contacted Ginnie. The bay at Resolute was full of ice, she said, and added that a Japanese man and wife, with a boat equipped with sail and outboard had been waiting there for two summers to cross Barrow Strait. This was his *third* year, she pointed out, so *I* shouldn't be impatient. That kept me quiet for a few hours but, when we were still in the little bay three days later, I began to get itchy again.

Each day more ice floes appeared along our protective sandbar. Some smaller ones sneaked over it at high tide and crunched against the side of the whaler but they were as yet too light to do much harm. Nonetheless, it would be foolish to be caught in the bay like a rat in a trap with floes pressed up solidly against our sandbar exit.

On the morning of the third day a skein of new ice sheened the water all about the whaler, a sinister reminder of pending winter. In eleven days or so the remaining open sea would begin to freeze.

In a week Giles and Gerry would arrive at Resolute with the Twin Otter and help guide us through any pack-ice in our way. But a week was too long to wait and, by a lucky stroke, an old friend of ours from the Arctic training days happened to come to Resolute for a month's pilot work. Dick de Blicquy, most famous of Canada's

Arctic bush pilots, met up with Ginnie and learnt of our predicament. He agreed to guide us across the strait as soon as the weather looked right.

On the fourth morning of our stay in the fjord, the wind dropped, the mist lifted and we sneaked over the ice-choked sandbar, sped round Somerset Island to our cache at Cape Anne, picked up fuel and within three miles had entered the pack-ice.

For four hours we responded to radio instructions from Dick who circled above with Ginnie and Simon in the PCSP Twin Otter. Sometimes it was necessary to push floes apart with oars and our feet; sometimes a route that looked good from above proved a cul-de-sac from the boat's point of view. But in the end we won through and reached the mouth of Resolute Bay two hours before fog banks poured over the cliffs of Cornwallis Island and blanketed the pack-ice.

The Japanese gentleman, hearing of our arrival, treated it as a talisman and left to head south. Things were not to go too well for him but we heard no more of his progress for a while. Tugaluk was as big as Bothie now and only happy when destroying some useful item like a mukluk or a set of vital maps.

"I thought you were going to get rid of it here," I reminded Ginnie.

"I am. Don't flap. We'll be around for at least another week and there are plenty of folk here who would sell their back teeth to own such a beautiful dog."

Within a few hours of our arrival a wind change brought pack-ice back into the harbour, nearly crushing the whaler. This prevented our departure towards Alert for four critical days of mist and sleet.

During this stay I received a message from our Chairman in London suggesting that my route be north of Resolute to the northern end of the Wellington Channel, where there was a narrow neck of low land blocking the sea route. Here we should abandon the whaler and camp until the sea froze, then carry on to Alert by skidoo. In case the Chairman's suggested course became necessary, I asked Ginnie to check out our light inflatables with skids which would be portable across the narrow isthmus west of the Douro Range, because they struck me as a better bet than skidoos for the conditions of ice *and* water which characterise early winter.

Ginnie exchanged messages with Ant Preston in London who told us that Dr Hattersley-Smith, the polar regions expert, had again stressed to our Chairman, "that I have always been very sceptical

about the feasibility of this journey in one season and told Ranulph
so three years ago".

I walked over to the Resolute meteorological research station and
questioned a technician there. Could we get through the strait east of
Bathurst Island? No. It was jammed solid with ice and likely to stay
that way. How about out into Lancaster Sound and up the east coast
of Ellesmere Island? Again, No. Likely to be ice *and* storm-bound.
How about a giant detour around Devon Island and through Hell
Gate to Norwegian Bay? Possible, but inadvisable owing to the
hazardous sea conditions off Devon Island's east coast. All in all the
met. man had discounted all options beyond spending the winter in
Resolute.

The one thing I could not countenance was doing nothing, so I
plumped for the easiest looking option, a race around Devon Island
for 600 miles as soon as the ice allowed our whaler out of the
harbour.

Ginnie was unable to contact our Chairman but got a message
through to Colonel Andrew Croft whose Arctic experience was
considerable. He replied with approval for my plan.

It might seem strange that I should check such moves with the
Committee back in London. Surely the man on the ground knows
best? This is often true, but I had never been in the North West
Passage before, nor had Charlie, so it seemed prudent to sound out
the opinions of people with experience. Having received such opinions I felt the final choice should rest with me. Maybe this was wrong.

Charlie's view:

*Ran runs the show. He is the leader in the field but you've got to
remember he has a Committee back in England. They run the
expedition. This does cause problems, as you can imagine. In the
sense that if Ran wants to do something, he does it, and the
board of directors, the Committee, they try and change it. I think
that this is the first time Ran has had a Committee who feel they
should be organising him. This is unfortunate for him. He now
feels the strain. I can see it. Because he has to be diplomatic. He
can't say, "Well, I'm going to do this or that without telling the
Committee."*

With 900 miles to cover in six days, there was no time for delay yet
pack-ice seemed to surround us and contrary advice slid in from

every quarter. The decision was mine and poor Charlie would have to suffer the consequences should my decision lead us into trouble. The journey so far had been wet, cold, bleak and we'd frequently been short on sleep. Now it was getting even colder and the way ahead looked dicey. It was a tense time for all of us. No wonder Simon wrote that Charlie seemed "overtly brash and friendly but needles underneath".

Early on 25th August the ice moved out of the harbour and hung around a couple of miles off the coast. Before a south wind stirred to bring the pack back in again, we went in silence down to the harbour in our boat-suits and set off to the east.

An American geologist, the founder of the Arctic Institute of North America, watched us leave. He wrote to Andrew Croft: "When we were in Resolute the Fiennes group came through. They moved off in a snowstorm when the harbour ice had cleared sufficiently – but I tell you none of us would have changed places with them, sitting high without benefit even of windscreen."

All that day the mist remained alongside or near to the gaunt cliff-line that we followed east. At the sheer cliffs of the Hotham Escarpment we left Cornwallis Island and crossed the stormy seas of Wellington Channel.

Relieved to make land and the shelter of the cliffs of Devon Island, we steered into an inlet called Erebus Bay. *Erebus* and *Terror* had been the two sturdy ships of Sir John Franklin, the sixty-year-old leader of an 1845 expedition who with 129 men had set out to locate the North West Passage. A few days before the expedition began Franklin's wife, spotting him dozing off in a chair, had tucked him up with a flag she was sewing for the expedition. He awoke startled and cried out, "Union Jacks are for corpses."

Both ships and all the men disappeared and despite forty separate search expeditions, many of them great feats of endurance in their own right, over the next ten years, no survivors were found. The disjointed discoveries of the searchers put together some idea of the drawn-out suffering of Franklin's men, but they also produced new mysteries.

Did Franklin's senior officer, Crozier, die with the rest or did he, because of his unique personal knowledge of the Eskimo tongue and methods of survival, live on with an Eskimo family? Why were two of the skeletons, found in an abandoned ship's boat, missing their skulls and why did each hold a rifle that had fired a single shot? Did

Eskimo hands pull down the survivors' cairns and destroy their records? Did they murder the stragglers?

Both ships were immensely strong. *Terror* had once spent three months stuck on a floating iceberg but had survived and returned to England. Six years after the ships left for the Arctic, there was an official sighting by the master and crew of the English brig *Renovation*. They reported seeing two three-masted ships, black in colour, marooned high on a passing iceberg off the northern coast of Canada.

Did some of the survivors resort to cannibalism? Dr John Rae, one of the searchers, recorded: "From the mutilated state of many of the bodies and the contents of the kettles it is evident that our wretched countrymen were driven to the last desperate alternative as a means of sustaining life."

I felt a twinge of sympathy for the terrible fate of Franklin and his men who had died so slowly and hopelessly in this hostile land.

On the eastern side of Beechey Island we anchored and waded ashore where an old ship's bowsprit protruded from the gravel beach. On benchland some way above the high tide mark were the crumbled foundations of a small shack and, all about, the shattered remains of wooden barrels and rusty iron hoops. Beyond the bowsprit were gravestones. Some of Franklin's men had died here, of scurvy perhaps, but the majority had continued on to die further south.

Charlie cut his name into a slab of slate and left it on the beach. For an hour we sat together and stared at our desolate surroundings. Then on for 160 miles to Croker Bay. En route we crossed the mouths of many bays and looking north saw the crown of the high ice-field which lies over the eastern half of Devon Island and sends its tentacles down the coastal valleys to calve into the sea fjords as icebergs.

As evening closed in we moved under the cold dark shoulder of huge cliffs through an ink black sea. There were seals and whales and many birds and, increasingly, icebergs of great height and length. At Croker Bay, as night fell on us from the ice-laden cliffs above, a storm rushed north over Lancaster Sound and caught us ten miles short of shelter. The propellers struck unseen ice with heart-stopping thuds. To be immobilised between the jostling icebergs would not be healthy.

"Monster to port," Charlie shouted in my ear. I stared into the gloom where he pointed and saw the foaming silhouette of a giant wave strike a nearby chunk of ice. A wall of spray rose above us. The world kicked and danced in unseen turmoil and I strained my eyes at the rock heights to spot the indent of Dundas Harbour, once the site of a Hudson Bay Company store, but now abandoned to the elements. I found the entry but icebergs large and small ground together in the high swell across the bay mouth and only with a goodly slice of luck did we thread our way safely through to the haven of shallows and the wonderful sight of three little shacks by a low bar of shingle.

One was almost rainproof and Charlie soon had a log fire spitting under our stewpot. For an hour we lay chatting of army days long ago in Arabia, candlelight flickering on our sodden suits hung up to dry.

East of Dundas the inland glacial mass poured ice down towards the sea: a million water-coloured chunks floated off the coastline like lethal frogspawn. Waves broke against the seaborne giants all about us. Spray shrieked by in horizontal sheets. The storm raged along the southern coast of Devon Island all day and from Resolute, Ginnie reported drifting snow and overlying ice. With but four days to the end of the month I decided not to wait for improvement.

An hour after setting out we rounded the gaunt rocks of Cape Warrender. Waves smashed the shore in a thundering welter of surf. A course running parallel to the cliffs and 400 yards out seemed least dangerous. Several times the boat shuddered as unseen ice hit the hull or propellers. Then a shear pin went: Charlie closed down the now useless port outboard and we limped on at half power, gradually drifting nearer to the cliffs. For four miles we found nowhere to land but knew we must change shear pins quickly. At any moment the other propeller might strike ice. Then we would be the fibreglass version of matchwood in minutes. A tiny defile with a shingle beach appeared between cliff walls. I sighed with relief. On our way in we passed several hundred beluga whales, then we nosed between madly jostling ice blocks and grounded bergs to fight through to the little beach.

Charlie grabbed my shoulder and pointed dead ahead. One of the grounded bergs on the beach, at the very point selected for our landing, turned out to be an adult polar bear. Perhaps the bear knew the beluga, its natural prey, were wont to bask in the shallows off the beach. To disturb a hunting perhaps hungry polar bear is generally a bad idea but we had no alternative. Unbroken cliffs stretched twenty miles to the east according to my chart.

Charlie nosed the boat in as far as he dared and I went overboard. One of my suit leggings filled up with water to the thigh for it had developed a tear. Holding the bow painter I trod the slippery rocks whilst Charlie unsheathed his rifle. The bear, unfamiliar with shiny white eighteen-foot long whalers, withdrew slowly and disappeared among boulders which ringed the beach.

For thirty minutes I struggled to hold the boat as steady as possible whilst Charlie worked with freezing hands to replace the shear pin and both propellers, for we discovered they were hopelessly battered and one had a blade missing. I kept a wary eye open for the bear. As we left the beach it passed us swimming with nose and eyes only above the water. Startled, it dived. For a second its great white behind rose skywards, then nothing.

The waves beyond the immediate lee of the cliffs were as big as any I had ever seen. For 120 miles we bucked and rolled between heaving icebergs, mesmerised by the size and power of the waves. Bergs bigger than bungalows rolled about like beach balls in the sixty-knot gale and I held my breath many a time as we squeezed between highly mobile ice monsters. Freezing sleet, fog and gale-force winds forced us to spend a night at Cape Sherard but on 27th August at midday we left the coast of Devon Island and crossed Jones Sound to Ellesmere Island; an anxious journey.

At Craig Harbour, under dizzy cliffs, we paused to relax beside a king-berg complete with blue arched caverns. Then on and on until, feeling much like soggy bacon rind looks, we reached the deep and shadowed reaches of Grise Fjord, the only Eskimo settlement on the island.

Back in Resolute, Ginnie, fully aware of the dangers of Devon Island's east coast, had waited for my call for twenty-eight hours. Simon explained in his diary: "Ginnie's face getting more introverted, frowning and bitter all day as she heard nothing."

I fixed an antenna up by two Eskimo houses, threading my way through wooden stretch frames of drying harp seal pelts. Ginnie's voice was faraway and faint but I heard the happiness in it as she acknowledged our position.

The last three days of August passed by in a blur of black cliff, freezing spray and, above all, increasing ice. At the mouth to Hell Gate, escape route from Jones Sound and beneath a cliff called Cape Turnback, I decided the conditions looked evil and the currents treacherous. We turned west and by Devil Island, north into Cardigan Strait. Again, hours of anxiety in wind-writhed waves but once through the strait, our long detour was over. In Norwegian Bay we were once more on our original axis north from Resolute Bay. The gamble had paid off and still there were forty-eight hours in which to cover the final 400 miles.

That evening the surface of the sea began to freeze for the first time, congealing silently and fast. We must speed on. A twenty-mile bay bites into Ellesmere Island to the south of Great Bear Cape and there we again hit pack-ice. Again and again we nosed up channels and leads. To no avail: the pack became more solid to seawards and impenetrable within the bay.

There was nothing for it but to retreat. Again new ice covered the open sea in oily sheets. We beached in an unnamed bay and talked little that evening.

I radioed Ginnie. She reported a sixty-mile belt of pack in Norwegian Bay that stretched west to Axel Heiberg Island. Our Twin Otter had still not arrived and so could not help us through the ice barrier. But an hour later Ginnie came back with great news. Russ Bomberry, one of the finest bush pilots in the Arctic and a chief of the Mohawk Indians, was in Resolute Bay with his Twin Otter. He had agreed to give us two hours 'ice flight' the next day.

The mist stayed away. The temperature dropped. I slept little that night. Only 320 miles to Tanquary Fjord, but we could be one short day too late if this last ice belt delayed us long enough to snare us in the new ice of the coming winter.

At dawn we were up, teeth a-chatter, and loaded the whaler in readiness. At mid-day Russ circled overhead and we left for the ice belt. The new ice was already thicker and filled every open lead in the pack. The young frazil ice and ice rind burgeoned like active yeast. In places the whaler could no longer plane through but meshed with it like a bumblebee in a spider's web.

In the middle of the bay a light wind arose and opened channels in the ice rind. This helped. Russ ranged in wide circles north east over the Bjorne peninsula and north west towards the snowy peaks of Axel Heiberg Island.

Whilst he was gone we nosed about in the centre of the pack. I wondered, if Russ did not return or a fog closed in, how long it would take us to extricate ourselves from so complex and ever-changing a labyrinth. Once back, Russ wasted no time, he knew the only way it could be done. To get us north to Great Bear Cape he took us west, east and even south a good deal of the time. From the air our course must have looked rather like a dish of spaghetti. Three hours later Russ dipped his wings and left us. We were clear of the close pack. The rest we could handle.

A mile or two out of the pack the steering linkage packed up. Charlie glared at it, smoked two cigarettes in contemplation of its mechanics, then fixed it in an unorthodox but effective fashion. We slept five hours during the next two days. For the rest we moved north through narrowing channels. A hundred miles up the winding canyons of Eureka Sound to Eureka itself, an isolated camp set up by the Canadian government purely as a weather station. A strong wind kept the new ice at bay in the fjords during the night of 30th August and next day we began the last run north up Greely Fjord for 150 miles to Tanquary Fjord itself, a cul-de-sac deep in glacier-cut mountains.

Tiers of snowcapped peaks shaped the horizons as we snaked ever deeper into a twilit world of loneliness and silence. Wolves stared from shadowed lava beaches, but nothing moved except ourselves to sunder in our wash the mirror images of the darkened valley walls.

Twelve minutes before midnight we came to the end of the fjord. The sea journey was over. Within a week the sounds behind us were frozen.

12

Over the Ellesmere Icecap

AUGUST–SEPTEMBER 1981

We are the pilgrims, Master: we shall go
Always a little further: it may be
Beyond that last blue mountain barr'd with snow,
Across that angry or that glimmering sea.

JAMES ELROY FLECKER
(SAS *regimental memorial*)

Five great icecaps surround the head of Tanquary Fjord on Ellesmere Island but it is possible to reach Alert, 150 miles to the north east, by a chain of stream valleys. On our arrival at Tanquary these valleys were snow-free, but the streams themselves had frozen. There was a temptation to set out at once before the temperatures began to plummet. But this could not be because the gravel strip and three little huts at Tanquary Camp were to form one of two bases for the Twin Otter during our coming attempt to cross the Arctic Ocean. It had been Ginnie's idea to use Tanquary as an additional base to Alert. The mists in April and May were so bad at Alert, she said, that we would save weeks by having Tanquary stocked, beyond the reach of sea mists.

Giles and Gerry were due in a week's time with the first of the base equipment from Resolute. This would need careful sorting and re-packing for some must stay at Tanquary and some go on to Alert.

This I must do before leaving. And another reason argued for delay: Charlie and I were body weak from more than a month of inaction in a cramped boat, and in no condition for a land journey on foot.

Ginnie and Bothie had flown in the previous day by Twin Otter from Resolute. Simon and Tugaluk stayed behind to run things for the aircrew.

There can be few places in the world as remote and idyllic as Tanquary Camp. I walked with Ginnie along the frozen course of the creek that tumbles from Redrock Glacier. Bothie gave chase to Arctic hares. Yapping with joy, he ignored Ginnie's orders to return and scampered away over moss-clad benchland unaware of his danger.

Two wolves, white like Bothie, and probably attracted by his barking, loped down the hillside towards him. Ginnie fired her pistol in the air. The wolves ignored her and closed the gap to Bothie. Ginnie screamed. So did I. Bothie took no notice but lost the hare trail and turned back. The wolves stopped, gazed at us, and then moved away towards the camp. That night three adult wolves with three cubs came down to the huts. We watched them through a window. The wolf cubs looked cuddly but we resisted the temptation to go outside and see if they liked to be stroked. Arctic wolves are slightly smaller than their southerly neighbours, the timber wolves. They often prowl alone but, when hunting caribou, their main source of food, they operate in packs. Not long ago all wolves were shot on sight in the Canadian Arctic but now only the Eskimos can kill them and sell their pelts.

On 6th September Giles and Gerry arrived with a full load of cargo from Resolute and a great many letters from London.

From these letters I gathered that Oliver's wife had seemed happier, so he had written to the Committee to say that he thought he might be able to join us at Alert for the North Pole crossing. However the Committee felt that if he returned to the Transglobe expedition, he must be able to guarantee uninterrupted service until the completion of the whole journey, however long it might take, and must resign from his present job. But when Oliver had taken on his new job, he had told his new employers that he was through with Transglobe and was joining them permanently as a fulltime career. He therefore did not feel that he could categorically guarantee what the Committee wanted. After all the Arctic crossing might take two years, if ice conditions were bad.

I could see both Oliver's and the Committee's problems, so I reluctantly accepted that it would be best if Charlie and I got on with the task and Oliver continued to help the London end of our organisation whenever he could. Charlie, too, was sad Ol would not return, although he pointed out: "I personally, if I had left, would not be coming back. The whole point of the expedition is to circumnavigate the world. If you leave and miss out one part of it, you might as well not do it."

On 11th September Charlie and I set out to cross Ellesmere Island from Tanquary Camp to Alert on foot, 150 miles carrying eighty pounds of gear apiece on our backs. I also carried a pistol and Charlie a .357 magnum rifle. Because the Viking Icecap blocked our way north, we trudged south east along the valley of the Macdonald River which in reality was a piddling little iced-over stream that meandered along gravel beds.

The first day's going was easy with a light breeze and clear sky. Mountains rose on both sides but the valley was wide and grazed by many Arctic hares. To us they were just white rabbits, pretty and comical. Some would carry on feeding until we were a mere ten yards away. Then off they went on their hind legs only, holding their front paws up daintily like old ladies poised with teacups. Musk-oxen, in groups of two or three, munched at the sere sphagnum, cow-sized shaggy bundles with stubby legs and runtish horns. As we approached they pawed the mossy ground, heads lowered in defiance. The explorers of eighty years ago shot many musk-oxen on the island: they took the soft wool that lies beneath the long brown hair. This *qiviut* was valuable to the Eskimo and the meat vital to the continued existence of any man so far north.

We put nearly two miles behind us each hour for four hours. Where the melt water from the Redrock Glacier enters the Macdonald Valley we stopped beside a frozen pool. Our tent was light and small, easy to set up. Charlie smashed the ice with his knife and collected water in his mug. The sole of one heel was blistered but he showed no concern.

Next day the valley narrowed down. Now the sunlight was shut away by canyon walls. We turned north west up a side valley that climbed for six miles to an unnamed glacier. This tumbled down from the Viking Icecap in a shambolic icefall which landed in our valley and turned it into a cul-de-sac. Summer floods had burrowed a tunnel underneath this barrier. Arriving at the resulting culvert, I found there was plenty of room to pass through it if well bent over, but the ceiling looked insecure and I paused to wait for Charlie.

In a while I heard him shout my name. There was a note of urgency but I could not see him for the ice chunks and boulders all around. I shrugged off my rucksack and scrambled back down the valley. I realised I'd left my pistol behind and there might well be a bear, but deciding not to stop, I plunged on round a corner. There was Charlie hunched over a rock in the middle of the frozen stream. No bear but plenty of blood. His head was leaking from below his hairline and one eye was full of blood. He had slipped on the ice and come down with his head hard against a sharp-edged rock. He looked white. I removed the tiny first-aid pack from his rucksack, plastered a gauze pad over the cut and had him shove his head low until the dizziness went. The plaster seeped blood for a day or two but the wound stayed healthy.

He had received a nasty jolt and moved a bit more slowly. I took the tent from his pack in exchange for my sleeping bag. After eight hours we had covered eleven miles but a mist came down and snow had settled on my tracks. I could not see Charlie behind, so I stopped and put the tent up. He arrived after forty minutes. Blisters on both his soles had broken and several had formed on his toes. He said he ached all over.

There was a big bump on my right calf above the boot rim. It was squelchy to touch but painless. My underclothes were wet with sweat. Our boots and socks and trouserlegs were soaking from breaking through the ice crust time and time again into the stream below. But it was easy going and the weather was still only slightly below freezing. We were in good time. There were no problems.

Charlie, a rugged individualist, did not need my walking just ahead of him to encourage him. So long as he could see which way I had gone he preferred to be left to suffer alone. My own preference was to carry on at the pace which suited me best, not to dawdle. Charlie knew this and never complained.

The film crew could not understand why we did not walk together like normal folk. Why did I not hold back with Charles as a good leader would? At Alert they asked Charlie about this. Did he hate walking? Charlie answered:

> *Yeah, I don't like it. But I wouldn't say I hated every step of the journey. I mean the first step was OK and the last step was absolutely beautiful. The rest of it was hell. I knew it was going*

to be hard keeping up with Ran. He has always punished himself
in the walking field. There was a race in Wales we all used to
train for and he was always up front. He is always pushing
himself. He can't do it the easy way. I don't know what drives
him but he always pushes himself. I'm not that way inclined. I'm
a slow plodder. I will do the trip but in my own time. Ran must
do it in the fastest possible time. It's a mental thing. I knew I was
going to do it in my time, but if I tried to keep up with Ran, I
wasn't going to make it. Whereas Ran can kill himself each day, I
can't. I have got to space myself out.

Does that bother Ran?

The speed difference would bother him for the simple reason
that he would have to wait for me. He travels for two hours then
he stops. I might be half an hour behind him in which case he has
got to wait for me and therefore he is going to get cold. That
would worry him.

The third morning dawned grey and dismal. Ice crystals lined the
tent for the first time but we were a mere thousand feet up into the
mountains. Snow covered the valley floor. Charlie's left eye was
almost closed and the skin about it was puffed up in yellow swellings.

He told me his back and knee and blisters all hurt. The blisters
looked very nasty. The whole of his right heel was raw and weeping.
He no longer wanted his rifle. "How about the bears?" I asked him.
"If a polar bear attacks me," he replied, "it'll put me out of my
misery."

The first ten minutes of the day's walk must have been purgatory
for Charlie but he kept at it and we covered fourteen miles in ten
hours. I missed one Y-junction of valleys in the mist but picked up the
second without trouble and forked further north up the Very River
bed. Gravel benches fashioned by the retreat of long ago glaciers gave
us shelter from a bitter wind and Charlie cooked a delicious re-
hydrated stew. With it went two kinds of army biscuit: biscuits plain
and biscuits sweet. If you were sufficiently hungry it was possible to
detect a faint difference in taste between the two types.

The Very River moves down its own flood plain with a chain of
pools or lakes leading to its mouth at Lake Hazen. But a mixture of
fine sand, ice and snow covered the lakes and the lonely moraines all
about them. A strong wind came down from the icecaps to our north
and whipped up the dust of the sand bowl. With a sickly lime light

sifting wan and sombre through the storm and our boots sinking deep in the grey-white dust, we might have been on the moon. −7°C.

Gradually the valley opened out until the lake itself was visible, forty miles long and up to six wide; it was bounded to the south by rolling tundra, spattered with streams and pools, to the north by the towering ramparts of the central icecap. I chose to follow the lake's northern flank because half-way along was a single deserted hut by the lakeside put there twenty years before by scientists. A fairly flat gravel bench beside it was said to be suitable for a Twin Otter and I felt we ought soon to change from rucksacks to pulk sledges, from walking boots to canvas mukluks and skis. Two weeks earlier we might have completed the journey on old crusted snow and bare tundra but new snow now lay thick in windscoops indicating the conditions likely at 2,000 feet, to which height we must soon climb.

We stomped along beside the lake all day, crunching the ice underfoot with odd zing and twang sounds until evening when we set up our tent. All night long a sound similar to Rice Krispies reacting to milk lulled our intermittent sleep; new ice forming in the shallows along the beachside and rafting, slab upon slab.

Charlie's left eye was by now quite closed and swollen over. Both his knees were watery and his feet were balloon-like. He was worried that they might not fit back in his boots the next day. He found the mornings especially painful: putting his raw heels and bloody toes into frost-hardened boots made him grit his teeth together. Late on 15th September I reached the old hut below Omingmak Mountain. A family of nine musk-oxen galloped snorting off the hillside. Two hours later Charlie arrived looking half dead. It was obvious that his feet were getting worse so we changed the bandages and he took penicillin lest the blisters turn septic.

Next day Giles flew in to the little strip beside the hut bringing our pulk sledges, skis and snowshoes. He removed Charlie's rifle and gave him a pistol. I made weak contact with Ginnie. She warned me communications were fading fast. She had spent two days alone at Tanquary earlier in the week and, although she found the white wolves most attractive to look at, was not altogether happy with the way they stood up at her hut windows during the night and looked in at her. Nor did she enjoy their loud and discordant howling which made sleep difficult. They themselves seemed to sleep little since five of them followed her about the camp all day, ignoring her pistol shots. She took to using my FN rifle instead but firing that frightened her more than it did the wolves. Part of the problem seemed to be the two dogs. The wolves had obviously decided Tugaluk and Bothie would provide good eating and hung about the camp waiting their chance. Ginnie's voice faded out and I was unable to raise her or anyone else again for the next two days, despite alterations of frequency and antenna. The polar sun was soon to disappear for the winter and communications are often poor at this time of year.

There were yellow-paged books in the hut which Charlie read, with his poor feet propped up on a bench. Giles had taken one look at his knees and feet and suggested we wait at least a week before continuing. After two days there was little sign of improvement.

I loaded the two pulk sledges with care. With enough food for ten days, the loads came to 110 pounds apiece, an easy pull. Whilst waiting for Charlie's feet to heal, I harnessed myself to a pulk, donned a pair of cross-country skis and climbed up into the foothills beneath the looming icecaps. I soon found the skis awkward, so changed to basket-work snowshoes which made uphill work much easier.

The air was cold and clear. To the east lay mile upon mile of rock and ice, the weird tundra polygons of Black River Vale and, fifty miles away, the frozen cliffs of Robeson Channel. The sad remains of Fort Conger, itself but fifty miles south of Alert, still stand beside the channel, mute testimony to two brave Arctic pioneers. The great American, Admiral Peary, who tried five times to reach the Pole had had seven gangrenous toes cut off at Conger in 1904. Twenty years earlier, Lieutenant Greely, also American, had experienced the hardships of an Arctic winter along the same coastline. Greely and his men ran out of food and suffered intense cold and bitter frost, disaster and slow starvation, insanity and death. To these unpleasantnesses historians have added the probability of cannibalism because the rescue party found corpses with large chunks of flesh missing. Only seven out of Greely's twenty-five men survived to be rescued by the relief ship. One of these, who had lost his hands and feet through gangrene, soon died.

Despite the inhospitable terrain and the climate, humans have survived on eastern Ellesmere Island on and off for centuries. Now no one lives there but 700 years ago Vikings are believed to have settled in the area; later Eskimos from Alaska are thought to have migrated east and colonised parts of the island before moving on into

Greenland. Up to about 1950, about 300 Eskimos lived by hunting polar bear, seal, walrus and whale, scattered in small settlements to the north of Thule. Existence was harsh for all: food was scarce: weak husky puppies were thrown to the pack as food and old dogs were killed. Aged and infirm members of the tribe were simply left outside to die: food was too precious to waste on non-productive members of society.

Then civilisation came to Greenland and in particular to Thule and the surrounding region. Drink and venereal diseases were introduced for the first time along with refrigerators, skidoos and outboard motors. The young preferred to gain a technical education in Denmark rather than to follow the traditional ways of life.

From Tanquary Fjord to Lake Hazen we had passed no single man-made object, no paths, no refuse, nothing: it was comforting to have been somewhere where humans have left no lasting mark whatsoever on their environment. The sun passed behind the outline of a glacier. It was time to head back down the mountain. Back at the hut Charlie showed me his feet. The swellings had subsided and the blistered areas looked clean. It seemed to me that even if we hung around for days until new skin replaced the raw places, the sores would re-open after the first mile or so. We might as well go on now. Every day the temperature dropped and the hours of darkness increased.

"If you feel OK tomorrow, we should set out early."

Charlie made no comment.

Wearing canvas mukluks and snowshoes put less pressure on Charlie's sore feet. The weight we dragged now was on pulk sledges behind us, not on our backs; this also helped him. At first he went well and we made good time. But the cliffs beyond the Abbé River came down to the lake, leaving no narrow shingle beach to trudge along. I detoured up a ravine in a thick mist. The slopes were steep and icy but under the balls of our feet, attached to our snowshoes, were metal claws and these helped us to get a good grip which made the pulks easier to pull. For several miles we pushed through dense fog along cliff ridges, down snowfields and rock gullies. Twice I tried to swing back to the lakeside, twice I was again forced uphill where there was no beach. By late afternoon however the hills receded from the lake leaving us some reasonably flat going.

The temperature dropped four degrees and our beards were now frosted. Once I waited forty minutes after only an hour's travel.

Seething inwardly, I pummelled my hands and feet about. What the hell was holding Charlie? When he arrived, I asked him.

"The pulk keeps overturning on boulders."

"Perhaps you've stacked it wrong," I suggested.

"It makes no difference," he replied.

I unloaded his pulk, repacked it and lashed the kit down tightly. Perhaps it would make no difference but anything was worth trying. All the time I realised that the fault was entirely mine: Charlie was suffering considerable pain moving at all. I should be moving at his pace, then I wouldn't have to freeze my noodles off waiting. There was no answer to this. Once or twice I did try setting off slowly but I just couldn't maintain such a desultory amble. It was like trying to suck Maltesers instead of chewing them.

That night the temperature dropped to $-18°C$ and the lake froze. We began to travel over its surface which was excellent for Charlie's feet and knees and we made good time. The ice often buckled, protesting noisily; if you trod where the ice was weak, it shattered. At noon on 21st September we left the lake behind and entered a wide featureless valley. Many musk-oxen, startled by our sudden appearance through the yellow murk, thundered off, their wide hooves sinking into drifts, their loose fur coats swinging kilt-like.

I took the line of least resistance and counted my paces. Without lake or closed valleys or river line for boundaries it would be easy to get lost, so I began to use the compass with care as the north magnetic pole was now a long way to our south. The needle was sluggish but seemed to settle with some consistency. I followed a magnetic bearing of 130° and ignored the temptation to take easier-looking routes which veered off this course. Ice hid all pools and we crossed the three mile long Lake Turnabout without even knowing it for the snow cover had made it invisible.

Musk oxen snorted and stamped as we loomed up through the freezing fog. We progressed through this snow-covered tundra at no more than one mile an hour as we were climbing much of the time over rough hummocks, our snowshoes often sinking in deep or jamming in potholes. We finished the lake water in our water bottles during the morning and grew thirsty. I tried eating handfuls of snow but that did little to slake my growing thirst. Charlie kept close now which was just as well for sometimes there were streams where the glass ice left no mark of my passing and he could easily have lost my meandering spoor.

Charlie too was thirsty. We listened in the gloom and once, hearing the tinkle of water from an iced-over stream through the heavy silence, plunged our knives into the ice. There was no water. Towards evening we found a slow trickle two feet below the iced surface. We drank greedily and filled our bottles with the muddy liquid, keeping them inside our shirts so the water would not freeze.

After twelve hours' travel, fat snowflakes began to fall softly through the mist. We set the tent up. It was a wet snow and our clothes were sodden. One of Charlie's little toes hurt him.

"Still," he reflected, "it takes my mind off the usual aches and pains."

I contacted Ginnie, who had flown from Tanquary Fjord to our old huts at Alert, and told her our rough position but conditions were too bad for anything else. Then the cooker would not start as there was no pressure in the pump. We found ice around the plunger leather but by covering it with margarine, eventually got it to come to life so we could get warm and dry.

Visibility was poor again the next day and distinguishing landmarks nil. My dead reckoning might be way out but without proof either way, I carried on up and down the valleys until I came across the prints of musk oxen climbing a narrow defile up one side of the valley system. By hauling our pulks up backwards six feet at a time we finally reached a ridge top so that I could get some idea of the lie of the land. This ridge turned out to be attached, like a rib, to a main spine which led west for a mile, cutting through a labyrinth of canyons to a high plateau of snowfields, with a lake leading northeast. Happily this placed us on the map where the dead reckoning had indicated.

The pulks partially broke through the ice-crust of the lake and sludge clung to their hulls. Once in contact with the air this sludge froze solid. We now dragged jagged-bottomed sledges which effectively doubled their weight. We chipped the ice-clay away with difficulty and, after four murderous miles, they ran free once more. For the next five hours we climbed steadily through deep soft snow. My snowshoes sank in twelve inches, sometimes double that, before the surface solidified enough to take my weight and the transferred drag of the sledge, which itself dragged low. We lurched and tugged our way along until late that afternoon when we reached the foot of the Boulder Hills at 2,200 feet and camped beside a frozen gully.

Here there was no water so we melted snow, a process wasteful on cooker fuel.

For three long days we plodded through deep snowfields with temperatures at −20°. Because the exercise was unbroken we wore but two layers of clothing, as for walking in the Welsh hills, and only felt cold when we stopped for more than two minutes to drink or eat snow. The stillness was immense. No musk-oxen now. Nothing and no one.

On 23rd September we camped at the foot of the great Eugenie Glacier, its well-formed snout armed with layers of glistening teeth, stalagmites from a previous summer's brief melt. Mist rolled over the plateau from the east but now the very rim of the Grant Icecap brushed our left flank and, spurred on by the increasing cold, we limped at last to the northern tip of the plateau. There were many steep snowbanks to climb up or slither down. On one of these Charlie bruised his hip but, after a short rest, continued as before. In awe we laboured beneath the towering icefalls of Mount Wood where twin glaciers tumbled 2,000 feet down to a lonely lake. Here everything had a contorted temporary look, gigantic blocks of ice, scarred and smudged with alluvial muck and blackened walls of ice, reared up like monster waves frozen in the act of crashing against some puny dam. In the wary hush of this place where no birds sang, some new and cataclysmic upheaval seemed imminent. Crane your neck up to ease the pain of the sledge harness and the skyhigh icefalls appeared to teeter from their summits.

Thankful to leave, I sought a tiny stream outlet from the lake. Fingers of frost crept over the primordial environs of the lake and we stumbled by good luck into a corridor, some ten yards wide, between two boulder outcrops. This narrow rock-girt passage immediately descended, in curves and steps, to the west-north-west. There could be no doubt we were in the upper canyon of the Grant River, a winding ravine that falls for thirty miles to the sea. Once in it there was no further need to navigate, there being no branch-off valleys. The only place to camp was on the river ice. All game followed the river too and myriad little hoof prints of fox, hare, lemming, caribou and wolf, dented the snowdrifts all about.

The metal spikes of our snowshoes, long since blunted by rock and slate, no longer gripped the sheet-ice. Every few minutes evil language echoed off the narrow canyon walls as one or other of us slipped and crashed over onto the rocks. Often our snowshoes smashed through the ice and dropped two or three feet down to the streambed. Thanks to the snowshoes, awkward though they were, there were no sprained ankles.

Our pulks plunged through the ice too and, wetting their hulls, clogged up as they had on the plateau lake. More scraping and cold fingers. The sledge harnesses broke from the violent stop-start effect of jamming against boulders, overturning and crashing into sharp rocks. Using parachute cord we repaired the breaks and carried on.

The canyon kinked and snaked, was blocked with high black boulders and once even seemed to climb. But this must have been an illusion. One night was spent in a bottleneck some twelve feet wide between high black walls. Our tent stood suspended on ice above a neat round pool. We swallowed our soya bean stew and bet each other how far it was to the sea. Already there was far less snow. In places we hauled the sledges over nothing but rock for hundreds of yards. Despite the hills all around there was good contact with Ginnie at Alert. I fell asleep thinking blissfully of the warmth of the huts there.

On 26th September, towards noon, the river bed plunged thirty feet down a frozen waterfall. From the top of this cleft we looked out at the Arctic Ocean where an inlet, Black Cliffs Bay, edged in to meet the mouth of our river valley. A jagged vista of contorted pack-ice stretched away to the polar horizon.

Travelling along the edge of the frozen sea we came by dusk to the four little huts that we knew so well, the most northern habitation on earth.

We had travelled around the polar axis of the world for 314° of latitude in 750 days. Only 46° to go; looking north at the chaotic ice rubble, thirty feet high in places, there was no doubt in my mind: the hardest nut was yet to be cracked.

13

Northern Winter

SEPTEMBER 1981–FEBRUARY 1982

To be alive at all involves some risk.

HAROLD MACMILLAN

For five days before our arrival at the Alert huts Ginnie had slaved away to make them habitable, for no one had wintered in them since we ourselves had back in January 1977. The main shack was a garage just big enough to take two Land Rovers. This was to be used for our skidoos, all outdoor stores and, in one half, the generators which Charlie would have to run now that Ol was absent.

A small kitchen hut faced the garage across twenty yards of snow and on a nearby slope three one-room living huts acted as bedrooms. One for Ginnie and me, one for Charlie and, when spring came, one for the aircrew and Simon.

The dogs were to live in a tiny shack on the slope between the huts which was also to be our lavatory, with straw on the floor and a bucket with a plastic seat which we had had sent out specially from England. I say dogs, for of course Ginnie had not had the heart to leave Tugaluk behind in Resolute. She was now prancing about, a monstrous black affair, at least three times as big as Bothie.

"Don't flap," said Ginnie, "she's probably fully grown as she's two months old now."

The thought of the creature's great black paws tearing up our square of lawn back in London made me shudder.

We had arrived during autumn when the temperature hovered around −20°C, a few hours of sunlight still graced each day and life was a delight. It was a far cry from the first bitter January night we had spent at Alert back in 1977. Of that mid-winter nightmare Oliver had written:

> *The huts are deplorable. Two of them are just habitable, the remainder full of ice or snow. Our predecessors must have left in a hurry, many years ago. No heater and so, so cold. I slept wearing ten layers of clothing. It is impossible to get warm.*

Two days later, after settling in a bit, he had added:

> *Have now had time to take in the environment. It is pitch black most of the time and even the moon has pissed off for two weeks. Apparently, it gets light on 2nd March. Everything and anything freezes solid. Tins, toothpaste, food, apples, paper, pens, metal, engines, human flesh. My hands are already a great problem.*

Soon after we arrived Major Reg Warkentin, in charge of the main camp, two miles to the south, called on us by snow caterpillar. Later on a Roman Catholic padre held a Thanksgiving Service for our safe arrival in Alert, home of the "Chosen Frozen" as the denizens, Canadian soldiers and weathermen, call themselves. They are proud to be the most northerly men on earth: the nearest manned base is Eureka, 300 miles to the south. There is no possibility of visitors by sea or land, nor, when the weather is bad, by air. The battered remains of a transport aircraft and the nine graves of its occupants rested close to our huts, a mute testimony to the hazards of reaching Alert.

We heard from the Resolute Canadians that the Japanese husband and wife team who left Resolute soon after us had been caught up in the pack-ice of Barrow Strait. They had later escaped south only to have to call for the help of a Canadian Coastguard icebreaker which steamed 700 miles through ice to reach them. They found that they were well but the boat was aground on a shoal. The Japanese asked them to remove his wife, so they pulled him off the shoal, took away his wife and he carried on with his journey. How far he got we never learned but the ice probably trapped him by Cambridge Bay.

Giles and Gerry managed to bring all our supplies into Alert in the first week of October. Before Giles left I asked him to drop a cache of fuel and rations a hundred miles west of our camp, along the coastline. The Twin Otter had no skis fitted, only tundra tyres. These were standard for a Dakota (DC 3) which uses a much wider tyre than the Twin Otter. With these Giles could land on fairly rough ground or on ice but not in soft snow. What was the terrain like where I wanted this cache, he asked? I was uncertain.

We took off at the beginning of the daily quota of sunlight, by then only three hours, and flew west. This flight marked Giles's one thousandth flying hour for Transglobe. I looked down to see a rough coast, exceptionally hostile to travellers. The sea-ice was broken, rearing up in huge waves of rubble that smothered the shoreline. The mountains were steep-sided and mostly hidden by active glaciers. Deep fjords cut into them. Giles inspected Cape Columbia, the dark promontory where I intended to turn north on to the sea-ice when the time came to start for the North Pole. There was nowhere remotely suitable for a landing. Giles veered back east. The next feature, Cape Aldrich, was also out of the question but, four miles further south, he circled over an unnamed glacier that flowed east from Mount Hornby. Close to its snout on the beach of Parr Bay we came in fast and low landing on an uphill slope of hard ribbed snow. There were bumps but we hardly felt them for Giles was no ordinary pilot. Quickly we unloaded the rations, jerry cans and orange marker flags. When next Charlie and I came here, there would be no sunlight.

This was Giles' last flight for Transglobe. Karl Z'berg would be replacing him and flying for us in the spring with Gerry. Giles said that he had enjoyed it all and offered to return at short notice if ever we needed him. He finally took off for England with Simon and Gerry on board and circled once, diving low over the three of us waving from the cold foggy strip.

We were not alone for long for David Mason flew in for two days in a Hercules sponsored by Bob Engel of North West Territorial Airlines. We unloaded over 200 drums of fuel, four skidoos we had last seen at Ryvingen and a good deal more ex-Antarctic gear. The work involved with transporting it all to London from the Antarctic, servicing and repairing it, then getting it up to Alert via Thule, Resolute or Montreal — all at no cost — had taken David many long months and late nights.

On arrival at Alert he was fuming about the drinking habits of RAF outposts. The RAF had agreed to fly some of our cargo from their Brize Norton base to Thule via an RAF outpost in Goose Bay. At the last minute the Bay airmen had considerably upped their Christmas order for beer and cigarettes. This took unquestionable priority over David's sledges and ice rations which had to be abandoned.

After leaving us, David flew back to Thule with a further load of stores destined for Ginnie's most remote radio base, Station Nord in East Greenland, a place she would fly to in the Twin Otter if and when we ever reached the North Pole. His work well done David returned to London.

The Alert base commander Major Reg Warkentin sent two tracked bulldozers with scoopblades from his camp to help me move the 200 drums off the airstrip, also ten volunteer soldiers. They wore fur-lined parkas and we worked in the dark for three hours. One of them, an expatriate Scot, started suffering exposure symptoms and was driven off to the camp sick bay. I nearly ended up there myself but not because of the cold. The drill was for three of us to roll three drums onto the lowered scoop of a dozer and signal 'Ready' to the driver up in his cab. He would then work his hydraulics so that the steel scoop tilted, the blade's rear end lowering to the ground and the sharp end rising so that the drums stayed on the blade. At the critical moment and without my realising it, one of my mukluks strayed to just beneath the pivotal part of the blade as I signalled 'Ready' to the driver.

Too late I felt the steel weight descend onto my foot and begin to press it down into the ice. At that second I *knew* my toes and the front half of my foot were about to be crushed flat. I screamed but the driver was looking elsewhere with his cab door closed against the intense cold. For some heaven-sent reason he released his lower-control with the blade still an inch or two off the ground. I thanked God for the driver's sloppiness. Without a doubt I was more thankful and more aware of my luck at that moment of the expedition than at any other. It would have been most difficult to complete the journey with one and a half feet.

I woke suddenly one night. Ginnie was moaning with stomach pains, which had become increasingly frequent, but something else had startled me. As I looked around, I noticed a horizontal gap along the edge of the ceiling through which I could see moonlight and stars. The roof had parted company with the walls by a good four inches. At that moment the whole hut shook as a violent gust struck the camp. For two minutes the camp hummed with the rattle of antenna wires and the clash of metal on metal from the stores hut. Then, as suddenly, silence. Throughout the night successive windstorms slammed through the camp hurling a thick carpet of snow into our room. Next day, as I lashed the wooden roof down with wire and ropes, I glimpsed huge black rents in the pack-ice. I checked the thermometers in our beehive screen: $-4°C$. Such warmth so late in the year did not bode well for us. We needed a cold hard winter to make the ice grow thick and solid, the better to resist the rupturing stresses of the winter storms.

Alert has no resident Mountie, so the current Station Warrant Officer is always appointed Sheriff, complete with handcuffs and arresting powers. The Commanding Officer and the Sheriff invited us to the camp's winter festival, a sort of "goodbye-to-the-sun" ceremony. Later we invited fourteen of the Canadians to tea in our kitchen hut. Charlie baked seventy scones which he redesignated rock cakes in deference to their consistency. Ginnie tried to scrub the kitchen floor but, before she could soak up the dirty water, it froze to the linoleum so she scraped it off and began again. It was equally pointless to wipe down the table before a meal as the resulting veneer of ice acted as a skid pan from which plates and mugs went skittering.

Because of the obvious dangers of frostbite, exposure or simply getting lost in bad weather, the soldiers were not encouraged to wander around outside the camp during the dark months; many preferred the indoor life anyway. There was a gym in which to keep fit and apart from the journeying between the centrally heated huts, the majority of the inmates spent the 183 days of their tour much as they would have done in any mainland base. They managed, nonetheless, to savour a touch of the local atmosphere from time to time. A dozen Arctic foxes lived under the camp huts and one of the soldiers, against Standing Orders, was wont to feed them. One nipped him, to show its gratitude, and he spent the next fourteen days on a rabies prevention course receiving four deep and painful injections per day. The poor fox was trapped and its head sent to Ottawa for analysis. Ginnie was worried lest Bothie or Tugaluk, who roamed loose about the camp, should be bitten for rabies is endemic in the area.

Normally on Remembrance Sunday I join my mother outside Westminster Abbey for the two-minute silence. On 11th November at Alert we went to the camp gymnasium where the national anthem,

'O Canada', was sung half in French, half in English, followed by 'God Save the Queen' to the wrong tune. Then, with forty Canadians in six snowcats, we drove in the midday darkness past the airstrip on to the headland, where nine Canadian airmen lay buried. Headlights silhouetted the forlorn huddle of grave slabs as the Commanding Officer laid wreaths and the padre intoned the ageless words: "At the going down of the sun . . . we will remember them." His breath rose into frost smoke and we were silent for a while beneath the pole star.

Soon Ginnie would have to begin her VLF recordings again as she had done in Antarctica, so we erected the mast out on the sea-ice beside a tiny portable hut in which the equipment was set up. But when all was ready and switched on, a loud humming sound was emitted over the headsets so we had Charlie stop the little generator in our garage. Still the humming. In the cause of science the Commanding Officer agreed to switch off the marker lights along the airstrip but even this had no effect.

Determined to find somewhere out of reach of the source of the hum, yet daily attainable by skidoo, Ginnie made up a mini version of her receiving antenna and we set out in a borrowed snowcat with goniometer amplifier and recorder at the ready. Bumping around over the snow covered tundra like an errant television detection unit we could find nowhere, even four miles north of the main camp, to escape the hum. With the Canadian Operations Officer we drove up the long winding track that led to a hilltop transmission site. Halfway between camp and site we stopped.

"This should be OK," said the driver. "It's so quiet here you could hear a flea belch." But the electric hum was as strong as ever so the VLF programme was abandoned whilst Ginnie remained in Alert.

When we returned to camp Ginnie discovered the thick coaxial cables she had painstakingly set up for her HF radio sets were lying in chewed pieces outside our door. Tugaluk stood nearby in the snow wagging her long black tail.

In the last week of November, Alert meteorological station recorded −9°C, the warmest temperature on record by eight degrees so late in the year. Bad news for our hopes. But it is an ill wind that blows no one any good and the dogs loved their mild starlit wanderings in fruitless search for fox and hare. Bothie followed Tugaluk nose to tail wherever she led.

By mid-December, one of the coldest winters ever recorded in

Britain with temperatures on the *south* coast of −33°C, we were basking in Alert at a mere −28°C.

Throughout that winter the three of us, Ginnie, Charlie and I, lived in a fair state of harmony. There were no arguments and few awkward silences. What did we talk about? The goings on up at the main camp. News from England and especially from the Transglobe ship, then berthed in Southampton for a refit. About this time we learnt that Walt Pedersen, the American hoping to race us to his second Pole, had been refused permission by the US authorities to use their McMurdo sea transport although they had originally agreed that he could.

On a cool night in December we went up to the camp on two skidoos to a party given by the men of a group called, against all spelling probability, the Fourskin Club. When Ginnie and I left it was midnight and a balmy −32°C. Charlie said he'd return later.

Next morning when I shouted outside his hut that breakfast was ready, there was no reply. I went in and found him in bed.

"What's up, Charlie? Lost your voice?"

"Shouting hurts," he replied. "I came off last night on the way back."

He had skidded on an icy bend and ended up in the ditch. His back hurt him badly but he could move. A few hours motionless in the ditch and he would have quickly frozen unnoticed, for nobody else used the road by night. I pulled his leg: this was the fifth time he had come a spectacular cropper off his skidoo – twice in the Arctic, three times in Antarctica. But this might not be so funny for in seven weeks we must both be fit and ready to go. Travel over rough sea-ice does not endear itself to injured backs. For days Charlie hobbled about painfully and slowly like an old man. I gave him Deep Heat embrocation but it did him little good; his coccyx was, he thought, bruised.

In the evenings after supper we played cards or dominoes but the kitchen hut was usually too cold to stay in for long. Sometimes Alert Radio spewed forth taped versions of the World News from Ginnie's transistor. Snow storms over Europe; a lifeboat lost off Cornwall with all hands; repression in Poland; unemployment rife all over the place. It made you think the Arctic wasn't such a bad place after all.

I spent long hours each day in the garage preparing every item for the coming journey, weighing, greasing, modifying and packing. I checked pistols and rifle after leaving them loaded outside for a couple of days. I mock-loaded the 8′ 6″ steel sledges as well as the fibreglass man-haul pulks. Since the smaller steel sledges had performed so well in 1977, I had made no alterations to them despite the problems with the larger versions in Antarctica. I cut up and re-designed aluminium bridges with which to cross frozen sea-leads. I checked my hand compass for variation when used on the skidoo and off it, with engine running and switched off; held in my left hand wearing a quartz-powered watch; and in the right hand above metal spiked snowshoes. Snow clearance and fuel drum work took time too and served to keep me fit. Charlie tried to rest to help his back recover, when not giving the generators their weekly service.

Whilst we worked slowly at our preparations four other groups announced their intention to reach the North Pole in the spring. A French team intended to travel with skidoos from eastern Greenland to the Pole and thence to Svalbard. A group of Spaniards aimed to sledge from Svalbard to the Pole and three Russians held a press conference in Montreal to announce a plan to cross from Siberia via the Pole to Canada. All these schemes were due to begin in a mere nine weeks' time, for 1st March is the optimum start date. A year previously four Canadians under one Larry Dexter set out from Cape Columbia but, six kilometres out from the coast, gave up and were evacuated at great cost. Not until Christmas time did we learn of a three-man team, a Canadian Eskimo and three Norwegians, under the leadership of Ragnar Thorseth, Norway's best-known contemporary explorer.

The Christmas Canadian Hercules brought mail to Alert which included some news cuttings about a month old sent by Ant Preston. A Norwegian paper, *Aftenposten*, in early November:

RACE TOWARDS NORTH POLE

Ragnar Thorseth who aims to lead the first Norwegian expedition across the ice to the North Pole, will be in competition with several foreign expeditions. Simultaneously with Thorseth, British, French and Russian expeditions will also set out for the Pole. "We aim to win the race and arrive first," Thorseth says. "It is only fun with a little competition. We'll be going nearly parallel to the British and French and on a collision course with the Russians, but we aim to reach the Pole first. There is only one time to make a start and that is the beginning of March. Earlier it is too dark and later the Spring thaw starts.

The next cutting, from the *Svalbardposten* in late November, added a new ingredient:

> *The Scott–Amundsen duel looks as if it is going to be repeated in the New Year. It will of course be at the other end of the world but will be, as before, Norwegian and English expeditions in a race to a Pole. As far as we know the English expedition is aiming to leave from the same place as Thorseth. The leader of the English is a lord who is very well-equipped. It is rumoured that on a recent North Pole attempt he took prostitutes with him so that the hardships would not be too severe. Scott had horses with him on his tragic South Pole expedition. The question now is whether prostitutes will bring better luck to the expedition team than horses.*

In mid-December the *News of The World* pricked up their ears and announced:

> *ARCTIC TEAM BLASTS SEX SLUR*
> *Members of the Arctic expedition sponsored by Prince Charles are furious at allegations that they are taking good-time girls with them. The claims are made in a Norwegian paper under a banner headline "Lord to North Pole with Prostitutes". The Lord is Sir Ranulph Fiennes who is leading the expedition. A Norwegian expedition with the same aims will depart at the same time and the allegations are part of a dirty tricks campaign to stir up hostility between the two teams.*
> *Robin Buzza, the British team's representative in Spitsbergen said the allegations were "a load of old codswallop". After Buzza complained, the relevant editor printed an apology saying he had been given wrong information. But he added, "Competition does exist and the race is starting long before they hit the ice."*

"Good old Buzza," I said.

"Who is Buzza?" Charlie asked.

"He's our representative in Spitsbergen."

"How do you know?"

"It says so here," I replied, tapping the cutting.

"I know, but who appointed him as our representative?"

"Good question. But it doesn't matter, he's doing a grand job. Probably appointed himself." Charlie became unusually silent.

"I know what you're thinking, Charles," I said, "get that wistful look off your face. We'll be taking quite enough baggage as it is and anyway there are certain things that are impractical at −40°."

Back in London our Committee had already heard about the Norwegian endeavour. The minutes of their meeting had recorded: "Members were agreed that competitive urges should be deplored ... A message to Sir Ranulph advocating his disregard of the Norwegians was proposed."

Whilst we sweated out our apprehension caused by the fatally warm winter and suffered nightmares about thin ice ahead, in North America a record cold front killed fifty-eight people in a week. Chicago suffered an all-time record low of −32°C and Atlanta, at −21°C, its lowest since 1899. Travellers were stranded in Ohio, Pennsylvania and Indiana in the most severe cold wave of the century. In Poland a mountain of broken ice caused the River Vistula to flood and heavy snow paralysed Austria, Belgium, Britain and West Germany.

I visited the little met. station on the edge of the main camp. The met. man was not enthusiastic about our chances. "Warm weather means less ice thickness. Taking last week's measurements, we have thinner ice, even in the sheltered bay by your huts, than at any previous Christmas since 1978 which as you may remember resulted in open sea the following summer." I winced inwardly and thanked him, not wishing for elaboration.

On Christmas Day we went up to the camp. Reg, the Commanding Officer, stopped Ginnie in the 'main street' and warned her against speeding. He was togged to the nines in traditional Father Christmas gear. His own white beard suited the role well. He may have had no reindeer but he was nearer the North Pole than any of his counterparts.

He showed us a radio message he had received from Ottawa. It was from Bill Berry, who had been the Commanding Officer at Alert when we had last wintered here:

I understand you have as neighbours a group of delightfully mad English persons hanging around the Polar Shelf Camp, waiting for a sunrise departure for the Pole. Please tell them from me: "I was convinced back in '77 that you folks were absolutely stark raving mad. Having watched your exploits since then I remain more than ever convinced ... but you're not stupid. If anyone

*can complete the journey, you will. If I can help in any way, you
need only pull my chain."*

As the old year faded I walked to the end of the isthmus over wet,
ill-formed snow. Forty mile an hour gusts blew from the south but
the temperature remained around −16°C. I listened. From beyond
the great angular inshore ice chunks, whose sinister silhouettes could
be seen in the semi-darkness of the moonlit noon, came a rushing
sound as though gravel was pouring from a great height on to
concrete. In a while my eyes grew more accustomed to the darkness
and I perceived wide rashes of black sea not far beyond the coastal
rubble. Then followed sounds of muted struggle, muffled thuds and
the splintering crash of ruptured floes as wind countered tide. I
thought of climbing over the immediate ice blocks to get a better look
but an old saying flashed through my mind, "Sufficient unto the day
is the evil thereof." I retired to the protection of the huts.

In mid-January, three short weeks before we must set out onto the
sea's creeping crust, I again saw the met. man. His news was bad. The
bay ice was only eighty-seven centimetres thick, thinner than that
of any previous January on record, the average being 105 centimetres.

The true coldness, that crackles the nose and ears like burning
parchment, congeals the blood in fingers and toes like rapid setting
glue and fixes the sea-ice slowly but surely into a precarious platform
to the Pole, finally came. Better late than never. A whole host of tasks
could now be done which I had left for the advent of the cold. The
tent must be erected on the bay-ice and the naphtha heater tested for
fumes. I bedded down in it that night with Ginnie. The ice about us
spat, cracked and boomed as the floes contracted.

Up at the camp that week they recorded −51°C with a ten-knot
breeze, and fixed safety lines between the huts. In our kitchen we ate
in duvets, boots and woolly caps for the hut was really a metal-sided
caravan and the cardboard slats I had taped to the walls provided
scant insulation. But our morale was now high for the sea-ice was
surely growing out there. And it might not be too late.

Ginnie's mouth swelled up for her gum was poisoned. Soon her
cheek was also swollen but we gave her penicillin pills and it
subsided. She received a message from Peter Jenkins at Sheffield
University Space Physics Department which delighted her: the initial
results of her long hard hours at Ryvingen had been analysed and

showed a recording quality even better than those obtained by the professionals at the British Antarctic Survey base at Halley Bay.

Charlie's back had slowly mended and we began to take daily exercise together. He ran through the details of skidoo servicing and repairs with me. The vehicles were precisely the same, apart from having different carburettors, as the ones we had used in 1977. I took him up on the hillside with a theodolite to shoot some stars. Each evening I practised morse with a key and a recorded tape prepared by Ginnie.

Back in London our sponsors, the *Observer* newspaper, held a reception for the rest of the media at which the editor, Donald Trelford, made it clear he wished for no monopoly in covering the news of our progress. Prince Charles, who presided at this reception, radioed through to Ginnie and mentioned he had heard rumours of a race with the Norwegians.

"No racing," he told me.

"No, sir," I replied, "we will not race."

But suddenly I remembered how he loved a race whether briefly during polo matches or out on hazardous four-man cross-country steeplechases and I knew he would not object to our indulging in a little healthy competition in a quiet way. I determined that whatever the Russians, French and Spanish might do, we must not let the Norwegians complete the Arctic Ocean crossing before us, even if they were to reach the Pole first. In a small way it would be nice to avenge Scott's much heralded defeat at the hands of Amundsen three-quarters of a century ago.

The rest of January stayed cool for us. It now took longer for Ginnie to knock up our meals. Although the larder was in the centre of the kitchen and well insulated, she had to use a hammer to batter frozen soup out of bowls stored there and place tins of fruit into boiling water to thaw out in time for lunch. Raw eggs emerged from their shells like golf balls although they did not bounce quite as well due to their shape.

To offset my mania for an open window at night, Ginnie began to use a hot water bottle under her duvet. One night a fox outside our room barked us awake and Ginnie found her bottle frozen solid by her feet. But none of us minded these little manifestations of the cold: it was all in a good cause.

We remembered with much mirth our fear of the cold when we had first come to Alert in 1977. How in our greenhorn state we were wont to touch metal without mitts on, a mistake not usually repeated since uncovered flesh sticks fast to metal and, if torn away, leaves the skin behind burning the hand just as though it had touched a flame. Much laughter, too, over the memory of Ginnie visiting our lavatory shack and the plastic seat slipping off the rim of the metal bucket. She had received a long *cold* burn down the left cheek of her backside and rushed back to our hut to comfort the afflicted area in front of our iron stove. Sadly she had got too close for comfort and branded herself with an even worse *hot* burn on her other cheek. The closer our departure date, the easier it became for each of us to laugh at the others, without fear of causing offence.

On 29th January I saw clearly for the first time the *aurora borealis*, not just an electric flicker on a summer night such as is common in the Scottish Highlands, but the full brilliant display of green and white curtains evolving from one marvellous pattern to another and fading away only after an hour of, for me, almost hypnotic fascination.

With no moon and an average temperature of −41°C, a succession of crisp clear nights provided some good navigation practice, my favourite target stars being Regulus, Arcturus and Vega, all too bright and easily located to be mistaken for other nearby bodies when pinpointed in my theodolite's narrow field of view. I must record on my Rolex watch the precise second at which one star moved across the horizontal line in the centre of my theodolite's eyepiece, and then do the same for two others. After which I would compute back-bearings from all three which should then enable me to work out my own position on the surface of the earth. Very simple in normal conditions. But doing this in the dark and cold had become no easier, despite my 1977 and Antarctic experience. The same problems still bedevilled my efforts: the vertical and horizontal bubbles in the alcohol moved sluggishly and insensitively, with slow lurches to left or right because of the cold, so it took me some time to get them to settle centrally to ensure the theodolite was correctly set; my mouth and nose dribbled involuntarily because of the cold so ice formed from my bottom lip to where my balaclava fitted into my wolfskin parka. This set hard and stopped my neck moving or me looking upwards; my eyelashes would stick to the metal of the scope, despite a chamois leather covering over the eyepiece itself, and my nose would feel as though it was succumbing to the first symptoms of frostnip. If I breathed anywhere near the eyepiece it froze instantly and I would have to extricate a gloved finger from my inner mitten to rúb the lens. Other difficulties centred round the small eyepiece used to view the instrument's graticule scales. I thought how much simpler a sextant would be. Wally Herbert, however, who was adept with both instruments, had counselled us strongly against the less accurate sextant.

In England what would have taken me twenty-five minutes, here took me well over an hour: the cold frustrated each of us whenever we tried to complete the simplest task. After each practice session with my theodolite, I would return to the warm hut to thaw out myself and my clothes, leaving the instrument outside to avoid condensation. I often wondered about my ability to keep track of our position in the drifting floes of the Arctic Ocean. So long as the sun was out there should be no problem but, given too many foggy days . . . I would shrug off such thoughts at this point.

By the last day of January, I needed to make up my mind exactly when we would set out to cross the whole ocean and reach faraway Spitsbergen. To reach this decision I thought of the overall problem, of those who had tried before us and of our own failure in 1977 when we had tried to travel as far as the Pole, less than half the distance which faced us this time. We had failed convincingly. Then four of us had left in early March but the cold had caught out Geoff, eight of whose fingers were frostbitten. So, three of us had set out again in mid-March. After fifty unpleasant days we'd found ourselves 160 miles short of the Pole, surrounded by a sea of moving slush ice too thin to travel over.

This time we must get further sooner. To be precise, we must reach the Pole by mid-April at the latest. Once in its vicinity we would be out of the grip of the Beaufort Gyral current, which floats ice backwards towards Alert, and into the pack-ice of the Transpolar Drift current which heads over the top of the world and down towards Greenland and Svalbard. Thereafter, for some 2,000 miles of floating travel, we could expect to move wherever the by then fractured pack might take us. Hopefully, the *Benjy B* would be able to penetrate the pack along its southern fringe and so remove us somewhere in the region of Spitsbergen without herself getting crushed.

Could such a journey be made in one Arctic summer season? Impossible to predict since it had never been done before. Wally Herbert, the only man ever to have crossed the Arctic Ocean, had taken two seasons.

Back in England at the time, he commented to our film team:

I think the big physical problem of crossing polar pack-ice is that, at least initially, you travel in very cold weather and, in order to get to your destination before the ice breaks up, you have to put in a lot of travelling time, which means being exposed to temperatures of −45°, −50°, for up to fifteen hours a day. Now −45° is not very cold by Northern Canadian standards but if you are exposed to it for that length of time and you have to knock your way through pressure ridges and across open leads, then it is a big strain. At the times when you really need to push hard, it is going to be twilight, or even dark. It is going to be a lot colder and you will be moving a lot longer across moving ice which can swallow you up at any time or which physically needs a lot of effort to knock down. So you might be burning up in the region of 7,500 calories a day. That is pretty high going.

Our own north polar adviser, Andrew Croft, said: "You will not be able to start for the North Pole, without excessive tribulation and breakages, until late February. That will be the time to start."

Charles Kuralt, writing about the four-man Plaisted group, the only men to have reached the Pole without dogteams, said: "There is only a short span of time, mid-March to mid-May, when man can safely walk on the Arctic ice. Earlier in the year darkness and severe cold can make travel hazardous. Later the rising sun turns the ocean snow cover to mush and high winds break the ice-pack into thousands of individual floes."

Back in 1977 our final start date had been 14th March. Now I decided to cut this by a month, to 14th February, and then to subtract a further week for good measure and unforeseen teething troubles. I'd aim to start in the dark in the first week of February. What worried me most was the likelihood one or other of us might get frostbite in the dark. The *only* way of avoiding amputation of a frostbitten limb would be evacuation to an intensive care hospital with the right equipment. Until sun-up in early March, this would be totally out of the question, since even an efficient ski-plane like our Twin Otter, with a brilliant pilot such as Karl Z'berg, would not land on the Arctic pack-ice in pitch blackness. Nonetheless I continued to aim for 7th February.

Three things occurred to frustrate this during the last week of January. The Twin Otter sustained damage to an aileron in its hangar at Farnborough; Gerry Nicholson began to suffer severe abdominal pains which were diagnosed as a hiatus hernia; and half of one of my teeth fell out one evening, followed by half the neighbouring goofer the next morning. Inside the resulting cavities were black rotten places; the nerve ends were bare.

The weekly Alert/Thule Hercules left that morning and would be returning to Alert on 9th February three days before our Twin Otter should arrive, so I caught it in order to visit the young Danish dentist at Thule. He spent one and a half hours in my mouth and fixed me up with two 'new' teeth.

Whilst waiting for my return Hercules, a United States Army Colonel took me around the missile warning centre.

"All kinds of things here have been screwed up because of this warm weather," he told me. "Normally, we have a drivable ice 'road' across the bay. It saves a long detour. But this year the ice is only three feet thick, instead of the normal six or seven feet. So no road. Usually the whole bay is solid in October. This winter she only began to freeze in late November."

On my return flight to Alert, the navigator let me sit beside him in the cockpit as he pointed down at the sea just off the coastline.

"Those areas of darker shading," he shouted in my ear. "They're either open water or freshly formed ice."

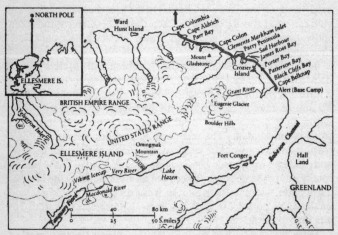

Alert to the North Pole

I digested this unhealthy news and grinned back in sickly fashion.

Karl now informed us that he could not arrive at Alert until the 15th but that he would be bringing Simon with him in the Twin Otter to replace the ill Gerry. Rather than wait five days, I decided to set out within forty-eight hours, as soon as the sledges were packed. Laden trials the next day indicated that the loads were too heavy, so we were delayed until the 13th. My diary for that day records: "Poor Ginnie has a sharp and persistent headache which really stuns her. This is despite four Parahyphon pills in the last twenty-four hours. She's really down-and-out and tired tonight and looks miserable. I hate the thought of leaving her."

The night before we left, a radio message came from Wally Herbert in the form of a rhyme.

> With my very best wishes for the final dawn.
> I send tips to help win the fight:
> Beware of the calm that follows the storm
> And the floes that go bump in the night.
>
> Never trust ice that appears to be dead,
> And if you want peace of mind,
> Steer well clear of the bear up ahead
> And cover that bear behind.

I left Ginnie a file of details on camp logistics to give Simon. Included was a note suggesting, should anything happen to Charlie and me, that he and David Mason should carry on from where we left off. Simon would as usual be working with Ginnie and David, when he arrived, running Tanquary Fjord.

The weather was clear as Charlie and I left Alert to cross the Arctic Ocean via the North Pole: we rode in open, heavily laden skidoos, each of which towed a sledge laden with 600-pounds of camping equipment, fuel, spares and gear. The thermometer read $-45°C$ and the prevailing wind brought this down to the actual temperature of $-90°C$ so we were well muffled up in our full Antarctic sledging gear. For four hours, shortly after midday, there would be enough twilight to travel by for a man with a touch of experience and common sense. The camp Commanding Officer and six others came down to see us off, their hand torches darting about below the haloes of freezing breath. They had been good to us.

I said but a quick goodbye then to Ginnie. We had spent the

previous night in our hut closing our minds bit by bit to reality. Over the years we have found it better that way. The wrench of leaving her was perhaps worse than in Antarctica, for we both knew that the southern crossing would prove to have been a rose garden compared with the journey ahead.

As I jerked my sledge away and headed out of the pool of light between the huts, I saw Ginnie crouch by the dogs and look up at the passage of darkness by which we had left. I kept the memory in my head like a photograph, as a squirrel will keep a last nut for the winter ahead.

Using the brief hours of twilight and the memory of our previous journey along the same coastline five short years before, we made good speed and no mistakes. There was nothing clever about this, for simple familiarity makes light of even the worst conditions, whereas the ignorant can founder at the easiest fence. The second morning, in Patterson Bay, we spotted the round pug-marks of a bear. They are known to range this coastline when there is open water for them to fish in. Two scientists had been dropped by helicopter for research work, not far west of our location, some years before. Both had been badly mauled. We checked our individual weapons and kept them close to hand. The ice pressure against the shoreline was in places heavier and higher up the beaches than previously. In others it was clear going where before there had been walls of rubble.

Until Cape Delano I held to the route as planned but bare patches of gravel west of Dana Bay, murder for our soft Tufnol sledge runners, forced me too far north over the mountain passes of the Feilden Peninsular. As the twilit hours dwindled I found myself caught on a sheer-sided slope between Mary Peak and Mount Julia. Charlie tried to follow my trail but that is often more difficult than taking a virgin route which offers more purchase for the skidoo's slithering tracks. Twice Charlie's sledge overturned. Both times he managed to right it by himself, but each time he was a touch lower down the snowfield below which were the cliffs of a narrow ravine.

With great caution we skirted this cliff and reached another steep slope down which we lowered the sledges bit by bit. It was dark by the time we camped along the rim of James Ross Bay. There were no animals and no birds about. Spring after all was a long way off. On 15th February we sneaked through a defile between mountains on the Parry peninsula and descended to Sail Harbour, surrounded by snowfields on every side. New snow lay soft and deep in this bay and the going was slow.

The hills fell away on either flank to reveal a view of frozen wonder, Clement Markham Inlet, a giant sea loch ten miles wide at its mouth and penetrating deep into the interior mountains. Although the sky was dark enough to see the major stars, the air was clear all the way to the looming bulk of Mount Foster, the western sentinel of this wild majestic fjord. We camped eighteen kilometres west of the fjord in bitter cold. So easy to make a little mistake in the darkness, to allow the creeping nip to stay that little bit too long in a finger or a toe.

Of the rare and time-scattered men to travel west along this coast some were never seen again. As recently as 1936 Kruger, leader of the German Arctic Expedition, was lost along the coastline further west with two companions. No trace of them was ever found. In 1983 David Hempleman-Adams, an experienced mountaineer, was to set out from this same coast on 10th March, well after sun-up, but was soon evacuated back to his base saying: "These last nine days were the hardest in my life. I am physically, mentally and psychologically marked by them." Yet he had climbed the notorious Eiger, to me an unthinkable challenge.

It is not necessary to be a weak-minded person, nor ill-equipped nor even inexperienced to die quickly in the Arctic, temperatures well above −20°C will kill in broad daylight.

A *Daily Telegraph* report in Oslo in 1983 ran:

Two British servicemen froze to death during a NATO exercise in Norway. Marine Jacques and Royal Naval Surgeon Lieutenant Hodgson were on a winter survival course in the Gundsbrandse Valley with twenty other troops when surprised by severe blizzards and temperatures which plunged well below zero. Five others suffered frostbite. Both men had served with 42 Commando.

They had set out for a one-day ski march in south west Norway but were caught in a blizzard and whiteout. They decided to stay overnight in an emergency shelter but there was a heavy drop in temperature. On the way back to base the two men died. "There will be an official enquiry," said a spokesman, "but all the men were properly equipped and had had Arctic training."

The longer a man is out in the field and eating dehydrated sledge rations, the less his strength and his resistance to the cold becomes. It is therefore obvious that a polar traveller must become more and more cautious the longer he has been away from warmth and solid food to avoid making simple fatal errors.

Late on 16th February I spotted the food and fuel cache Giles had left well south of our route over the Cape Aldrich ice shelf. We spent an hour there replenishing and repacking, then camped a short distance to the north: it was dark and −46°C.

Next day we set out early. The coast steamed with the brown murk of frost-smoke, a sure sign of open water in the vicinity; at a guess the coastal tide creek had opened up during the night. Open water in the depths of winter, long before sunrise and at a point of maximum coastal pressure, was ominous. Skirting the steaming slits, I kept as near to land as possible when rubble fields forced me out onto the sea-ice. Every few minutes I turned in the seat to check that Charlie never faltered, never fell out of sight for long. Between the encroaching walls of pressure ice from the sea and the tumbling glaciers which descended from Mount Cooper Key there was a narrow corridor, in places merely ten yards wide. Into this we crawled for there was no other way west.

To our right frozen waves of snow lay shoulder high where five years before I had seen pellucid green blocks, piled layer on layer to a height of twelve metres, a testimony to the great driving and cutting power of the pack-ice. Peary, in an account of his journey along Greenland's northern coastline, tells of pressure ice stacked a hundred feet high against the cliffs. We had no trouble in the gloomy corridor and emerged at the foot of a steep snow slope just short of Cape Columbia. This we ascended to its bonnet and I spent a while observing the immediate area since, any time now, I must find a route north on to the sea-ice.

The black slab of Cape Columbia stood out to the south, the site of Monzino's base camp for his 1970 dash to the Pole, and still littered with the remains of his camp, Parcol huts, fuel cans and bric-à-brac of every sort. The Italian count, a millionaire and professional explorer, had set out with 150 dogs, thirteen Eskimos and seven others. After a week or two half of the Eskimos, a Dane and a Canadian returned separately. There was much disappointment and dissent. But, with the daily help of a spotter aircraft and a Hercules C130 transport plane, Monzino made his goal. Asked if he would do the journey again, he shook his head vehemently, saying, "Too much; too much of everything. Too much danger. Too much cold."

Asked why he flew all his dogs back to civilisation from the Arctic at great cost, when he would never use them again and no one wanted them, he simply said, "Beautiful dogs. Very fast."

A short distance west of Cape Columbia the rolling white layers of the Ward Hunt Ice Shelf thrust north into the sea for over ten miles. The ice shelf was formed by thicknesses of sea-ice forming off the coast and attaching themselves, in most places still afloat, to the original coastline. Each year the shelf grew upwards because sea water with a low saline content froze to its lower surface at the same time as summer melt water from inland re-froze to its upper surface.

As with all Arctic ice, the ice shelf was subject to immense strain and could fracture with no warning. In 1961 massive calving from the Ward Hunt Ice Shelf reduced its area by some 600 square kilometres. The resulting islands floated away east and west and an aerial study of their routes suggested that Cape Columbia lay at the spot where westerly and easterly currents separated. This would make it the best start-point for anyone wishing to travel north as the route inland would not be powerfully influenced by the pull of either current.

At the base of our hill were large chunks of pressure ice, piled in places to a height of forty feet. They formed a wall between snowfield and frozen ocean, but in places there were narrow gaps. We descended the hill, slithered down a ramp after some easy axe work to bridge a twenty-foot void and – we were at sea.

Already we had covered a hundred miles or more towards our goal, albeit on a somewhat devious route but we had managed to set out many days earlier than any of our predecessors. On 17th February, two weeks before sun-up, we camped for the first time on sea-ice.

I remembered my thoughts following the bitter acceptance of defeat five years before. I had known I would come back. It was wrong to be beaten. Peary once wrote: "The true explorer does his work because the thing he has set up for himself to do is part of his being and must be accomplished for the sake of accomplishment."

After one of his two-year polar attempts had failed he said: "The lure of the North is a strange and powerful thing. More than once I have come back from the wild frozen spaces . . . telling myself I have made my last journey thither . . . It was never many months before the old restless feeling came over me and I began to long for the great white desolation."

Dr Frederick Cook, his arch-rival and co-claimant as first man to the North Pole, was equally emotional: "A new and absorbing passion which ever since has dominated my life – the voice of the Arctic, the taste for the icy response of the polar sea. Something keeps calling, calling, until at last you can stand it no more and return, spell-drawn by the magic of the North."

The Danes have a word for this polar attraction – *polarhullar*.

As we erected our tent 300 yards out from the coast on the edge of a seemingly limitless field of impenetrable rubble and I pressed one mitt to the raw end of my nose, I felt not the remotest tinge of *polarhuller*, merely a ghastly realisation of what was to come and a host of crowding memories of what had passed last time we tried to pit our wits against the power of the Arctic Ocean.

14

The Fringe of Failure

FEBRUARY–APRIL 1982

*Even a man with perfect circulation and the
best clothing combination designed by man will
suffer terribly under the worst Arctic conditions.*

WALLY HERBERT, 1974

As a result of our 1977 failure to reach the Pole I had this time planned a pessimistic schedule, which allowed for initial progress of only half a mile per day. During the first day's twilit labour we fell short of this scheduled distance, but only just, for we cleared 800 yards of rubble. The 'motorway' we axed and shovelled was exactly the width of a skidoo and zig-zagged between ice walls and isolated boulders. During the next six months there were many times when we felt truly at the end of our tether, but not once did we consider giving up. The thought of facing the crew of the *Benjy B* having failed was not something I could even contemplate.

Would it have been more sensible, more responsible, to have given up? Who can say? As will be seen, even our Arctic experts were to counsel evacuation, and with good cause. In those first twilit days, however, we did not think of anything but the next few yards of slow and frozen toil.

According to Wally Herbert we would have to travel 825 miles in order to cover the 474 miles bee-line distance to the Pole – a seventy-five per cent detour. Wally, and nobody knew better than he for nobody else had ever crossed the Arctic Ocean, said we were unlikely to succeed unless we reached the Pole before 17th April. With this date in mind we could afford minimal delays.

No man has ever crossed the Arctic Ocean without re-supply by air. Wally's support came from Canadian Air Force C 130 aircraft. If our own lifeline, the Twin Otter, was off the road for any reason at any time, it could critically delay our progress. Charlie and I had set out before the Twin Otter had arrived at Alert but its welfare was seldom far from our thoughts. We hoped all had gone well on the long flight from England.

Ever since Giles and Gerry had so nearly been marooned in the midst of Antarctica by engine start problems, there had been concern that our aircraft suffered from some major but intermittent technical fault. Karl was an experienced engineer as well as a pilot but he had to sleep sometime; he could not always be tinkering with the engine. Karl's diaries tell of his mounting worries:

> *The English engineers at Farnborough worked long hours to find the problem but with no success and I found it not too amusing because I know, as soon as I hit the Arctic temperatures of $-35°$ to $-45°C$, that the problem could be very serious. Anyway, we flew to Stornoway. The weather was OK to cross to Iceland. But on the start-up of the port engine I had a problem of no light-up and got the engine running only with a cross-generator start which is advisable only in an emergency.*
>
> *From Iceland we made it to Frobisher Bay via Greenland and stayed one night. Next day was bitter cold, steady at $-45°C$. The port engine would not even start when I had a heater warm it up to $+45°C$. With a local engineer friend we worked for an hour before it was OK. We came to Resolute Bay and there I mounted car heaters and wiring on boards that we could plug into generators for when we came to Alert.*

Karl and Simon reached Alert in darkness on 15th February. Karl's notes continue:

> *Simon had to do his own job in the camp fixing skidoos, generators etc. Ginnie worked the radios and kept track of the ice group. As pilot and engineer I had to look after the aircraft alone. I was very worried about the starting problem. I knew if I could*

*not solve it soon, it could get serious. With some bad luck I could
burn an engine to a crisp on start-up. This would be a big delay.
So I worked for two days at temperatures of −40°C in the
darkness of the polar night and at last I could trace the electrical
problem. I was very, very pleased.*

*To get the aircraft ready for a flight took me four hours. I had
to dig the fuel drums out of hard-packed snow, wobble-pump the
fuel into the tanks by hand with no good filter. This made me
uneasy as I didn't know then if the drum fuel was well filtered.*

Any droplet of water in the fuel system could have stopped both
engines in mid-flight without warning.

On 19th February we axed our way north with a fifteen-knot
breeze and −42°C. By the end of the twilight hours a further 200
yards were hacked away and I decided to bring the skidoos up the
one thousand prepared yards from our first coast-site camp.

Despite the work we had done, there was pushing and pulling,
bouncing and sweating. The sweat turned to ice particles inside our
underwear as soon as we stopped. I broke off half a finger nail but felt
no pain as the finger was cold.

Like me Charlie weighed 185 pounds, so between us we could, by
using our weight jointly and sensibly, shift the 800-pound laden
skidoos and 600-pound laden sledges bit by bit over each new
blockage. But progress was hardly the word for it: more like a couple
of geriatric snails on a Sunday outing. Luckily the visibility remained
passable during the hours of twilight so we did not lose track of our
hard-wrought motorway.

Much damage was done to the skidoos, since there was no way of
negotiating the 'cleared' route other than at full pelt, rebounding off
walls and iron hard ice rocks.

Just short of the roadhead my drive axle snapped.

That did it. I decided to switch to manpower and abandon the
skidoos.

The previous winter in Alert, preparing for just such a switch, I'd
tested out two eight-foot long fibreglass man-haul sledges and
light-weight survival gear to go with them. That night I asked Ginnie
to get the new equipment to us the next day in the Twin Otter. We
would try to find a flat place where Karl might drop the kit without
smashing it. In the tent I wrote out lists of small items we would also
need. Although we lay in a dark deep freeze there was enough light to

see by from a polythene bag hanging on a string from the tent's apex. The bag was filled with luminous beads called Beta-lights which threw out a green and restful, if somewhat satanic, light.

In the morning Charlie worked to change the sheared shaft. At prevailing temperatures not at all the easy job it would be in a nice warm garage. I ferried the sledges slowly back to the coastline and was lucky enough to find a 400-yard strip of flat ice without a bump or imperfection of any sort.

It struck me that here, at the very mouth of Clements Markham Fjord, was a unique spot where a skiplane might land even in the semi-dark, since the lack of perspective, fatal on a bumpy landing strip, would not be as critical on such a dead flat floe. This proved to be a poor choice later on but initially it seemed like the proverbial answer to a maiden's prayer.

I axed down to forty centimetres and struck no water. After twelve hours the weather luckily cleared to coincide with the time of twilight. No wind; blowing ice crystals but no mist, −37°C. Perfect conditions but nonetheless there was probably a mere handful of pilots in the world who could have, and would have, landed in those circumstances. Karl did. We shook hands with him and his duvet-covered passenger, Simon. The pulks and ancillary gear were off in a trice and our steel sledges loaded together with boxes and fuel.

"Leave the skidoos and the big tent here," Karl said, "and I'll come back later when it is light to collect them."

I asked Simon to get ready the two light skidoos, only 250 cc and easily manhandled by one person unaided. When the rubble zone ended, or at least cleared up a bit, I hoped to try them out to see if, as I had been so often told, they were indeed better than our own heavy 640 cc models.

Karl Z'berg:

I left there some kit and food for the team. The temperature was −43°C and the faces of the ice crew were all frosted up and I was glad not to join them for their journey but instead to climb back into my plane and turn back for a warm base camp . . . Before heading east, I tried to find a passage through the ridges from the air, but it looked everywhere the same, and it didn't do any good to go further east or west. This recce was of course also very hard because we had only twilight.

So on 22nd February in semi-darkness we began the long haul. I thought of Wally Herbert's words: "There can be few forms of polar misery more physically exhausting than hacking a route through pressure ice when it is cold and there is scarcely enough twilight to see the joke."

After eight hours our underwear, socks, facemasks and jackets were soaking wet or frozen, depending on which part of the body they covered and on whether we were hauling or resting at the time. Each load weighed 190 pounds. The new North Face tent was only nine pounds, compared with our 100-pound Antarctic tent, and was difficult to keep 'warm'. Small and igloo-shaped, there was little room for drying clothes other than on a suspended net from which the drips fell on to us, our bags and the evening stew. It was never possible to dry clothes out but, with a bit of effort, they could be improved from wet to damp.

Our eyes stung when the cooker was burning but never as badly as during 1977, since we burnt clean naphtha at all times, never petrol. There was the occasional fire alarm resulting from re-filling the cooker tank inside the tent, as some fuel invariably spilled and ignited but was usually quickly doused with a sleeping bag. I was forever putting sticky tape over holes burnt in my bag and our beards were usually dusted with feathers.

For four long days of twilit gloom we hauled, sweated and froze over the endless rubble. I suffered from the problem which you get in warmer climes through sitting on hot radiators or wet grass and this made the constant vicious tugging at my harness an altogether unpleasant experience. Charlie's legs and back were also displeased with life. But by the end of the four days we had completed eleven long miles. That doesn't sound very impressive unless you have seen pressure rubble for yourself and travelled through it in the dark and in the −40°Cs.

The previous year a team of four sturdy Canadians set out for the Pole from the same spot as us, but with the benefit of sunlight. After five miles they were evacuated, one with bad frostbite. They were well-trained and sensible but their luck was out.

As on Ellesmere Island and even back on the Welsh mountains four years before, Charlie plodded on at his own slow but solid pace. Unable to go any slower than my 'natural' pace, I ended up every hour stomping around in circles banging my hands violently together, kicking my mukluks hard against the nearest ice block and singing loudly. At such times my thoughts often wandered to the local fauna. On the move it was stupid to keep glancing over your shoulder to check on polar bears as this could cause painful trip-ups. Sheer exhaustion overcame any fear of bears most of the time but I often mused about the best action to take if attacked, remembering the words of a friendly Greenlander in Thule: "The old bears, going blind, die slowly of starvation as they roam the pack-ice, less and less able to find a meal. But they retain their scent for hot-blooded animals and a human will suffice if they happen to smell one." I kept my pistol readily available on the pulk at all times.

On 27th February we came upon a wide pan of smooth ice thick enough to be a 'multi-year' floe, the normal term for ice three or more years old. Karl and Simon flew that day to check on the conditions back at the site of the abandoned skidoos. From there they flew north. Long hours of toil for us was but a five minutes flip to them. They came in low to inspect our 300 yard strip. We had walked up and down to check for hidden cracks or bumps and put jerry cans as markers at each end. Very rudimentary of necessity.

Karl had landed once before sun-up but that was on smooth one-year ice with nary a bump. He trusted me so he came in. Simon wrote:

> I was preparing to drop the rations and had roped myself down, put on the rear intercom headset and started to remove the temporary starboard door. But Karl called me forward. "The ice group," he said, "are in a large paddock. Ran reports a good surface with Charles and him stood at either end." After one low pass we landed. The roughest landing I've ever had or hope to have. Hard ice ridges underlying soft snow. Bounced off one hump fifty feet after touch-down and then again with a blow that threw me to the limit of my safety harness and sounded like the plane's nose was broken up.

Karl's description:

> We were ready to do a free drop when Ran told me they found a suitable spot for a landing and I trusted Ran's word because I mentioned to him before that I can't see enough in the twilight and, since the first landing site was good, I had no doubts that this one could be different. After looking the place over and checking the markers I landed by the first one, but thirty yards

past it I hit a fair size of an ice hump which threw me twenty to thirty feet back in the air and I had no more air speed for an overshoot and I came crashing down and finally came to a stop . . .

First I was just sitting in the aircraft for three minutes dumbfounded, raging mad and also afraid to step out and check the damage. I was very lucky and everything was OK and I began to breathe normally. Ran knows how mad I was at the time and I then made the rule that I will only land when I have sunlight.

Back in Alert I started to have disagreements with Ginnie because of the landing. Sure I was the pilot and have to know what I am doing, but in such circumstances you have to have support from everyone on the ground too, otherwise you are just bound for a disaster. I felt sad that Ginnie and I could not communicate any better. She couldn't understand me and I couldn't understand her.

Morale in base was low for a while and the conditions even for simple camp work were unfavourable. Simon wrote: "I am very stiff and sore. My hands are black and chafed."

We struggled to part ourselves from the mountains but they seemed to move with us. The day when we could no longer see them would mean much to us both. We longed for some visible sign of progress. I tried to avoid stopping in rubble fields. How stupid to be caught napping by a sudden storm. Yet it was often tempting to camp wearily on a small slab in a field of rubble liable to instant crack-up and massive fracturing. Often, exhausted and sore, I gave in to my weakness and camped in just such fragile places in full knowledge of the danger of it. The safest sleeping places were chunks of consolidated pack-ice where many floes were frozen together. They were never completely flat but, if made up of older multi-year floes which had somehow survived disintegration for several summers, proliferated with well-rounded hummocks polished by years of wind and sun. You could cut away chunks from the yellow-white hummocks on these old floes and find, on melting them, that the water was salt-free or as near as made no difference.

On 2nd March we woke as usual with steaming breath, feeling cramped. Outside the tent the temperature held at $-44°C$. Inside our body heat improved matters to $-38°C$ but to be honest I noticed little or no difference. We did not start the cooker in the mornings but quickly drank down a mug of coffee brewed the previous night and kept in a padded flask. This was breakfast and gave us the courage to unzip our bags and climb into frosted clothes and boots.

At this time we were dragging behind us, man for man, as much as Scott and his team. If we could have counted upon the Twin Otter finding us when we needed it and if we had unlimited fuel for it we could have lightened our loads. As it was, we carried the minimum required for reasonably safe progress. Amundsen, of course, used dogs and so did not normally experience long periods of man-hauling. The difference between our clothing and Scott's was minimal, except for our footwear which was superior so long as the boots were carefully dried out when camping. I wore a pair of cotton socks under woollen stockings, a cotton T-shirt under a zip-up windproof jacket and a pair of army windproof trousers over a pair of cotton long johns. Charlie wore much the same. We both wore face-masks.

Our cooking habits were about the same as Scott's, save that we ate only in the evenings and, a vital difference, our dehydrated rations were supplemented by two vitamin pills each per day.

The weather conditions for us were, for three weeks, far more severe, in that we travelled in lower temperatures and in semi-darkness. Like Scott we were spurred on by the knowledge that a team of Norwegians shared the same goal and details of their progress to our flank were not known to us. The terrain that we struggled over was of course ribbed with high walls of ice and pitfalls of soft snow which Scott did not face in Antarctica. But this horrific region stretched a mere one hundred miles ahead of us before it would improve a touch and we would hopefully be able to have our skidoos brought in by Karl. Whereas the comparatively easier surface Scott struggled over would face him for 800 miles to the Pole and 800 back to his base. He took snowmobiles with him but abandoned them soon after leaving Scott Base.

Our main peril lay in thin ice and the crushing motion of the floes; Scott's in the hidden crevasses which we had ourselves so disliked in Antarctica. He would fear unseasonable blizzards; we were worried about abnormally warm and loose pack conditions. He could suffer by not locating his pre-laid depots; we by a single electronic failure of our pocket beacon which sent a pulse some forty miles into the sky. If the beacon failed due to the cold or a malfunction, or if my navigation erred by over forty miles, not too difficult on drifting pack-ice after many days in thick mist with no landmarks, then we could be lost for ever in five million square miles of ever-shifting rubble. In such circumstances no amount of searching aircraft would necessarily locate us. Scott moved over land-girt ice and his route was predictable. Ours must move for six long months very largely at the whim of the floating ice floes on whose skin we hitched a lift. Our means of navigation, like Scott's, were a compass and the sun, its position and its altitude. As regards radios, they seldom helped us travel from A to B, whilst their fragility and weight was not something our predecessors had to cope with. As many a modern polar traveller has discovered, radios break down easily in cold temperatures. Two recent North Pole expeditions have had to be withdrawn *because* their radios ceased to work – the Simpsons and Hempleman-Adams.

If a man is injured in a crevasse or through frostbite he needs to be evacuated if he is to avoid death yet, during much of our Antarctic crossing, sastrugi would have prevented Giles landing near us had we required evacuation and, in the Arctic, darkness, mist, rubble or slush would likewise have prevented Karl from reaching us more often than not. Polar journeys which postdate the invention of the radio should not be relegated to the status of picnics. As we struggled on day after day, week after week, neither radio nor aircraft brought us warmth or comfort: we were pitting ourselves against the elements just as our predecessors had been.

On 3rd March, despite a slight lowering in the temperature, our world took on a new rosy glow as the blood-red ball of the sun slid briefly along the rim of the frozen sea. The sun was of course our number one enemy. Its ultra-violet rays would soon begin their deadly work upon the ocean's skin, eating at the sea-ice, melting the thinner sections until, in a few weeks' time, we would float along at the whim of whatever floe we might choose as host body. Nonetheless, after four months' absence, the sun was for a while a welcome friend.

Whether the coming of the sun made me unusually optimistic or whether the surface did that day begin to improve for the first time, I cannot say, but I felt there was a chance we could now progress using light skidoos. Our normal 640 cc machines were still where we had abandoned them. When Karl had last flown over them he reported: "I will not be able to land for at least ten days for the ice looks like a shattered window with the skidoos sitting in the middle of it. I hope that the movement stops or we could lose them."

However, there were two little toy-like machines called Elans at Alert and Ginnie said they would be brought to us the next day, weather and ice conditions permitting. Simon went out to the stores garage to prepare the Elans. He decided to leave them inside for the night. Easier to start in the morning.

At three a.m. Ginnie's alarm went off and she climbed off her bunk to listen in for the ice group, as was her wont. By then a field telephone had been rigged between her room and the Canadian camp two miles to the south. Just before four a.m. its bell jangled. It was the duty watchman. "I think there is a fire somewhere by your huts," he said. "I can see flames down at your place." Ginnie thanked him and looking out of her own frosty window saw an orange glow from the garage. The dogs sensed something was amiss. The big black Tugaluk cowered under Ginnie's table but little Bothie put up a strident yapping.

Ginnie, forgetting the temperature, which was $-40°C$, rushed across to the garage and tried to pull back the main sliding door. "It was just one big fireball inside," she said later, "with smoke issuing from all the seams in the walls and flames filling the windows. I shouted 'FIRE!' but nobody heard me. I moved round to the rear end of the hut where there were eight forty-five-gallon drums of gasoline stacked beside the wall. We had once tried to remove them but they had been there many years and were frozen deep into the ice."

She hoped to rescue the precious Elans but found she was too late. The garage was a mass of flames from end to end. The scientific gear, including a valuable seismometer was already destroyed, as were machines, spare parts, rations and all the items I had modified during the winter, including ladders to see us safely over 'porridge-ice' and open canals nearer to the Pole. Ginnie used four fire extinguishers but she might as well have spat into Hell.

Rushing down to the other huts she woke Simon, Karl and Beverly Johnson, one of the film crew. But none of their efforts was any good. Karl, no stranger to Arctic bases going up in flames, wrote:

> *4th March brought the first glorious sunrise after the long Arctic night. Ginnie woke up Simon and me by knocking on our door and saying the garage was on fire. I jumped out of bed in my underwear and looked out the door. But when I have seen the*

*flames shooting out and licking on the roof I could see that all
hope of saving anything was going up with the flames. Maybe
our hopes to complete the expedition were buried also in the
ashes. I dressed in a hurry with warm clothes for the −40°C and
then we could only watch as everything went up in smoke.*

As they watched, the eight drums of gasoline exploded and soon
fusillades of rocket flares and 7.62 FN bullets further enlivened the
scene. Within an hour of the fire's peak, we later learned, American
signals interceptors picked up Soviet messages to the effect that a fire
had been spotted at Alert. If Ginnie had not been alerted by a
watchful Canadian, the Russians would have known about the fire
before she did. We will probably never know the cause of the fire.
Simon believed it was probably something to do with the electrical
wiring.

There was an unforeseen side effect. The expedition had managed
to cross Antarctica in sixty-six days and navigate the entire North
West Passage in four weeks without causing a ripple of interest in
Britain or anywhere else. Suddenly, newspapers and television
screens all over the world mentioned us, "Conflagration at Polar
Base" and "Polar Expedition in Flames". After the night of the fire
every action that we took, and one or two that we didn't, became
news from London to Sydney, from Cape Town to Vancouver.

But out on the ice we had other things to think about when Ginnie
told us that *everything*, the result of seven years of painstaking
sponsor-getting and equipment-testing, was burnt.

Within an hour of assessing the damage Ginnie began to react.
After much trouble, for communications were always poor at the
time of the sun's return, she got a message to David Mason in
London. He was due to fly out to Alert that week to be ready as our
first reserve and to man our alternative mist-free airstrip at Tanquary
Fjord. Now he agreed to delay his coming for as long as it took to
obtain the more vital replacements for our fire losses. Prince Charles
sent us a message of sympathy, as did the crew of the *Benjy B*.

Out on the sea-ice we had food for eight days, so we tried to close
our minds to the disaster at Alert and concentrate on the job of
immediate concern, that of haulage over the next few miles or, to be
precise, the next few painful yards. As our resistance lowered
imperceptibly day by day, the effects of the unremitting cold began to
tell and our pace to slacken. I found the worst of it was the

trail-breaking, the sinking of each snowshoe at every step into the deep soft snow on the floes and the deeper traps of hidden holes between ice blocks. My legs ached and the pain of the piles made life difficult to enjoy. Our shoulders were chafed from the day-long tug of the sledge traces. My nose, red-raw at the nostrils for two weeks now, had become frost-nipped on its bridge. This too now lacked skin and bled as the rough and frozen material of my facemask rubbed across it.

As in 1977 we failed to solve the facemask problem to our satisfaction. Heavy breathing and the continuous involuntary dribble from nose and mouth resulted in a plaster cast of ice around the neck to which my beard froze solid. I could not wipe my nose to stop this happening since, being raw, it preferred not to be wiped.

By night we thawed out the armour plated facemasks above the cooker where they soaked up the smell of our rehydrating meal. So every day we slogged along breathing in the aroma of yesterday's supper. This was frustrating since we ate nothing at all by day, being unable to force food through the little mouth hole in our masks and unwilling to open up the masks once they were frozen into position for the day. Attempts at re-affixing a frozen but disturbed facemask usually failed to prevent frostnip to nose, forehead or cheeks. So daytime snacks were out.

The worst troubles at night were also to the face. Generally speaking, polar travel would be quite pleasant if one didn't have to breathe. If you tried to snuggle down inside your sleeping-bag tying up the drawstrings above your head, then your breath formed a thick rime of frost all around your head, particles of which fell down your neck or settled on your face and in your ears. If, on the other hand, you left a hole at the top of the bag just big enough to frame your nose and mouth *and* you managed to keep them in that position through the sleeping hours, then your nose grew most painful as soon as the temperature descended to around −40°C which it did once the cooker's heat faded away.

By 7th March, on which day I was thirty-eight years old, we had lived and hauled for three weeks at temperatures much colder than a deep freeze with winds usually above fifteen knots. Both of us now knew why people do not venture about on sea-ice in these latitudes before the coming of March. It had taken a lot out of us; perhaps too much.

Charlie said of those days:

*Instead of drinking something like six pints a day, which we
needed, we were only getting about two pints, so we suffered
from dehydration. As you get dehydrated you get weaker. If you
are out for a long period of time and don't stop to recuperate you
get weaker and weaker, until you simply can't even pick up an
axe . . .*

*You start hammering away and after about five minutes you
collapse and gag and don't know what to do with yourself. You
start to suck ice and snow. I can remember times when Ran and I
couldn't pick the axe up: we both had to go back absolutely
exhausted to the tent because we could not pick an axe up any
more. We were absolutely shattered; so tired. We dragged our
way back, hardly raising our feet off the snow and crawled into
the tent and went to sleep like dead mutton. But there is always
the light at the end of a tunnel and this is what you've got to
think about the whole time you're killing yourself.*

On 8th March Ginnie advised us that the French had arrived in
Greenland to start their Arctic crossing attempt. The Norwegians
had set out on skidoos three days earlier, four men including an
Eskimo, from Resolute Bay. Their resupply flights were to be provided partly by chartered Twin Otter and partly by the Royal
Norwegian Air Force with C130 aircraft. She thought they would
set out from the coast at more or less the same spot as ourselves.

Late that day, in a brief gap between snowstorms Karl found us in
a flat but narrow 'alleyway'. He managed to land and off-loaded two
skidoos – not the Elans we wanted since they had been burnt – but a
slightly heavier model called a Citation, also made by Bombardier.

Man-hauling we had averaged six to seven miles per day and
covered over a hundred miles of the worst sort of pressure ridging.
Now, with skidoos, we reverted to one mile on the 9th and two on
the 10th. Admittedly there was non-stop whiteout and high winds,
but that was not unusual. The problem was the old one: skidoos,
unlike dogs and man-hauled sledges, simply will not negotiate small
heaps of rubble let alone walls of ice blocks. So the days passed in
endless hauling and pushing, bogging down and overturning with
inevitable breakdown delays. And all to little avail in terms of
progress.

Charlie's back became most uncomfortable from the strain of
dragging the 400-pound machines up rubble walls. This was alarm-

ing: we needed a sprained back like we needed a pain in the backside.

Just south of a twenty-foot-high wall, the top of which was lost in mist, my skidoo's drive system showed signs of malfunction. A reconnaissance on foot, with both of us heading separate ways along the west-east barrier, proved fruitless since neither of us could spot a possible route in the thick fog. So we camped and waited and all the while floated slowly back towards the coastline from which we wanted so much to distance ourselves.

When Karl brought us the Citations he removed our manhaul sledges so now we could carry on only with these ineffective machines or, if Karl could ever retrieve them from the ice, by waiting until he brought us our original old Alpine models. It was a four-day wait because the whiteout stayed damped down about the pack and the winds increased. During that time we managed to reach a slightly bigger floe with a possible airstrip down its middle, but in doing so the drive shaft of my vehicle sheared.

I used the enforced delay to take a look at our overall chances. It seemed that the time was ripe to encourage our London end to put plans into action that might cope with our failure to meet the tight schedule ahead. If we should succeed, there would be no problem but, if not, I did not want sudden panic at home among the sponsors, especially the owners of the Twin Otter and the *Benjy B.* Best to make them well aware of troubles before they occurred.

The alternative would be an optimistic assessment of our chances. I remembered the advice of the Roman sage, Publius Syrius, "Never promise more than you can perform," and sent Ginnie a message couched in terms intended to worry the Committee and Ant Preston into immediate action. They must make ready fuel and food enough for an extra year back at Alert in case we failed to reach the Pole before ice break-up, likely to occur in mid-May. They must also make preparations in case we reached the Pole at the end of April, and so needed extra food and fuel for the remote Greenland base of Cape Nord. I ended the message with the words: "I fully appreciate that a delay in our schedule will mean a difficult decision for sponsors, Committee members and members of the expedition team, whether on the ship, aircrew or Londoners. It will mean extra requests for financial aid and materials, mainly food and fuel. I feel we cannot too quickly put the likely eventualities to all concerned. This way, if key sponsors do drop out there will be time to replace them."

This note, despite being sent off so early in the day did not, unfortunately, have the required effect. Everything had gone too well in Antarctica and the North West Passage and a dangerous attitude prevailed at home which was soon to cause critical troubles.

All about our floe, as the wind steadied around forty knots from the west, a sound of roaring water came to us through the fog and the blown snow. The pack was on the move but there was no knowing in which direction. It was easy to worry yourself sick inside the tiny tent. At times the wind tore away the windward side of the fly sheet. I shovelled a wall of snow around us and double-pegged the guy ropes but each new crack and boom from outside made my ears prick up and the skin crawl slightly down my back.

Prince Charles had made a radio broadcast after our Antarctic crossing. One of his comments passed more than once through my head as we waited out storms in the Arctic:

> I think a great lesson to be learned is that the power of nature is still immense and that it should remind us of our frailty as human beings, that we aren't as great as we think we are, that out there still is something so much more powerful than we are, even with our sophisticated technology and our ability to communicate to people so rapidly and create vast and deadlier weapons, that nature is even more deadly in many ways than we are, and we should respect that and recognise our place within the natural environment because if we lose that I think we should lose touch with everything.

I found it very easy to agree with this when sitting in a tent amongst the crashing floes with 17,000 fathoms of cold sea just beneath my sleeping bag and remembered Hemingway's words, "Cowardice, as distinguished from panic, is almost always simply a lack of ability to suspend the functioning of the imagination."

The four days of wind, acting upon sea-ice far less compacted than it would be after an average winter, caused widespread fracturing over thousands of square miles and vast regions of open water where, for at least another two months, the ice should have remained solid. Fortunately we were not able to see a satellite photograph of our overall predicament.

Although we could not know it, the Norwegians arriving at Yelverton Inlet, not far west of Cape Columbia, had found to their astonishment nothing but sea water where solid fields of rubble should have pressed up against the Yelverton peninsula. The Eskimo and one of the Norwegians decided they should give up so risky an enterprise at this point. The Eskimo was brave as a tiger when it came to facing polar bears or extreme low temperatures but, like many of his kind, he had relatives or friends who had died out on the sea-ice and he could sense more clearly than the Norwegians, that things were far from normal this year in the Arctic Ocean.

On 14th March Karl and Simon managed to rescue the two stranded skidoos at some considerable risk and flew north to our battered floe. Within ten minutes of his leaving us a fogbank closed over the floe and the wind rose, moaning over the shattered pack. But we were keen to press on now that our old skidoos were back. Heavy and battered they might be, but we knew their every idiosyncrasy: we had after all crossed the Southern Continent with them.

So we set off into a curtain of snow blown from the north west which settled over the many slits and trenches freshly opened up by the wind. I could see very little to my front due to flying ice particles that stung my eyes. Twice I lurched down into camouflaged patches of sticky *nilas* and held my breath as the skidoo tracks slithered and clawed for purchase. Both these places were invisible due to a dusting of blown snow. I should have been warned but it was so good to be moving again that I carried on into the gathering gloom of dusk. Each time a new split caught me unawares I signalled wildly to Charlie who shoved a hand up to acknowledge the warning and took care to avoid my route.

The canals began to proliferate and widen. Soon there was a spider's web of open canals cunningly concealed by the poor light and the newly fallen snow. From time to time I turned to check the whereabouts of Charlie in the twilit murk. This I did once too often and narrowly missed a wide canal zig-zagging across my front.

No sooner did I come clear of this cutting than a divergent channel with four-foot high banks barred my new course. Again I swerved. This time too late. Skidoo and sledge skidded into the trough flinging me towards the far bank. My legs broke through the snow's crust and water filled my boots but my chest was against the further wall and I scrambled out.

The skidoo was beyond my reach and already settling fast like a cow caught in a quagmire. Within minutes it was gone, its 900 pounds laden weight pointing down at the black ocean floor far below. Slowly the steel sledge tilted despite the air trapped between items inside the sledge boxes. The front of the sledge was just within reach and I grabbed at a lashing strap. With a twist around my leather mitt, the strap could not slip.

I shouted for Charlie. He was twenty yards away unaware of my problem and unable to hear me above the noise of his skidoo. I could not stand up to attract his attention but did so lying down with my free hand. Charlie saw this and came up at once. "She's going down," I shouted somewhat unnecessarily. "Try to save the tent."

The tent was in a rear-mounted box. Each box had a separate lashing strap and, since the sledge had already been briefly immersed in salt water ditches that day, the straps were covered with a sheen of hard ice.

Charlie found he could only just reach the rear of the sledge and with thick mitts could not unlash the straps which held the tent box. So he took his mitts off, a thing we *very* rarely do outside our tent, and began to work at the frozen strap.

As he did so the sledge settled slowly but surely and my arm began to feel stretched to its limit. I could not hold on much longer. My body, laid out on the ice bank, was slowly pulled over the edge.

With my free hand I opened the second box and pulled free the radio and search beacon.

Charlie could not get at the tent but he loosened the lashing of another box and retrieved my theodolite. He also removed a bundle of tent rods tied separately to the sledge. But by then one of his hands had lost all feeling and my own arm could take it no more.

"I'm letting go," I warned him and did so. If my arms had been measured just then and turned out to have been of equal length I would not have believed it. Within a minute the sledge had silently disappeared. The tent went with it.

We had long ago learnt that warmth must be very quickly applied to frozen limbs. Warmth meant a tent even though it was unusually mild that day, −33°C with a twenty-two-knot breeze. I connected the long aluminium tent poles and pushed their ends into the snow to form the skeleton of a small igloo. Over this I flung the light tarpaulin with which Charlie normally covered our skidoos at camps. With Charlie's shovel I covered the tarpaulin's edges with snow to keep it taut over the skeleton. All cooking equipment and half the rations were on my sledge somewhere below us, but Charlie carried a spoon, mug, a spare tin pot and a spare petrol cooker. Also a spare set of navigation almanacs.

Whilst I fixed up the shelter Charlie worked hard to keep his worse hand alive, flinging it from side to side trying to force some blood down his arm and into the white unfeeling fingers. Once the spare cooker was alight we bundled what gear we had into the shelter and Charlie began the wonderful but painful process of regaining his fingers.

The temperature fell back to −40°C during the night.

Two of us could in no way fit into Charlie's down sleeping bag but it came with an outer waterproof cover and an inner cloth liner both of which Charlie gave me and this kept some of the cold at bay. There was much chattering of teeth that night and halfway through it I made us a cup of coffee.

Charlie's face staring at me in the dim light from a candle balanced between us looked skull-like.

"You look half dead," I told him.

"Thanks. You don't look too healthy yourself."

I had made a stupid mistake and we both knew it. In my zeal to press north whatever the conditions, I had lost precious equipment and, very nearly, some of Charlie's fingers. Each day since we had left the coast I had recorded details of the ice conditions, incidence of open water, dimensions of major pressure walls and apparent age of floe systems. All my records had sunk along with my photo of Ginnie, personal gear and spare clothing. Gone, too, was my oilskin container with the only two items to have travelled every foot of the way with me, Gnome Buzzard and Eddie Pike's china mouse.

Still, we were both alive and no further from our goal. We had certainly fared better than a Thule Eskimo hunter whose story we had heard of. He fell through sea-ice close to his sledge. Searchers found the place later the same night through the howling of his dogs. The moon lit up an expanse of ice fragments made during his last struggles. His body was retrieved with hooks and his torn nails showed how, clutching at the ice, he had fought to climb out.

At midnight, with my little radio none the worse for its brief immersion, I called Ginnie on our emergency night schedule. As usual she was listening and picked up my faint call sign through the permanent crackle, static and plethora of morse signals.

She sounded calm but concerned when I told her of our situation. Since all our replacement gear was destroyed in the fire, I feared a bad delay. But, Ginnie said, the sledge Ollie had always used, with its standard load, had been in the snow clearing outside the garage. She promised to get it, the camp 'run-about' skidoo and a tent belonging to our film crew as soon as possible. If I sunk that, she said, there would be nothing else; even our skis had been burnt.

As soon as the weather cleared Karl set out and found a clearing half a mile from the site of my accident where he landed . . . just. I cannot imagine many other pilots even considering such a site.

On his way back to Ellesmere Island Karl warned us that the ice was now horribly broken. He reported: "Whole areas of open sea."

The wind soon dropped to eighteen knots and a new fogbank swirled about us, messing up my navigation and slowing our progress to a blind limp. I counted seven wide leads of grey jellied ice that flexed beneath our skidoos and broke under the heavier sledge runners. In such places we crossed at different points and at maximum speed, 'swimming' the sledges across on long tow ropes with less danger to skidoo and rider.

Pressure ridges averaged a height of twelve feet, sometimes reaching twenty-five feet, with two or three to a mile; between them lay rubble fields through which a criss-cross of alleyways often snaked, enabling us to progress without the non-stop preparatory axe work necessary in the more southerly pack.

On 16th March we woke to find a forty-knot wind battering the tent and showering the layer of frost from the inside of our flysheet on to our faces and into our bag openings, where it promptly melted. In semi-whiteout we nosed north. There was no sign of the sun so I applied an error of some 92° to my compass bearing and hoped for the best. The temperature had shot up to −6°C, a sinister sign and unprecedented so early in the year. By evening conditions resembled a lily pond with ourselves hopping from one floating leaf to another. The powerful west wind fortunately ensured that most ice chunks touched each other at some point. If they did not, we retraced our route and tried a new one. There was inevitably a great deal of west-east travel involved as we zig-zagged north and much axing of ice blocks to make bridges.

Not long before dusk our best bridging efforts failed to span a twelve-foot wide lead and, when we tried to get off the floe the way we'd arrived, we found our tracks led into a new canal which opened further even as we watched. So we camped in the centre of our floating islet. I climbed a thirty-foot high hummock and looked around. Leads meandered all about us. The wind rose to fifty-five knots as we set up the tent and the sound of shattering ice vied with the roar of the elements. We both knew that small isolated floes are highly susceptible to crack-up, not only when larger neighbours weighing millions of tons begin to nip them, but simply because of lateral wave action bending and straining the natural flaws in the ice. Sleep avoided me for much of that noisy night.

On one of our brief radio contacts Ginnie warned me how the press at home was enjoying cataloguing our setbacks. I decided to alter my approach to the crossing attempt. I would forget the various other teams racing us across the Pole, even the Norwegians. I would no longer press on as far and as fast as we could stand the pace. I would from now on try to conserve our strength day by day and concentrate on the long-term aim; simply to reach the ship before winter brought a new freeze-up, probably in October. That way I might avoid any more dangerous foul-ups which so set the wasps buzzing back in London: buzzing which might very well make some of our sponsors begin unhealthy reassessments.

All day on 17th March we remained cut off and a new crack opened up some twenty yards from the tent. Although this happened soundlessly we both felt the sudden temperature change as warmer air emanated from the un-zipped sea beside our tent. The temperature lowered a touch to $-26°C$ and the wind held at fifty-two knots. The main lead to the north was now a wind-whipped river some forty feet across. To sleep in such conditions might not be difficult for folk with no imagination at all but for less fortunate souls a sleeping pill would be the only way to catch up on much needed rest. The noise and the vibrations were truly spectacular once the ice began to move. We refrained from taking pills only because of their day-time after effects on our state of alertness. The fracture and pressure sounds were many and varied but the most awe-inspiring were the booming and crunching type. Like the pipes and drums of an approaching enemy horde, the distant rumble and crack of invading ice-floes that grew louder and closer, hour by hour, was horribly difficult to ignore.

The minor noises, too, had a chilling effect on the tent-bound listener. After hours of silence the sudden sharp trill or zing of a violin note immediately below our ears, as we lay on the thin mats upon the ice, could bring us instantly alert and ready to run – were it not for the clumsy constriction of our zipped-up, laced-up sleeping bags.

The ice beside our ears acted like a huge acoustics chamber, ensuring that each fine nuance of the tiniest sound was fully appreciated as we lay there and wondered.

Next morning the wind dropped as did the temperature, to −36°C. At seven a.m. I scouted around our floe and found a narrow junction point at its southern extremity. There was a deal of grinding and whining at this point and much flaking off of ice from our side of the touchpoint. An hour later we were packed and, with a little axe work, managed to manoeuvre the sleds across the moving junction of the floes. Only a few miles to the north we entered a miasma of brown gloom, a certain sign of open water, and soon afterwards stopped before a sea of dirty sludge that moved across our front. In the mist we could see no limit to this marsh.

After thirty hours of work in bitter cold conditions and using an old fibreglass kit, Karl and Gerry repaired the damaged wing tip and then went for a trial flight. They flew high over our own area, around 85°N and 70°W.

Karl wrote:

The ice is very rotten and much in motion. I am sure that the ice group are stuck for a week or more, until the ice can settle and re-freeze. They are in a trap. To their east, north and west there are high ridges and open water all around. I can see only one way out. They must retrace their tracks for half a mile and then go west for one and a half miles where I can see some ice bridges. Then they can try to go north. If they miss any part of my prescribed track there is no way out.

Ginnie made contact with a pilot operating out of Cape Nord in north east Greenland, the area we must float past sometime during the next six months. At this time of the year it should be mostly solid pack-ice. He reported: "No ice older than second-year floes and all the younger ice appears thin, weak and broken up. Even 300 miles north of here the sea is like a watery mosaic."

That night Ginnie said: "When I look to the north of the camp here I should see an expanse of unbroken ice. All I see is open water to the horizon."

Back in London Ant Preston wrote: "At this stage it is fair to say that there is no one immediately involved in the expedition who would give much for its chances of reaching the Pole this year."

From our camp by the sludge marsh we went out on long journeys on foot taking with us weapons and axes. The first two trips led us through much impressive scenery and evidence of wide upheaval. I thanked God we had not been camped anywhere in this region during the recent high winds. It was as though the floes had been shaken through a great sieve and dropped back into the sea like croutons into chilled consommé. A most unpleasant region to travel through, even on foot.

We retreated to the tent and I took down detailed advice from Karl following his recent over-flight. His route was complex but we followed it, even though it meant filling in two twenty-foot deep ditches that took us four hours, during which time the blocks about the ditches shifted a good deal, causing us some fright. But we stuck to it and after fourteen hours' travel progressed six miles to the north before a new lead stopped us.

Karl later wrote: "I was very, very curious if they could make my route and I must say in that respect Ran is an excellent navigator because next morning Ginnie told me they had made it out of the ice jungle and were some miles north of it."

The next ten days passed in a haze. Brief excerpts from my diary may give some idea of what our lives were like:

We have come nine miles today to 84° 42'. Only 318 miles to the Pole. Another thousand or so on the other side but that is not even worth contemplating yet. It was at this point that the Simpson Expedition gave up and turned back. Plaisted's first attempt with skidoos petered out sixty-six miles to the south and Peary's first two attempts -- Eskimos, dogs and all -- got to 84° 17' and 83° 38' respectively.

For a while this evening we bridged our way over a multi-year floe with great splits in it just narrow enough to fill in with shovel work. Looking down you can see twelve feet and more to the level of the sea. We are stopped here by a two-mile field of green, ridging blocks. Spent an hour axing a path before coming back and erecting the tent. Quite a few rips in the flysheet now.

My chin was numb when I came in and lit the cooker. Must have pulled my frozen facemask off too hard. When thawing it out and picking the ice bits from around the mouthpiece I found a one inch diameter tuft of my beard complete with skin implanted in the bloody ice. It took a while to remove this from the wool. Where the skin has come away there is now an open patch of raw flesh the size of a large coin. In a while my chin warmed up and began to bleed. Now it is just weeping liquid matter.

A big switchback wall held us up this morning. After a rough time we got over. I saw Charlie's track looked wrong. One track adjuster bolt had sheared and I left him to fix it. For an hour I scouted and chopped as necessary and then went back. Charles was cursing away, unable to fix the new bolt in place without damaging its thread for the angle of the female sleeve was wrong. Together we heaved at the track until at last the bolt screwed home. Charlie's fingers took a while to revive before we could continue. Mechanical work at −44°C with a twenty-knot breeze is no fun . . .

Both sledges were dunked today and now all our lashings are frozen stiff. You need to crack the ice off with the back of an axe to get at the buckles. If we used ropes it would be hell to undo knots, even with needle-nose pliers.

Tonight we've had a fire. Charlie re-started the cooker but a leak around the pump caused flames all over the safety blanket and on the tent floor. We chucked the flaming cooker out of the tent in case the tank decided to explode, then we beat out the flames. Now we are using the spare cooker and patching up the holes in our bags with black cloth cut from a marker flag.

One of Charlie's tow ropes frayed through today but we had a spare. Two hours of axing and shovelling were necessary in a rubble field just north of here before camping. So our clothes are wet and steaming above the cooker. My chin aches non-stop now but it is all right by day when it is normally numb . . .

Charlie's leg went through the ice into the water today as we tried to pull out a sledge jammed in a moving trench. Dead on −40°C all day and wind steady from the north west bang into our eyes. All the world is misty. We've been out here well over a month and I cannot wear goggles on the move; they mist up and navigation becomes impossible. I just can't spot that vital line of least resistance through the murk which is the key to success or failure. At mid-day, clouds of black steam rose up right across the northern horizon. There is no noise, just the steam. I find it impressive and a touch uncanny. The equinoctial tides may well be shifting the sea and so fracturing the ice.

Have just finished trying to patch up my chin. The raw place is

*now down to the bone; I can see it in the mirror of my compass. I
look a disgusting sight. Charlie confirmed this . . .*

Ginnie's signal was so weak it was almost unreadable on 21st March.
I had an antenna laid out cut to 4982 mhz; perhaps too low. But I did
not start chopping and changing as that usually leads to confusion. I
kept to Ginnie's frequency programme and hoped the weakness was
just due to equinoctial interference. She said the Norwegian team had
needed fuel and had called in a chartered Twin Otter fitted with
tundra tyres. Thinking the surface to be fairly solid snow the plane
landed but could not take off again. One of the crew began to suffer
frostbite. After a two-day delay another Twin Otter, carrying spare
skis, arrived and eventually 'rescued' the first one. Karl had been
called in to help when the rescue plane was unable to locate the
Norwegian's camp. Karl spotted them and guided the other Twin
Otter down. Later the Norwegians ran out of naphtha and Karl
dropped them some of ours. All this delayed them badly and two
were already keen to give up.

The French team, Ginnie said, had bickered amongst themselves whilst preparing to set out from their base in East Greenland. This resulted in a serious schism and they had flown back to
France.

It struck me that perhaps the French leader had selected his team
from experts. A doctor perhaps, a mechanic, a navigator, a radio
operator, a scientist or two or, most troublesome of all, a cameraman
and film crew? In short, a nest of prima donnas and the likely
ingredients for internecine strife.

Our expedition had from time to time certainly suffered from its
lack of experts, but that to my mind was the lesser evil. Quite apart
from the prima donna aspect, experience from past expeditions had
taught me that it is a natural temptation for cameramen, reporters
and film crew to see trouble where there isn't any, because trouble,
especially between leader and team, is newsworthy stuff. Fortunately
for me, the back chatter and critical gossip from Bryn Campbell and
the film team during the three years of our journey was minimal. I
was extremely lucky to have them especially since, professionally
they had no peers.

On 22nd March, fearing our days of drifting had taken us too far
east into the looser conditions above the outflow channel west of
Greenland, I steered 15° to the west of north. Charlie's starter rope

broke so he had to keep his skidoo ticking over all day. It was unusually cold and my duvet jacket's zip gave up the ghost; I used some string as a belt but my heat loss all day was considerable and did me no good.

That night I slept not at all as my chin throbbed like a tom-tom. Not having any more antibiotic cream, I applied the cream I used for my haemorrhoids. Charlie found this highly amusing. "He's got piles on his chin," he shrieked with mirth. It was lucky that we shared a weird sense of humour.

Then we had our first good day: fifteen miles in eight hours, though not all of it to the north. We were finally brought to a halt by a great barrier of blocks averaging twenty-five feet high and over 200 yards from side to side which stretched west and east beyond the limits of my vision. We clambered up the wall and agreed it would take a day at least to axe a route to the other side.

Leaving the sledges we drove east through a maze of high sculptured blocks and, after a mile, came to a wonderful sight. The Israelites must have felt equally grateful when the Red Sea upped and parted down its middle. Somehow an acre or two of four-foot thick floe-ice, in the grip of hidden forces, had been forced twenty or thirty feet upwards without fragmenting and formed a ready causeway over the barrier wall. For two hours we chopped and hammered with our axes to make a ramp by which to descend the other side of the wall. My axe slipped and cut through one mukluk but I felt no pain and assumed my inner boot had protected my toes. Winding our way, soaked with exertion, back to the sledges we erected the tent on this paddock and soon had the meat rehydrating. It was not an old floe and the water was very salty. Charlie looked at my foot. The axe blade seemed to have cut right through the nail of one toe and deep into the meat beneath. But there was not too much blood and Charlie bound it up with gauze and plaster treated with 'cure-it-all' piles cream.

Another good day followed. In the morning my chin was swollen up like a golf ball so Charlie gave me Bactrim broad-spectrum antibiotic pills. After covering the raw chin with piles cream and gauze plus a tissue, I placed a stocking-bandage over my head from chin to the back of my skull as though I had toothache. Then on went the two facemasks. But within twenty miles of leaving the tent the facemasks had once more begun to freeze into position and I had accumulated a matting of ice from nostrils to chin. The discomfort of

long hours of travel *into* the wind, which averaged eighteen knots at
−40°C, was well worth it for we needed the cold to repair the ice and
stave off further break-up.

At mid-day we stopped at a fifteen-foot high barrier and trudged
towards it with axes and a shovel. Charlie grabbed my arm. "Listen," he said. A grinding, squeaking moan, as from a concrete mixer,
issued from the wall of ice and, despite the intense glare of the sun, we
watched fascinated as blue-bellied blocks the size of small bungalows
spewed up from the wall's centre and fell down its leading edge. At
the same time splits appeared in the floe itself and green water surged
up and along the foot of the moving wall. At the time there was little
or no local wind but great shearing powers were at work to cut and
shift those heavy blocks. The theory that pressure ridging results
from the squeezing of newly frozen leads and not from the interaction between the grinding edges of two senior floes did not tally with
the impressive activity of that particular ridge.

Since there was no way round and no point in waiting indefinitely
for the movement to cease, we gingerly worked at the blocks as they
slithered and fell, taking great care to avoid being crushed. A few
minutes before we were ready to attempt a crossing, all movement
ceased and there was absolute silence.

The wind rose again during the afternoon and Charlie was frost-nipped along the bridge of his nose; myself on one eyelid. Navigation
was becoming almost instinctive with or without the sun. Perhaps
unknowingly I was responding to the lie of the ridges or the wind or
even the direction of the light source which I could not consciously
determine. Wally Herbert once told me: "It is essential that all of you
should be excellent navigators." This is not the reckoning of distance
covered, which is simple to tally, but the ability to keep to the correct
direction when on the move without necessarily seeing the sun and
without constantly checking the compass as one would in a mist
when hiking in Europe.

On 27th March it was −41°C with twenty-three knots from the
north west. Every hour we had to stop to restore the blood to our
hands and feet. Fingers got numb with axe work. My neck glands
were now puffed up and swollen like my chin, so I kept taking the
Bactrim pills. I noticed in my compass mirror that the whites of my
eyes were all red. I still could not wear my goggles although much of
the day iced rain fell, little freezing nuclei particles in the air which hit
my retina as tiny spicules and stung.

We camped at five p.m. on a solid enough floe, though a small one. There seemed to be no movement about. Yet at six p.m., just as Charlie had boiled the ice water and made coffee, a violent shudder passed through the floe like an earth tremor and, within a second, a shock wave of air, precisely similar to a distant bomb blast, grabbed at the tent and caught at our breath. Immediately, coffee spilling all over the floor, we tore at the tent zip in readiness to rush outside, for we feared that a giant floe had hit ours and was about to raft over us. Outside there was no wind, no movement and no sign of anything untoward. Warily we re-zipped the entrance flap and mopped up the coffee puddles.

"Odd," I said.

"Strange," said Charlie.

We felt uneasy on that floe. I still have a tape recording of a weird conversation we had in the tent about Charlie's toe. Typical of many of our discussions, it was as though our brains were in neutral.

"Very strange," Charlie observed. "Right at the end. My feet are dead. No feeling. Very strange."

"Can you feel that there's no feeling?"

"I can feel there's no feeling."

"What sort of feeling is it?"

"No feeling."

"Yes, I know the feeling."

During the night of 28th March we awoke sweating inside our damp bags. The atmosphere was oppressive and there was deathly silence. I thought briefly of a line from Wally's doggerel: "Beware the calm that follows the storm." As I moved outside in the morning I knew at once that something unusual was happening. Our rubble-strewn paddock was entirely surrounded by mottled marshes of steaming sludge. The light of the sun, a sickly yellow, appeared to flutter and fade from minute to minute. Neither of us spoke as we raised camp and tightened the lashings of our sledges.

To the north east a brown-skinned lake disappeared into the gloom. Elsewhere the marsh was broken by floes similar to lumps of melted cheese on the surface of onion soup. I heaved a lump of ice on to the skin of this marsh. It settled slowly into the jellied crust then, in a leisurely manner, disappeared. I looked at Charlie. His eyebrows lifted and he shook his head slowly. We walked to the eastern side of our island and slung a chunk out into the brownish skin of the lake. There was a rippling motion away from the point of impact but no break-through. Again I looked at Charlie. He remained expression-less. I shrugged and we made for the skidoos.

There followed five hours of hell. God was exceptionally good to us that morning. By rights we should not have tried to travel. Our route was about as straight as a pig's tail and went where the perils of the moment dictated. To stop would mean to sink. For a thousand yards we moved over this first lake, which was in reality more like a wide river, with a sludge wash spreading out in front of our slow advance. The brown skinned lane ended in open water which hissed with curling vapour on both sides of us. A solitary floe chunk with one low edge gave us brief respite. From it we listened for signs of what lay ahead in the yellow murk.

A soft squeaking and grinding emanated from nowhere in particu-lar. Satan's private cauldron could hardly have produced so evil an aspect. Often that morning we lost sight of each other in the fog. Sometimes we moved on foot, Charlie waiting on some bump suspended in the marsh half-way from the skidoos and shouting to guide me back. We were frightened lest a new fracturing cut us off from the sledges. If that happened we could not expect to live for long. By noon we were weary with apprehension since the marsh, for all we knew, stretched on for many miles. Then the mist grew less dense and in a while, thank God, it cleared away altogether and fourteen miles of *solid* ice rewarded our morning's efforts.

I felt wonderfully good and forgot about my chin and nose and toes and all the vast distance ahead. For nothing could surely ever be so bad again. If we could travel over that marsh we could cross anything. Such a sense of elation and conceit did not last long but was fine whilst it did. We stopped at 87° 02' within nine miles of our furthest north in 1977 and forty days earlier in the season. If our aim had been solely to reach the Pole we could perhaps have felt confident. That night in a new fog bank I took a little while to work out to my satisfaction exactly in which direction Ginnie was in order to lay out the radio antenna on the correct plane. If I got it wrong I was, of course, less likely to make contact. At first I had no luck but after changing the antenna length to a cut of 5592 megahertz I heard her Strength 2 but fading in and out like the noise of the seashore. The Spanish team, she said, had set out on their journey to the Pole from West Svalbard. After progressing three miles from their camp beside Longyearbyen airport, their siedges gave trouble so they abandoned them and returned to Madrid.

The Norwegians on the other hand had covered an astounding 120 kilometres in a couple of days and were now but 176 miles to our south awaiting resupply by the Norwegian Air Force. Quite how they had stormed through the worst possible pressure zone which had taken us weeks I learnt some days later. The break-up which had held them up at Yelverton Inlet, froze solid during the ensuing cold front and presented them with a virgin highway to the north. Taking their chance, they had carried on mile after mile without sleeping until at length they came to older ice and ridging and fractures. But 176 miles is a long, long way on the Arctic Ocean, so I decided to observe Prince Charles' winter advice and cast aside any thoughts of racing.

"The Norwegians may catch us before we reach Spitsbergen but not before the Pole," I told Ginnie.

"Be careful," she replied, "remember the convergence."

This was not a feature I was likely to forget, since it was stage one on the way to Nirvana as far as our crossing attempt was concerned. Once past the convergence we would be out of the Beaufort Gyral, the current that flows in a giant clockwise circle between the Pole and the top of Canada. For a while we would be in a sort of no-man's-land where floes might or might not find themselves shoved back into the gyral. But within a few miles of the Geographical Pole we would enter the Transpolar Drift proper which heads over the Pole from the USSR and down towards Greenland. Where these two currents meet and diverge there is, of course, corresponding surface disturbance which, in places, tears floes apart, in others jumbles them together. We believed this highly mobile belt to be at around 88°, 120 miles short of the Pole.

As we crept north in early April the general movement and noise of the floes increased. It seemed as though we were rushing pell-mell in an unseen tide-race to an invisible sink-hole, the maw of the world.

Keen to keep tabs on our position and warned by Karl of the unpredictable behaviour of the Twin Otter's navigation system, I checked out my theodolite on 2nd April, shortly before Karl was due to drop us rations. Three sun's altitude shots gave me a position of 87° 21'N, 76°W. But when Karl came in his Omega put us at 87° 23'N, 75°W, a difference of some five miles. The Omega I decided was more likely to be accurate, so I asked Karl to bring in my second theodolite once we reached the Pole. This had been kept in

Ginnie's hut and so was not burnt, although two others of different types had been destroyed.

Karl managed to land at our strip, although it was far from even and Simon was able to collect eight bags of snow for a pollen check for the Polar Shelf Project. When Karl left, I tried to make up time by setting out at midnight. A wearisome and bitter ten miles, with much axing through rubble with no perspective to indicate possible routes. We camped amidst a hopeless muddle of blocks. The sting of the ice rain, the glare of the whiteout and the fumes in the tent made my vision poor. I don't think I had even a hint of sun blindness but something was wrong. However much I blinked I just saw an indistinct haze up ahead. I prayed hard in the tent for my sight to come back properly. It did.

For three days we struggled on with some good old floes, many breakdowns and two nasties — occasions when a sledge sunk into a lead and its skidoo was jammed in the sludge simultaneously. So long as both of us were close by when this happened we could usually tow the stricken units out frontwards or backwards. But there were many near squeaks. Not good for the nerves.

At 87° 48′N we were stopped by the most massive wall I had ever seen in the Arctic. Not in height but in sheer bulk. First a ten- or twelve-foot moat, fortunately frozen, then a sheer-sided twenty- to thirty-foot high buttress a hundred yards in depth. Then a jagged rubble belt ending in another rampart which almost twinned its parallel neighbour. There was no causeway over this barrier and no detour round it, so we fashioned a devious zig-zag route over it and four hours later bounced down the far side to eighteen miles of better going and no leads of any consequence.

Throughout the day black shadows along the line of the horizon, similar to rainstorms seen on steppe-lands, helped me steer clear of open water. A helmsman in polar seas knows by ice blink, a portion of brightness in an otherwise dark ocean sky, just where ahead he will find floes. Conversely black smoke, known as steam-fog or frost smoke, tells the ice-bound pilot where he may find an escape route from the pack. The steam comes from cold air striking warmer water: it is the rapid and visible discharge of moisture and heat into the atmosphere.

Ginnie came through clearly on 4th April. The Russian expedition, she said, had never set out because the Canadians refused it a 'landing permit'. The Norwegians were doing well but no longer closing on us. Dundee University had sent Ginnie a message describing a satellite picture of the sea-ice ahead. For weeks they had told her nothing owing to fog or clouds, but now a clear picture was available. At 88° 30′N and again at 89° 20′ massive surface disintegration was under way and both areas appeared to consist only of thin ice.

Given that the first such zone might be the convergence belt, we tried to speed up our progress and next day managed twenty-one miles despite open canals, wide rubble fields and much axework. We were operating well together and the magic of knowing we were north of 88° worked wonders.

7th April: A real fight today. To think we have believed for years that a flat and smooth highway existed to the north of 88°. Charlie said this morning that today's conditions were as bad as anything we met along the coast. He may well be right but at least up here there are a few good bits between the zones of chaos.

Charlie nearly sank this morning. After two hours hacking through an eighteen-foot high wall we filled a sludge ditch with cutaway blocks. As he drove onto them they disappeared under water. He leapt off and together we hauled until his rubber tracks were clear. How many more cat's lives? . . .

8th April: Crossed sixty-two sludge cracks today and two major ridge features. But the bit is between our teeth. Twenty-one miles done and no more than thirty-one to the Pole . . .

9th April: Charlie's sledge swam for twenty yards today but the breaking nilas never quite caught up with his skidoo. This area is a dreadful mess. My neck swelling has gone and my chin is almost healed, so no more antibiotics . . .

Suddenly, some twenty miles short of the Pole, the ocean's surface improved and remained almost unbroken with hardly an obstacle in sight. At mid-day on 10th April, a theodolite sighting put us at 60°W. Our local noon was at 1630 hours Greenwich Mean Time. The last miles to the Pole were flat but with three narrow leads that caused no problems. I checked the miles away with care after the noon sun shot, not wishing to overshoot the top of the world. We arrived there at 2330 hours GMT and I contacted Ginnie at 0215 hours GMT on Easter Day 1982.

I had to think for a while when laying out the antenna to point due south at her since *every* direction was due south. The temperature was −31°C. We were the first men in history to have travelled over the earth's surface to both Poles but apprehension over what lay ahead overshadowed any sense of achievement we may otherwise have felt. The *Benjy B* was still many hundreds of miles and many cold wet months beyond our immediate horizon.

15

The Circle is Complete

APRIL–AUGUST 1982

Luck and strength go together.
When you get lucky you have to have the strength to follow
through.
You also have to have the strength to wait for the luck.

MARIO PUZO

Following our arrival at the Pole the *Daily Mail* commented: "On the anniversary, almost to the day, of Robert Falcon Scott's tragic death in Antarctica in 1912, there is something very satisfying about Englishmen beating Norwegians at the other end of the globe. For it was Norway's Roald Amundsen who vanquished Captain Scott at the South Pole."

I remembered on first reading Scott's diary my feeling of empathy at his comment: "On the second hour of the march Bower's sharp eyes detected what he thought was a cairn . . . Soon we knew this could not be a natural snow feature. We marched on and found it was a black flag . . . The Norwegians have forestalled us and are first at the Pole. It is a terrible disappointment and I am very sorry for my loyal companions . . . All the daydreams must go; it will be a wearisome return." And later, with some presentiment of the horrors to come, "Great God! This is an awful place and terrible enough for us to have laboured to it without the reward of priority."

Of course, when our own self-confirmed competitors arrive here at the North Pole, unlike Scott and his companions, they will be able to plant their flag in virgin ice because, within twenty-four hours of our ceremony, our flag and its resting place will have floated away to the south.

I thought of the Vikings' famous saying, their equivalent of not counting chickens until they are hatched, "Praise no day until evening, no wife until buried, no sword until tested, no maid till bedded, no ice until crossed." We had not crossed our ice nor even reached the halfway point.

The sea-ice break-up, after which we would be unable to travel and must look for a solid floe on which to float, was unlikely to occur before mid-May. This gave us four weeks in which to zig-zag a thousand miles to the edge of the ice and the safety of the *Benjy B*. At the Pole the weather for once was excellent but we could not take advantage of this because, back in London, an arrangement had been made for the *Daily Mirror* to send two of their staff to the Pole by Twin Otter. David, Simon, Bothie, the journalists and the film crew were to spend a few hours at the Pole with us if the weather stayed fine. But Ginnie and Laurence Howell must remain at their respective radio watches at Alert and Tanquary Fjord as Karl's rear links. The landing was made on 12th April. Karl said the ice all about the Pole was decidedly suspect, but he landed nonetheless. He was proved right a few days later when another Twin Otter, chartered at great expense by a group of Japanese tourists determined to land at the Pole, came down safely enough but then sank through the ice and disappeared. I admired the way Karl continued to work with us, although summer was rotting the pack faster each day, and he had the memory of losing a Twin Otter the previous year in very similar sea-ice conditions.

The *Daily Mirror* men brought us a message from HRH Prince Charles: "What wonderful news on Easter Day ... you have achieved a remarkable feat and we are all praying for endless square miles of solid smooth ice between the North Pole and Spitsbergen."

We also heard that Buzzard Weymouth, deckhand extraordinary on the *Benjy B* and Annie, his New Zealand plunder, had been married in a little church in Bedford. The church was full of Transglobers. She wore a long white dress and carried a bouquet of spring flowers. I closed my eyes to imagine it; another world from ours. They were to honeymoon briefly then return to the *Benjy B* which, under Ken Cameron, was refitting feverishly in Southampton. In three weeks they were to set out for the North Sea and Spitsbergen.

The aircraft Omega and the flight calculations both indicated we were within 600 metres of the geographical North Pole. Bothie was unimpressed. He trotted about on the floe and pee'd close to, but not on, the Union Jack and the other flags which we had planted there: the flags of the Explorers' Club of New York, New Zealand, Cape Town, the Special Air Service Regiment, Jacky McConnell's home town of Pouce Coupé, Canada, the Sultanate of Oman, Blue Peter, C. T. Bowring and Marsh and McLennan Inc.

Karl took a walk over the airstrip and checked the holes that Charlie had drilled for ice depth. He was not happy. Taking me on one side before he left he advised me to head down the Greenwich meridian itself for at least a hundred miles from the Pole and then aim off to the east to counteract the prevailing westerly currents.

Once the Twin Otter and our friends had gone away, we packed up and set out in the evening for I had decided to travel by night and sleep by day. That way the sun would be behind us and would throw the shadow of my body ahead of the skidoo allowing me to use it as a sundial and so dispense with a compass for much of the time. Also there would be less glare and more perspective.

Our new 'day time' was hardly welcomed by the rest of the team back at Alert, since it seriously curtailed their daily sleep quota. As far as they were concerned our travel hours were from two p.m. until two a.m. with a radio safety schedule at five a.m.

I like operating on simple schedules based on solid information, but for the next phase of our journey I had none. I wanted to travel across the Arctic to a place where the *Benjy B* could reach us, by a route with the thickest ice. Where exactly should I aim for this mild warm year? Which way would be safest?

Uncertainty as to the best course for us was crystallising in London. The Chairman, and one or two others, counselled an attempt to reach the coast of north east Greenland and then to sledge over the icecap to some part of the coast which the *Benjy B* might reach. But Andrew Croft disagreed and suggested we keep to my original plan to head east towards the northern coast of Spitsbergen.

Although I trusted Andrew Croft, I feared the current signs of an unusually early break-up. At Cape Nord, an American meteorologist had announced that the pack-ice was more broken north of Fram

Strait than at any time in the last thirty-seven years, since the first observations had begun.

This being so, I was equally shy of heading too far west *or* too far east. It seemed safer to stay halfway between Greenland and Spitsbergen almost on the Greenwich meridian, where the southerly current was thought to be strongest. So I made up my mind to heed local evidence rather than outside opinions.

Two expeditions in history had travelled south from the Pole in this region, but neither could be treated as a safe yardstick from which to draw conclusions applicable to our own route. The weather alters radically year by year, and anyway the other two expeditions were evacuated from extremely hazardous sea-ice conditions in a manner not available to ourselves.

In 1937 Ivan Papanin had been deposited by a Soviet ski-plane, with three companions and a prefabricated hut, at the North Pole, near the end of May and they had drifted slowly south down the east coast of Greenland in the succeeding winter darkness. They had chosen a multi-year floe of size and solidity but by mid-February it had all but disintegrated. At this point Joseph Stalin had made the might of the Soviets available and three Russian icebreakers had crashed through the ice-pack to rescue the stranded men just west of Jan Mayen Island. We had no icebreakers at our disposal, nor could we expect the might of the British to be sent to our rescue. Mrs Thatcher was not in the business of helping lame ducks.

I had all my hopes pinned on the *Benjy B* but I knew she could not penetrate pack-ice the way an icebreaker could. The only way she might reach us was through the skill and spirit of skipper and crew acting in unison with Karl, as their eyes, in daylight and summer conditions. Such conditions exist only for five or six weeks in an average year, from late July until late September, so we must reach at least 81° of latitude and preferably well east of the Greenwich meridian by that period, otherwise even the best endeavours of the *Benjy B* would be to no avail. For the ship to linger after the end of the short Arctic summer would be to invite disaster upon herself.

Apart from Papanin and his crew, the only other men to have travelled south from the North Pole on this side of the world were the four members of Wally Herbert's 1968 team. With some forty huskies, they had left the Pole on 7th April but by late May had been cut off by the ice break-up from their goal, a landfall on the Svalbard coast. However, two of the team had managed to scramble onto a tiny island some twenty miles north of Svalbard to retrieve some granite rock symbolic of their success. In increasingly broken mush they had floated west to a rendezvous with HMS *Endurance*, ice patrol vessel of the Royal Navy, whose helicopters had managed to uplift men and dogs to the safety of the mother ship.

Our skidoos could not cope with mush ice and open water because, unlike dogs, they were not amphibious. The *Benjy B* could not penetrate pack-ice as well as the far larger HMS *Endurance*, nor did she possess any helicopters. Therefore, it would be foolish for me to attempt to follow Wally Herbert's route, even assuming the 1982 break-up was to be in late May – as it was in 1969.

I decided to steer a central course. The Roman philosopher, Cleobus, had a lifelong dictum "The middle course is best". This seemed to fit the bill best for me too. To head south under our own steam at a speed comparable to Wally Herbert's, whilst the temperatures remained reasonably low and the pack relatively stable. But once local conditions deteriorated to the point where I considered a break-up imminent, then I would search for a floe as solid as Papanin's on which to float south towards the best pick-up point, somewhere close to the Zero meridian, not too far west or east of it. This way we might reach the *Benjy B*s limit-of-penetration point before winter darkness and new ice forced her out of the Arctic. No man had crossed the Arctic Ocean in one summer season before but, given a few more weeks of solid ice and skilful handling of the old *Benjy B*, we might conceivably make it.

For four nights of travel from the Pole, surface conditions were better than ever before, the weather was warm and pleasant, never below $-28°$ and, despite signs of recent upheavals, there was no open water to be seen. We averaged twenty-two miles of southerly sea travel each night without pushing the pace.

During the night of 22nd April I noticed the prints of an Arctic fox at 88°N, many hundreds of miles from the nearest land. Although there were no bear prints in evidence it was safe to assume that the fox could only have survived so far from the source of any natural prey, such as hares, by shadowing a bear and feeding off its leftovers. Bears have been spotted by air only a few miles from the Pole itself.

As we moved away from the Pole, our distance from Alert was at the very limit of Karl's operating distance, so Ginnie decided to start closing down first Tanquary Fjord and then Alert in readiness to move to her next base, Cape Nord in East Greenland. David Mason had to return to England because his father was ill, leaving Laurence Howell alone at Tanquary Fjord. On 16th April Karl was to fly there to evacuate Laurence and the radio equipment but, just as he was about to take off from Alert, his starboard engine failed.

Owing to bad weather and David's early departure Laurence was benighted at Tanquary for two and a half weeks but was not, unfortunately, quite alone. A pack of wolves moved down to the camp and stayed with him. His only weapon was Ginnie's .38 Smith and Wesson revolver. The persistent attention of the wolves by day and by night did little to make Laurence's vigil enjoyable. Once he forgot to take his revolver to the isolated lavatory shack and was marooned there for an hour before he deemed it safe to make a dash back to the radio hut. When Karl was finally able to relieve poor Laurence, six wolves chased the Twin Otter down the airstrip in broad daylight.

One hundred and six miles from the Pole we needed fuel and Karl managed to land a mile away from our camp on a narrow lead. He reported broken conditions not far to the south and mentioned the existence of an ice island only 130 miles to our south. Nicknamed North Pole 22, this floating tabular iceberg had for several summers been manned by Russian scientists living in huts beside an airstrip. However, North Pole 22 was now, after years of wandering in mid-ocean, headed for the perils of Fram Strait and the last Russian occupants had finally abandoned it a week previously.

On the night of 18th April we crossed a narrow lead between two pools of green water. Then a belt of grey sludge, or nilas, confronted us which bubbled cauldron-like. As we watched, this sludge moved slowly to the south west, transporting a load of broken floe bits and pieces. The noise of a giant heartbeat emanated from this canal and we listened fascinated at its edge. Two skins of nilas rafted one over the other with rhythmic jerks and this we decided was the source of the cardiac beats. Long ago we had learned that a single skin of nilas was liable to collapse beneath a skidoo but two, buckle and bend as they might, usually held our weight. So we headed out and across the canal. That day we made thirty-one miles in fourteen hours, probably our best night's travel. Over the next three nights of twenty-four, twenty and twenty miles respectively, conditions slowly deteriorated. There were many regions of ridges, and rubble as bad as any to be found off the Ellesmere Coast.

"Makes you laugh," said Charlie as we axed our way through a twenty-five foot high blockage. "Both sides of the Pole between 88° and 89° have great heaps of this muck just where we have always expected good going."

He was right; Peary and Cook and Plaisted and Herbert all experienced a marked improvement to the north of 88°. Perhaps we just happened to hit unusual conditions.

From 88° down to 86° was a continued decline. Rubble fields grew more frequent, with many more open water leads. Potential airstrip floes were correspondingly rare. I had grown accustomed to keeping an eye open at all times for airstrip potential, just as in Arabia I had subconsciously noted every piece of dead ground as we drove by in case of sudden ambush. You never knew when you might need to seek cover. In the Arctic no one could tell when a flat floe of at least twenty-four inches thickness might not become a life-saving necessity. Through the nights of 20th and 21st April for forty miles there was no potential strip of any sort. The pack-ice was far too broken and, for huge areas, too thin. Nothing I saw in all that time could have served us for a floating platform on which to head south.

The temperature was by now in the −20s and rising daily. It was no longer necessary to wear a facemask. By rights I could count on four more weeks until break-up, given normal conditions. But this was no normal year and I became daily more wary as the weather grew more balmy. For the first time I felt there would be no great risk should one fall through the ice when on foot patrol. As long as it was possible to clamber out, frostbite would no longer be a risk.

Open water, pools and leads began to occur many times each mile, with no signs of new ice forming over them. Often I walked ahead with an axe to find a way through webs of canals. Charlie would station himself halfway between the sledges and me and within sight of both. If and when he saw some canal become active he would shout and signal and I would run back to him as fast as possible so we were not cut off. There was, of course, no one to keep close watch on the channels between Charlie and the sledges but that was a risk we could not avoid. There were many acrobatics and near-misses those last days, many wet sledges and legs and, on two occasions, skidoos caught wallowing in mobile ridge joints with but a minute or two for Charlie and me to haul them out before they sank.

On the night of the 21st a whiteout closed over us as we camped in a tiny paddock we had reached by dint of a tortuous route through sludge fields and 'lily pond' conditions. The wind rose to twenty-five knots and blown snow brought visibility to nil. In such broken ice it would be silly to travel so we remained there for forty-eight hours. In the evening of 23rd April the wind rose to thirty knots from the south. The whiteout lifted enough for a wan yellow light source in the north west to provide a means of navigation. The temperature had risen to −14°C.

Two hours of axing through low walls of green rafted blocks gave us access to a weird region of winding couloirs of new-looking ice. All around were black pools of wind-ruffled water. The whole area looked ready to go. Several times, approaching grey sludge, I sank into water-logged ice which had seemed firm. Along the side of one narrow canal I tripped and fell headlong. The hand holding my axe shot out to ward off a heavy fall. It disappeared through the surface, as did my arm up to the elbow and somehow one leg up to the knee. I was partially soaked but the snow-covered sludge held my overall weight. The axe sank.

Seven miles later sea water cut us off in all directions, so we camped. The wind still blew at thirty knots with the temperature steady at −13°C. Chunks of ice, floating across pools and along canals, all seemed to be heading east.

In the tent I told Charlie I would start searching for a floe suitable for a float south. For three days no sun shot had been possible but a rough estimate put us at 86° 10′N. Charlie was most unhappy. He felt we should not attempt a float-out until we had travelled to at least 83°, another 190 miles. Any less and he felt we might not make it in time. Charlie did not argue strongly that we should not stop. He acknowledged that the decision was mine but wished to dissociate himself from it. I could see his point of view. After so many weeks out on the ice the one thing we both wanted was to get the hell off it as soon as possible. Indeed to risk stopping so early and so far north must have seemed like wilful masochism to him.

But for many hours over the past three days I had been turning over and over in my mind the pros and cons of my alternative courses. To my mind everything must come second to whichever course of action promised the greatest chance of eventual, not short-term, success. I tried to make Charlie see things my way but he could not. I decided that he must be mentally exhausted and unable even to consider any course which did promise speedy removal from our current environment. He in turn felt that I must be mentally exhausted with the stresses of day to day travel and simply wanted to stop regardless of our chances of escape from the Arctic Ocean. Despite our contrary views of the dilemma we did not argue. This I credit to Charlie's strength of character. He must have badly wanted to dissuade me from my course but he did not so much as attempt to do so. On the other hand he would not allow himself to agree with my reasoning. He simply made his position quite clear. If I decided we would at once begin our search for a suitable floe, so be it; but I should remember in the days ahead that it was my decision not his.

What would he do, I asked him, if the decision was his?

"I would continue until mid-May," he replied, "providing the temperature stays at $-12°$ or below. But I would keep a sharp watch and, should a sudden rise in temperature and wind conditions become severe and indicate a break-up, I would at once adopt the float mode."

"But Charlie," I argued, "adopting a float mode is not something you can do at once because there are, as we have seen for the last fifty miles, very few suitable floes on which to float. I, too, would like to carry on further before floating but the choice I face is either stopping *after* the break-up signs have become apparent as you suggest, in which case it is likely no suitable floe will be attainable, so I will be in the position of a 'foolish virgin' being wise too late in the day. Or, I can risk accusations of over-caution and try to find a reasonably safe floe whilst it is still possible to get to one." After thirty-eight years of behaving like a bull in a china shop, deriding the canny and the cautious, I had decided to join their ranks.

Whether it was the right decision was, of course, quite another matter. The outcome of starting to float too soon, from too far north might make us end up well short of the ice edge and out of reach of the *Benjy B* when the new winter ice formed in September or October. If so, the fingers would point fairly and squarely at me.

It was clear that nobody at all wanted us to stop yet. The decision had to be mine alone and I could see that the popular course all round would be to 'bash on'. But Ginnie and I had each put ten years of our lives into this expedition and we were at last on the home straight. The current was now with us. My natural instinct to hurry on conflicted with an inner intuition to be careful; an intuition developed over fifteen years of expeditions.

Of course, it was one thing to decide to float and quite another to locate a suitable floe or, better still, the recently evacuated Russian ice island. For a week I had simply been heading between 15° and 30° to the east of due south whenever the terrain allowed.

By the evening of 24th April the wind had softened to ten knots. There was light snow and the temperature hovered at −15°. That night, bathed in a pale pink light, we stumbled over an obstacle course of streambeds that bounced, sludge mires, cracked canals, the banks of which moved laterally in opposite directions, and wide plains of thin new ice ready to fragment at the least pressure from wind or current. A precarious place to travel over and one where, at any time, we were liable to enter a cul-de-sac from which our exit might crack away as fast as a portcullis descends.

Many times that day, on reaching open water, we split up to check both ways for a crossing point. Meeting again in the middle we would report our finds and decide on a solution. If no natural bridge was available either way, we would follow the obstacle for two or three miles until some narrow place gave us a chance to build a bridge. More often than not these narrow places moved apart as we worked and the chunks we flung in simply submerged and floated away. I noticed pools, protected from the wind, where the water lay quite still, yet no new frazil ice platelets formed upon their surface. The winter healing process appeared to have stopped.

Around midnight, crossing a deep ditch in which we had made a clumsy ramp, Charlie touched his engine kill button by mistake and came to a halt at the critical moment he needed momentum. His sledge quickly began to sink. I slung him a medium size tow rope, something both of us carried at all times close at hand, and he clipped it on to his towbar within seconds. Then he pulled his starter rope and, with both our skidoos straining and slithering, the sinking sledge came clear, water surging off its flanks as off a wet dog emerging from a river.

Despite long hours of travel we managed a mere five miles that night and won through to a medium sized floe of first year ice, the first viable airstrip I had seen in sixty miles or more. But not old enough ice for a floating home. At that camp Charlie woke to feel the floe shudder under the impact of an unseen collision.

A wide lead delayed us for some hours at the far side of this floe next night but we crossed it on sludge and, to my delight, landed on a good sized second or third year floe dotted with well rounded hummocks which, apart from two easy fracture lines, allowed us easy progress for four miles to the south. An odd looking lead of two

colours, grey and brown, put a stop to our advance. We patrolled far
to the west and east but found no improvement. The river of sludge in
fact seemed narrowest where we first ran into it, at which point it was
only a hundred yards across.

Charlie's description of our attempt to cross the lead:

*It wasn't completely open. There was ice on it, bad ice rather like
sponge rubber. We tried to cross it. I gave Ran a bit of a start
then followed. But I saw him stop, swing round and turn back
towards me and at the same time I felt a motion beneath me
rather like being on a roller-coaster. I looked back. The ice was
actually breaking into waves and I realised the same thing must
be happening to Ran. He was trying to get off. When these two
waves meet, mine and Ran's, I thought, I don't want to be on this
lead. So I turned in a big sweep and managed to run up on to
some firm ice and Ran went past me and got back to the floe
where we'd left it. We chatted about this. We had been on this
sort of ice before but we have never encountered such big liquid
ice waves before.*

There being no way around or over the lead, we camped on the floe
and for the next four days walked out periodically to check it with an
axe. Once I reached some two-thirds of the way across before the
surface was obviously too rotten to take my weight. However, I
knew a skidoo could cross where I could not, so I told Charlie all was
well and we packed up. Back down on the lead the temperature was
$-24°C$ and I felt sure the nilas, though still of an odd tinge, part grey
part brown, would by now hold our weight.

Charlie watched carefully as I ran over the grey stuff and headed
obliquely towards the weaker brown band in the centre. To my
surprise my sledge cracked straight through the grey sludge where I
had only an hour beforehand been happily walking. I swerved
immediately back towards Charlie and the bank. We put up the tent
again some ten yards from its last position.

That night I spent a good deal of time re-reading the records of the
Russian, Papanin's drift. I noted in my diary: "If we float from *here* at
Papanin's rate, we will get to 80°N 8° W by 15th August."

I walked to the edge of the floe at the narrows and climbed up a
twenty-foot high ice boulder which gave me a clear view to the south.
The ice looked as mouldy and riven with pools, canals and mush
zones as the sixty miles to the north of the floe. Dark patches on the

underneath of clouds showed where open lakes were reflected in the sky. It was apparent even then that the overall conditions were those of an early break-up, despite the continuing low temperatures. This can only have been due to the abnormally warm winter of 1981.

Six days after our arrival, we were still on the same floe. I managed to walk right across to the far side but it still felt tacky; the same sticky texture which, during colder weather, would have firmed up within twelve hours. As the days passed I began to accept that Providence had brought us a reasonable piece of real estate and we must make the best of it. On the other hand, if the Russian's ice island was nearby it would be worth trying to reach its greater security. On 30th April Ginnie closed her base at Alert, bade a sad farewell to the Canadians up at the camp who had been such kind friends for so long, and joined Simon and the aircrew for the flight over the Robeson Channel and the Greenland Icecap to Cape Nord. Cape Nord was a military radio base, manned by five Danes, serving as the northern depot for the Syrius dog teams which patrol the north east coast of Greenland every summer. Whilst Ginnie began to set up her radio gear, Karl flew north to try to locate the ice island. There was no sign of it. He flew over our own beacon and gave us a position of 85° 58'. After three weeks of poor visibility and strong north winds we had floated some forty-four miles further south than could be expected in normal conditions. Such helpful winds sadly never occurred again. Ginnie's first call from Nord confirmed that the *Benjy B* had set sail from Southampton for the North Sea, also that the Norwegian ice team, having finally reached the North Pole, had decided to give up their attempt to cross the Arctic Ocean. A Twin Otter managed to evacuate them to Cape Nord where Ginnie had a long talk with their leader Ragnar Thorseth, a strong individualist and a likeable man.

During the first week of May I sent a message to London via Ginnie. "Whether on the ice island or on this floe we must just rely on floating until the ship can get to us, or as close as possible to us, so we can close the gap. This will probably be in July or August."

For any 'gap-closing' travel my original plan had been to travel over mush ice, where skidoos would be as useless as walking or boating, by using water-shoes and towing light hand-sledges. The 'shoes' we ended up with did not fill me with confidence yet there was nothing else, for people do not normally wander about on mush ice.

So I asked Ginnie to procure a couple of light canoes. She radioed this to Ant Preston and warned him they must somehow reach Spitsbergen within three weeks or the surface of our floe would be too slushy for Karl to land on, and we could not drop canoes by parachute. Poor Ginnie's job isolated her for long hours alone as she waited for us to call in or struggled to get radio messages through to London and now, at Cape Nord, she was even lonelier for she was without Bothie or Tugaluk. Laurence Howell had taken them on the long journey back to England to spend six months in quarantine kennels. On 9th May the *Benjy B* arrived off Longyearbyen in Spitsbergen, the most important of a group of islands called Svalbard.

Back on the ice floe, we'd been twelve days in the tent. I then cricked my back and could move only with difficulty. Despite the continued whiteout, the surface of the floe was becoming slushy. Signs of last year's melt pools, shiny green patches, were daily more in evidence as the actual snow cover decreased. Radiation from solar rays was gnawing at our precarious floating platform and eating it from under us. Wally Herbert wrote: "There is no surface more unstable nor any desert more mistily lit than the Arctic ice-pack in the month of May."

On the night of 11th May and without a sound, our floe unzipped 500 yards to the east of our tent not, as far as I could determine, along the seam of an old ridge or any other faultline. Our territory was suddenly a third smaller than it had been the previous day. Bending over the new canal I saw that the floe was some five or six feet deep.

Early in the morning, after three months without seeing a bird or an animal, a single faint cheep awoke me. Peeping out of the tent flap, once my eyes were accustomed to the glare, I spotted a snow bunting, the size of a robin redbreast, perched on a ration box. Somehow I felt full of hope and certainty. The bunting soon departed into the damp mist, God knows to where. It ignored the bits of army biscuit I threw out onto the snow.

When Karl finally landed on the floe he brought us two eight foot by five tents. We tried to erect them end to end, so we could sleep in one half and eat in the other. This did not work because the surface wasn't level, so we left a small gap between them and agreed we would each live in one. I would keep the radio gear in mine and Charlie the cooking utensils. Quite apart from being together more or less non-stop for over six years, we had lived cheek by jowl in the same small tent, in slightly trying physical conditions, for the previous ninety camps. Tempers could be expected to be frayed.

We had one long discussion during which Charlie accused me of having a negative disposition. I stoutly denied this. Then he said I was highly devious. This I found more difficult to parry, since I knew he had heard both my mother and Ginnie accuse me of the same trait. I counterattacked that he was naturally argumentative, following a disagreement as to the direction of north west in relation to the position of our tent door. That was the most risky conversation we ever held: within minutes we were busily discussing the merits of putting snow around our tent skirting.

During the entire duration of our Arctic Ocean journey we had had no flare-ups nor bad atmospheres. Back in 1977, things had not been so trouble-free, but we had become older and wiser, like owls. Perhaps we recognised each other's stress points so well that we knew almost subconsciously when to steer clear of a delicate topic.

Chris Bonington wrote of journeys of far shorter duration than our own: "Most grievances on a mountain, taken out of their context, seem incredibly petty, yet all too easily they can get out of hand and undermine the morale of an expedition. On the other hand I am sure that a certain amount of grumbling and character stripping helps to relieve tension."

Charlie said of himself: "People either like me or dislike me. I have a manner which can be abrupt and I am basically a shy person – although nobody believes that. I myself either like or dislike people which is a terrible thing: I have tried to get myself over it. I don't like people who try to push themselves or me too far. There are limits to what I can take but if someone is a pain I will listen quietly, for I am good at listening."

Since the tents were cramped we could not stand up. The floors of axed ice were uneven and daily became more sodden with melt water. This made sitting impracticable so we lay in our sleeping bags to keep out the damp and cold. I raised mine above the melt water on ration boxes and a wooden board to help my wonky back.

Most days we were enveloped in sea fog and there was no chance of Karl landing on the floe even though the surface in mid-May was still firm enough. But one glorious morning the sun shone from a perfectly clear sky and we sunbathed beside our tents. Karl flew in with Bryn Campbell who spent an hour or two taking photographs.

On 17th May Ginnie reported that the *Benjy B* was stuck firmly inside Longyearbyen Fjord because of a wind change. This same roaring southerly pushed us back north towards the Pole and caused new fractures and a second major split right through the floe which effectively halved our original 'safe' area. By the end of the month we were well behind my schedule.

Each day I walked around the floe's perimeter. There was no sign of bears so I took only a pistol. Although I lost sight of the tents after a few yards there was no chance of getting lost for I could always retrace my own prints and anyway, there was now open water all around our floe, in places up to forty yards wide, edged with huge upright slabs.

Every night Charlie produced an excellent supper which he passed down to my tent and then came in himself; there was just room for both of us. On 1st June he plucked three grey hairs out of my mop: "Poor old man," he said, "getting past it." I reminded him that he was a year older than me and that his bald patch had doubled in size since we left Greenwich. He checked his diary and discovered this was the one thousandth day of the expedition.

It seemed as though we had been on that floe for aeons but strangely we weren't bored. A conversation about even the simplest matter seemed to take forever. That evening I remember we had a fifteen-minute discussion about faggots in Hyde Park and why a chunk of wood should have become a generic term for gay gentlemen.

Charlie's face and hands were by now black with carbon deposits from the cooker fumes. Our beards were wild and tangly and our clothes ragged. But the sores of our earlier travels were mostly healed up. Day by day my tent sank lower and became wetter and Charlie's grew more and more precarious as our mound melted slowly. The ice under the edges of his tent began to disperse and his bed slipped downwards and outwards into the open.

Late in May two members of the Committee flew to Longyearbyen from Copenhagen and then, with Karl, flew out over the sea-ice between Svalbard and our own area. Returning to London they warned the rest of the Committee on 2nd June that the chances of success this summer were remote. Conventional wisdom said we should be lifted out and within a fortnight, because after that our floe would be too sodden for the Twin Otter to land. Ginnie received a radio message from the Committee to this effect. It seemed pretty unequivocal, but when she managed to speak to them herself from Cape Nord it became clear that the original message left the final responsibility with me. Only then did Ginnie contact me and I sent a reply back assuring the Committee of our determination to carry on with the original plan and agreeing to take sole responsibility for the consequences.

The canoes arrived in Longyearbyen in the first week of June and even as Karl flew to collect them, Charlie looked about our floe for an alternative unsodden airstrip. He found a still solid patch starting twenty yards to the west of our camp and running for 300 yards towards the open water along our floe rim. Karl landed there on 3rd June and unloaded two light aluminium canoes with paddles and wooden ski adaptions for man-hauling over floes. By mid-June this second strip was also water-logged and we were cut off. As far as evacuation by any means was concerned we were now on our own.

My diary:

Strong westerlies on 6th June and average temperatures of −3°C. Non-stop fog. Last night our floe was blown against its easterly neighbour. Where they met, a fifteen-foot high wall of fragments has reared up. It is thirty metres long, noisy and spews up new blocks as you watch. I am bailing out the water from my tent floor every other day now. Communications are awkward to Ginnie: she has a black-out to England and to the ship and the Danes cannot raise anyone. I get through to Ginnie only with morse and then only on 9002 megahertz on the brief up-surges of that frequency.

We have been on the floe fifty days and nights but not a bear yet. On my evening walks it is too wet now to use snowshoes, so I wear waders and take ski sticks for balance.

15th June: To my surprise I heard Howard Willson of the Benjy B talking to the ship. He is manning a second radio set in a Portakabin, brought out from England, set up beside the Longyearbyen airstrip. When we get further south the Twin Otter crew and Simon will use this hut.

Ginnie says David Mason's brother was on board a Royal Navy ship, the Sir Galahad in the Falkland Islands war last week when it was bombed and set on fire. Many of the crew were killed or mutilated in the resulting furnace but Mason junior escaped unhurt.

We are spending twenty-one hours a day in bed. After my walk I found my pulse rate was 125. Getting old. And we're going scatty too. Every time a passing seagull shrieks in the mist outside we both shout back, "Hello, Herbert." All types of gulls are Herbert to us as we're not much good at identification without Ollie. I think our most common visitors are jaegers, kittiwakes and ivory gulls. No more snow buntings.

One thing was certain; sooner or later polar bears would find us, for their sense of smell was legendary. Eskimos say that they can smell a seal from twenty miles away. We had with us Canadian and Norwegian pamphlets which told us about the polar bear, stressing its great size and weight. Large males could weigh over half a ton, be eight feet long and tower to twelve feet tall when erect. Yet for all their size, they could glide over the ice with fluid grace and thunder along at thirty-five m.p.h. They were said to be able to kill a 500-pound seal with a single blow of the paw and might attack man, if they felt threatened, with supple leaps. In 1977 a group of Austrians with children camped at Magdalene Fjord in Svalbard. A polar bear wandered into the camp and snuffled at a tent. The man inside un-zipped the door flap and the bear seized him by the shoulder. It dragged him down to the sea and on to an ice floe where it slowly ate him in front of the other Austrians who did not possess fire-arms.

I was in my sleeping bag one evening when I heard snuffling sounds beside my head which was up against the single canvas skin of the tent. The noise went away in a moment or two but shortly afterwards, close to the gap between our tents, a ration box began to make scraping noises.

"Ran?" Charlie called.

His voice came from within his tent. He had not after all been snuffling around my tent nor scratching at ration boxes. My hackles rose at the implication. A third party!

"I think we have a visitor," I called back.

Donning waders and jacket over my long johns and vest, I grabbed my camera and revolver and peeked with great care out of the door-flap. All I could see was Charlie doing likewise. We emerged very slowly. Charlie was dressed precisely as I was and held his rifle at the ready. I thought of the Goon Show. I looked around his tent. "Nothing there," I said.

He peered at the end of mine: "Nothing by yours either."

We relaxed. Then I saw Charlie stiffen and his eyeballs seemed to grow larger all of a sudden.

"Correction," he said, "we *do* have a visitor."

A large polar bear stepped out from behind my tent. Its front legs were across the guy ropes some three yards in front of us. It licked its lips and impressed me with the length of its long black tongue. The official warning notes came back to me – "Do not allow polar bears to get close." There was not much we could do about that. Without remembering to focus or adjust the shutter speed I took a couple of photographs hoping not to irritate the great beast with the clicks. The bear eyed us up and down for a while then slowly walked away. Like a poodle that barks ferociously once a bulldog has left its immediate vicinity, I began to shout "Shove off" at our visitor when it was well clear of the camp.

Next time we were not so lucky.

Again, the bear moved about by the tents for a while with each of us thinking its movements were the other man working outside. When we twigged and emerged armed, the bear was close by Charlie's tent. We shouted at it and I fired my revolver over its head. All this was studiously ignored.

Charlie's .357 rifle was bolt-action and at the time he had only two bullets. I had plenty of ammunition but my .44 Ruger magnum revolver had been ridiculed by some Canadians as inadequate for effectively stopping an aggressive bear, so I had little confidence in it. For ten minutes the bear padded about us in a half circle between our ration boxes whilst we shouted abuse in three languages, clashed our pots together and sent revolver bullets past its ears.

After fifteen minutes Charlie lay down on a sledge and took careful aim. I stood behind and to one side and fired off a parachute illuminating flare. The rocket blasted by Charlie's head and struck the snow in front of the bear fizzing brilliantly. This was also ignored and the bear crouched down in the snow facing us, waggling its rear end slightly in the manner of a cat stalking a mouse. It began to approach us.

"If it comes within thirty yards, over that snow dip, I'll fire one shot at it," I whispered to Charlie.

The bear, a beautiful looking creature, continued to advance and I aimed the pistol at one of its front legs. The shot went low, through the foreleg and probably close to the paw.

The bear stopped abruptly as though stung by a bee, hesitated for a moment, then moved off sideways and away. There was no sign of a limp but splashes of blood marked its spoor. We followed it to the end of the airstrip where it jumped into the sea and swam across to another floe. Would it have been better to have killed the bear? A dead bear lying beside our camp or even floating in a nearby lead, might attract other visitors. Or should I have left it alone? *How* close should one allow a bear to get? To my mind, no closer than you feel is the distance where, if it does charge, you can shoot it dead with your available firepower before it can reach you. A single raking scratch from the paw of even a dying bear is to be avoided by individuals who cannot be evacuated by any means and whose first aid know-how would be sneered at by the Battersea Girl Guides.

A goodly number of bears wandered across our floe over the weeks ahead and eighteen came up close to our camp. Each one seemed to react differently to our scare tactics. Their visits kept us from being bored. So, too, did the shrinking nature of our floe. Any noise outside the tents had us listening intently. There were many false alarms. One night I awoke in a gale. Amongst the plethora of wind noises I heard a rhythmic scuffling that I was certain must be a bear. It turned out to be merely the sound of my heartbeat against the canvas earflaps of my night cap!

Shut away in her radio room at Cape Nord, Ginnie was finding communication becoming more and more distorted and difficult. Sometimes her contact with England was cut off. Sometimes she could only reach me by intricate tuning, frequency hopping and antenna changing. Powerful Russian 'woodpecker' jamming caused her headaches, the long vigils turned her into a zombie yearning for sleep. She felt all around were hostile, sapping her will, as she struggled on surrounded by non-stop noise.

Once in Antarctica I had spent an hour on listening watch awaiting a call from another winter base. All I heard was a low whine, a fuzz of crackle and a high pitched whistling that quickly deafened and irritated me. I turned the volume down but this made it impossible to pick up the low dah-dit-dah of the morse signals I was waiting for. Either you put up with the cacophony or, as likely as not, you missed the message when it came. For me an hour was more than enough. Most of the interference was a speciality of the polar regions and not the normal mush which ham operators anywhere in the world have to deal with. This is not a technical sort of book, but a brief background to Ginnie's problems should be given.

As in lower latitudes radio waves passing through the polar ionosphere are distorted and the spoken message carried on them can become hopelessly garbled. By using CW (morse) messages we could still operate because they remain intelligible on a narrower bandwidth. But from time to time the polar ionosphere reflects noises which do not trouble lower latitudes and these noises often correlate with disturbances in the earth's magnetic field. The disturbances can result from strong outbursts in the sun's activities or ionospheric storms. The behaviour of the aurora and of cosmic rays can also lead to troubles.

The main bugbears Ginnie grew to dread were SID (sudden ionospheric disturbances), AA (auroral absorption) and PCA (polar cap absorption). SID affects communications all over the world and caused Ginnie the least concern since they never lasted more than an hour at a time. AA was more persistent, being the result of electrons and protons entering the ionosphere. PCA was the worst condition. For one three-day period at Alert it blacked out all communications to mainland Canada. When sunspot activity increases so does PCA, starting about an hour after a solar flare. The absorption of HF wave energy is often so strong that all HF communications in a given area become impossible.

Ginnie had had a long history of migraines and spastic colon attacks and this increased as the stresses of her job built up. The uncertainties of our progress increased the strain and she had no one's shoulder to cry on and no one from whom to seek advice. She did not enjoy this part of the expedition at all. She kept steadily at her job but found it hard to appear cheerful.

Anton and Les Davis, the skipper of the *Benjy B*, knew that we were not far from the Marginal Ice Zone, or ice pulverisation area in Fram Strait. Two million square miles of the Arctic Ocean are covered by pack-ice and one third of this load is disgorged every year through Fram Strait, which acts as a giant drainage plughole. Very soon now our floe would enter a bottleneck where the surface currents increase by as much as a hundred per cent and rush their fragmenting ice burden south at an incredible thirty kilometres a day. Keenly aware of our approaching danger, they decided, with the full support of the crew, to try their luck without delay. On 28th June the

Benjy B reached the outer rim of the pack-ice to within 150 miles of us.

Les knew that damage to the ship within the pack could be fatal, far more so here in the Arctic Ocean than down in those Antarctic waters where he had successfully negotiated the pack of the Ross Sea. Antarctic pack is usually far younger and lighter. Normally only icebreakers have business in the northern pack and they have less need to heed the warnings of the Arctic Pilot, which are:

> *The Greenland Sea pack-ice is in general unnavigable. In the northern part the pack may be up to six and a half feet thick. As a result of pressure due to wind or current the pack-ice may be hummocked to a height of twenty-five, even thirty feet. Typical forms of damage to vessels by the ice are the breaking of propeller blades, rudders and steering gear, damage to stern and plating causing leaks in the forepart of the vessel and the crushing of the hull. Also due to ice pressure the buckling of plating and the tearing out of rivets causes seams to open and leak.*

For two days we lost contact with the ship but, on 2nd July, heard she had been forced back. After this failure Anton thought it best to stay close to the edge of the pack and so to moor at the tiny coastal settlement of Ny Alesund, rather than return to Longyearbyen. Les came round to agreeing with this and so our various expedition components were scattered about the Greenland Sea, with Ginnie at Cape Nord, and Simon and the aircrew at the little Portakabin beside the windswept Longyearbyen runway.

On 10th July I managed to shoot the sun at mid-day. We had been on the floe seventy days and our latitude was still north of 82°. Preparing the theodolite for the noon-day shot took me fifty minutes wading about in slush pools. Since the tripod legs kept settling slowly it was necessary to re-adjust the theodolite's levelling bubbles after nearly every shot and each re-adjustment took five or six minutes before the bubbles were reasonably level.

The sun was a faint white circle, too indistinct to be visible through a dark or even a blue prism, so I had to use the telescope with no protection against retina burns. From the noon latitude shot I also obtained my longitude because time equals longitude.

At around 82° a complete chunk of some two acres across broke away from our south east corner. Our northern neighbour rode up and over one sector of the floe over a forty yard front and eighty per cent of our floe was covered in slush which varied from eighteen inches to seven feet deep. New ridge walls rose up daily with a good deal of noise where we struck against our neighbours. Off our sea-side edges, the wind whipped up wavelets on the black water lakes where regattas of broken fragments sailed by before the wind. All around us the ice was bare of snow cover, so that weak seams now showed up clearly like varicose veins. Day after day there was no sign of the sun and the low-hung sky reflected the dark blotches of great expanses of open water to the south and north of our floating raft.

Dundee University had experienced trouble in getting satellite pictures of our area, partly due to cloud cover and partly because of a tall chimney on the University roof which blocked out reception of the crucial area. When in mid-July a reasonable picture was obtained and shown to our Committee there appeared to be a major loosening of the pack between our floe and the Greenland Sea. Captain Tom Woodfield, whose previous experience skippering British Antarctic Survey vessels included interpretation of satellite pictures of sea-ice conditions, took one look at the Dundee picture and wondered what all the fuss was about. Of course, the ship could get through that loose stuff! He offered to fly out to Longyearbyen and personally take the ship north into the pack.

By 20th July things were a touch unsettling on the floe. Hardly a day passed without a bear, sometimes two. We stood beside the tents waiting with guns, hoping that each new visitor was not a hungry one. For a while they came at us only from our remaining 'dry' side but as this narrowed down they took to swimming across the melt-water lake that hemmed us in. They could swim almost silently despite their bulk.

The noise of the wind and the surf sound of the sea was now joined by a gurgle of drainage for the melt pools had eaten away a network of sluices from pool to pool and finally off the floe into the sea. In the water all about us huge floating chunks jostled and humpback whales, surfacing with much resonant splashing, swam back and forth, much like dolphins save for their Moby Dick tails. Often they would snort like horses and by night their unearthly music floated clear over the misty ice fields: sometimes the eerie howl of were-wolves, at others a soulful dirge containing a whiff of all the sadnesses of life.

We were now separated by some distance from other solid bodies of ice, save when a strong wind blew our floe briefly against another, causing much peripheral damage. At times I woke suddenly and listened intently. Was it a bear close by or a new upheaval around the floe? For an answer more often than not came the plunging roar of many tons of ice breaking off our floe-rim followed by echoes as miniature tidal waves broke against the far side of the leads.

As we headed south into the maelstrom of Fram Strait, so the floe began to gyrate like a piece of scum descending towards a plug-hole. The sun hovered imperceptibly lower each day and by nights now the surface of the melt pools began to freeze.

Captain Tom Woodfield arrived in Longyearbyen and initially met some hostility. The skipper and crew had tried to reach us and failed, but they saw no reason why some ice maestro should be brought in from outside even if he was a member of our Committee and one of the Board who had three years previously selected most of the crew. But Tom Woodfield was no fool. He brought a peace offering of whisky, accepted the flak which came his way and openly discussed the situation with all and sundry.

Anton wrote of the ensuing attempt to reach us:

> *Tom is at the controls and hurling the ship at six to seven feet thick floes which are breaking without too much difficulty. But the ice is more solid and further to the south than on our last attempt. Evening: we are stuck solid at 82° 07'N, 01°20'E, 82 miles south of Ran. One or two people went overboard by rope ladder and Jimmy Young spotted a cracked weld in the stem. Ken and Howard have gone over with welding kit to fix it.*

The crew had set out with much excitement. It seemed as though, with Tom's success at crashing through medium pack nothing would stop the *Benjy B*. Bryn Campbell had arrived from London again and Mike Hoover, the leader of our film crew, had flown out from the USA to be in at the kill. Then the sea temperature dropped five degrees in twenty-four hours and the wind moved around to the south. The pack began to tighten up dangerously and, after four days battling the floes, the ship reluctantly turned away, having, by some ten miles, not even reached the most northerly point of her earlier attempt. Morale was very low: after so much hope, there was now disappointment.

Mike Hoover returned to the USA and Tom Woodfield went back

to London where he told the Committee there was nothing to be done but wait for the ice to ease off.

During the last week of July there were seven bears in our camp in five days. We could not hear them approach for a strong south wind prevailed and the roar of the surf drowned all sound but the crash of segments breaking from our floe-rim. All night on the 28th July I slept little, listening to the rumbling explosions from the sea; as though elephants were belly-flopping off skyscrapers. We were daily decreasing in size.

On the 29th Charlie warned me that the bare seams in the floe between our lavatory shelter and the tents were widening as were those between his tent and the nearest part of the melt-lake. We had now been on the floe for ninety-five days and our entry into the marginal ice zone was imminent. Les decided to sail at once to the edge of the pack and, at the first sign of its loosening up, to fight north towards us. So, on the first day of August, our seventh month on the sea-ice, the *Benjy B* slipped into the low mist. Shortly beforehand Ginnie, certain at last that she could communicate with our floe from the ship or Longyearbyen, had left Cape Nord and the kindly Danes. Now she too was on board and only Simon manned the little Portakabin.

Late in the evening of 1st August, I heard Anton speaking intermittently to Simon. The ship was forty-nine miles from our last reported position and moving slowly through medium pack and thick fog. Progress between the larger floes was hampered by wedges of ice small enough to be pushed under the bows but too tough to break. They had to be nudged aside and swept past by the draw of water from the propeller, a frustrating business that took considerable skill from the bridge. In fits and starts, with many detours, the *Benjy B* moved through an ever-changing and ill-lit icescape, occasionally startling seals and bears and Minke whales and gradually gnawing away at the edges of the floes that barred her progress.

"The shuddering and grinding of the hull," wrote Anton, "is a constant accompaniment; the lurch as we strike each new floe often throws us off our feet."

Many of the crew spent long hours on deck in foul-weather gear peering into the gloom and clinging to the rails. A cautious and expectant mood of optimism slowly surfaced. Late on the afternoon of 2nd August the fog rolled away from the *Benjy B* and Karl took off from Longyearbyen at once. After circling for a while he began to talk Les Davis through the labyrinth of broken floes and, with great skill, guided the ship to a jagged twelve mile lead heading north west towards our floe.

At that time the crew noticed ominous signs of a wind change and, within the hour, a southerly breeze had picked up. Any stronger and the pack would begin to close about the ship, which was now deep inside the marginal ice zone, too deep to escape if the floes concertinaed. Throughout the long night the whole crew willed the ship north, yard by yard, and despite much battering and many a retreat, the *Benjy B* squeezed through.

At nine a.m. on the 3rd I made contact with Ginnie. She sounded tired but excited.

"We are seventeen miles south of your last reported position and jammed solid."

I shouted the news to Charlie. We must be ready to leave by canoe as soon as possible. Both of us hoped that somehow the *Benjy B* would smash a way through right up to us. For us even half a mile of travel from our floe might prove disastrous for everything was in motion about us. Great floating blocks colliding in the channels and suspended nets of porridge ice marauding the open sea lanes.

At noon I shot the sun and sent our position to Anton: 80° 43.8'N, 01° 00'W. The ship was to our south east. To reach it we must move over the sodden surface of the racing pack for some twelve nautical miles and cross the Greenwich meridian en route. At two p.m. on our ninety-ninth day adrift, we stowed 300 pounds of gear, rations and our glaciological records into the two aluminium canoes and trudged away from our bedraggled camp.

I had a compass bearing to the ship at the time we set out: the longer we took to reach her the more this would alter. The wind was a stiff twelve knots as we paddled across the first choppy lead.

The wooden ski attachments for hauling the heavily laden canoes over floes broke off within the first hour. After that we simply dragged the naked hulls over the rough ice and prayed they would not wear through. As we arrived at each successive pool, river or lake, we lowered the canoes off the crumbling ice banks with care.

We had lain in our sleeping bags with scant exercise for so long that the strain of the haul was considerable. Charlie was nearly sick with the effort. Every so often I filled my water bottle from a melt pool and we both drank deep.

At one stage a swamp of porridge and floating fragments barred our way. Once into it we were committed. That hour we progressed only 400 yards. But normally, spotting such marsh zones well ahead by clambering up the high ridges, I took long circuitous detours to avoid their hazards. Melt pools several feet deep were no problem. We simply waded through them hauling on our two ropes. Trying to negotiate a spinning mass of ice islands in a wide lake, I looked back to check Charlie was following, just in time to see two high blocks crunch together. The impact sent a surge of water after my canoe. Fortunately Charlie had not yet entered the moving corridor and so avoided being flattened.

Our hands and feet were wet and numb but at seven p.m., climbing a low ridge to scout ahead, I saw two matchsticks upon the broken horizon along the line of my bearing. I blinked and they were gone. Then I saw them again; the distant masts of the *Benjy B*.

I cannot describe the joy of that second. I found tears smarting at my eyes and I yelled aloud to Charlie. He was out of earshot but I waved like a madman and he must have known. I think that was the single most wonderful and satisfying moment of my life. Until then I could never bring myself to accept that success was within our grasp. But now I knew and I felt the strength of ten men in my veins. I knelt down on that little ridge and thanked God. For three hours we heaved and tugged, paddled and sweated. Sometimes we lost sight of her briefly but always, when again we saw her, she was a little bit bigger.

Shortly before midnight on 3rd August Jimmy Young, up in the crow's nest with binoculars, shouted down to the bridge, "I see them! I see them!"

On the bridge, gazing into the low wan sun, one by one the crew identified amongst the heaving mass of whiteness the two dark figures that they had dropped off so long ago at the mouth of the Yukon River on the far side of the Arctic Ocean.

Down below decks a tired Kiwi, John Parsloe, was just turning in to his bunk when Terry, the bosun, rushed down the gangway shouting: "Up! Up! The boys are home."

At 0014 hours on the 4th August at 80° 31′N 00° 59′W, we climbed on board. The circle was complete.

Each one of us retained the image of that moment on our ship amongst the floes. We would never forget. At that moment we shared something no one could take from us, a warm sense of comradeship between us all, Swiss and American; Indian and South African; British, Irish and New Zealander.

Ginnie was standing by a cargo hatch. Between us we had spent twenty years of our lives to reach this point. I watched her small, tired face beginning to relax. She smiled and I knew what she was thinking. Our impossible dream was over.

Afterwards

And of what value was this journey?
It is as well for those who ask such a question
that there are others who feel the answer
and never need to ask.

WALLY HERBERT

Once on board the ship I radioed Longyearbyen and spoke to our base there. Karl wrote:

> *They are arrived! In my joy I could have made a somersault.*
> *Right away I woke up Simon and Gerry and with no hesitation*
> *went to my bag for my bottle of champagne which I carried over*
> *the whole North Pole route for this special occasion. I couldn't*
> *sleep any more and I paced the hut up and down and it felt so*
> *good because of the released pressures which I had carried with*
> *me for the last seven months.*

For twelve days the *Benjy B* strained to escape the pack-ice. But she was jammed solid. By good fortune the angles of the two floes that enclosed her accepted the transverse pressure and protected her from the enormous internal forces of the pack. Karl tried to help when visibility allowed but there was nothing he could do.

On 15th August the wind finally changed and the *Benjy B* was little by little released from the pack. We called at Longyearbyen Fjord to collect the base cargo and say goodbye to the aircrew who would begin their flight back to Britain at once. Karl wrote in his diary:

> *As the ship arrived Ran gave me a good handshake and Ginnie*
> *gave me a big hug and then I knew I did something right and I*
> *could almost cry. She is a great hardworking girl. So many times*

*over the months I thought she would break down in tears but she
never showed any signs of it. It sure has been an experience in a
lifetime. I have met a lot of great people and I won't forget them.
All the hardship is now over for us all.*

The 'real' world impinged upon ours with local drama. First, two
drunken Norwegian fishermen came aboard and broke into the
Buzzards' cabin. Ginnie saw them off with her most killing expression. But the fishermen were soon back. This time, surrounded by Les
Davis from Carlisle, Cyrus from Bombay and the Kiwi, Jimmy
Young, they were shoved down the stairway. I arrived just in time to
cool tempers, bearing in mind that there were but twenty Transglobers and over fifty Norwegian fishermen moored alongside.

That afternoon two Polish scientists with a portable radio
'escaped' from the inland base where they were working with the
Russians and sent a message to the Norwegians. The Russians
monitored the signal. Norwegian and Russian helicopters rushed to
the escapers' location. The Norwegians arrived first and the Poles
were given asylum.

The simplicity of three years away from it all looked like coming to
an end.

Next day, the cargo lashed in the hold, we moved away from the
wooden jetty. Our last leave-taking after three years of departures
from remote harbours and ports. We had made many friends in
many lands.

One of those who saw us off was Robin Buzza, the local expatriate
who had defended us against the allegations of taking prostitutes to
the Pole. He later wrote to me: "I felt sad on the day your band of
global adventurers left Longyearbyen for the last time. Transglobe
had sustained me for many months and I was only too glad to have
been of assistance to a really great expedition. When the *Benjy B*
sailed out of the fjord last week, a part of me went with her."

From the lonely islands of Svalbard we sailed south through the
Greenland Sea and finally the North Sea until the lone beacons of fire
from the oilfields and the orange night sky of Aberdeen passed us
by.

Cyrus noted with pride that the *Benjy B* averaged ten and a quarter
knots on the journey home, well above her normal best. "She always
does that," he said, "puts on a bit of speed when she's coming into
port for a rest. All ships have special characters you can't explain and

the older they are, the more they show it. The *Benjy B* is very special."

Cyrus, perhaps more than most, was going to feel the wrench when he had to leave the ship. He would not get his job back with the P & O Line and would not be the only one to join the ranks of the unemployed which, since we first left Britain, had increased to over three million.

On 29th August HRH Prince Charles joined us on the River Thames and brought the ship back to our start point, Greenwich, almost three years to the day since we had set out. The Thames glittered under a stiff breeze and the warmth of a lovely summer's day. Colourful bunting and 10,000 cheering people lined the banks.

The journey was over.

Our team has now melted away. Charlie is hard at work attempting to raise sponsorship for a boat to enter the 1985 Round the World yacht race. Ollie, happily married, works in London, Gerry has signed on as an administrator with the British Antarctic Survey, Giles is back with Britannia Airways and Karl with Bradley Air Services in the Arctic. The Buzzards now live and work at Mount Maunganui in New Zealand, Eddie Pike and Les Davis are back in the Merchant Navy and Simon is married and settled in Australia. Terry Kenchington works in his home town of Bath and Anton Bowring will be organising the occasional reunion so perhaps we will all meet again one day . . . to remember how it was.

A few months after our return Ken Cameron purchased the *Benjy B* from the Bowring Steamship Company. On a cold day in January 1983 he held a re-naming ceremony at a deserted quay in the London docks. The ship looked ghost-like. Ken only employed Cyrus and Dave Hicks; no one lived on board. They had reluctantly re-painted the ship. No longer the words BENJAMIN BOWRING and TRANSGLOBE stood out proudly from her familiar hull. Ginnie, with help from Dave Hicks, Ollie and Charlie, smashed a champagne bottle against the bow and re-named her *Arctic Gael*. The *Benjy B*, remaining link of our memories, was no more.

What will I do now? Join the army of novel-writers, I think. With fiction it takes less than ten years to produce a book. But I will try to keep fit, for one day Ginnie may come up with another idea.

Bibliography

compiled by P. M. Booth *Transglobe Research Assistant*

Amundsen Roald
  The Northwest Passage
  CONSTABLE, 1908
Arctic Blue Books 1875–76, HMSO
  1877
Arctic Pilot Volume III,
  HYDROGRAPHIC DEPARTMENT,
  ADMIRALTY, 1959
Armstrong, Terence and Roberts, Brian
  Illustrated Ice Glossary
  POLAR RECORD 52, January
  1956
Caswell, John Edwards
  *Arctic Frontiers (US Exploration of
the Far North)*
  UNIVERSITY OF OKLAHOMA PRESS,
  1956
Conway, Sir Martin
  The First Crossing of Spitsbergen
  J. M. DENT, 1897
Cook, Dr Frederick A.
  My Attainment of the Pole
  THE POLAR PUBLISHING COMPANY,
  1911
Cooke, Alan and Holland, Clive
  *The Exploration of Northern Canada
Chronology 500–1920*
  ARCTIC HISTORY PRESS, 1978
Croft, Andrew
  Polar Exploration
  ADAM AND CHARLES BLACK, 1939
Diubaldo, Richard J.
  Stefansson and the Canadian Arctic
  MCGILL-QUEEN'S UNIVERSITY
  PRESS, 1978

Franklin, John
  *Narrative of a Journey to the shores
of the Polar Sea
Sea*
Franklin, John
  *Narrative of a Second Expedition to
the shores of the Polar Sea*
  JOHN MURRAY, 1828
Hakluyt Society
  Voyages of William Baffin
  1881
Hattersley-Smith, G.
  North of Latitude Eighty
  CANADA DEFENCE RESEARCH
  BOARD, 1974
Herbert, Wally
  Across the Top of the World (British
  Trans-Arctic Expedition)
  LONGMAN GROUP, 1969
Johnson, Robert E.
  Sir John Richardson
  TAYLOR AND FRANCIS LTD, 1976
Kirwin, L. P.
  A History of Polar Exploration
  PENGUIN BOOKS, 1962
Mirsky, Jeanette,
  To The Arctic!
  UNIVERSITY OF CHICAGO PRESS,
  1970
Neatby, Leslie H.
  The Search for Franklin
  ARTHUR BARKER, 1970
Nobile, Umberto
  My Polar Flights
  FREDERICK MULLER, 1961

Parry, William Edward
  *Narrative of an attempt to reach the
  North Pole*
  JOHN MURRAY, 1828
Peary, Robert E.
  The North Pole
  HODDER & STOUGHTON, 1910
Ridgway, John
  Gino Watkins
  OXFORD UNIVERSITY PRESS, 1974
Ross, Sir John
  *Narrative of a Second Voyage in
  Search of a North-West Passage*
  A. W. WEBSTER, 1835
Scott, J. M.
  The Private Life of Polar Exploration
  WILLIAM BLACKWOOD, 1982
Simpson, Myrtle
  Due North
  VICTOR GOLLANCZ, 1970
Starokomskiy, L. M. tr. and ed. by
  William Barr
  *Charting the Russian Northern Sea
  Route*
  MCGILL-QUEEN'S UNIVERSITY
  PRESS, 1976
Stefansson, Vilhjalmur
  My Life with the Eskimo
  MACMILLAN, 1913
Sugden, David
  Arctic and Antarctic (A modern
  geographical synthesis)
  BLACKWELL, OXFORD, 1982
Thomson, George Malcolm
  The North-West Passage
  SECKER & WARBURG, 1975

JOURNALS
Polar Record
  SCOTT POLAR RESEARCH
  INSTITUTE,
  CAMBRIDGE
The Geographical Journal
  ROYAL GEOGRAPHICAL SOCIETY,
  LONDON

FACSIMILE
  *The 1806 Log Book Concerning the
  Arctic Voyage of Captain William
  Scoresby*
  CAEDMON OF WHITBY, 1981

ATLAS
Polar Regions
  NATIONAL FOREIGN ASSESSMENT
  CENTER, CIA (May be seen at RGS
  Map Room)
Times Atlas of the World
  (*Comprehensive Edition*)
  TIMES BOOKS AND JOHN
  BARTHOLOMEW AND SON LTD

Index